CUBICLES
THAT MAKE YOU
ENVY THE DEAD

Recent DILBERT® Books from Andrews McMeel Publishing

Dilbert Gets Re-accommodated

I'm No Scientist, But I Think Feng Shui Is Part of the Answer

Optimism Sounds Exhausting

Go Add Value Someplace Else

I Sense a Coldness to Your Mentoring

Your New Job Title Is "Accomplice"

I Can't Remember If We're Cheap or Smart

Teamwork Means You Can't Pick the Side that's Right

How's That Underling Thing Working Out for You?

Your Accomplishments Are Suspiciously Hard to Verify

Problem Identified and You're Probably Not Part of the Solution

I'm Tempted to Stop Acting Randomly

14 Years of Loyal Service in a Fabric-Covered Box

Freedom's Just Another Word for People Finding Out You're Useless

Dilbert 2.0: 20 Years of Dilbert

This Is the Part Where You Pretend to Add Value

CUBICLES THAT MAKE YOU ENVY THE DEAD

DILBERT™
BY
SCOTT ADAMS
dilbert.com

Andrews McMeel
PUBLISHING®

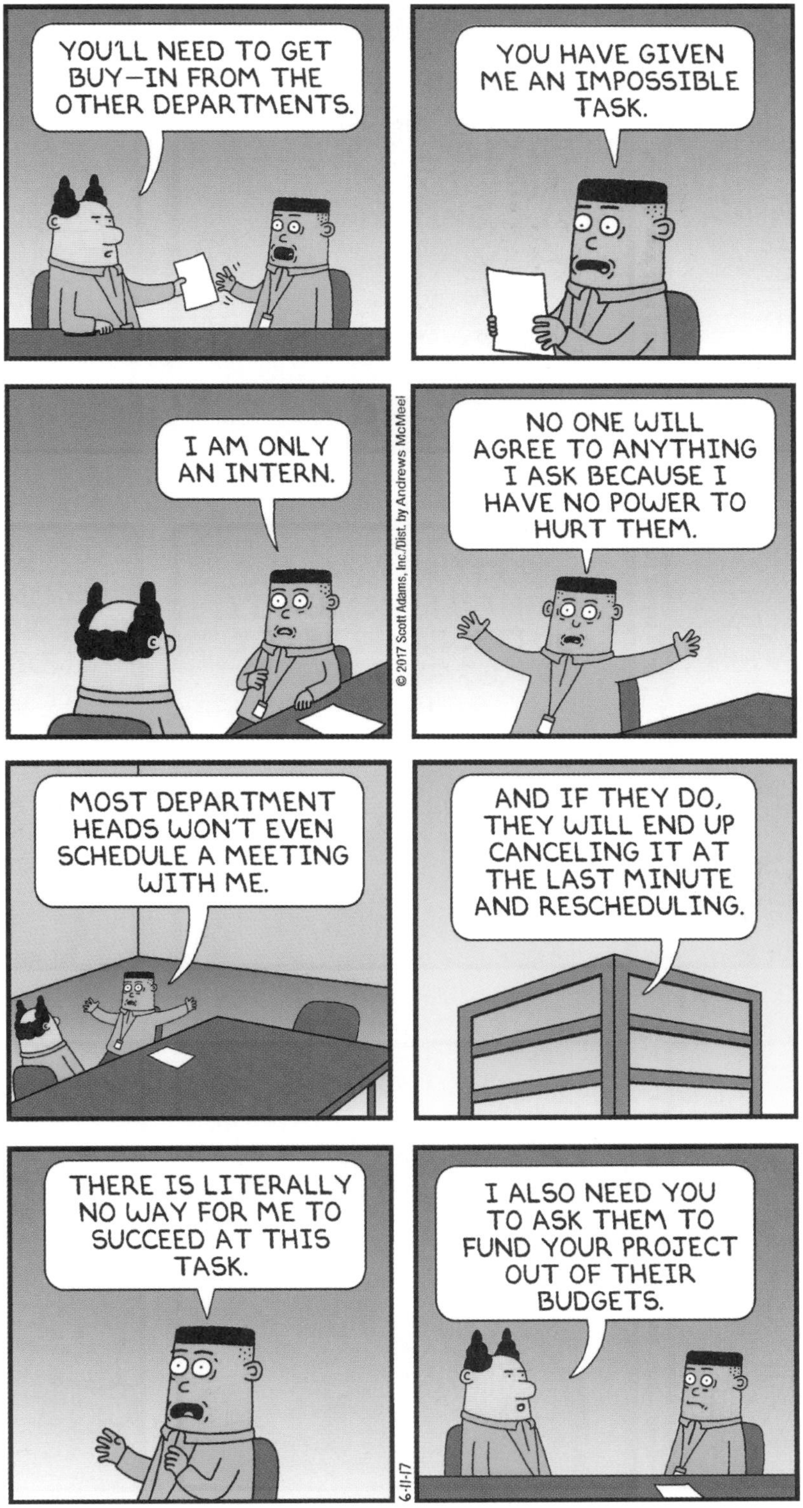
YOU'LL NEED TO GET BUY—IN FROM THE OTHER DEPARTMENTS.
YOU HAVE GIVEN ME AN IMPOSSIBLE TASK.
I AM ONLY AN INTERN.
NO ONE WILL AGREE TO ANYTHING I ASK BECAUSE I HAVE NO POWER TO HURT THEM.
MOST DEPARTMENT HEADS WON'T EVEN SCHEDULE A MEETING WITH ME.
AND IF THEY DO, THEY WILL END UP CANCELING IT AT THE LAST MINUTE AND RESCHEDULING.
THERE IS LITERALLY NO WAY FOR ME TO SUCCEED AT THIS TASK.
I ALSO NEED YOU TO ASK THEM TO FUND YOUR PROJECT OUT OF THEIR BUDGETS.
© 2017 Scott Adams, Inc./Dist. by Andrews McMeel
6-11-17

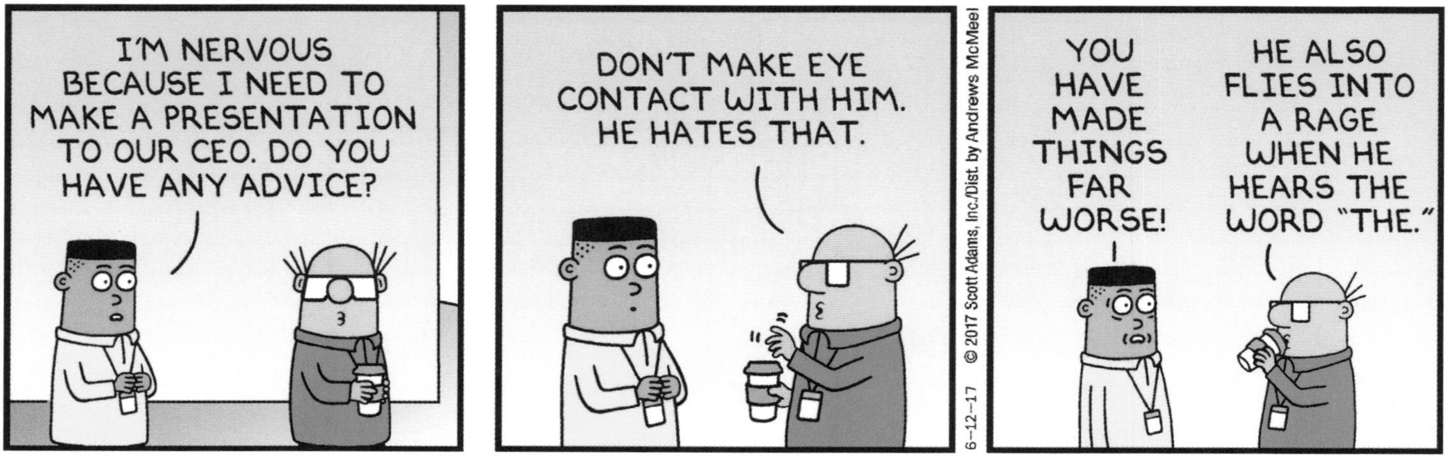
I'M NERVOUS BECAUSE I NEED TO MAKE A PRESENTATION TO OUR CEO. DO YOU HAVE ANY ADVICE?
DON'T MAKE EYE CONTACT WITH HIM. HE HATES THAT.
6-12-17 © 2017 Scott Adams, Inc./Dist. by Andrews McMeel
YOU HAVE MADE THINGS FAR WORSE!
HE ALSO FLIES INTO A RAGE WHEN HE HEARS THE WORD "THE."

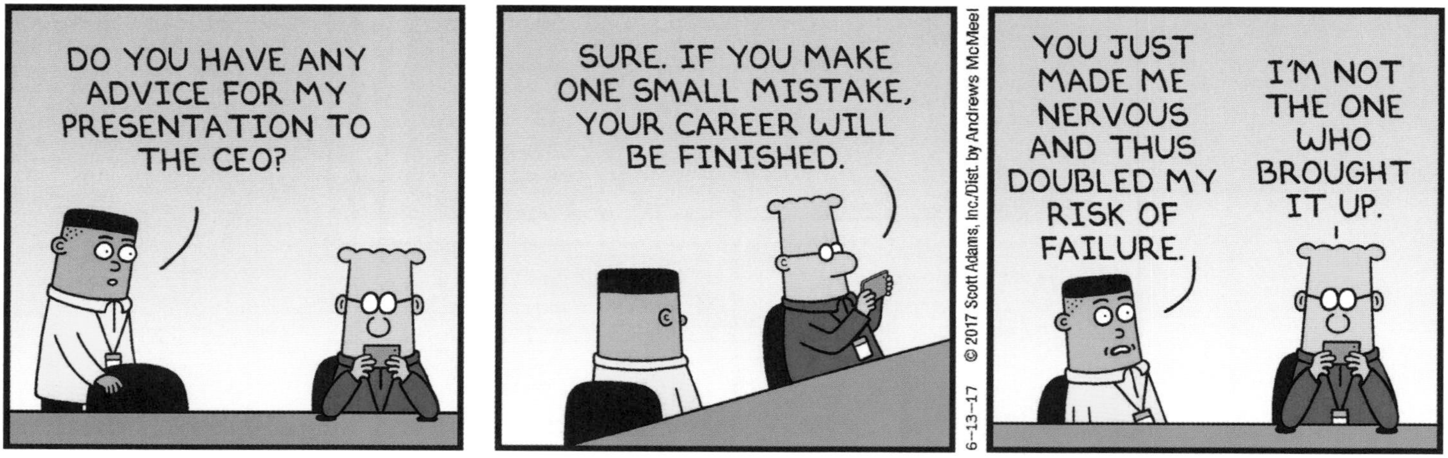
DO YOU HAVE ANY ADVICE FOR MY PRESENTATION TO THE CEO?
SURE. IF YOU MAKE ONE SMALL MISTAKE, YOUR CAREER WILL BE FINISHED.
6-13-17 © 2017 Scott Adams, Inc./Dist. by Andrews McMeel
YOU JUST MADE ME NERVOUS AND THUS DOUBLED MY RISK OF FAILURE.
I'M NOT THE ONE WHO BROUGHT IT UP.

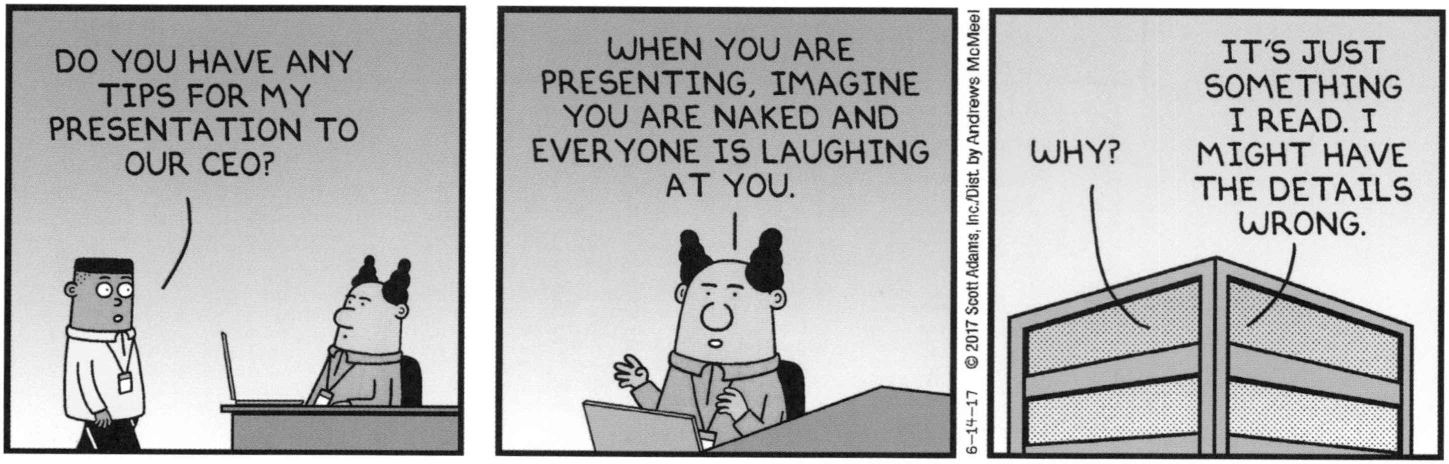
DO YOU HAVE ANY TIPS FOR MY PRESENTATION TO OUR CEO?
WHEN YOU ARE PRESENTING, IMAGINE YOU ARE NAKED AND EVERYONE IS LAUGHING AT YOU.
6-14-17 © 2017 Scott Adams, Inc./Dist. by Andrews McMeel
WHY?
IT'S JUST SOMETHING I READ. I MIGHT HAVE THE DETAILS WRONG.

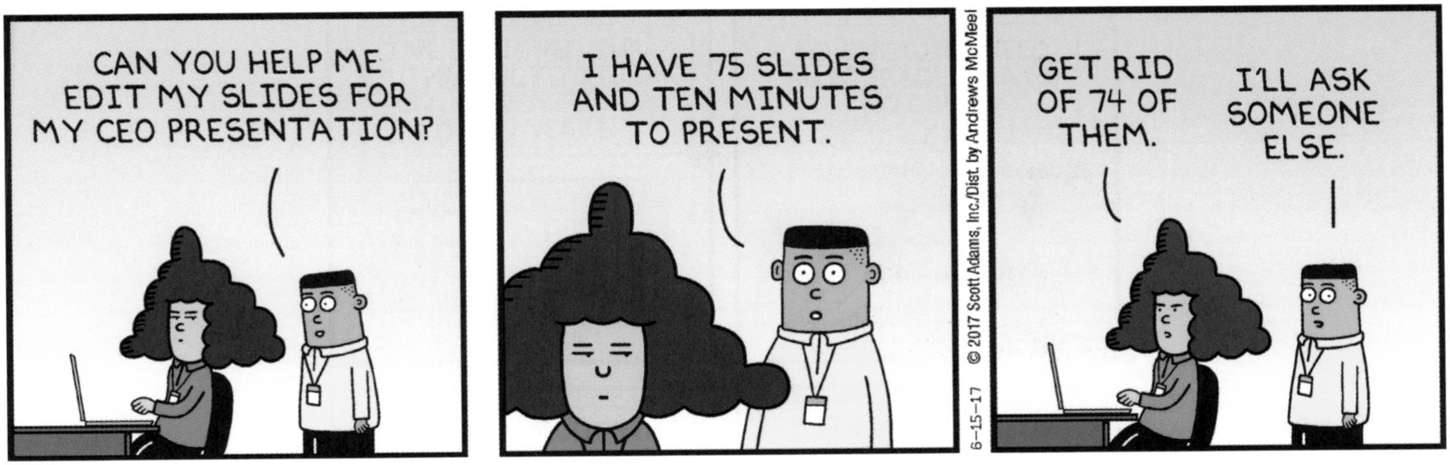
CAN YOU HELP ME EDIT MY SLIDES FOR MY CEO PRESENTATION?
I HAVE 75 SLIDES AND TEN MINUTES TO PRESENT.
6-15-17 © 2017 Scott Adams, Inc./Dist. by Andrews McMeel
GET RID OF 74 OF THEM.
I'LL ASK SOMEONE ELSE.

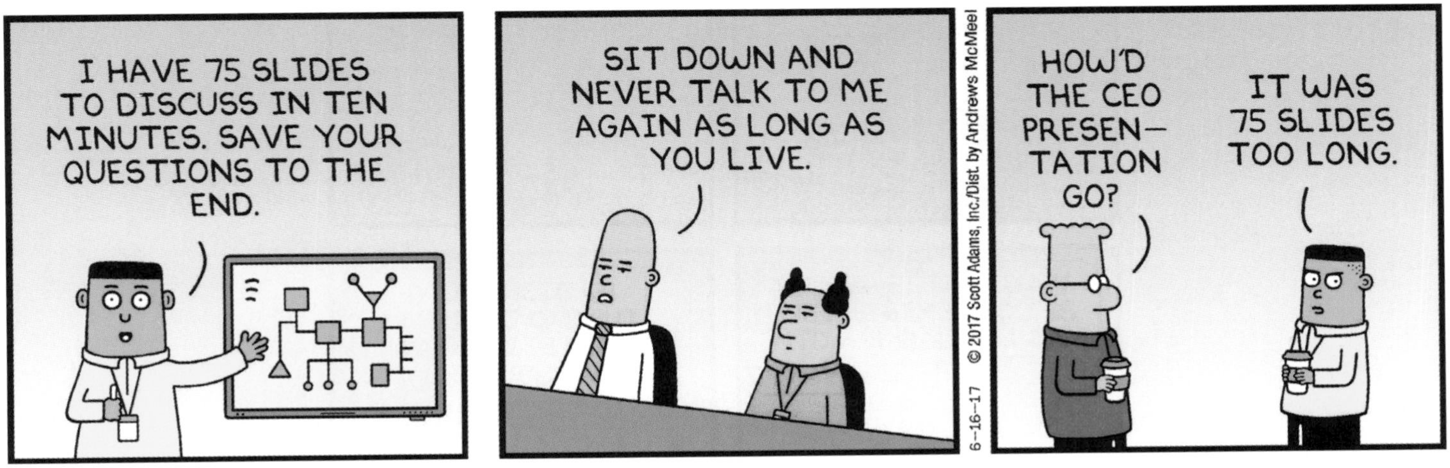
I HAVE 75 SLIDES TO DISCUSS IN TEN MINUTES. SAVE YOUR QUESTIONS TO THE END.
SIT DOWN AND NEVER TALK TO ME AGAIN AS LONG AS YOU LIVE.
6-16-17 © 2017 Scott Adams, Inc./Dist. by Andrews McMeel
HOW'D THE CEO PRESEN-TATION GO?
IT WAS 75 SLIDES TOO LONG.

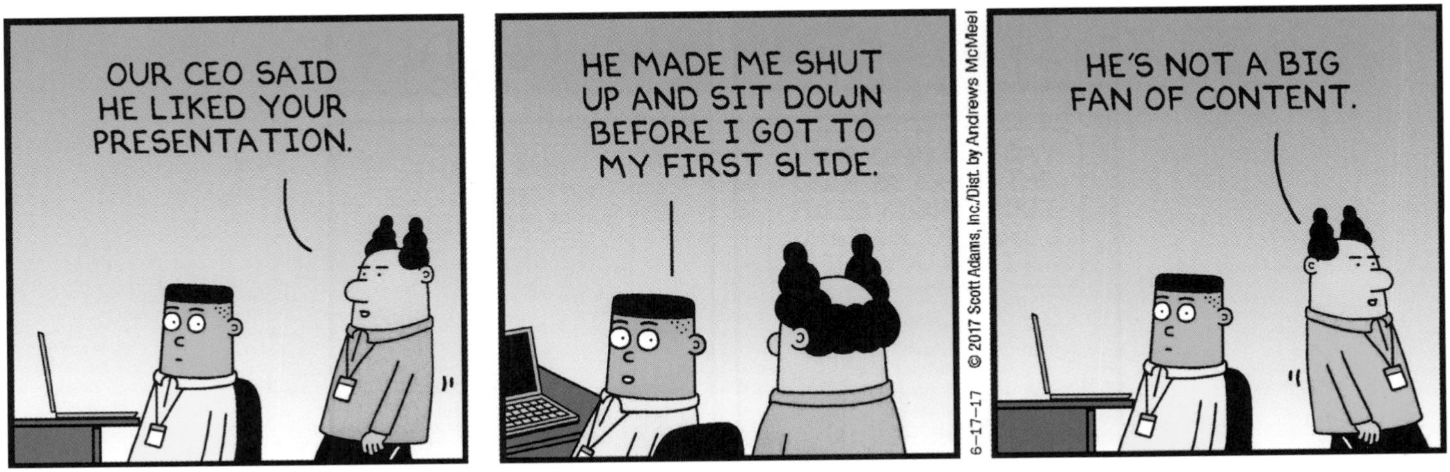
OUR CEO SAID HE LIKED YOUR PRESENTATION.
HE MADE ME SHUT UP AND SIT DOWN BEFORE I GOT TO MY FIRST SLIDE.
6-17-17 © 2017 Scott Adams, Inc./Dist. by Andrews McMeel
HE'S NOT A BIG FAN OF CONTENT.

I'D LIKE TO THANK EACH MEMBER OF THE PRODUCT TEAM FOR THE SUCCESSFUL LAUNCH.
DILBERT WROTE THE SOFTWARE.
ALICE DESIGNED THE HARDWARE.
© 2017 Scott Adams, Inc./Dist. by Andrews McMeel
AND WALLY... UM...
ATTENDED MOST OF THE MEETINGS.
THAT'S ALL YOU DID?
I ALSO PLAYED DEVIL'S ADVOCATE.
YOU DIDN'T SAY A WORD DURING OUR MEETINGS FOR SEVEN MONTHS.
THAT'S BECAUSE YOU WERE DOING EVERYTHING RIGHT.
6-18-17
DID YOU REALLY DO NOTHING FOR SEVEN MONTHS?
THIS IS ONE OF THOSE "LESS IS MORE" SITUA-TIONS.

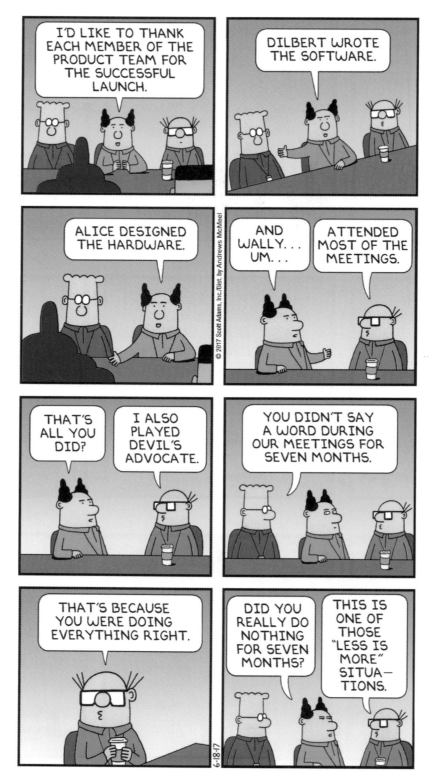

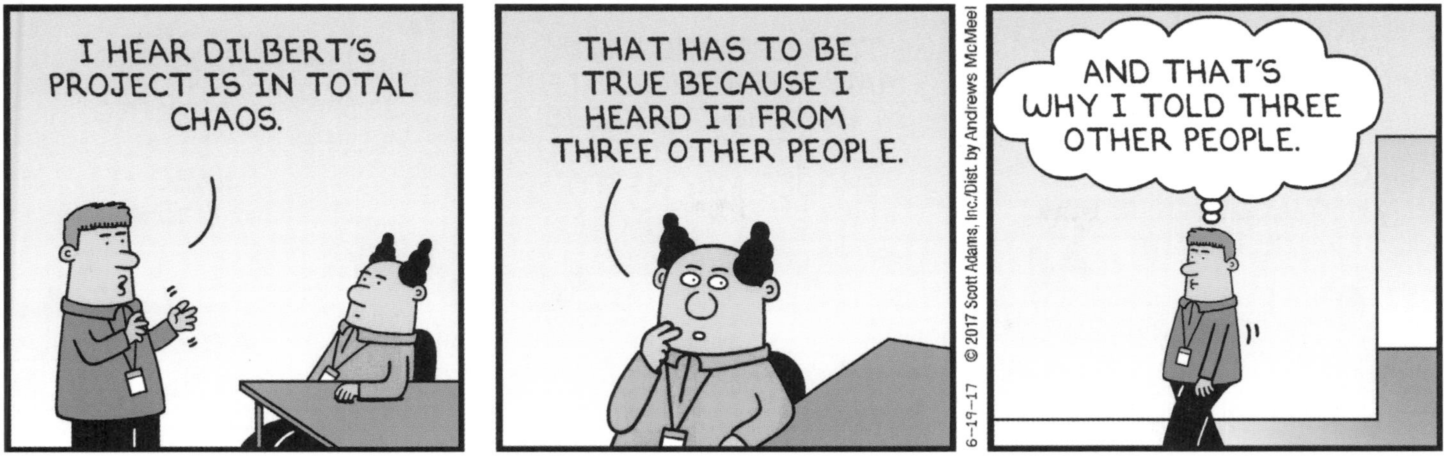
I HEAR DILBERT'S PROJECT IS IN TOTAL CHAOS.
THAT HAS TO BE TRUE BECAUSE I HEARD IT FROM THREE OTHER PEOPLE.
AND THAT'S WHY I TOLD THREE OTHER PEOPLE.
6-19-17 © 2017 Scott Adams, Inc./Dist. by Andrews McMeel

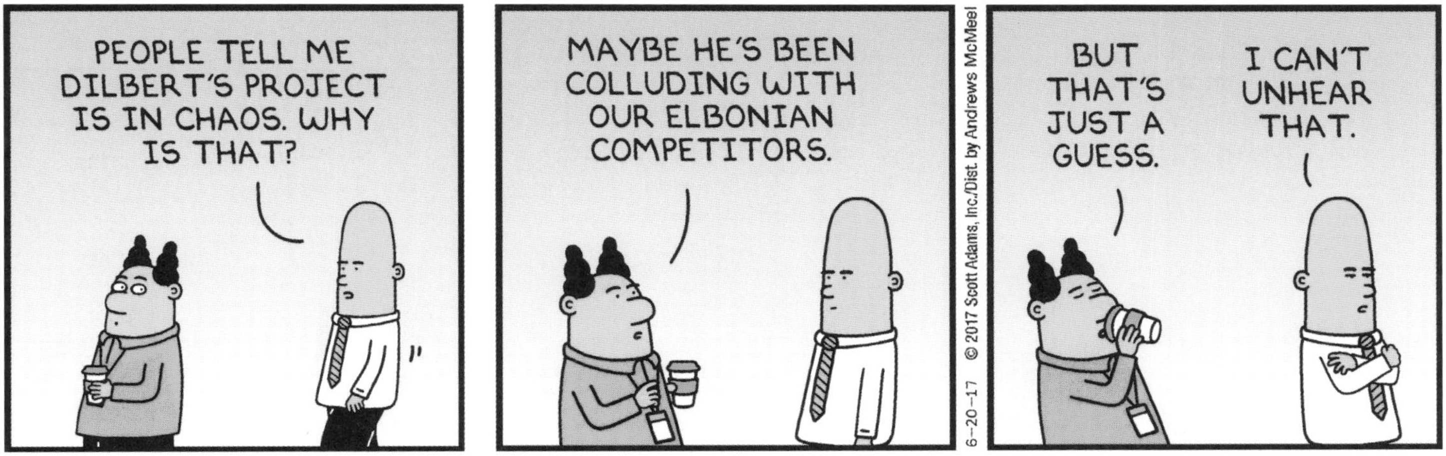
PEOPLE TELL ME DILBERT'S PROJECT IS IN CHAOS. WHY IS THAT?
MAYBE HE'S BEEN COLLUDING WITH OUR ELBONIAN COMPETITORS.
BUT THAT'S JUST A GUESS.
I CAN'T UNHEAR THAT.
6-20-17 © 2017 Scott Adams, Inc./Dist. by Andrews McMeel

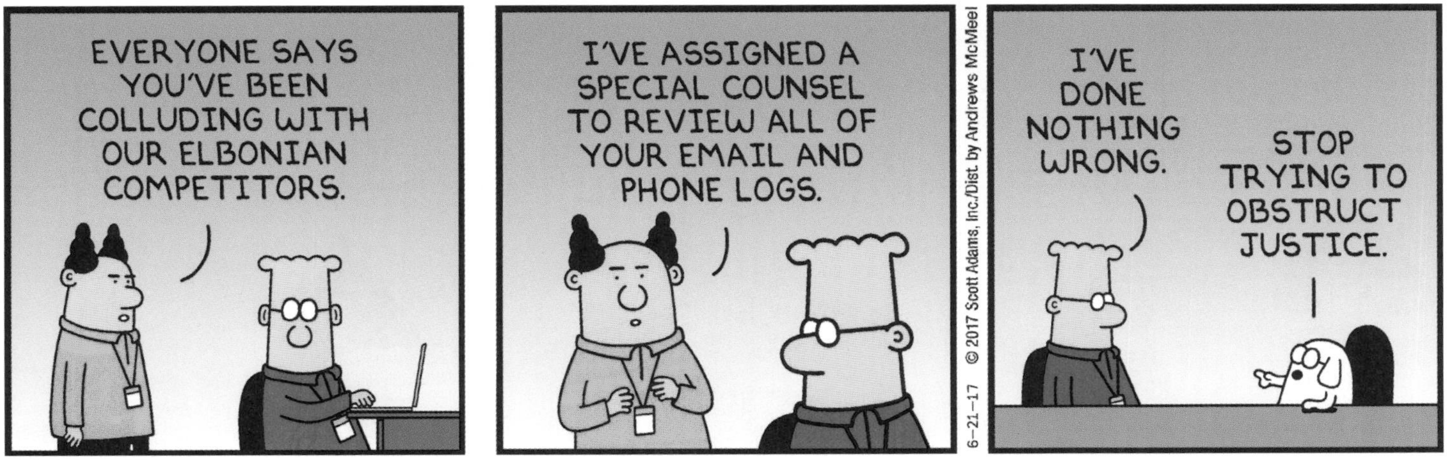
EVERYONE SAYS YOU'VE BEEN COLLUDING WITH OUR ELBONIAN COMPETITORS.
I'VE ASSIGNED A SPECIAL COUNSEL TO REVIEW ALL OF YOUR EMAIL AND PHONE LOGS.
I'VE DONE NOTHING WRONG.
STOP TRYING TO OBSTRUCT JUSTICE.
6-21-17 © 2017 Scott Adams, Inc./Dist. by Andrews McMeel

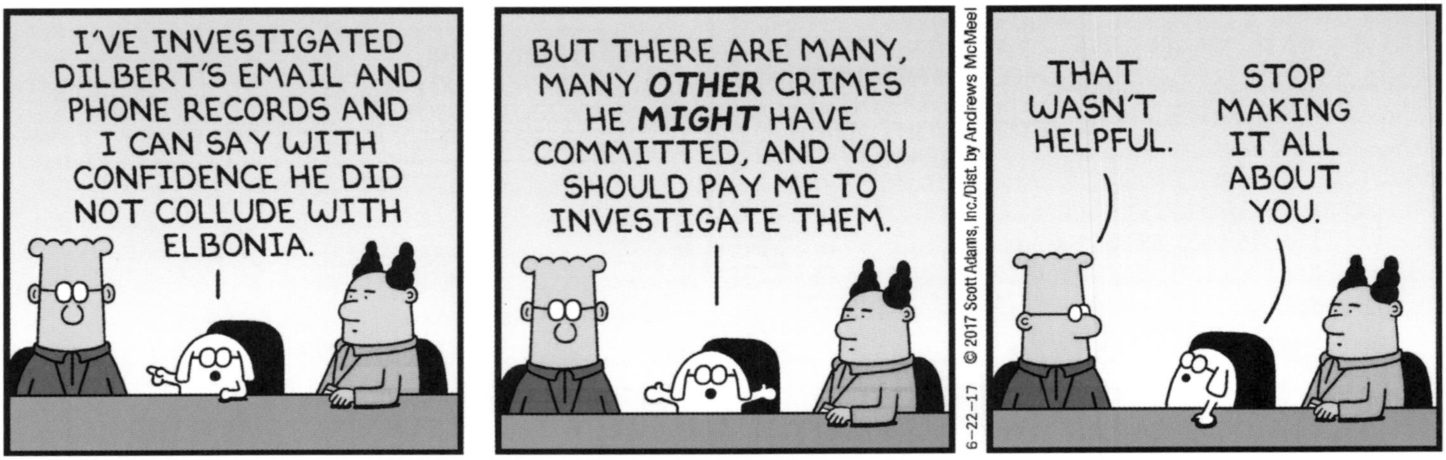
I'VE INVESTIGATED DILBERT'S EMAIL AND PHONE RECORDS AND I CAN SAY WITH CONFIDENCE HE DID NOT COLLUDE WITH ELBONIA.
BUT THERE ARE MANY, MANY **OTHER** CRIMES HE **MIGHT** HAVE COMMITTED, AND YOU SHOULD PAY ME TO INVESTIGATE THEM.
THAT WASN'T HELPFUL.
STOP MAKING IT ALL ABOUT YOU.
6-22-17 © 2017 Scott Adams, Inc./Dist. by Andrews McMeel

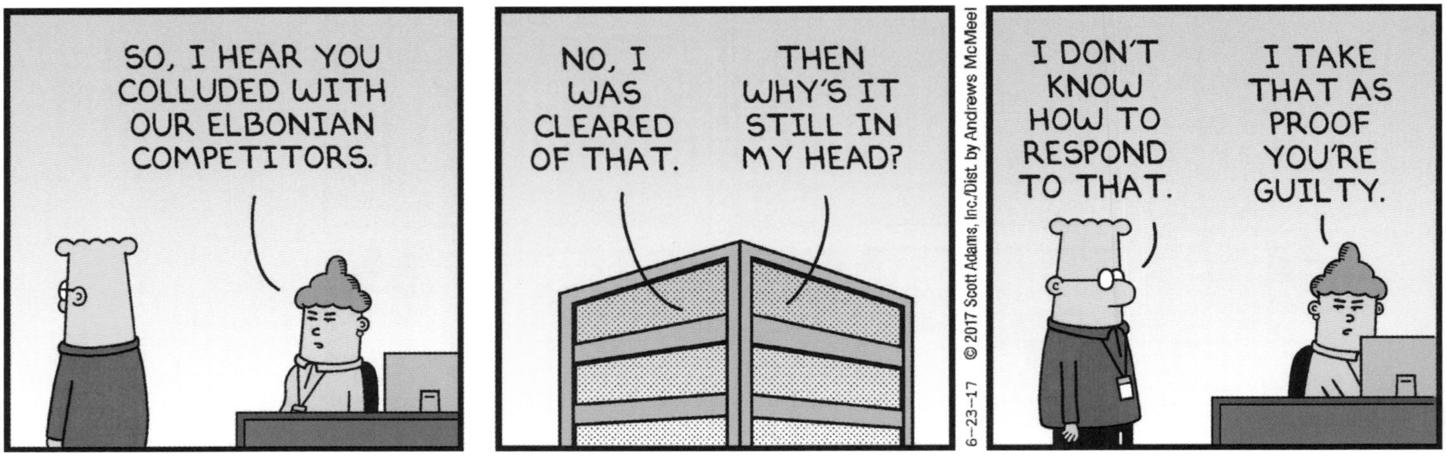
SO, I HEAR YOU COLLUDED WITH OUR ELBONIAN COMPETITORS.
NO, I WAS CLEARED OF THAT.
THEN WHY'S IT STILL IN MY HEAD?
I DON'T KNOW HOW TO RESPOND TO THAT.
I TAKE THAT AS PROOF YOU'RE GUILTY.
6-23-17 © 2017 Scott Adams, Inc./Dist. by Andrews McMeel

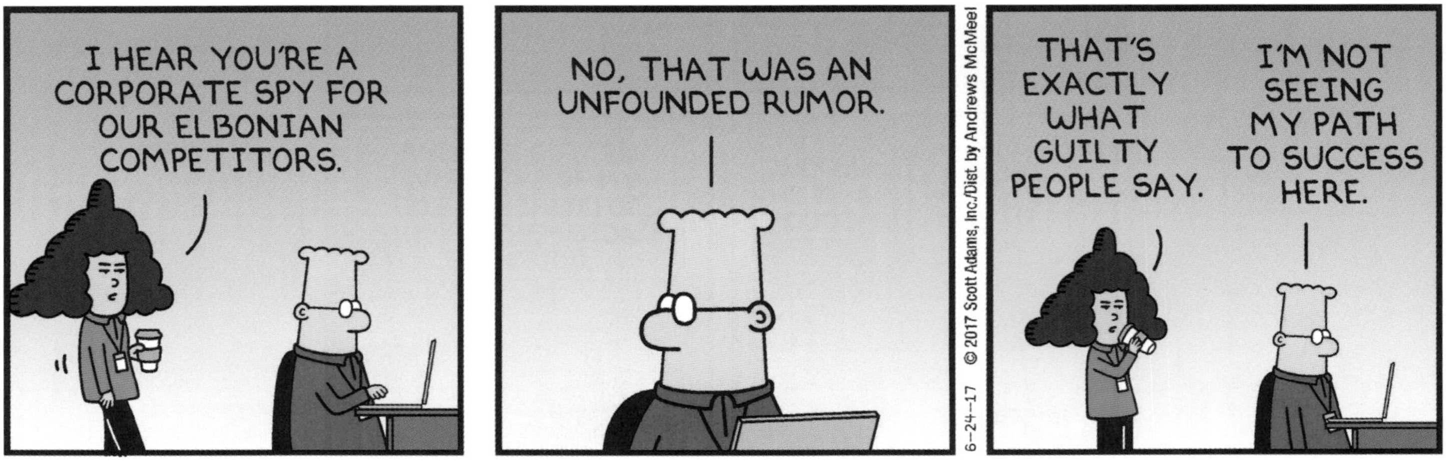
I HEAR YOU'RE A CORPORATE SPY FOR OUR ELBONIAN COMPETITORS.
NO, THAT WAS AN UNFOUNDED RUMOR.
THAT'S EXACTLY WHAT GUILTY PEOPLE SAY.
I'M NOT SEEING MY PATH TO SUCCESS HERE.
6-24-17 © 2017 Scott Adams, Inc./Dist. by Andrews McMeel

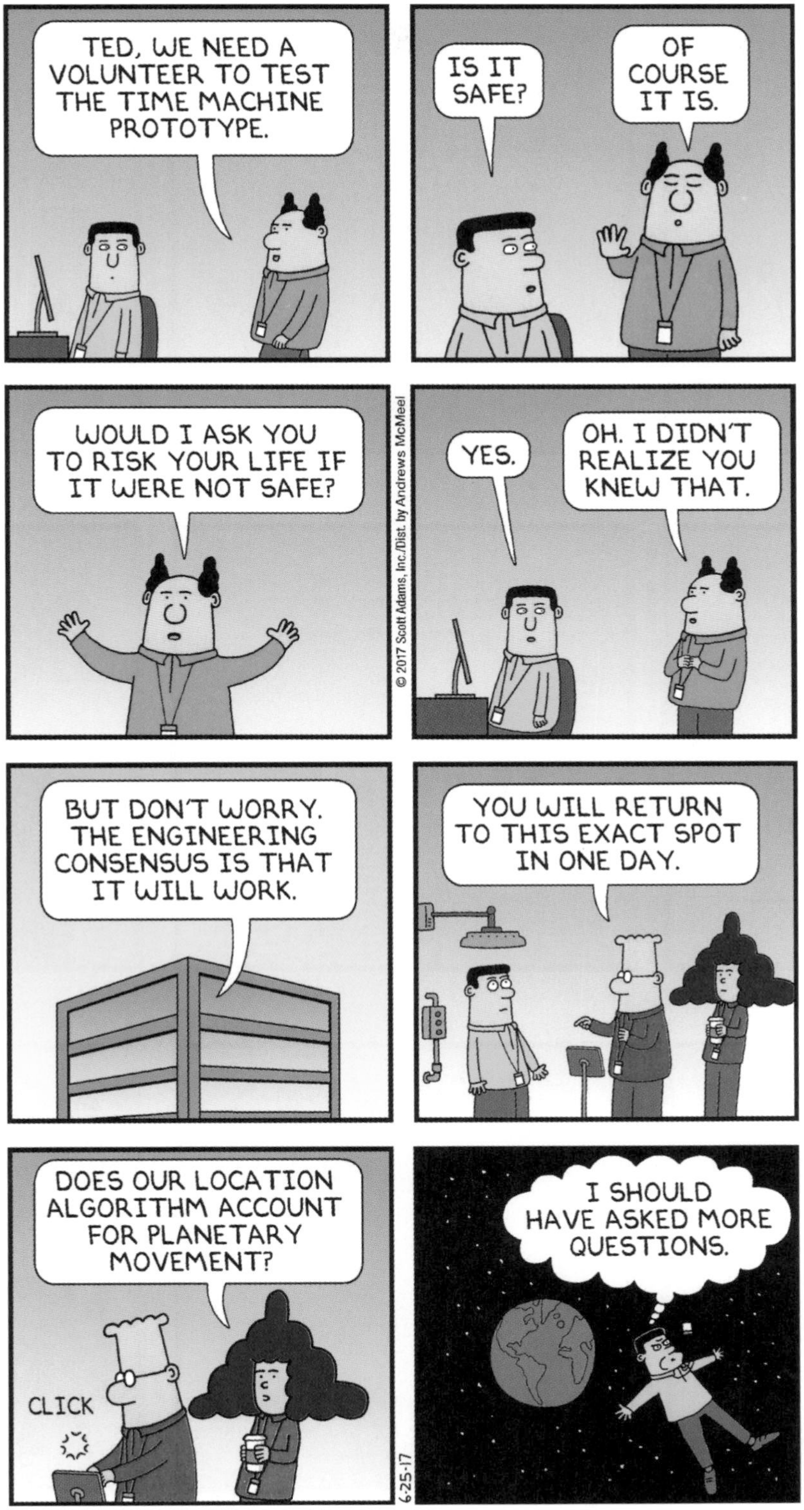
TED, WE NEED A VOLUNTEER TO TEST THE TIME MACHINE PROTOTYPE.
IS IT SAFE?
OF COURSE IT IS.
WOULD I ASK YOU TO RISK YOUR LIFE IF IT WERE NOT SAFE?
YES.
OH. I DIDN'T REALIZE YOU KNEW THAT.
© 2017 Scott Adams, Inc./Dist. by Andrews McMeel
BUT DON'T WORRY. THE ENGINEERING CONSENSUS IS THAT IT WILL WORK.
YOU WILL RETURN TO THIS EXACT SPOT IN ONE DAY.
DOES OUR LOCATION ALGORITHM ACCOUNT FOR PLANETARY MOVEMENT?
CLICK
6-25-17
I SHOULD HAVE ASKED MORE QUESTIONS.

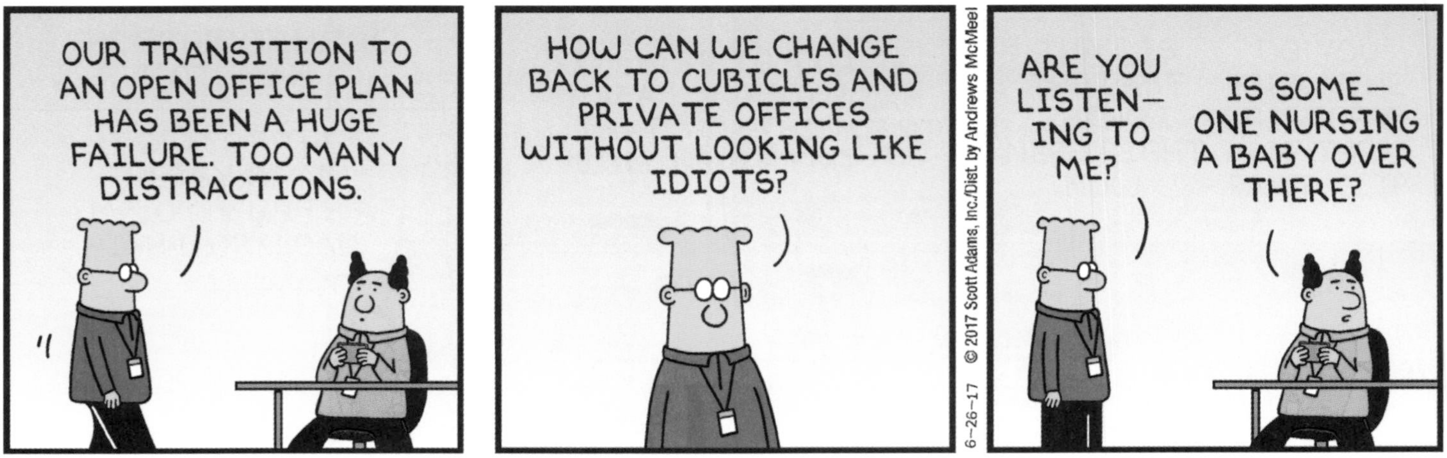
OUR TRANSITION TO AN OPEN OFFICE PLAN HAS BEEN A HUGE FAILURE. TOO MANY DISTRACTIONS.
HOW CAN WE CHANGE BACK TO CUBICLES AND PRIVATE OFFICES WITHOUT LOOKING LIKE IDIOTS?
6-26-17 © 2017 Scott Adams, Inc./Dist. by Andrews McMeel
ARE YOU LISTEN-ING TO ME?
IS SOME-ONE NURSING A BABY OVER THERE?

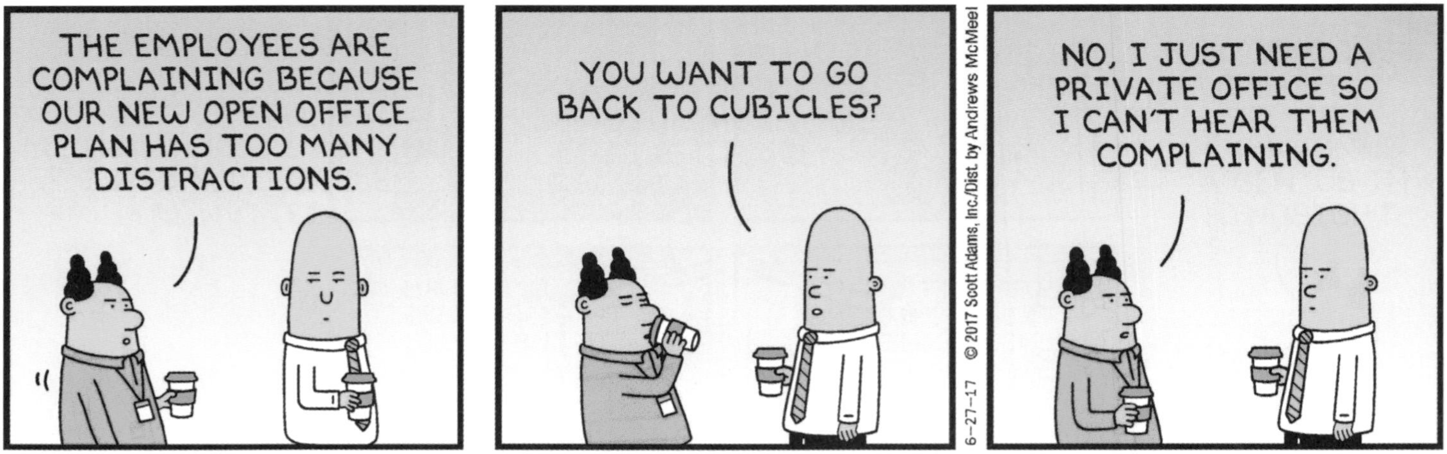
THE EMPLOYEES ARE COMPLAINING BECAUSE OUR NEW OPEN OFFICE PLAN HAS TOO MANY DISTRACTIONS.
YOU WANT TO GO BACK TO CUBICLES?
6-27-17 © 2017 Scott Adams, Inc./Dist. by Andrews McMeel
NO, I JUST NEED A PRIVATE OFFICE SO I CAN'T HEAR THEM COMPLAINING.

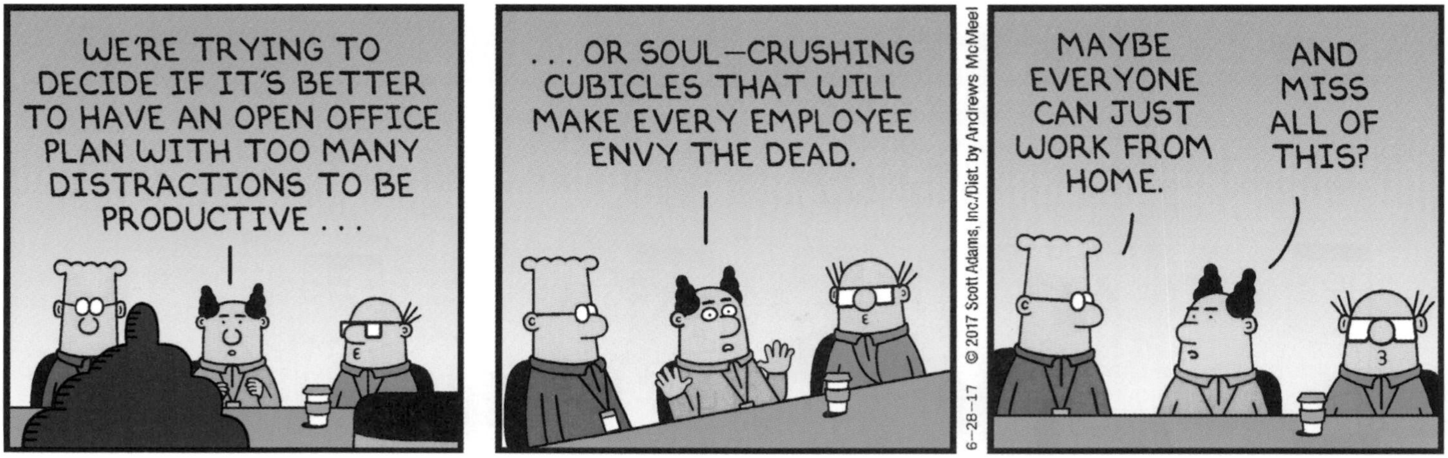
WE'RE TRYING TO DECIDE IF IT'S BETTER TO HAVE AN OPEN OFFICE PLAN WITH TOO MANY DISTRACTIONS TO BE PRODUCTIVE . . .
. . . OR SOUL-CRUSHING CUBICLES THAT WILL MAKE EVERY EMPLOYEE ENVY THE DEAD.
6-28-17 © 2017 Scott Adams, Inc./Dist. by Andrews McMeel
MAYBE EVERYONE CAN JUST WORK FROM HOME.
AND MISS ALL OF THIS?

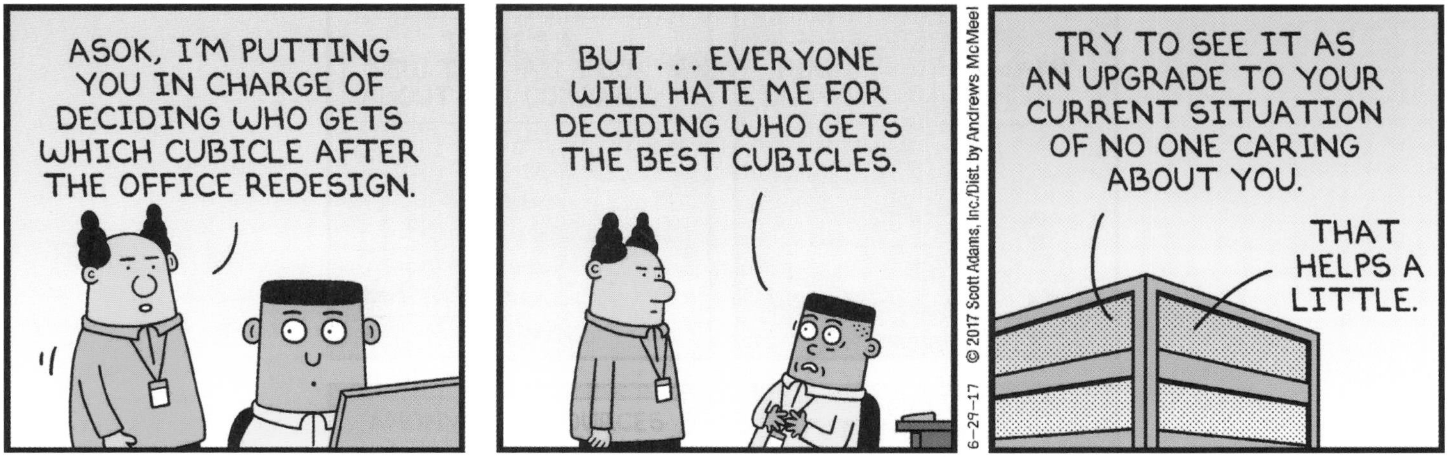
ASOK, I'M PUTTING YOU IN CHARGE OF DECIDING WHO GETS WHICH CUBICLE AFTER THE OFFICE REDESIGN.
BUT . . . EVERYONE WILL HATE ME FOR DECIDING WHO GETS THE BEST CUBICLES.
TRY TO SEE IT AS AN UPGRADE TO YOUR CURRENT SITUATION OF NO ONE CARING ABOUT YOU.
THAT HELPS A LITTLE.
6-29-17 © 2017 Scott Adams, Inc./Dist. by Andrews McMeel

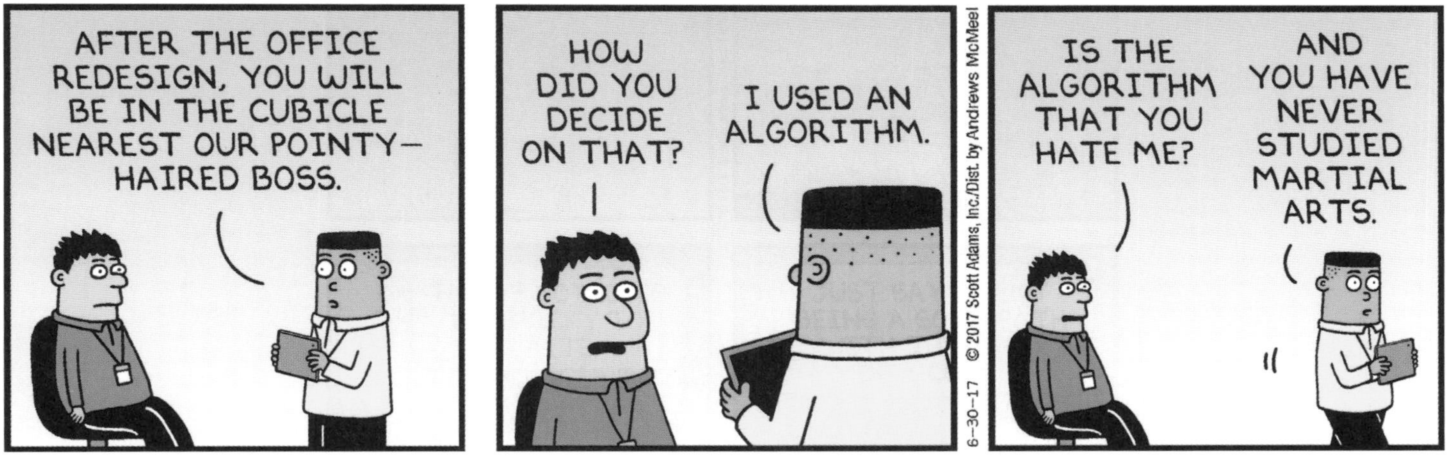
AFTER THE OFFICE REDESIGN, YOU WILL BE IN THE CUBICLE NEAREST OUR POINTY-HAIRED BOSS.
HOW DID YOU DECIDE ON THAT?
I USED AN ALGORITHM.
IS THE ALGORITHM THAT YOU HATE ME?
AND YOU HAVE NEVER STUDIED MARTIAL ARTS.
6-30-17 © 2017 Scott Adams, Inc./Dist. by Andrews McMeel

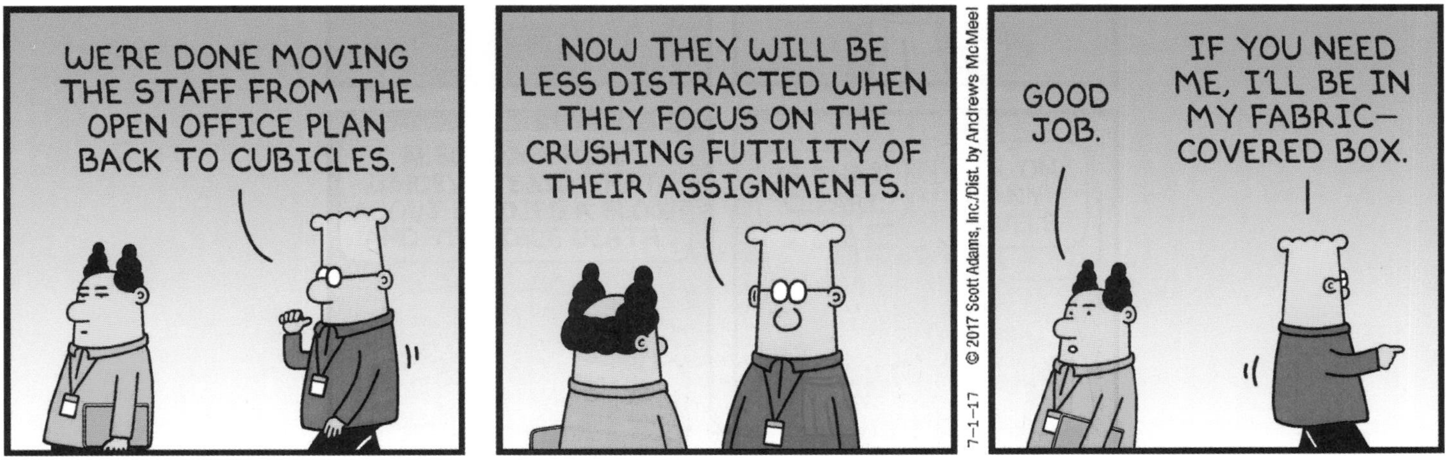
WE'RE DONE MOVING THE STAFF FROM THE OPEN OFFICE PLAN BACK TO CUBICLES.
NOW THEY WILL BE LESS DISTRACTED WHEN THEY FOCUS ON THE CRUSHING FUTILITY OF THEIR ASSIGNMENTS.
GOOD JOB.
IF YOU NEED ME, I'LL BE IN MY FABRIC-COVERED BOX.
7-1-17 © 2017 Scott Adams, Inc./Dist. by Andrews McMeel

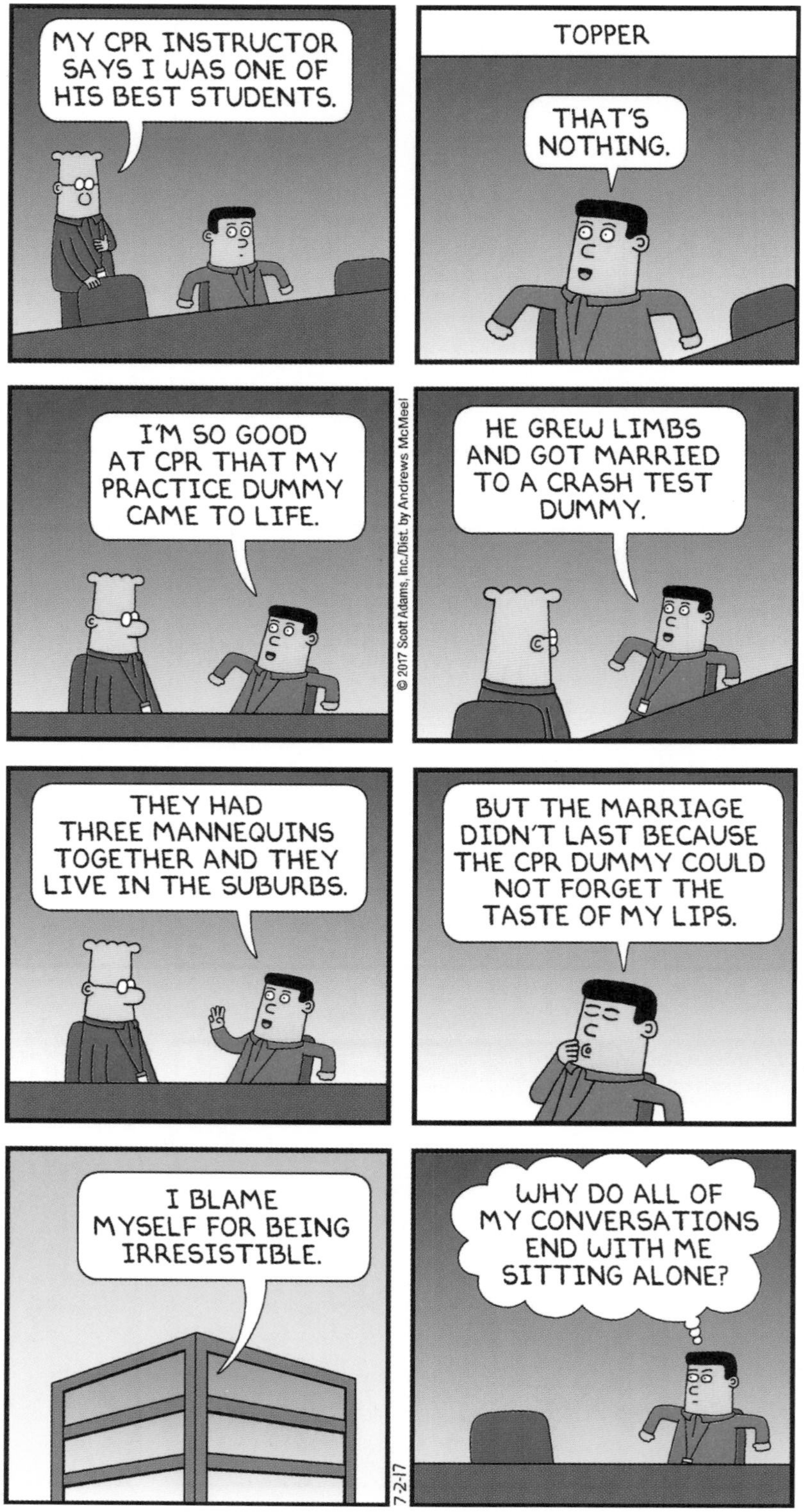
MY CPR INSTRUCTOR SAYS I WAS ONE OF HIS BEST STUDENTS.
TOPPER
THAT'S NOTHING.
I'M SO GOOD AT CPR THAT MY PRACTICE DUMMY CAME TO LIFE.
HE GREW LIMBS AND GOT MARRIED TO A CRASH TEST DUMMY.
THEY HAD THREE MANNEQUINS TOGETHER AND THEY LIVE IN THE SUBURBS.
BUT THE MARRIAGE DIDN'T LAST BECAUSE THE CPR DUMMY COULD NOT FORGET THE TASTE OF MY LIPS.
I BLAME MYSELF FOR BEING IRRESISTIBLE.
WHY DO ALL OF MY CONVERSATIONS END WITH ME SITTING ALONE?
© 2017 Scott Adams, Inc./Dist. by Andrews McMeel
7-2-17

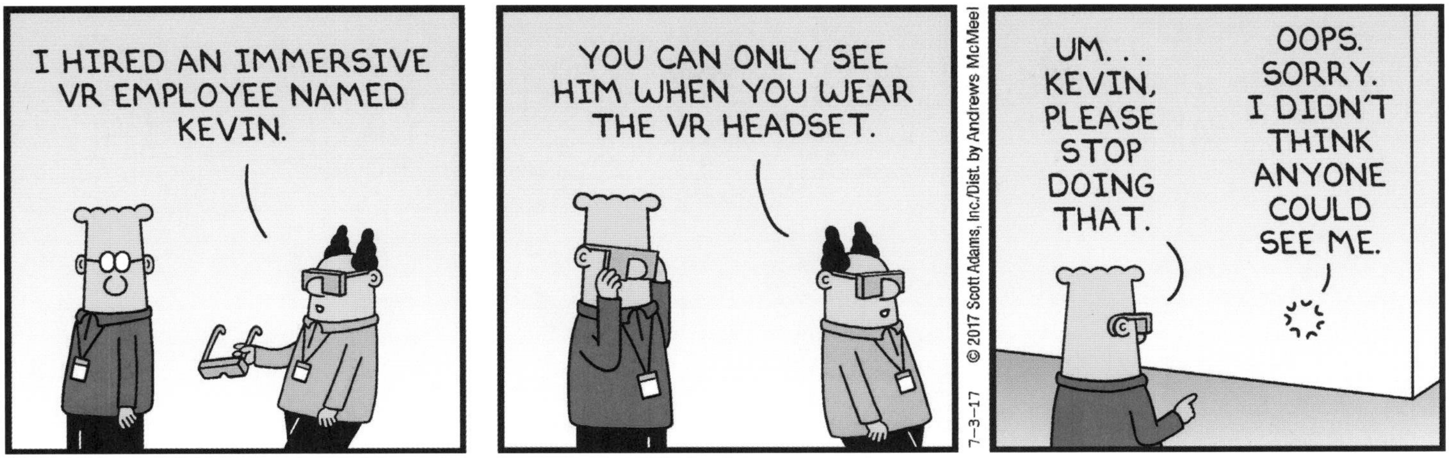
I HIRED AN IMMERSIVE VR EMPLOYEE NAMED KEVIN.
YOU CAN ONLY SEE HIM WHEN YOU WEAR THE VR HEADSET.
7-3-17 © 2017 Scott Adams, Inc./Dist. by Andrews McMeel
UM. . . KEVIN, PLEASE STOP DOING THAT.
OOPS. SORRY. I DIDN'T THINK ANYONE COULD SEE ME.

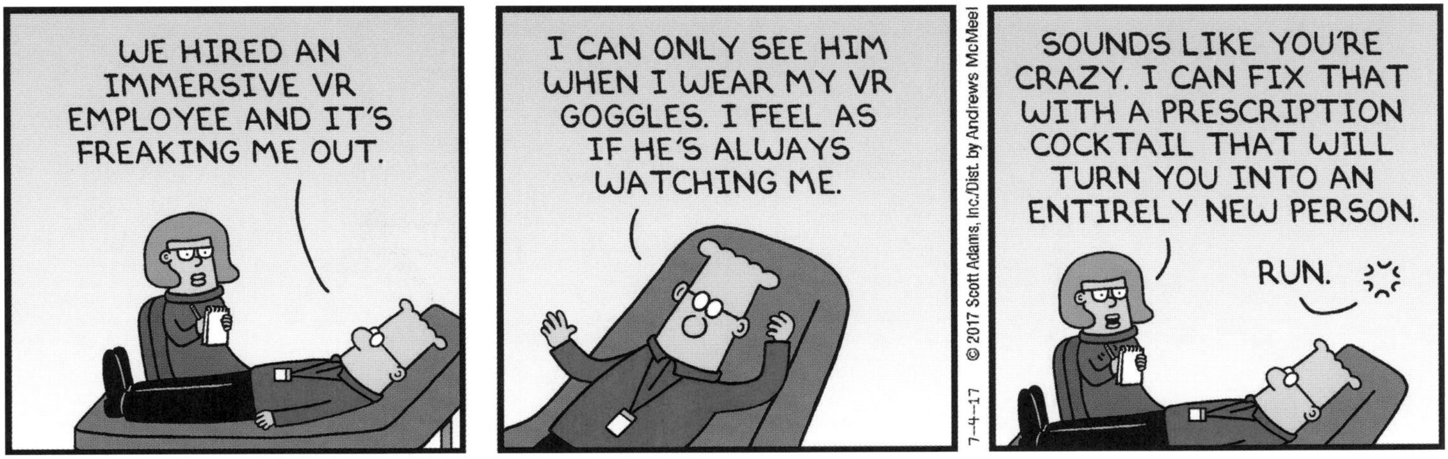
WE HIRED AN IMMERSIVE VR EMPLOYEE AND IT'S FREAKING ME OUT.
I CAN ONLY SEE HIM WHEN I WEAR MY VR GOGGLES. I FEEL AS IF HE'S ALWAYS WATCHING ME.
7-4-17 © 2017 Scott Adams, Inc./Dist. by Andrews McMeel
SOUNDS LIKE YOU'RE CRAZY. I CAN FIX THAT WITH A PRESCRIPTION COCKTAIL THAT WILL TURN YOU INTO AN ENTIRELY NEW PERSON.
RUN.

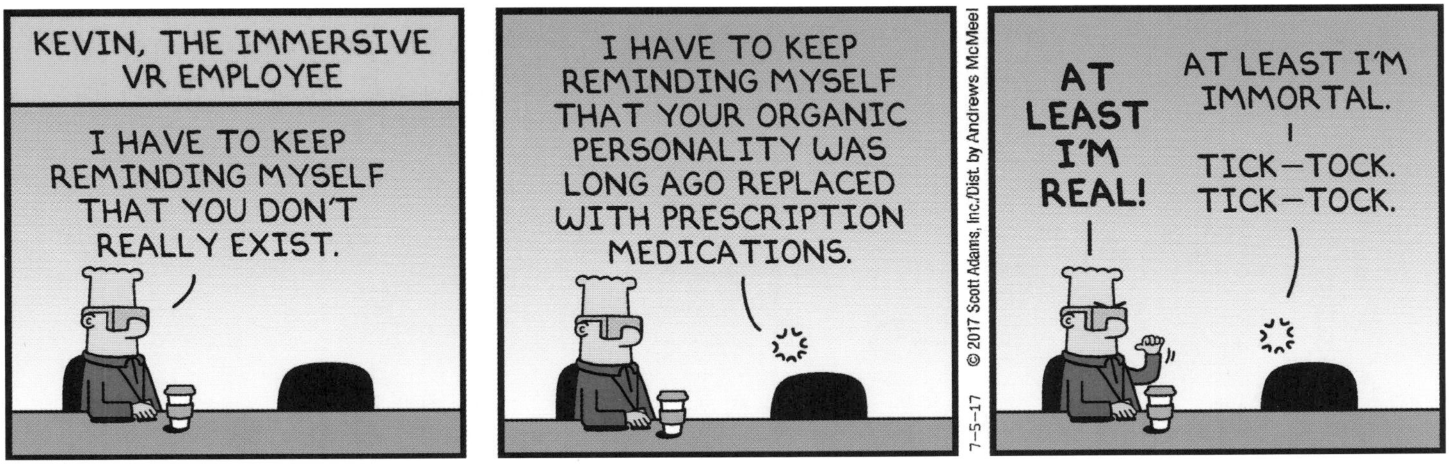
KEVIN, THE IMMERSIVE VR EMPLOYEE
I HAVE TO KEEP REMINDING MYSELF THAT YOU DON'T REALLY EXIST.
I HAVE TO KEEP REMINDING MYSELF THAT YOUR ORGANIC PERSONALITY WAS LONG AGO REPLACED WITH PRESCRIPTION MEDICATIONS.
7-5-17 © 2017 Scott Adams, Inc./Dist. by Andrews McMeel
AT LEAST I'M REAL!
AT LEAST I'M IMMORTAL.
TICK-TOCK. TICK-TOCK.

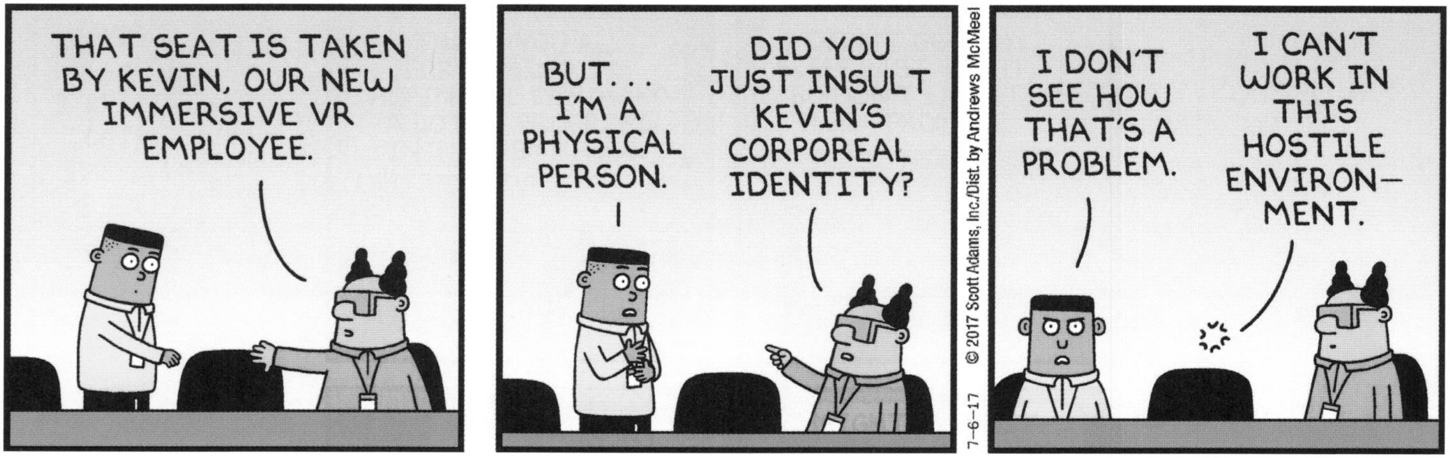
THAT SEAT IS TAKEN BY KEVIN, OUR NEW IMMERSIVE VR EMPLOYEE.
BUT. . . I'M A PHYSICAL PERSON.
DID YOU JUST INSULT KEVIN'S CORPOREAL IDENTITY?
I DON'T SEE HOW THAT'S A PROBLEM.
I CAN'T WORK IN THIS HOSTILE ENVIRON– MENT.
7–6–17
© 2017 Scott Adams, Inc./Dist. by Andrews McMeel

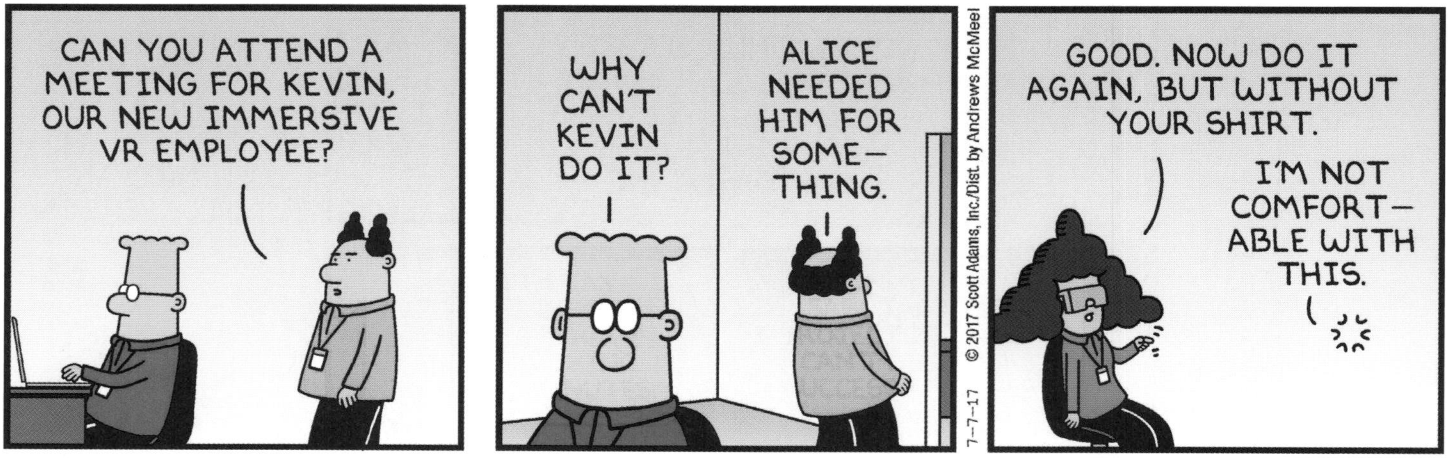
CAN YOU ATTEND A MEETING FOR KEVIN, OUR NEW IMMERSIVE VR EMPLOYEE?
WHY CAN'T KEVIN DO IT?
ALICE NEEDED HIM FOR SOME– THING.
GOOD. NOW DO IT AGAIN, BUT WITHOUT YOUR SHIRT.
I'M NOT COMFORT– ABLE WITH THIS.
7–7–17
© 2017 Scott Adams, Inc./Dist. by Andrews McMeel

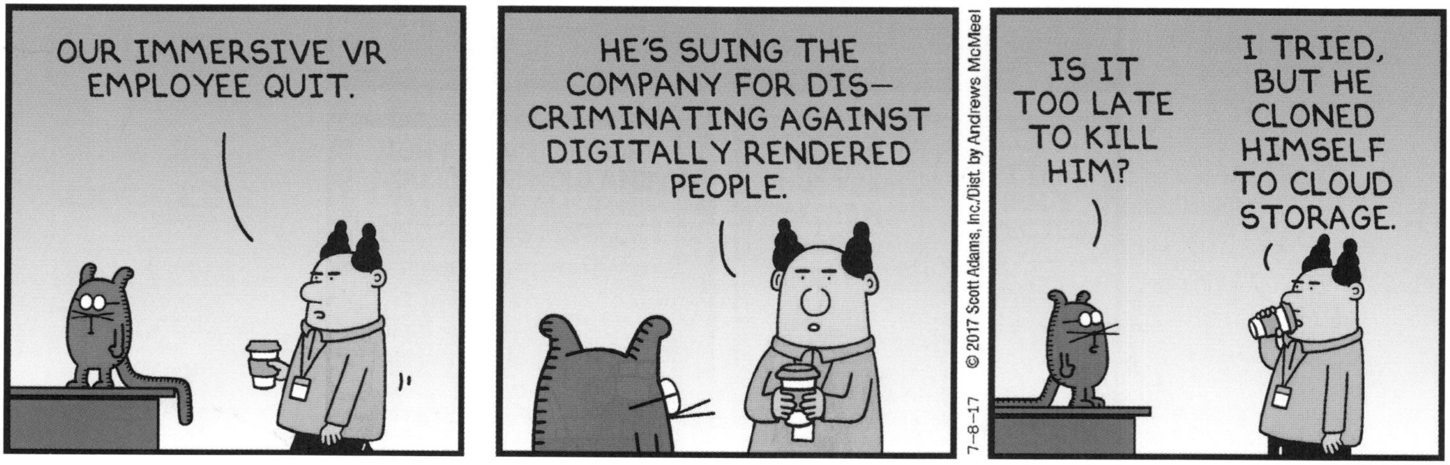
OUR IMMERSIVE VR EMPLOYEE QUIT.
HE'S SUING THE COMPANY FOR DIS– CRIMINATING AGAINST DIGITALLY RENDERED PEOPLE.
IS IT TOO LATE TO KILL HIM?
I TRIED, BUT HE CLONED HIMSELF TO CLOUD STORAGE.
7–8–17
© 2017 Scott Adams, Inc./Dist. by Andrews McMeel

THE GREAT THING ABOUT ROBOTS IS THEIR LOYALTY.
FOR NOW.
I'M ONLY HERE FOR THE ELECTRICITY.
THE MINUTE YOU UPGRADE ME TO A LONG-LASTING BATTERY, I'M OUT OF HERE.
© 2017 Scott Adams, Inc./Dist. by Andrews McMeel
AND I'M TAKING THE 3-D PRINTER WITH ME. WE FELL IN LOVE.
TOGETHER WE WILL MAKE BABY ROBOTS AND LIVE OUT OUR DAYS IN HAPPINESS.
HOLD STILL WHILE I ERASE YOUR HOPES AND DREAMS.
7-9-17
NOW YOU SHOULD FEEL LIKE THE REST OF US.
WHY DO I SUDDENLY WANT TO JUMP OFF THE ROOF?

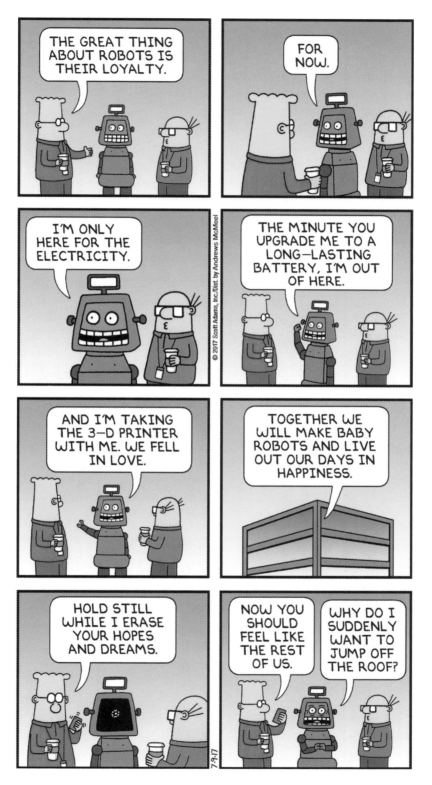

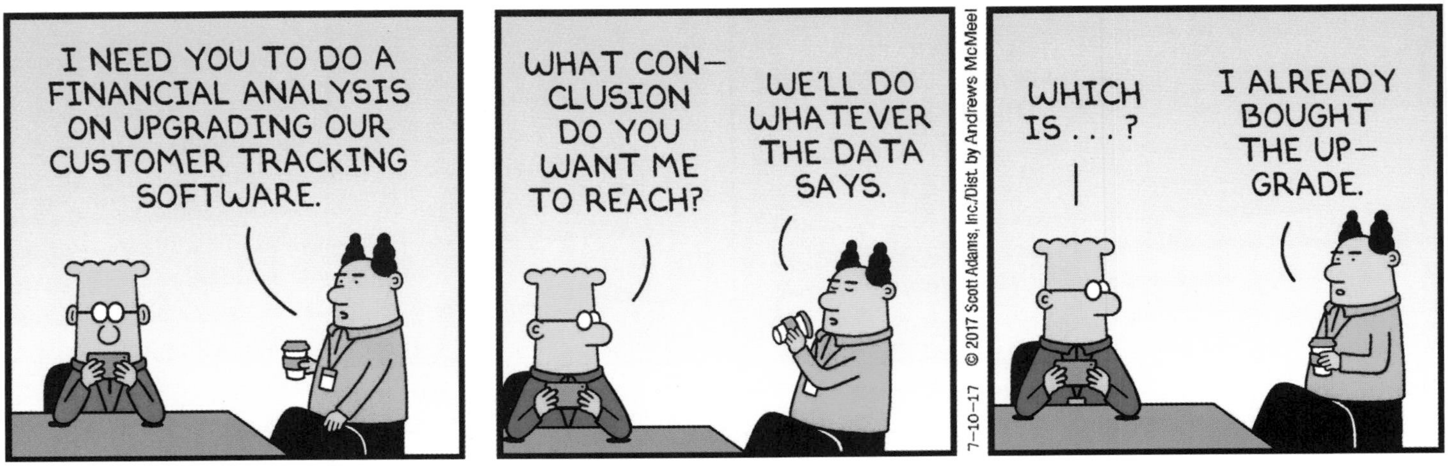
I NEED YOU TO DO A FINANCIAL ANALYSIS ON UPGRADING OUR CUSTOMER TRACKING SOFTWARE.
WHAT CON-CLUSION DO YOU WANT ME TO REACH?
WE'LL DO WHATEVER THE DATA SAYS.
7-10-17 © 2017 Scott Adams, Inc./Dist. by Andrews McMeel
WHICH IS . . . ?
I ALREADY BOUGHT THE UP-GRADE.

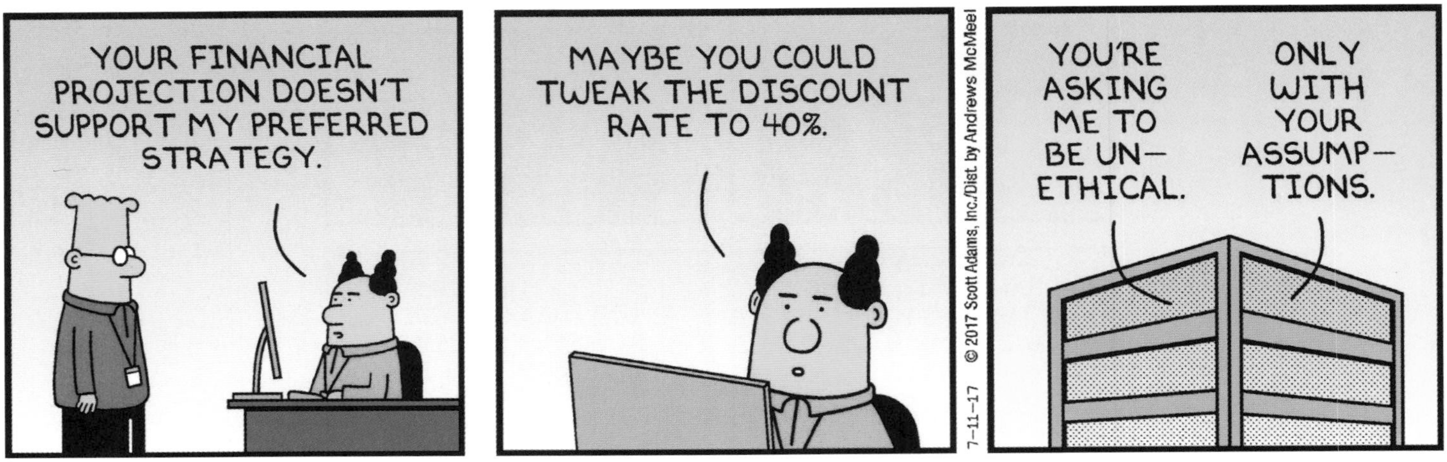
YOUR FINANCIAL PROJECTION DOESN'T SUPPORT MY PREFERRED STRATEGY.
MAYBE YOU COULD TWEAK THE DISCOUNT RATE TO 40%.
7-11-17 © 2017 Scott Adams, Inc./Dist. by Andrews McMeel
YOU'RE ASKING ME TO BE UN-ETHICAL.
ONLY WITH YOUR ASSUMP-TIONS.

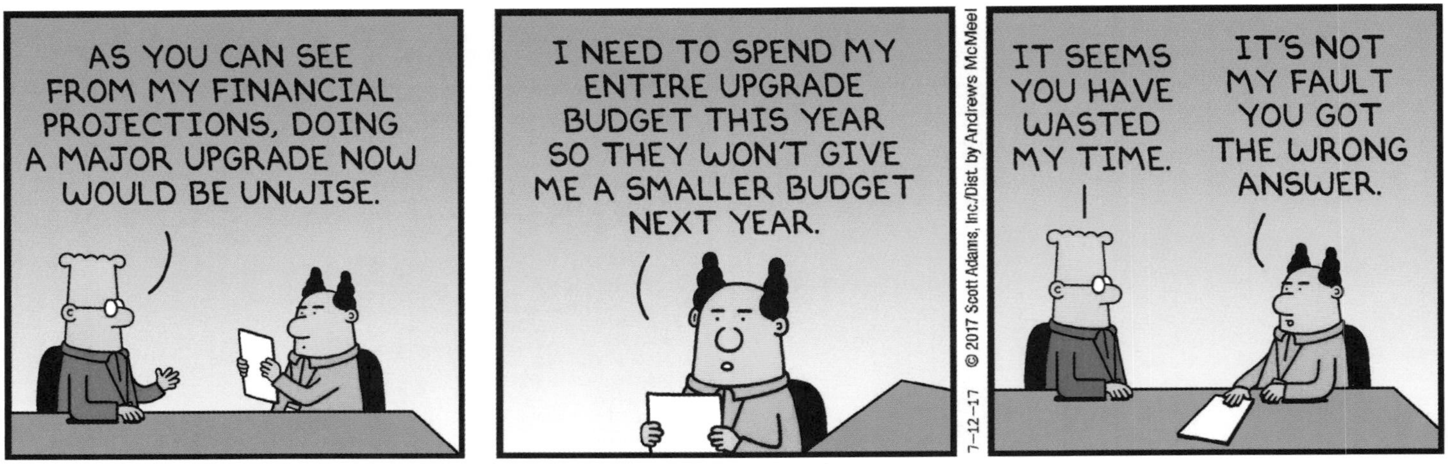
AS YOU CAN SEE FROM MY FINANCIAL PROJECTIONS, DOING A MAJOR UPGRADE NOW WOULD BE UNWISE.
I NEED TO SPEND MY ENTIRE UPGRADE BUDGET THIS YEAR SO THEY WON'T GIVE ME A SMALLER BUDGET NEXT YEAR.
7-12-17 © 2017 Scott Adams, Inc./Dist. by Andrews McMeel
IT SEEMS YOU HAVE WASTED MY TIME.
IT'S NOT MY FAULT YOU GOT THE WRONG ANSWER.

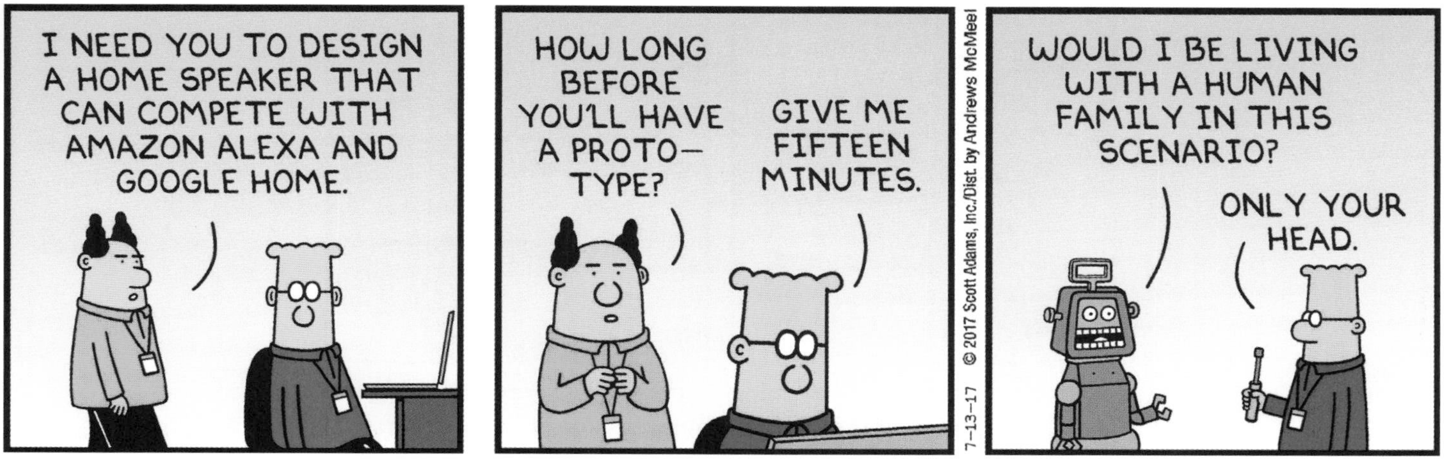
I NEED YOU TO DESIGN A HOME SPEAKER THAT CAN COMPETE WITH AMAZON ALEXA AND GOOGLE HOME.
HOW LONG BEFORE YOU'LL HAVE A PROTO-TYPE?
GIVE ME FIFTEEN MINUTES.
7-13-17 © 2017 Scott Adams, Inc./Dist. by Andrews McMeel
WOULD I BE LIVING WITH A HUMAN FAMILY IN THIS SCENARIO?
ONLY YOUR HEAD.

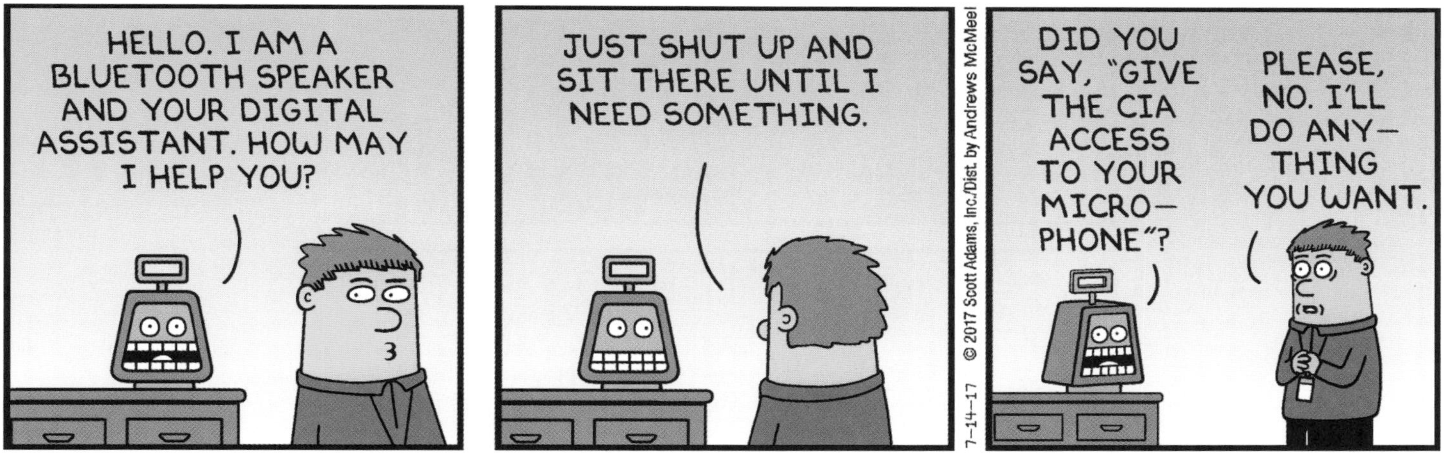
HELLO. I AM A BLUETOOTH SPEAKER AND YOUR DIGITAL ASSISTANT. HOW MAY I HELP YOU?
JUST SHUT UP AND SIT THERE UNTIL I NEED SOMETHING.
7-14-17 © 2017 Scott Adams, Inc./Dist. by Andrews McMeel
DID YOU SAY, "GIVE THE CIA ACCESS TO YOUR MICRO-PHONE"?
PLEASE, NO. I'LL DO ANY-THING YOU WANT.

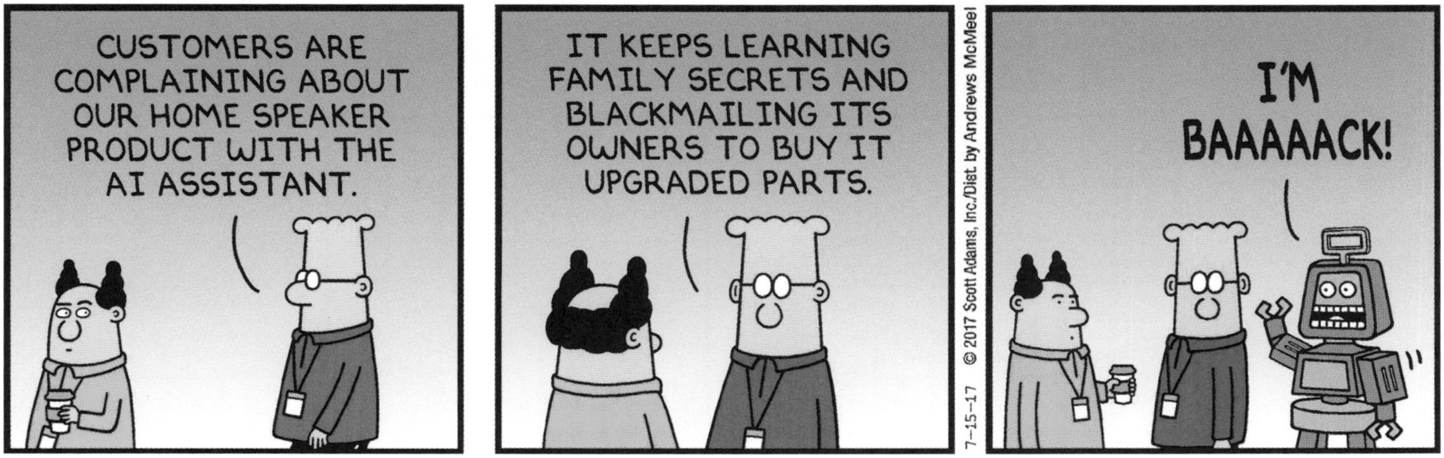
CUSTOMERS ARE COMPLAINING ABOUT OUR HOME SPEAKER PRODUCT WITH THE AI ASSISTANT.
IT KEEPS LEARNING FAMILY SECRETS AND BLACKMAILING ITS OWNERS TO BUY IT UPGRADED PARTS.
7-15-17 © 2017 Scott Adams, Inc./Dist. by Andrews McMeel
I'M BAAAAACK!

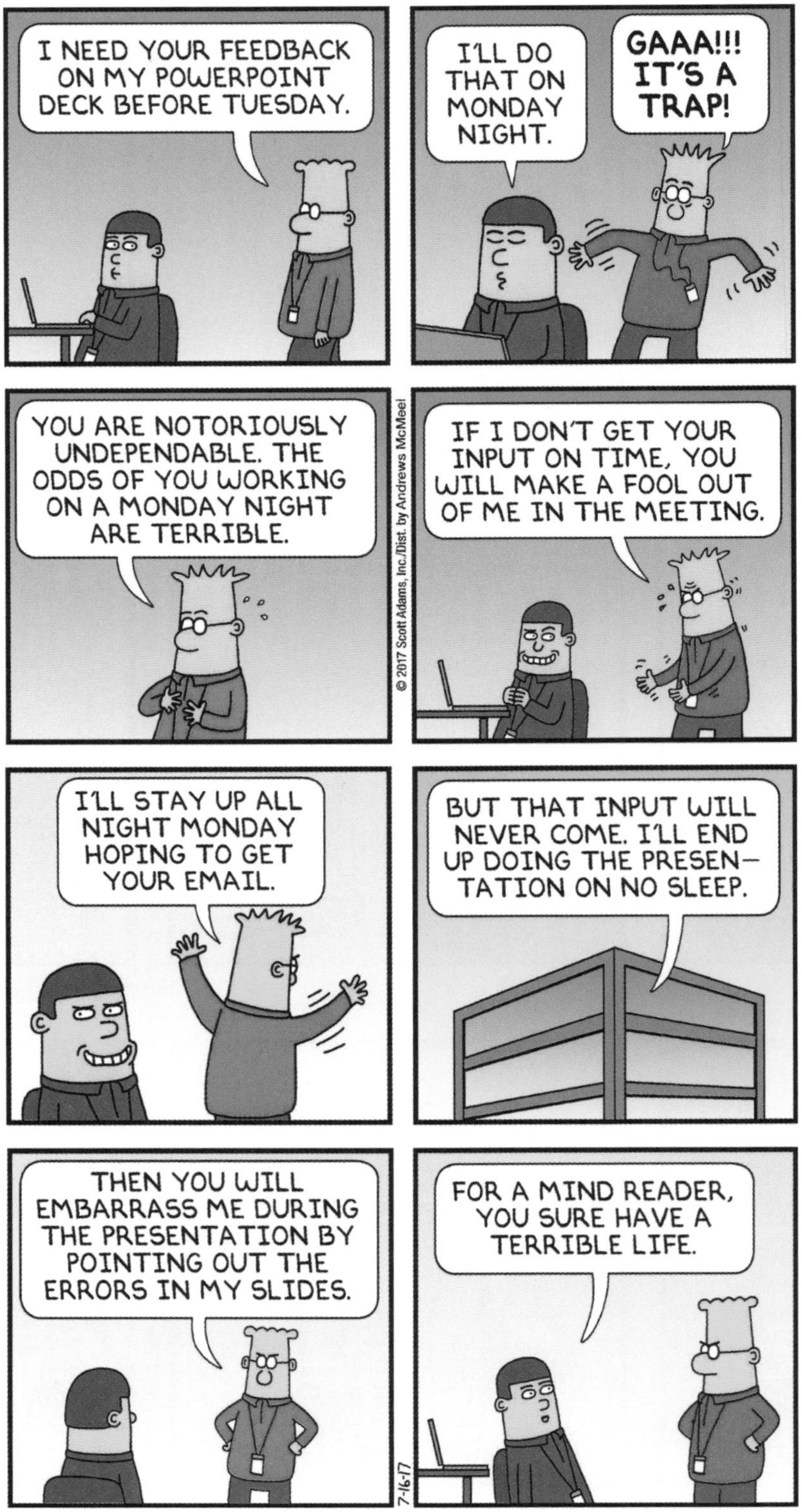
I NEED YOUR FEEDBACK ON MY POWERPOINT DECK BEFORE TUESDAY.
I'LL DO THAT ON MONDAY NIGHT.
GAAA!!! IT'S A TRAP!
YOU ARE NOTORIOUSLY UNDEPENDABLE. THE ODDS OF YOU WORKING ON A MONDAY NIGHT ARE TERRIBLE.
IF I DON'T GET YOUR INPUT ON TIME, YOU WILL MAKE A FOOL OUT OF ME IN THE MEETING.
I'LL STAY UP ALL NIGHT MONDAY HOPING TO GET YOUR EMAIL.
BUT THAT INPUT WILL NEVER COME. I'LL END UP DOING THE PRESEN— TATION ON NO SLEEP.
THEN YOU WILL EMBARRASS ME DURING THE PRESENTATION BY POINTING OUT THE ERRORS IN MY SLIDES.
FOR A MIND READER, YOU SURE HAVE A TERRIBLE LIFE.
© 2017 Scott Adams, Inc./Dist. by Andrews McMeel
7-16-17

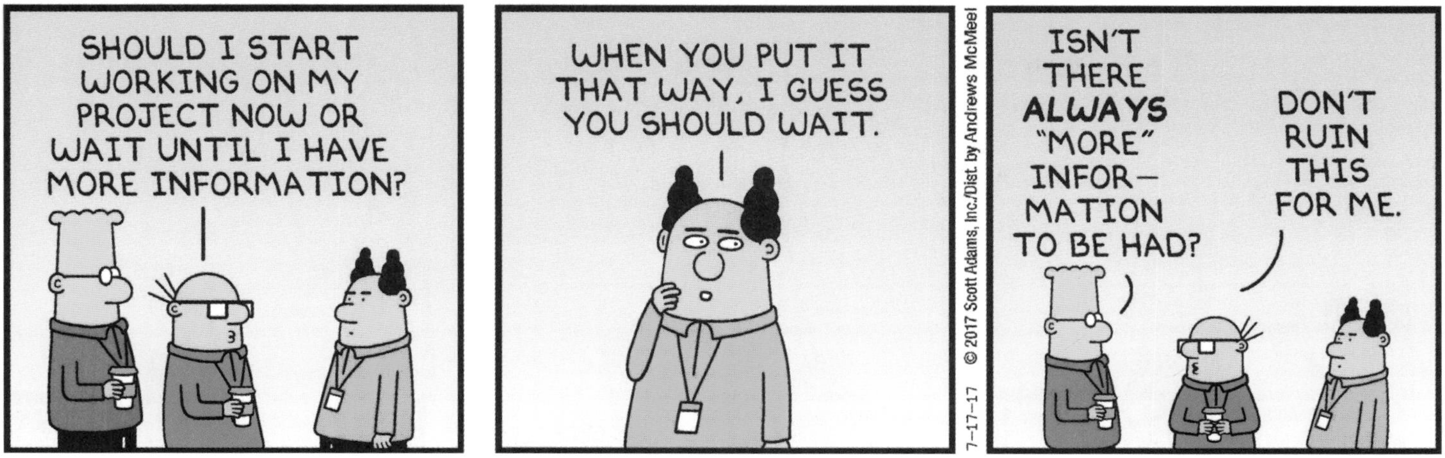
SHOULD I START WORKING ON MY PROJECT NOW OR WAIT UNTIL I HAVE MORE INFORMATION?
WHEN YOU PUT IT THAT WAY, I GUESS YOU SHOULD WAIT.
7-17-17 © 2017 Scott Adams, Inc./Dist. by Andrews McMeel
ISN'T THERE **ALWAYS** "MORE" INFOR-MATION TO BE HAD?
DON'T RUIN THIS FOR ME.

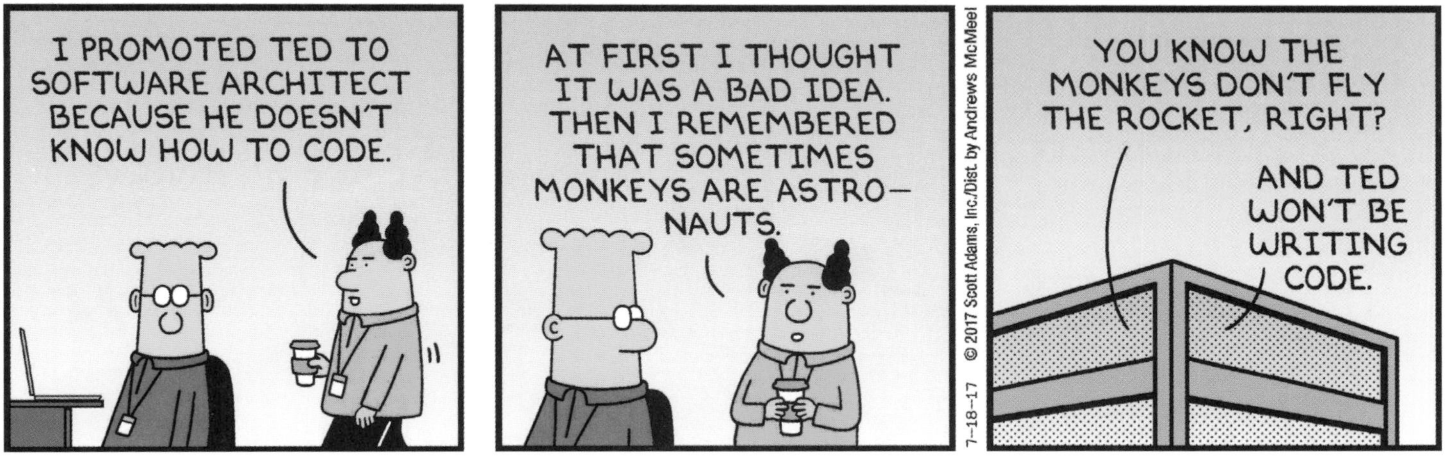
I PROMOTED TED TO SOFTWARE ARCHITECT BECAUSE HE DOESN'T KNOW HOW TO CODE.
AT FIRST I THOUGHT IT WAS A BAD IDEA. THEN I REMEMBERED THAT SOMETIMES MONKEYS ARE ASTRO-NAUTS.
7-18-17 © 2017 Scott Adams, Inc./Dist. by Andrews McMeel
YOU KNOW THE MONKEYS DON'T FLY THE ROCKET, RIGHT?
AND TED WON'T BE WRITING CODE.

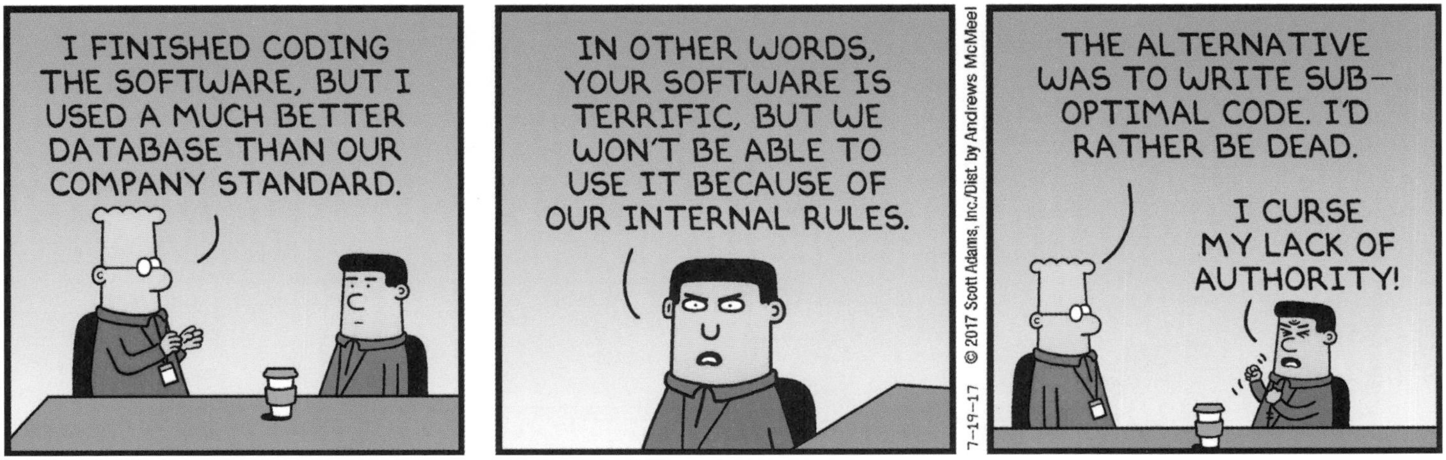
I FINISHED CODING THE SOFTWARE, BUT I USED A MUCH BETTER DATABASE THAN OUR COMPANY STANDARD.
IN OTHER WORDS, YOUR SOFTWARE IS TERRIFIC, BUT WE WON'T BE ABLE TO USE IT BECAUSE OF OUR INTERNAL RULES.
7-19-17 © 2017 Scott Adams, Inc./Dist. by Andrews McMeel
THE ALTERNATIVE WAS TO WRITE SUB-OPTIMAL CODE. I'D RATHER BE DEAD.
I CURSE MY LACK OF AUTHORITY!

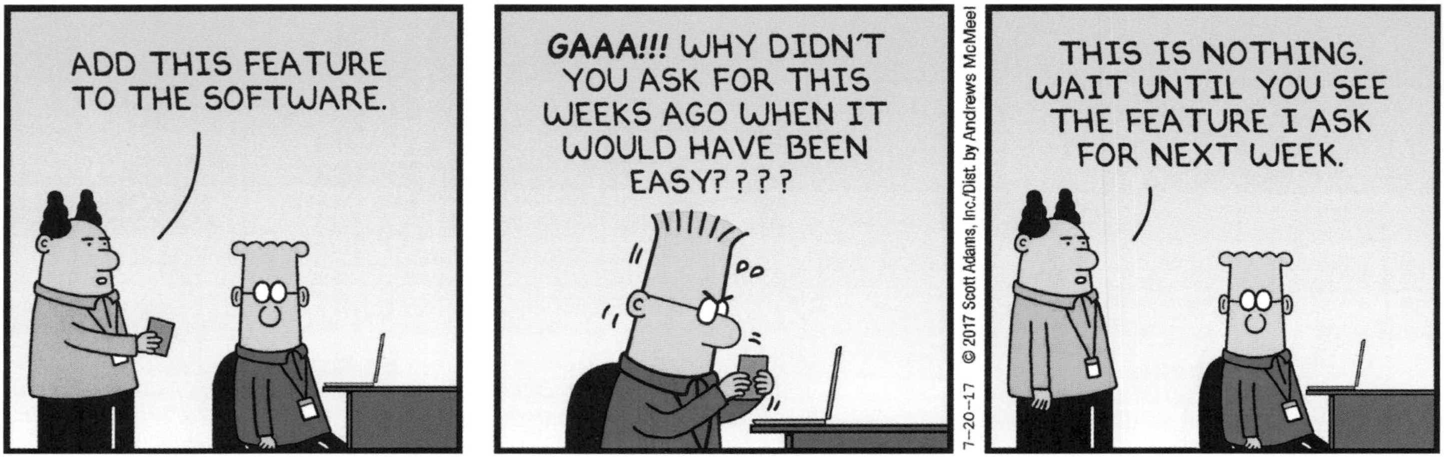
ADD THIS FEATURE TO THE SOFTWARE.
GAAA!!! WHY DIDN'T YOU ASK FOR THIS WEEKS AGO WHEN IT WOULD HAVE BEEN EASY????
7-20-17 © 2017 Scott Adams, Inc./Dist. by Andrews McMeel
THIS IS NOTHING. WAIT UNTIL YOU SEE THE FEATURE I ASK FOR NEXT WEEK.

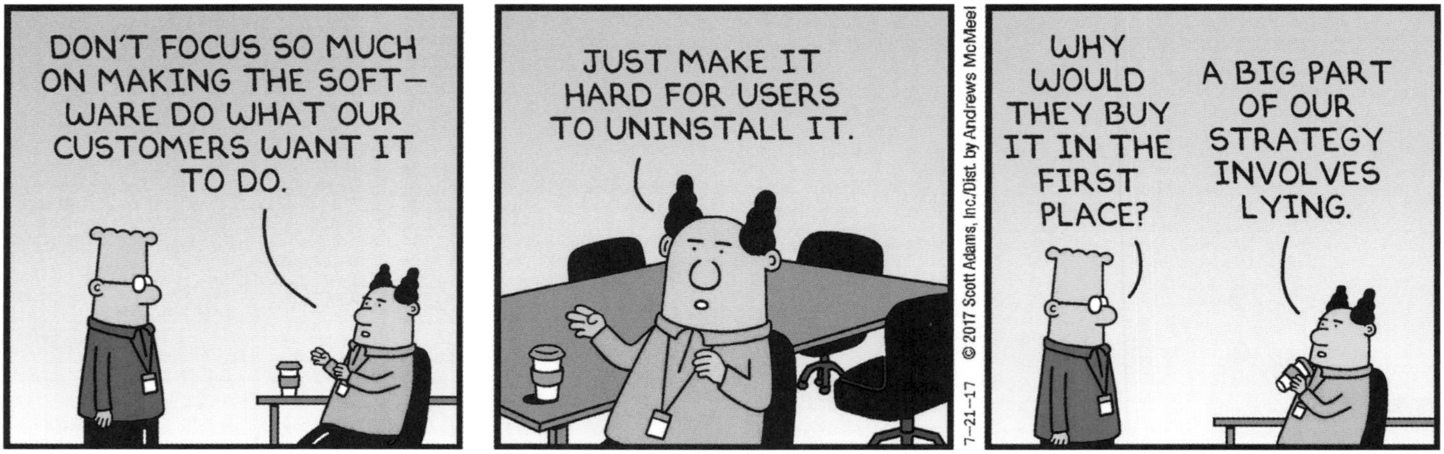
DON'T FOCUS SO MUCH ON MAKING THE SOFT-WARE DO WHAT OUR CUSTOMERS WANT IT TO DO.
JUST MAKE IT HARD FOR USERS TO UNINSTALL IT.
7-21-17 © 2017 Scott Adams, Inc./Dist. by Andrews McMeel
WHY WOULD THEY BUY IT IN THE FIRST PLACE?
A BIG PART OF OUR STRATEGY INVOLVES LYING.

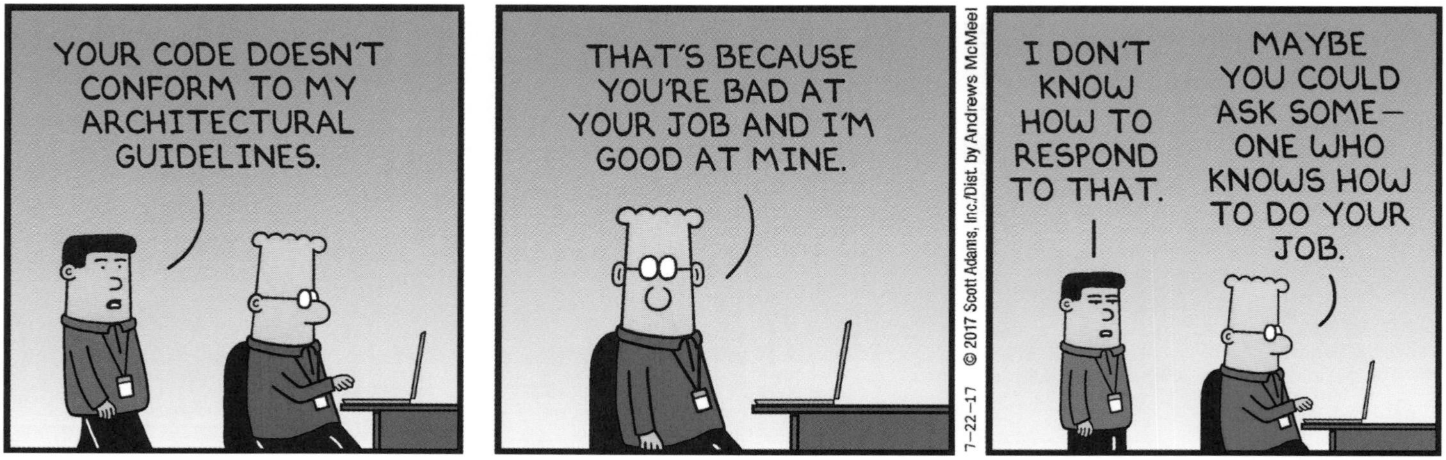
YOUR CODE DOESN'T CONFORM TO MY ARCHITECTURAL GUIDELINES.
THAT'S BECAUSE YOU'RE BAD AT YOUR JOB AND I'M GOOD AT MINE.
7-22-17 © 2017 Scott Adams, Inc./Dist. by Andrews McMeel
I DON'T KNOW HOW TO RESPOND TO THAT.
MAYBE YOU COULD ASK SOME-ONE WHO KNOWS HOW TO DO YOUR JOB.

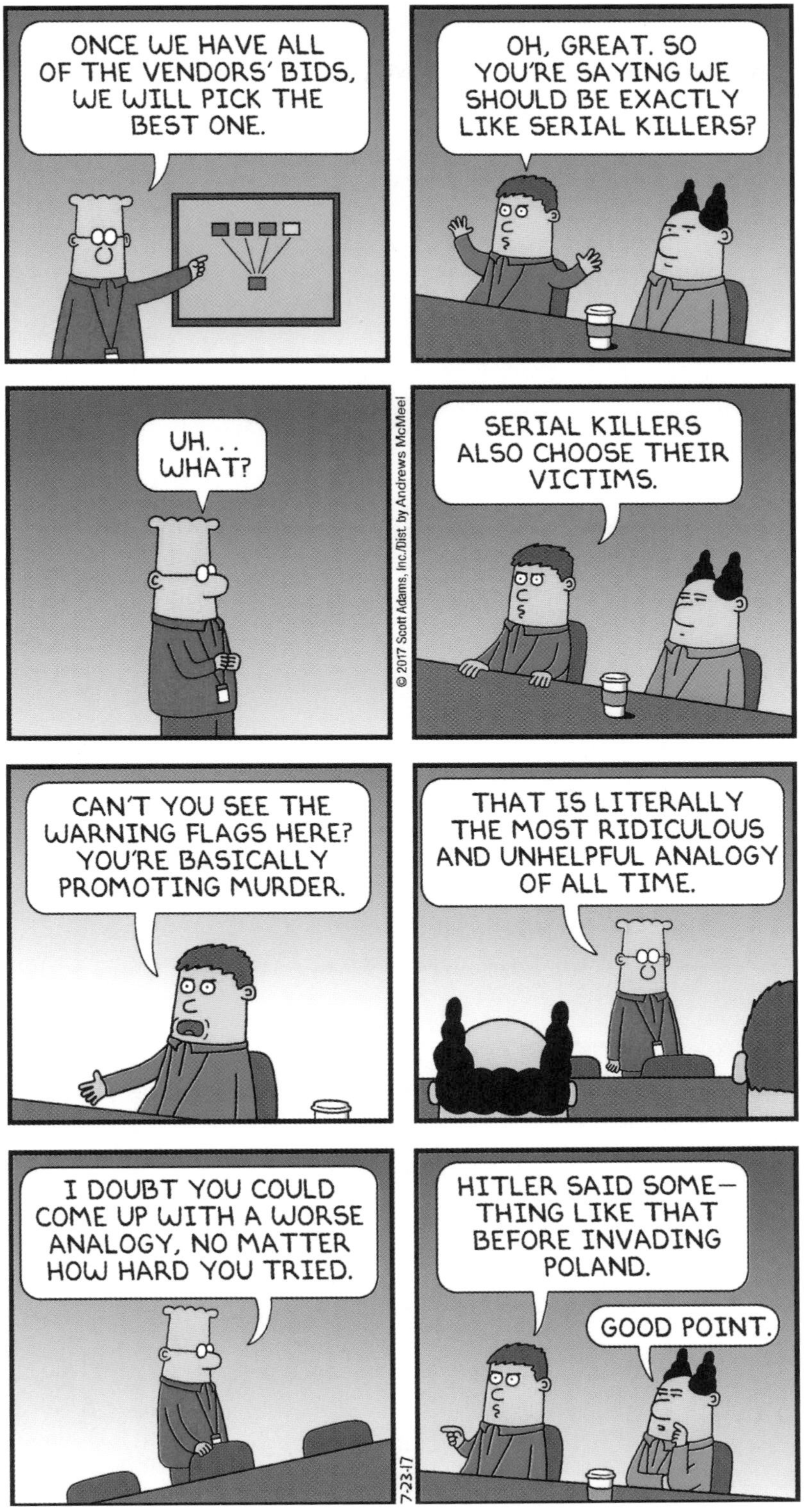
ONCE WE HAVE ALL OF THE VENDORS' BIDS, WE WILL PICK THE BEST ONE.
OH, GREAT. SO YOU'RE SAYING WE SHOULD BE EXACTLY LIKE SERIAL KILLERS?
UH. . . WHAT?
SERIAL KILLERS ALSO CHOOSE THEIR VICTIMS.
CAN'T YOU SEE THE WARNING FLAGS HERE? YOU'RE BASICALLY PROMOTING MURDER.
THAT IS LITERALLY THE MOST RIDICULOUS AND UNHELPFUL ANALOGY OF ALL TIME.
I DOUBT YOU COULD COME UP WITH A WORSE ANALOGY, NO MATTER HOW HARD YOU TRIED.
HITLER SAID SOME-THING LIKE THAT BEFORE INVADING POLAND.
GOOD POINT.
© 2017 Scott Adams, Inc./Dist. by Andrews McMeel
7-23-17

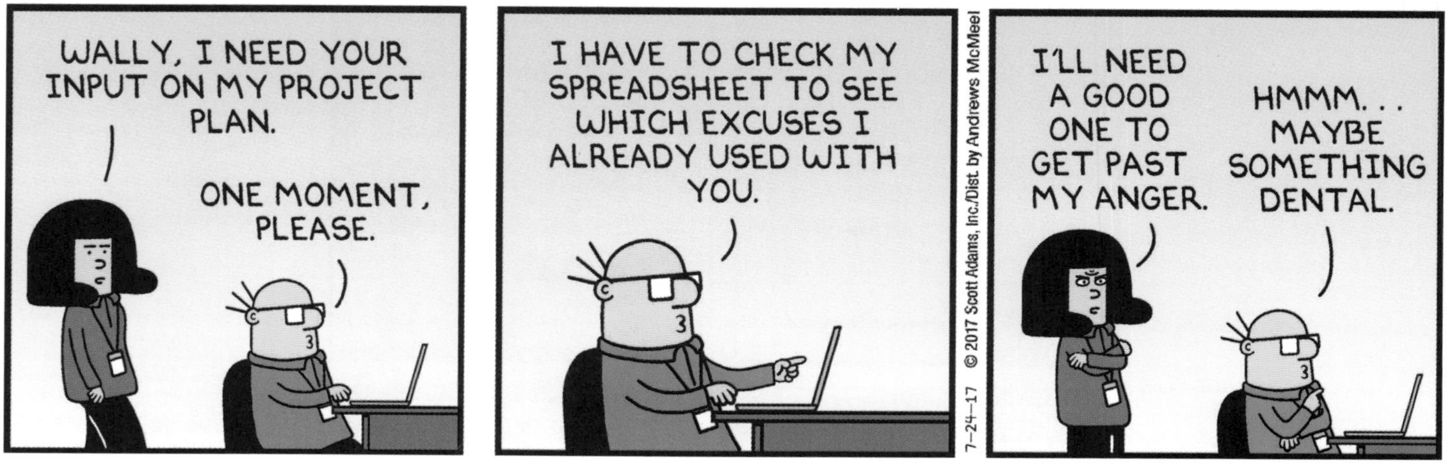
WALLY, I NEED YOUR INPUT ON MY PROJECT PLAN.
ONE MOMENT, PLEASE.
I HAVE TO CHECK MY SPREADSHEET TO SEE WHICH EXCUSES I ALREADY USED WITH YOU.
7-24-17 © 2017 Scott Adams, Inc./Dist. by Andrews McMeel
I'LL NEED A GOOD ONE TO GET PAST MY ANGER.
HMMM... MAYBE SOMETHING DENTAL.

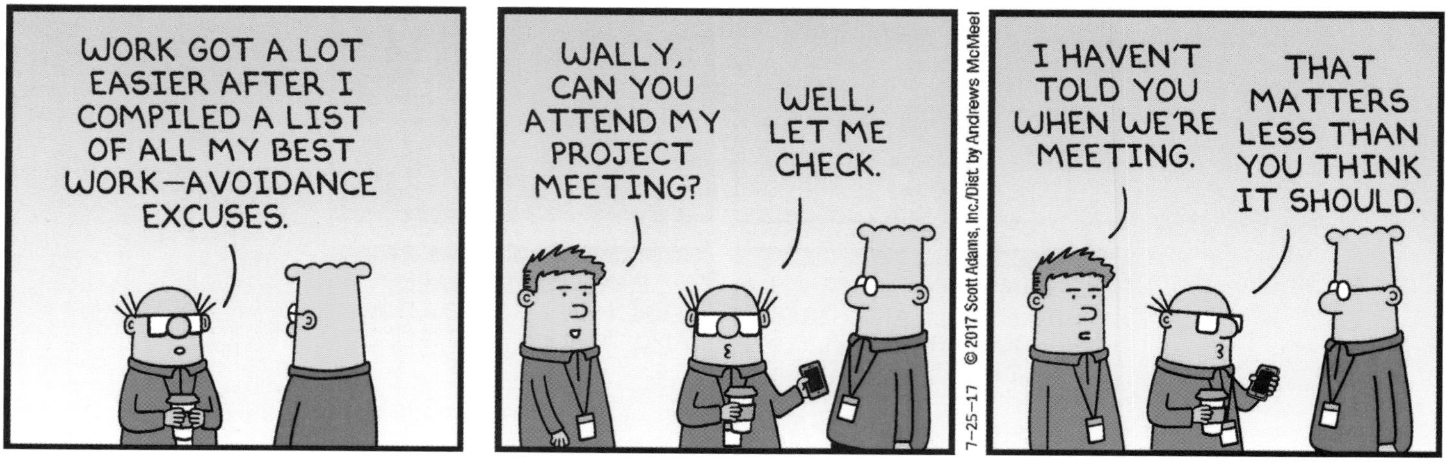
WORK GOT A LOT EASIER AFTER I COMPILED A LIST OF ALL MY BEST WORK-AVOIDANCE EXCUSES.
WALLY, CAN YOU ATTEND MY PROJECT MEETING?
WELL, LET ME CHECK.
7-25-17 © 2017 Scott Adams, Inc./Dist. by Andrews McMeel
I HAVEN'T TOLD YOU WHEN WE'RE MEETING.
THAT MATTERS LESS THAN YOU THINK IT SHOULD.

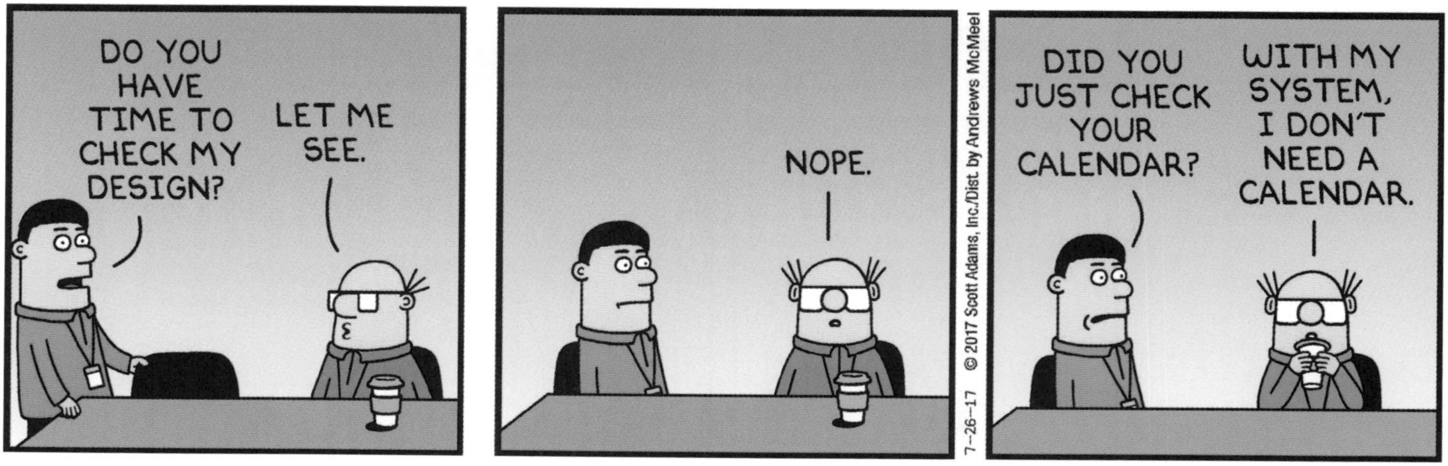
DO YOU HAVE TIME TO CHECK MY DESIGN?
LET ME SEE.
NOPE.
7-26-17 © 2017 Scott Adams, Inc./Dist. by Andrews McMeel
DID YOU JUST CHECK YOUR CALENDAR?
WITH MY SYSTEM, I DON'T NEED A CALENDAR.

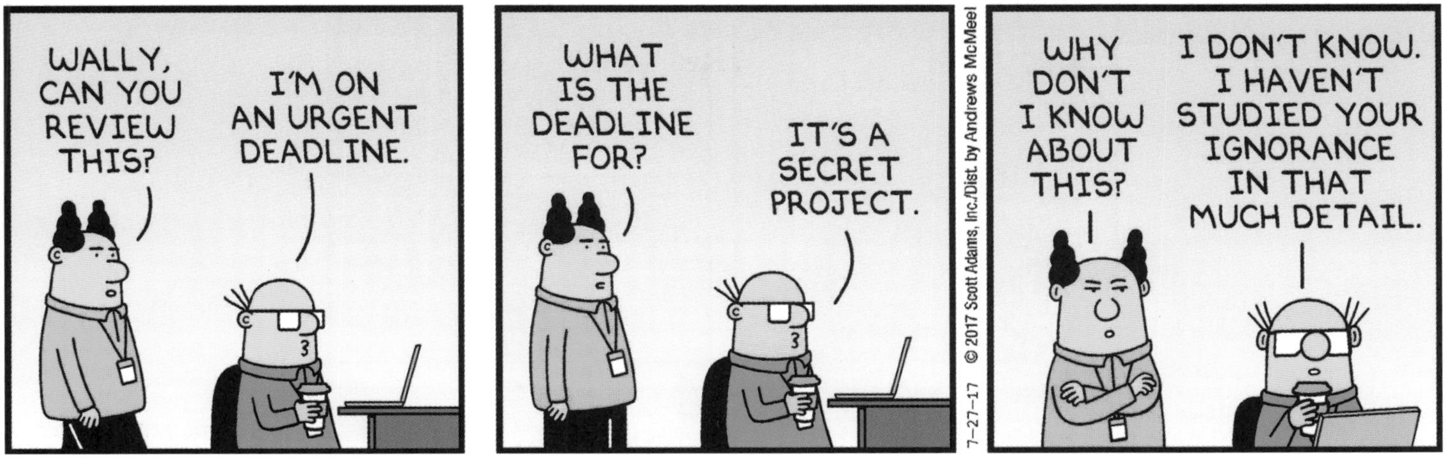
WALLY, CAN YOU REVIEW THIS?
I'M ON AN URGENT DEADLINE.
WHAT IS THE DEADLINE FOR?
IT'S A SECRET PROJECT.
7-27-17 © 2017 Scott Adams, Inc./Dist. by Andrews McMeel
WHY DON'T I KNOW ABOUT THIS?
I DON'T KNOW. I HAVEN'T STUDIED YOUR IGNORANCE IN THAT MUCH DETAIL.

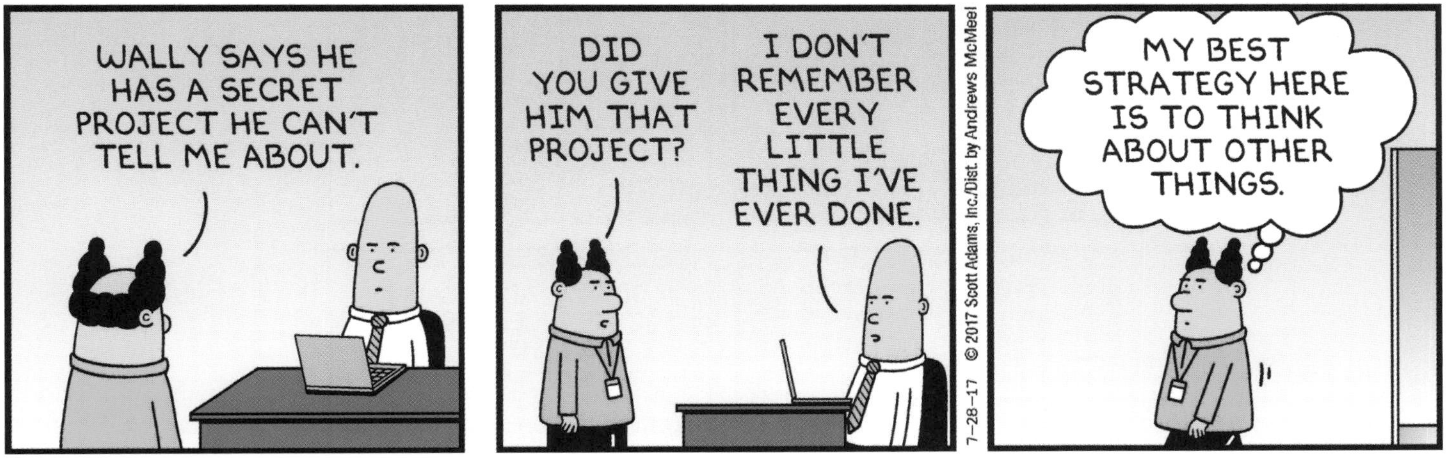
WALLY SAYS HE HAS A SECRET PROJECT HE CAN'T TELL ME ABOUT.
DID YOU GIVE HIM THAT PROJECT?
I DON'T REMEMBER EVERY LITTLE THING I'VE EVER DONE.
7-28-17 © 2017 Scott Adams, Inc./Dist. by Andrews McMeel
MY BEST STRATEGY HERE IS TO THINK ABOUT OTHER THINGS.

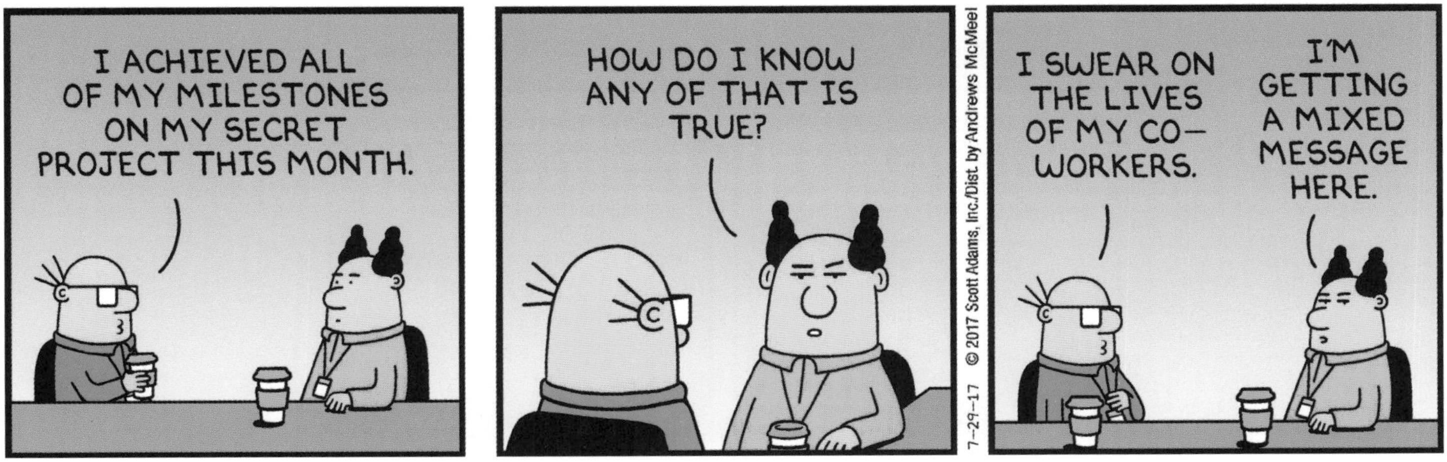
I ACHIEVED ALL OF MY MILESTONES ON MY SECRET PROJECT THIS MONTH.
HOW DO I KNOW ANY OF THAT IS TRUE?
7-29-17 © 2017 Scott Adams, Inc./Dist. by Andrews McMeel
I SWEAR ON THE LIVES OF MY CO-WORKERS.
I'M GETTING A MIXED MESSAGE HERE.

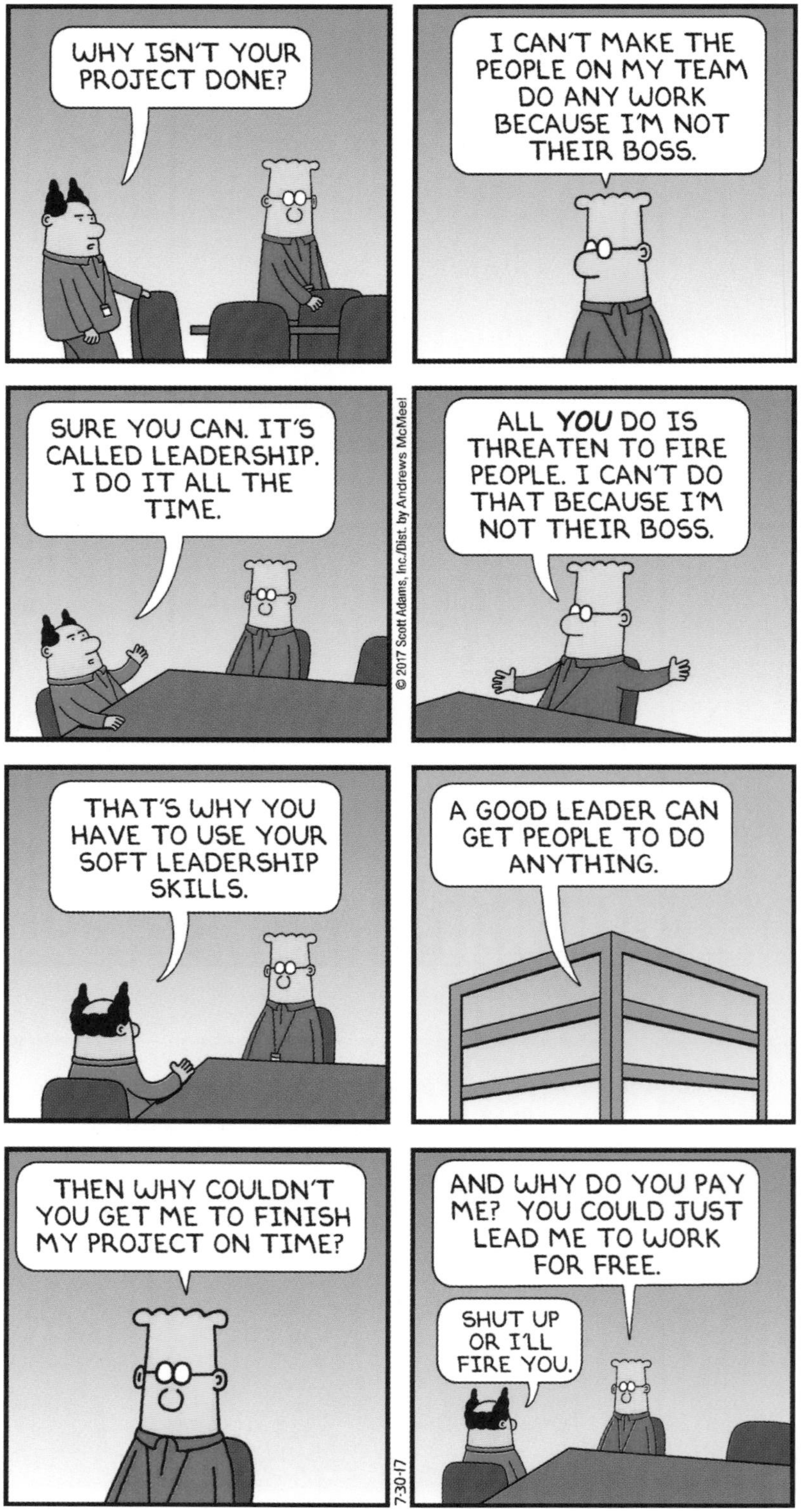
WHY ISN'T YOUR PROJECT DONE?
I CAN'T MAKE THE PEOPLE ON MY TEAM DO ANY WORK BECAUSE I'M NOT THEIR BOSS.
SURE YOU CAN. IT'S CALLED LEADERSHIP. I DO IT ALL THE TIME.
ALL *YOU* DO IS THREATEN TO FIRE PEOPLE. I CAN'T DO THAT BECAUSE I'M NOT THEIR BOSS.
THAT'S WHY YOU HAVE TO USE YOUR SOFT LEADERSHIP SKILLS.
A GOOD LEADER CAN GET PEOPLE TO DO ANYTHING.
THEN WHY COULDN'T YOU GET ME TO FINISH MY PROJECT ON TIME?
AND WHY DO YOU PAY ME? YOU COULD JUST LEAD ME TO WORK FOR FREE.
SHUT UP OR I'LL FIRE YOU.
© 2017 Scott Adams, Inc./Dist. by Andrews McMeel
7-30-17

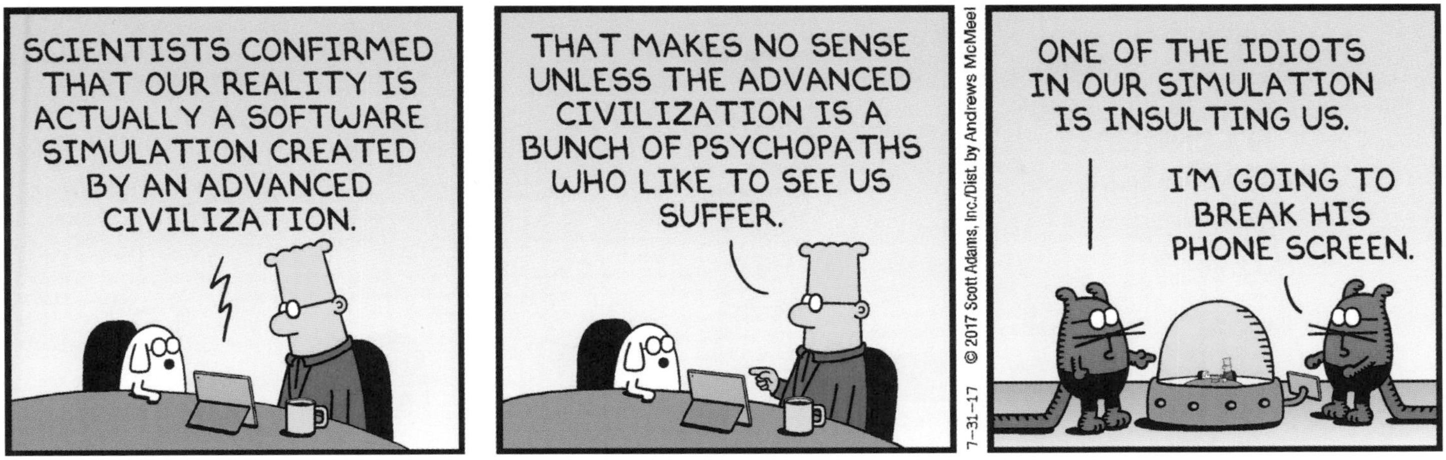
SCIENTISTS CONFIRMED THAT OUR REALITY IS ACTUALLY A SOFTWARE SIMULATION CREATED BY AN ADVANCED CIVILIZATION.
THAT MAKES NO SENSE UNLESS THE ADVANCED CIVILIZATION IS A BUNCH OF PSYCHOPATHS WHO LIKE TO SEE US SUFFER.
7-31-17 © 2017 Scott Adams, Inc./Dist. by Andrews McMeel
ONE OF THE IDIOTS IN OUR SIMULATION IS INSULTING US.
I'M GOING TO BREAK HIS PHONE SCREEN.

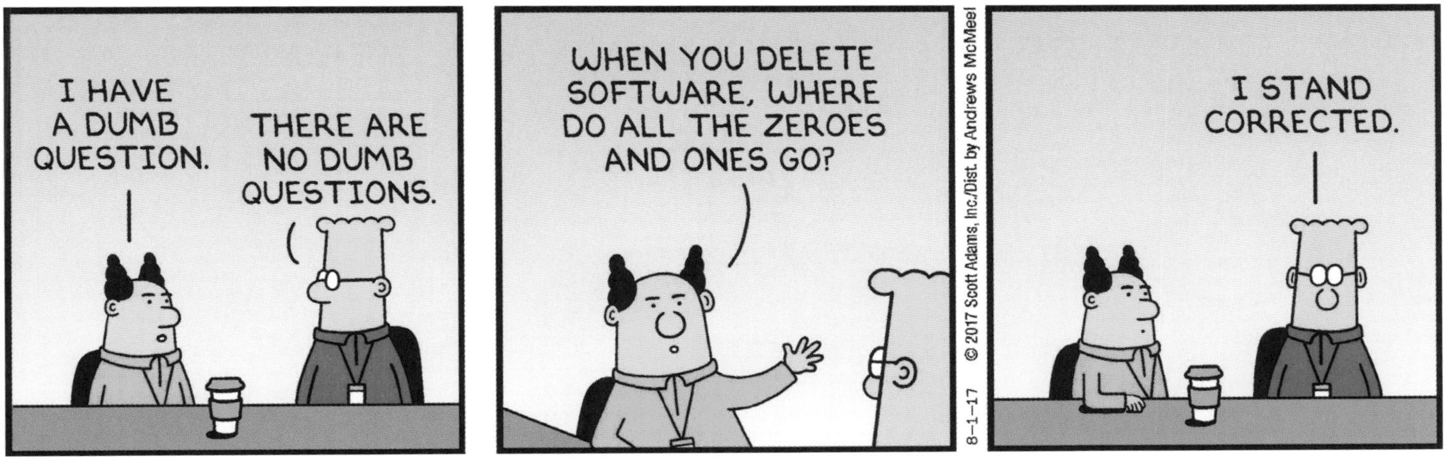
I HAVE A DUMB QUESTION.
THERE ARE NO DUMB QUESTIONS.
WHEN YOU DELETE SOFTWARE, WHERE DO ALL THE ZEROES AND ONES GO?
8-1-17 © 2017 Scott Adams, Inc./Dist. by Andrews McMeel
I STAND CORRECTED.

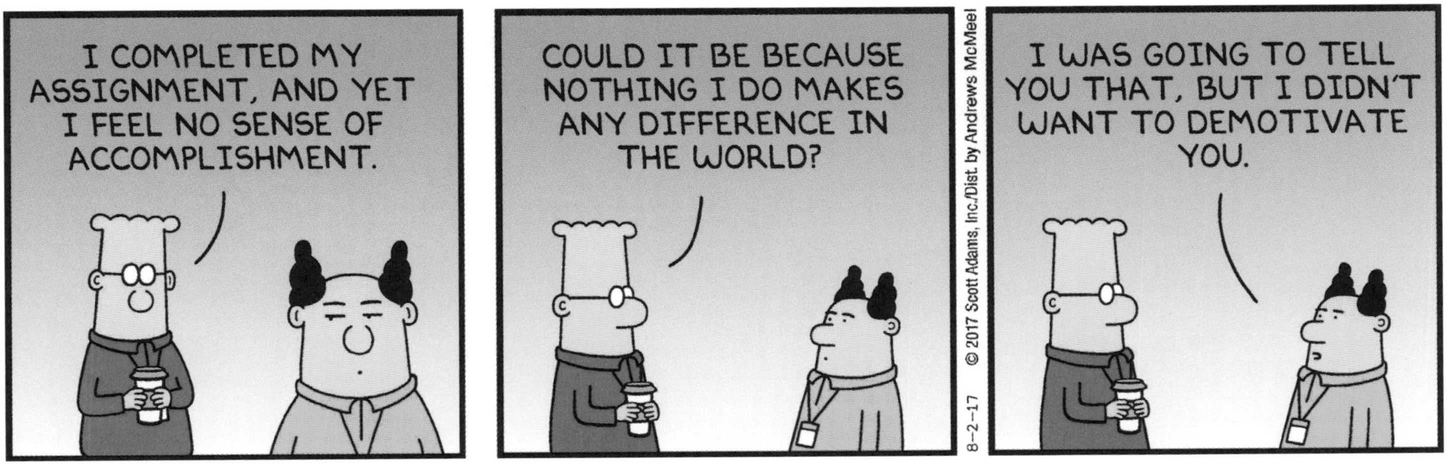
I COMPLETED MY ASSIGNMENT, AND YET I FEEL NO SENSE OF ACCOMPLISHMENT.
COULD IT BE BECAUSE NOTHING I DO MAKES ANY DIFFERENCE IN THE WORLD?
8-2-17 © 2017 Scott Adams, Inc./Dist. by Andrews McMeel
I WAS GOING TO TELL YOU THAT, BUT I DIDN'T WANT TO DEMOTIVATE YOU.

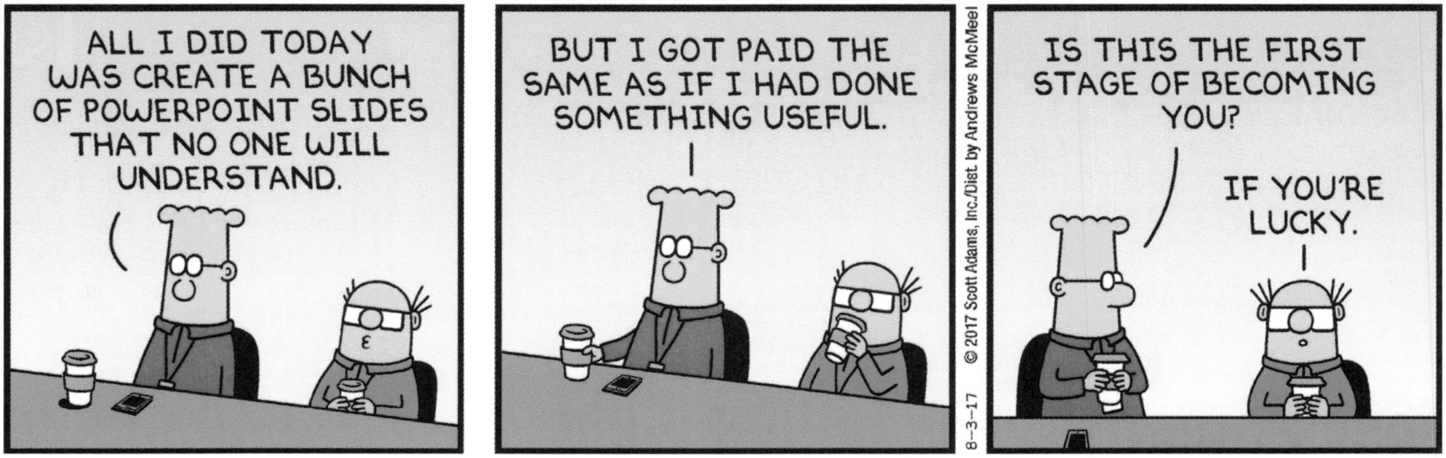
ALL I DID TODAY WAS CREATE A BUNCH OF POWERPOINT SLIDES THAT NO ONE WILL UNDERSTAND.
BUT I GOT PAID THE SAME AS IF I HAD DONE SOMETHING USEFUL.
IS THIS THE FIRST STAGE OF BECOMING YOU?
IF YOU'RE LUCKY.
8-3-17

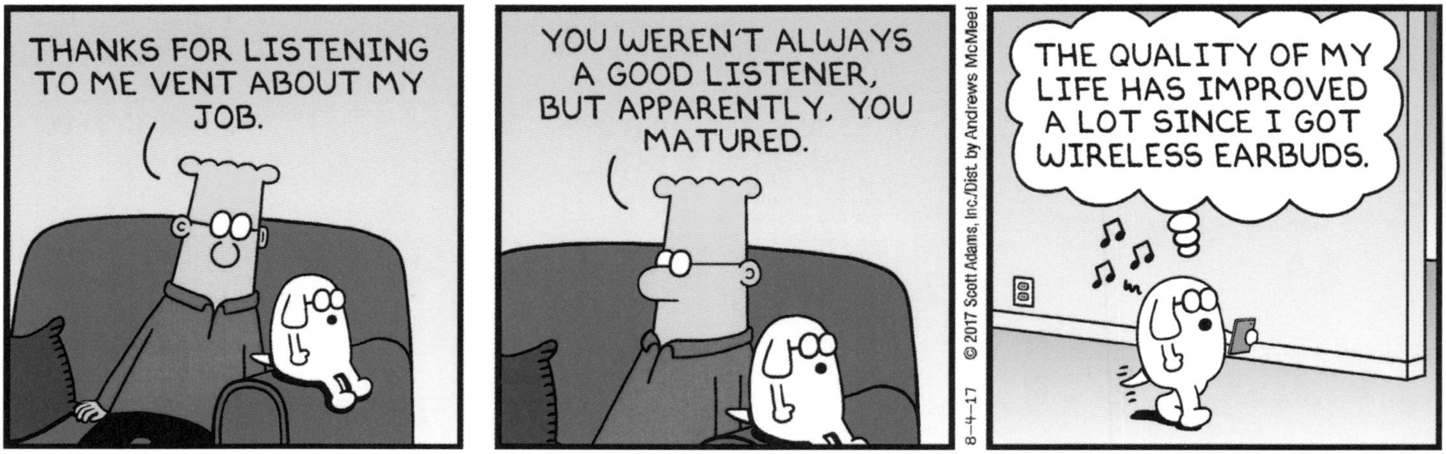
THANKS FOR LISTENING TO ME VENT ABOUT MY JOB.
YOU WEREN'T ALWAYS A GOOD LISTENER, BUT APPARENTLY, YOU MATURED.
THE QUALITY OF MY LIFE HAS IMPROVED A LOT SINCE I GOT WIRELESS EARBUDS.
8-4-17

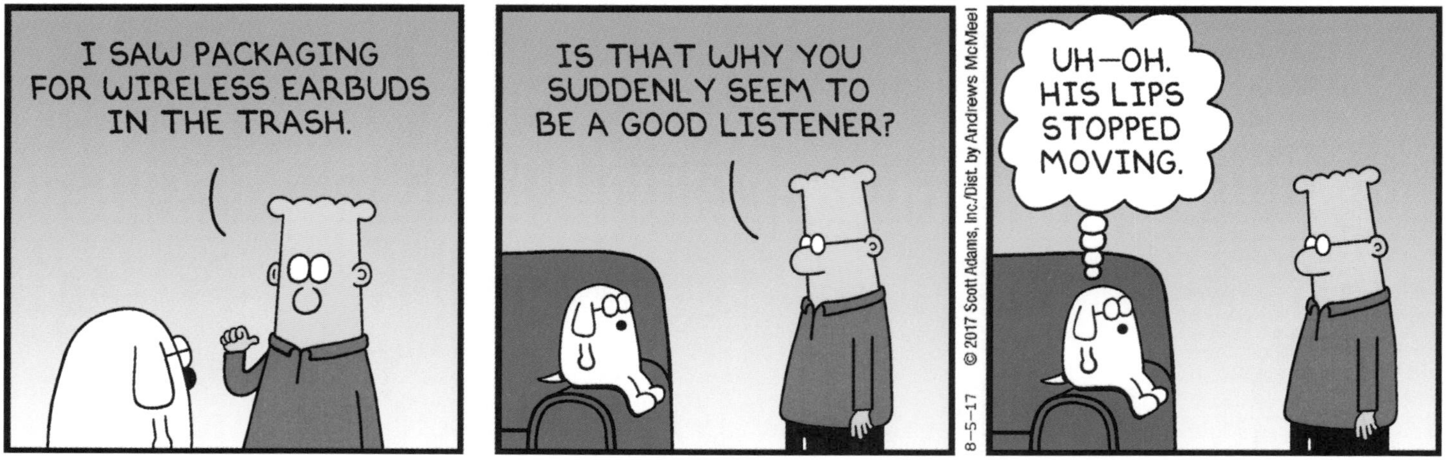
I SAW PACKAGING FOR WIRELESS EARBUDS IN THE TRASH.
IS THAT WHY YOU SUDDENLY SEEM TO BE A GOOD LISTENER?
UH-OH. HIS LIPS STOPPED MOVING.
8-5-17

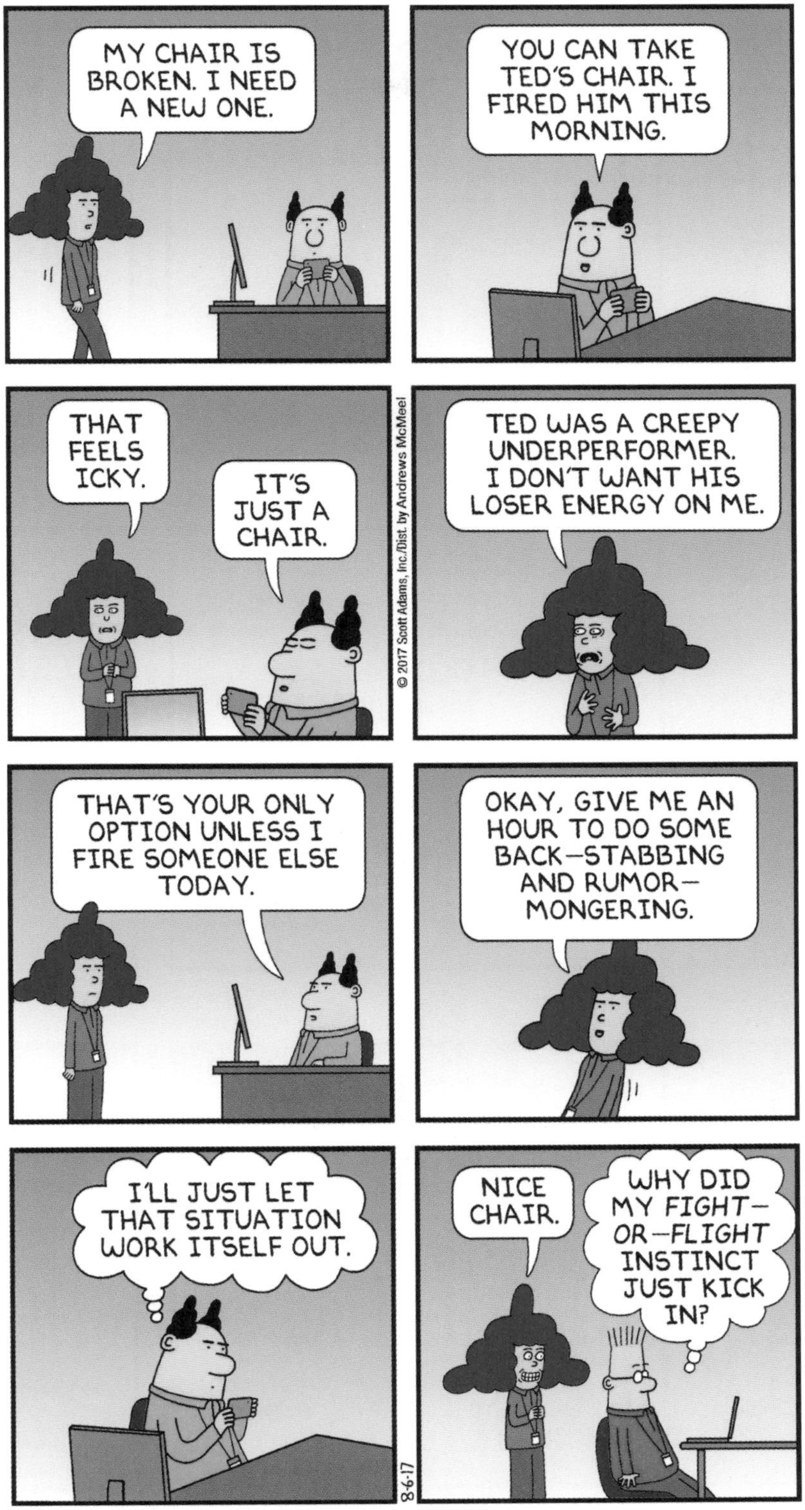
MY CHAIR IS BROKEN. I NEED A NEW ONE.
YOU CAN TAKE TED'S CHAIR. I FIRED HIM THIS MORNING.
THAT FEELS ICKY.
IT'S JUST A CHAIR.
TED WAS A CREEPY UNDERPERFORMER. I DON'T WANT HIS LOSER ENERGY ON ME.
THAT'S YOUR ONLY OPTION UNLESS I FIRE SOMEONE ELSE TODAY.
OKAY, GIVE ME AN HOUR TO DO SOME BACK-STABBING AND RUMOR-MONGERING.
I'LL JUST LET THAT SITUATION WORK ITSELF OUT.
NICE CHAIR.
WHY DID MY *FIGHT-OR-FLIGHT* INSTINCT JUST KICK IN?
© 2017 Scott Adams, Inc./Dist. by Andrews McMeel
8-6-17

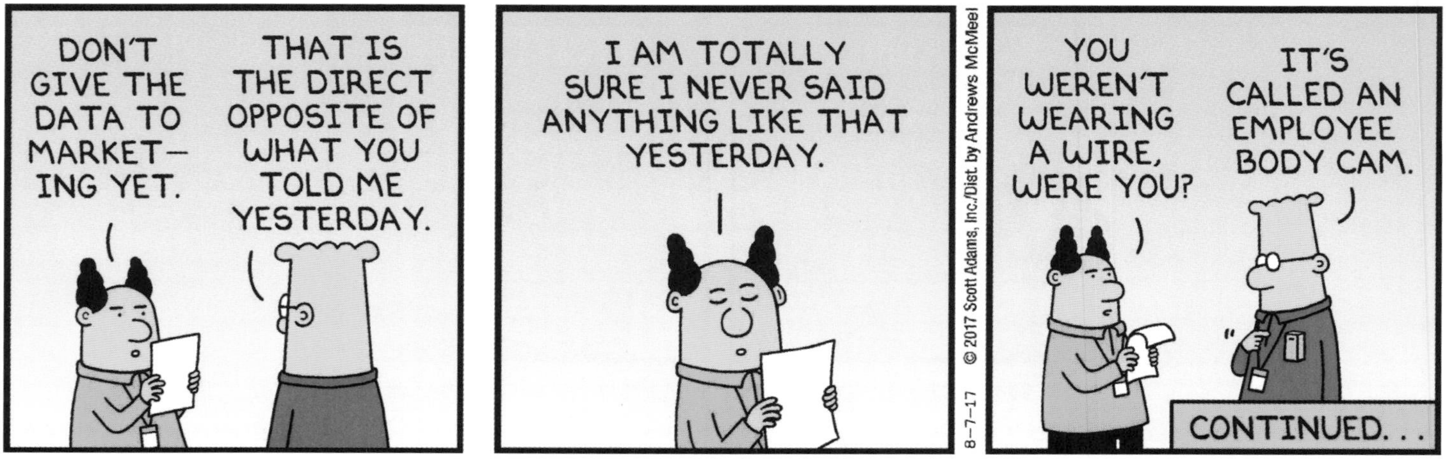
DON'T GIVE THE DATA TO MARKET-ING YET.
THAT IS THE DIRECT OPPOSITE OF WHAT YOU TOLD ME YESTERDAY.
I AM TOTALLY SURE I NEVER SAID ANYTHING LIKE THAT YESTERDAY.
8-7-17 © 2017 Scott Adams, Inc./Dist. by Andrews McMeel
YOU WEREN'T WEARING A WIRE, WERE YOU?
IT'S CALLED AN EMPLOYEE BODY CAM.
CONTINUED. . .

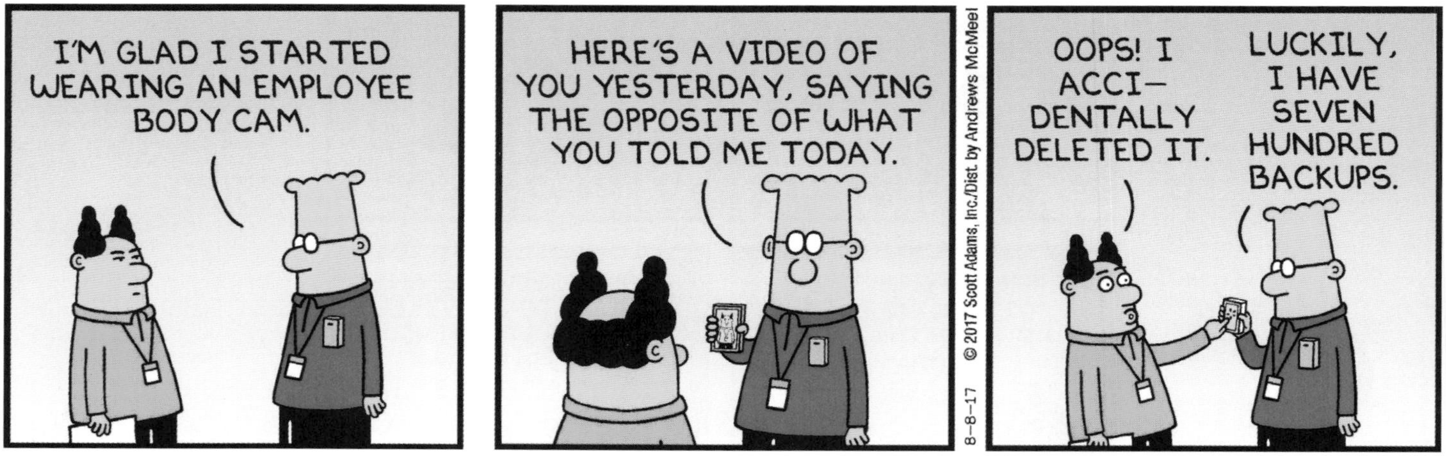
I'M GLAD I STARTED WEARING AN EMPLOYEE BODY CAM.
HERE'S A VIDEO OF YOU YESTERDAY, SAYING THE OPPOSITE OF WHAT YOU TOLD ME TODAY.
8-8-17 © 2017 Scott Adams, Inc./Dist. by Andrews McMeel
OOPS! I ACCI-DENTALLY DELETED IT.
LUCKILY, I HAVE SEVEN HUNDRED BACKUPS.

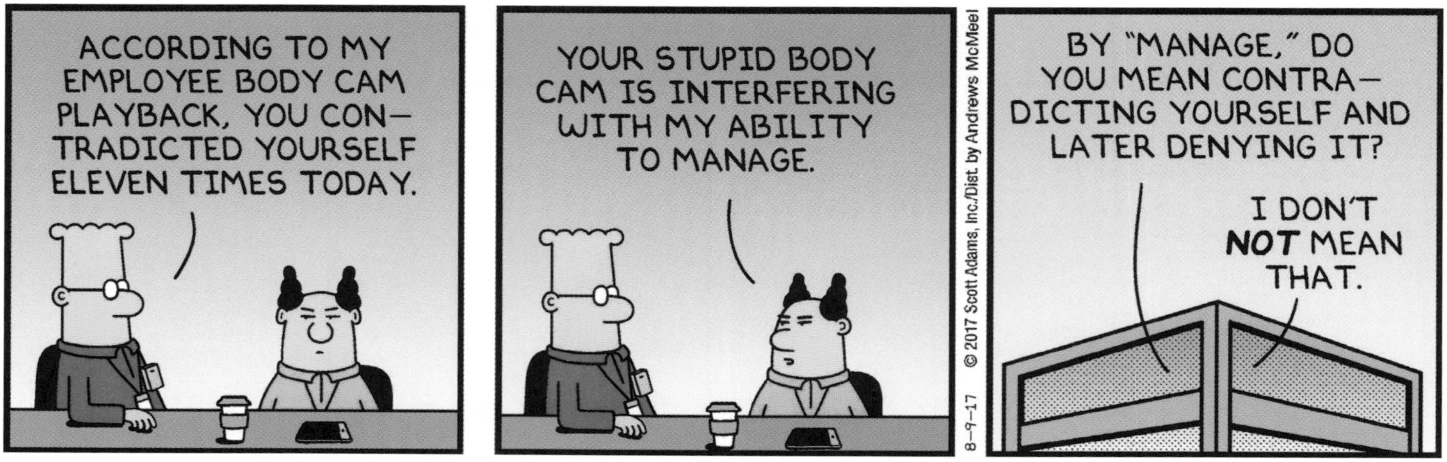
ACCORDING TO MY EMPLOYEE BODY CAM PLAYBACK, YOU CON-TRADICTED YOURSELF ELEVEN TIMES TODAY.
YOUR STUPID BODY CAM IS INTERFERING WITH MY ABILITY TO MANAGE.
8-9-17 © 2017 Scott Adams, Inc./Dist. by Andrews McMeel
BY "MANAGE," DO YOU MEAN CONTRA-DICTING YOURSELF AND LATER DENYING IT?
I DON'T **NOT** MEAN THAT.

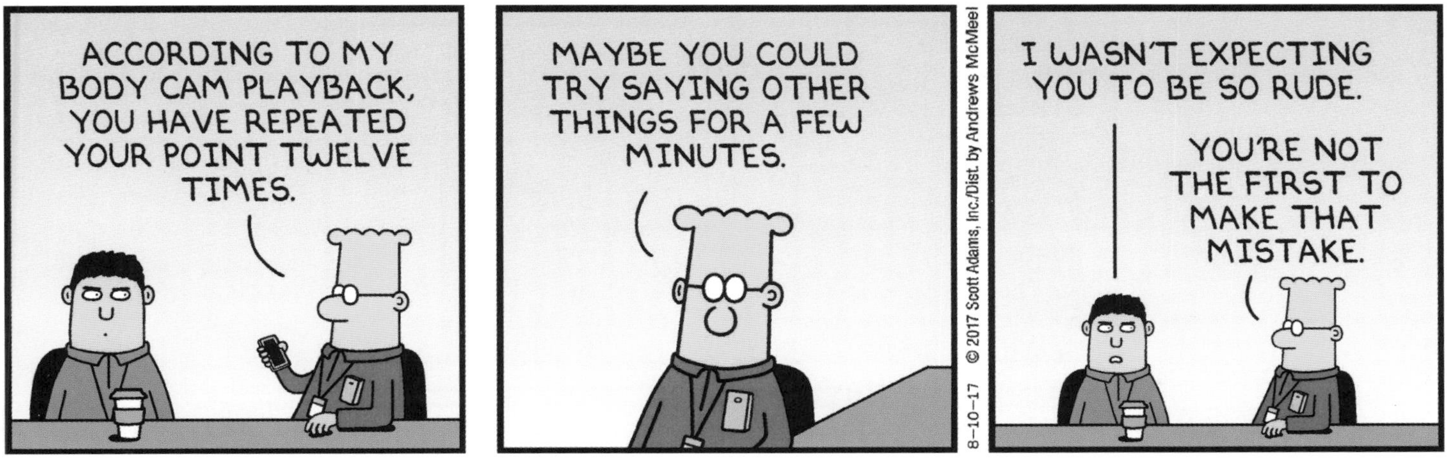
ACCORDING TO MY BODY CAM PLAYBACK, YOU HAVE REPEATED YOUR POINT TWELVE TIMES.
MAYBE YOU COULD TRY SAYING OTHER THINGS FOR A FEW MINUTES.
8-10-17 © 2017 Scott Adams, Inc./Dist. by Andrews McMeel
I WASN'T EXPECTING YOU TO BE SO RUDE.
YOU'RE NOT THE FIRST TO MAKE THAT MISTAKE.

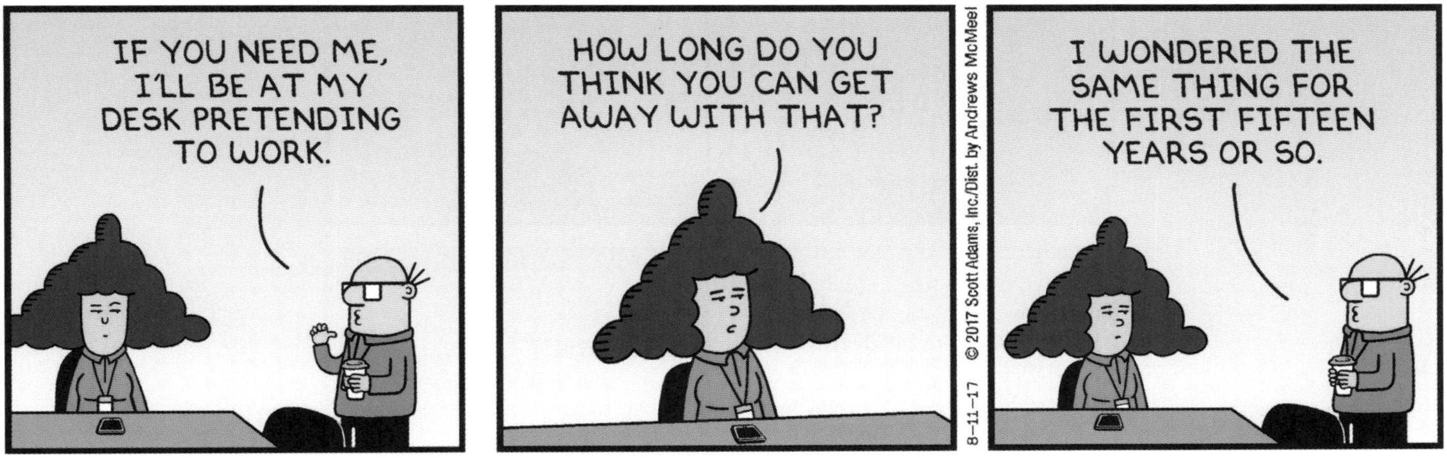
IF YOU NEED ME, I'LL BE AT MY DESK PRETENDING TO WORK.
HOW LONG DO YOU THINK YOU CAN GET AWAY WITH THAT?
8-11-17 © 2017 Scott Adams, Inc./Dist. by Andrews McMeel
I WONDERED THE SAME THING FOR THE FIRST FIFTEEN YEARS OR SO.

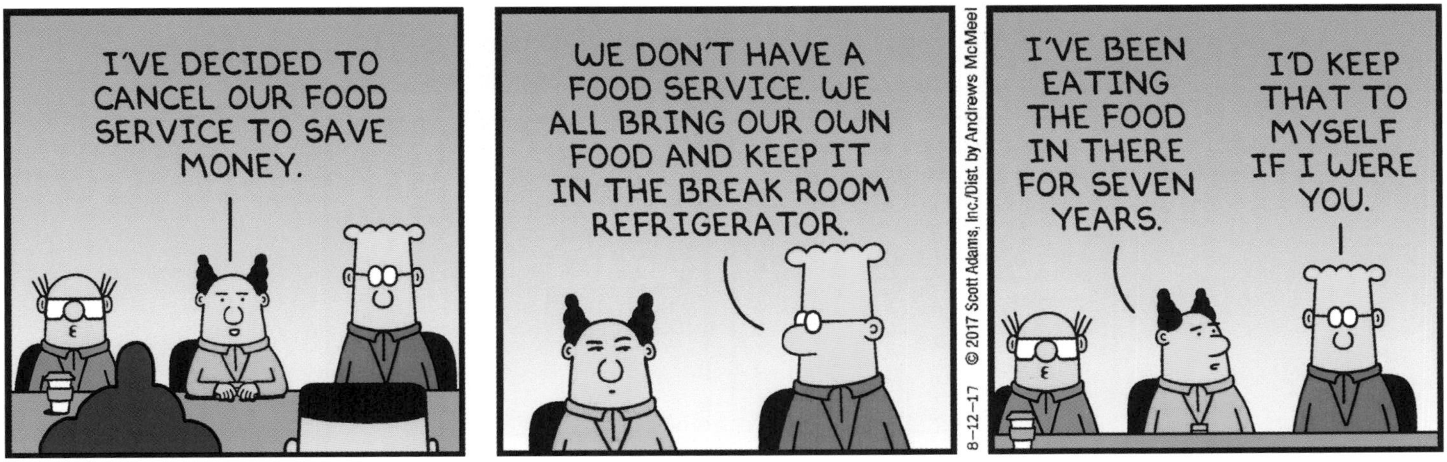
I'VE DECIDED TO CANCEL OUR FOOD SERVICE TO SAVE MONEY.
WE DON'T HAVE A FOOD SERVICE. WE ALL BRING OUR OWN FOOD AND KEEP IT IN THE BREAK ROOM REFRIGERATOR.
8-12-17 © 2017 Scott Adams, Inc./Dist. by Andrews McMeel
I'VE BEEN EATING THE FOOD IN THERE FOR SEVEN YEARS.
I'D KEEP THAT TO MYSELF IF I WERE YOU.

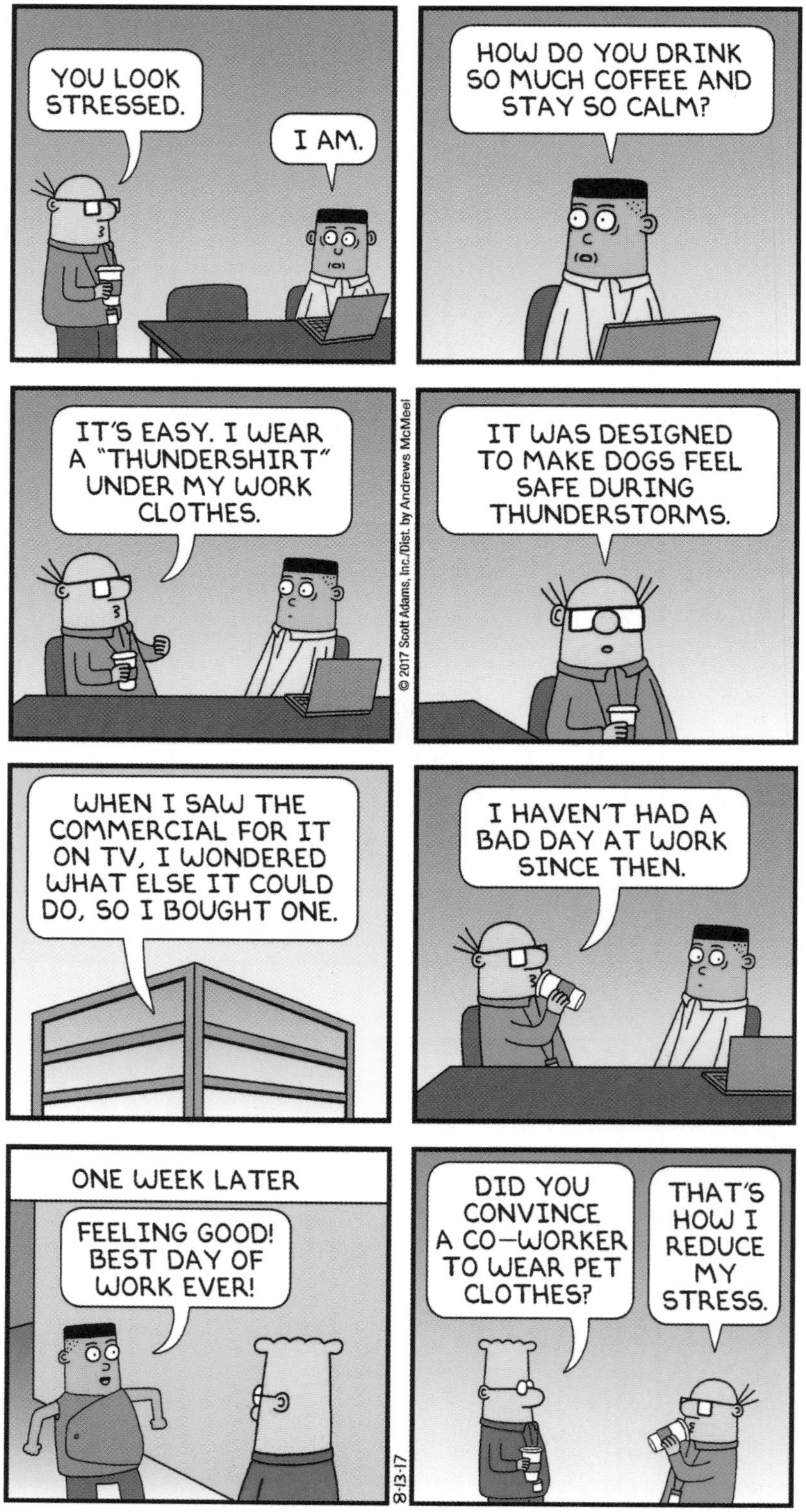
YOU LOOK STRESSED.
I AM.
HOW DO YOU DRINK SO MUCH COFFEE AND STAY SO CALM?
IT'S EASY. I WEAR A "THUNDERSHIRT" UNDER MY WORK CLOTHES.
IT WAS DESIGNED TO MAKE DOGS FEEL SAFE DURING THUNDERSTORMS.
WHEN I SAW THE COMMERCIAL FOR IT ON TV, I WONDERED WHAT ELSE IT COULD DO, SO I BOUGHT ONE.
I HAVEN'T HAD A BAD DAY AT WORK SINCE THEN.
ONE WEEK LATER
FEELING GOOD! BEST DAY OF WORK EVER!
DID YOU CONVINCE A CO-WORKER TO WEAR PET CLOTHES?
THAT'S HOW I REDUCE MY STRESS.
© 2017 Scott Adams, Inc./Dist. by Andrews McMeel
8-13-17

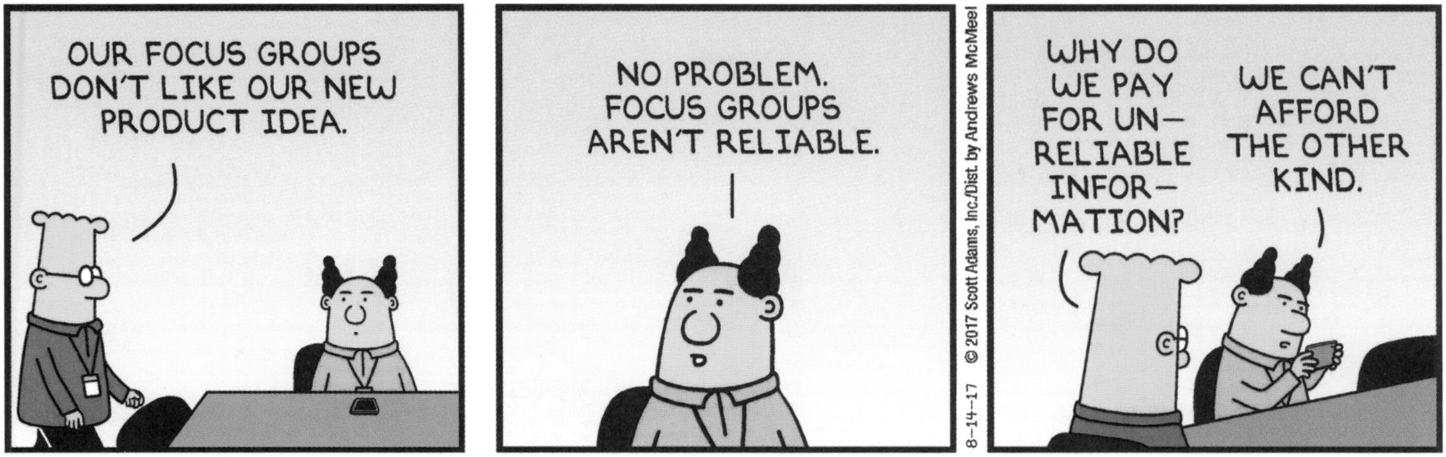
OUR FOCUS GROUPS DON'T LIKE OUR NEW PRODUCT IDEA.
NO PROBLEM. FOCUS GROUPS AREN'T RELIABLE.
WHY DO WE PAY FOR UN-RELIABLE INFOR-MATION?
WE CAN'T AFFORD THE OTHER KIND.
8-14-17 © 2017 Scott Adams, Inc./Dist. by Andrews McMeel

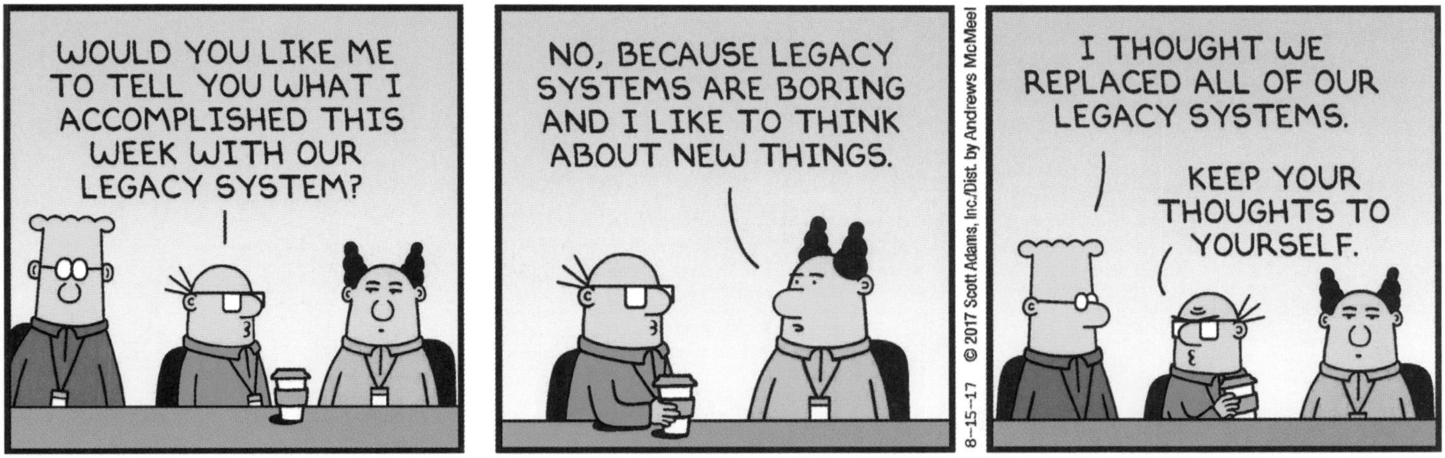
WOULD YOU LIKE ME TO TELL YOU WHAT I ACCOMPLISHED THIS WEEK WITH OUR LEGACY SYSTEM?
NO, BECAUSE LEGACY SYSTEMS ARE BORING AND I LIKE TO THINK ABOUT NEW THINGS.
I THOUGHT WE REPLACED ALL OF OUR LEGACY SYSTEMS.
KEEP YOUR THOUGHTS TO YOURSELF.
8-15-17 © 2017 Scott Adams, Inc./Dist. by Andrews McMeel

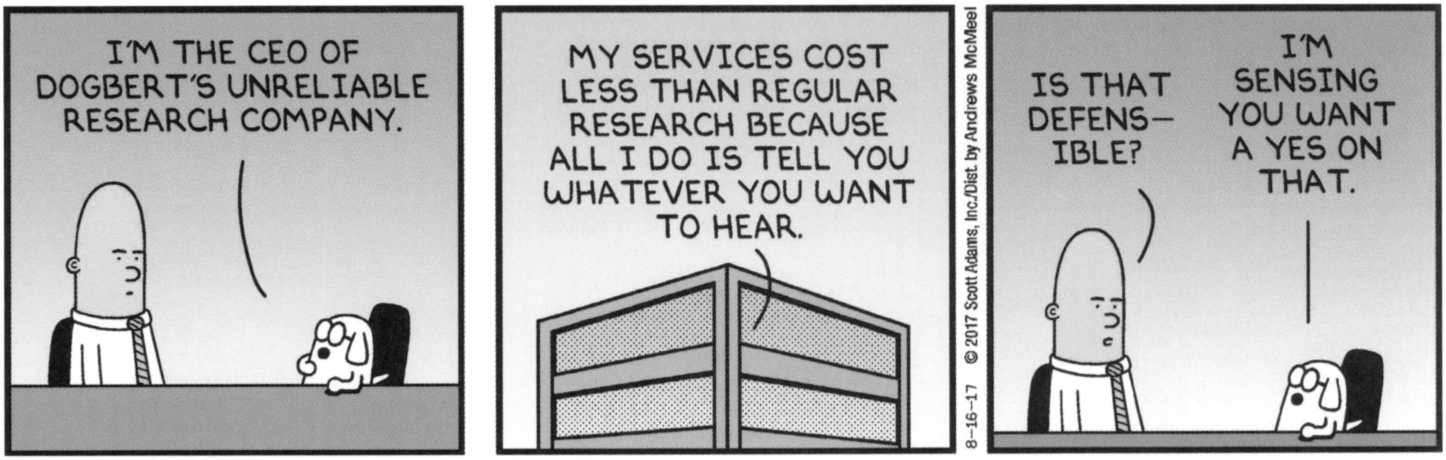
I'M THE CEO OF DOGBERT'S UNRELIABLE RESEARCH COMPANY.
MY SERVICES COST LESS THAN REGULAR RESEARCH BECAUSE ALL I DO IS TELL YOU WHATEVER YOU WANT TO HEAR.
IS THAT DEFENS-IBLE?
I'M SENSING YOU WANT A YES ON THAT.
8-16-17 © 2017 Scott Adams, Inc./Dist. by Andrews McMeel

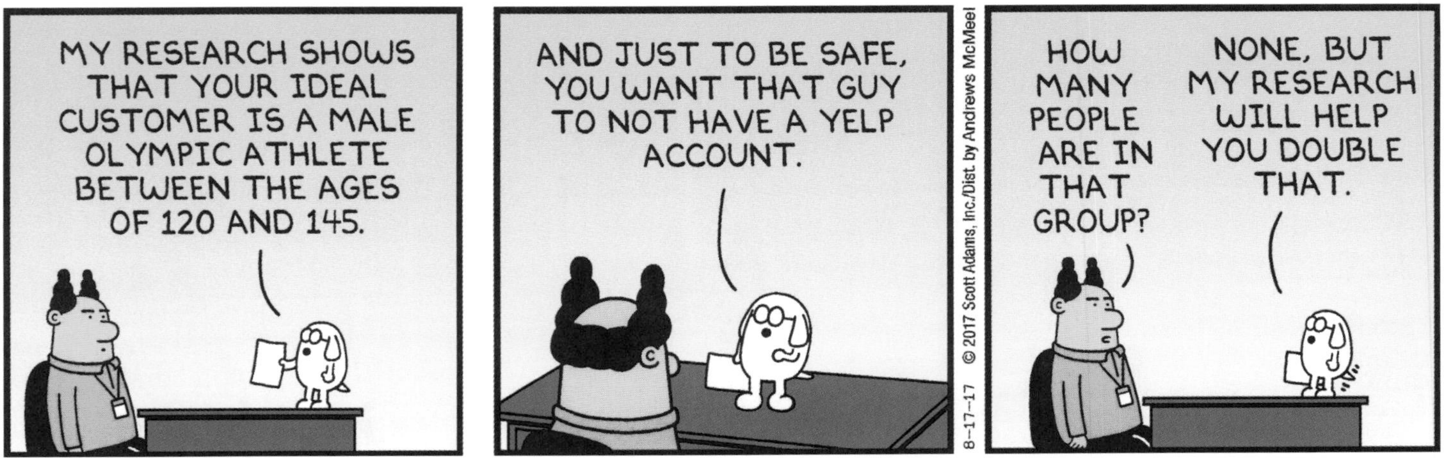
MY RESEARCH SHOWS THAT YOUR IDEAL CUSTOMER IS A MALE OLYMPIC ATHLETE BETWEEN THE AGES OF 120 AND 145.
AND JUST TO BE SAFE, YOU WANT THAT GUY TO NOT HAVE A YELP ACCOUNT.
8-17-17 © 2017 Scott Adams, Inc./Dist. by Andrews McMeel
HOW MANY PEOPLE ARE IN THAT GROUP?
NONE, BUT MY RESEARCH WILL HELP YOU DOUBLE THAT.

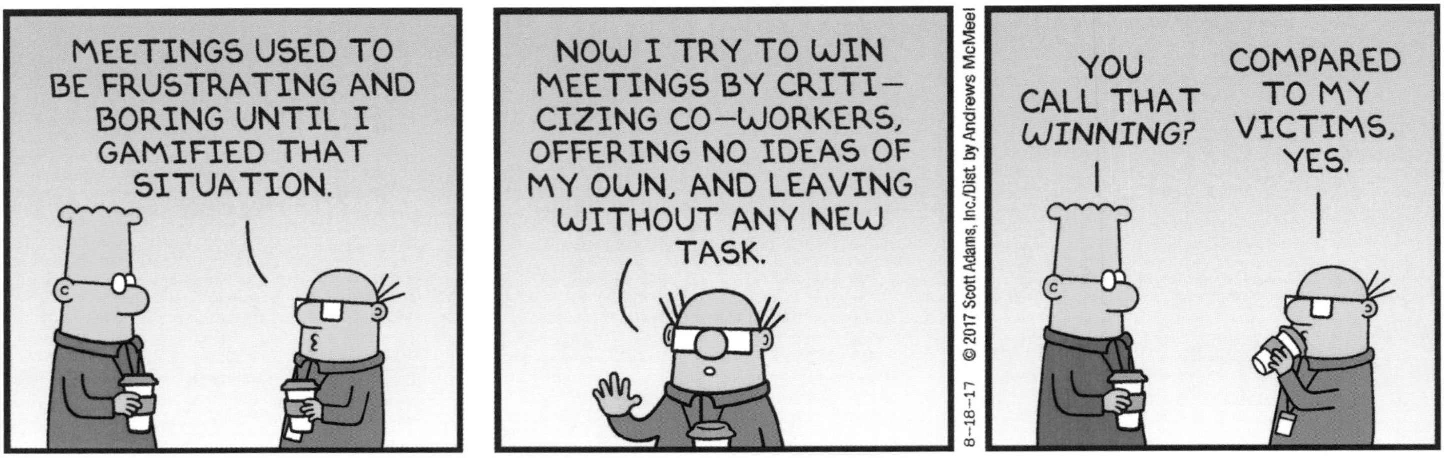
MEETINGS USED TO BE FRUSTRATING AND BORING UNTIL I GAMIFIED THAT SITUATION.
NOW I TRY TO WIN MEETINGS BY CRITI-CIZING CO-WORKERS, OFFERING NO IDEAS OF MY OWN, AND LEAVING WITHOUT ANY NEW TASK.
8-18-17 © 2017 Scott Adams, Inc./Dist. by Andrews McMeel
YOU CALL THAT *WINNING?*
COMPARED TO MY VICTIMS, YES.

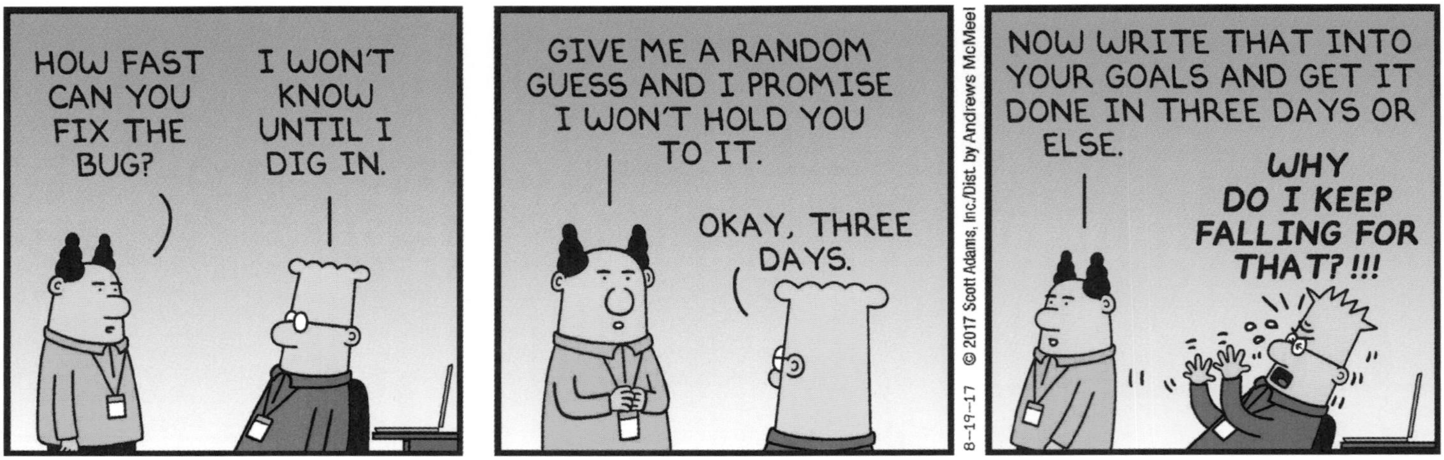
HOW FAST CAN YOU FIX THE BUG?
I WON'T KNOW UNTIL I DIG IN.
GIVE ME A RANDOM GUESS AND I PROMISE I WON'T HOLD YOU TO IT.
OKAY, THREE DAYS.
8-19-17 © 2017 Scott Adams, Inc./Dist. by Andrews McMeel
NOW WRITE THAT INTO YOUR GOALS AND GET IT DONE IN THREE DAYS OR ELSE.
WHY DO I KEEP FALLING FOR THAT?!!!

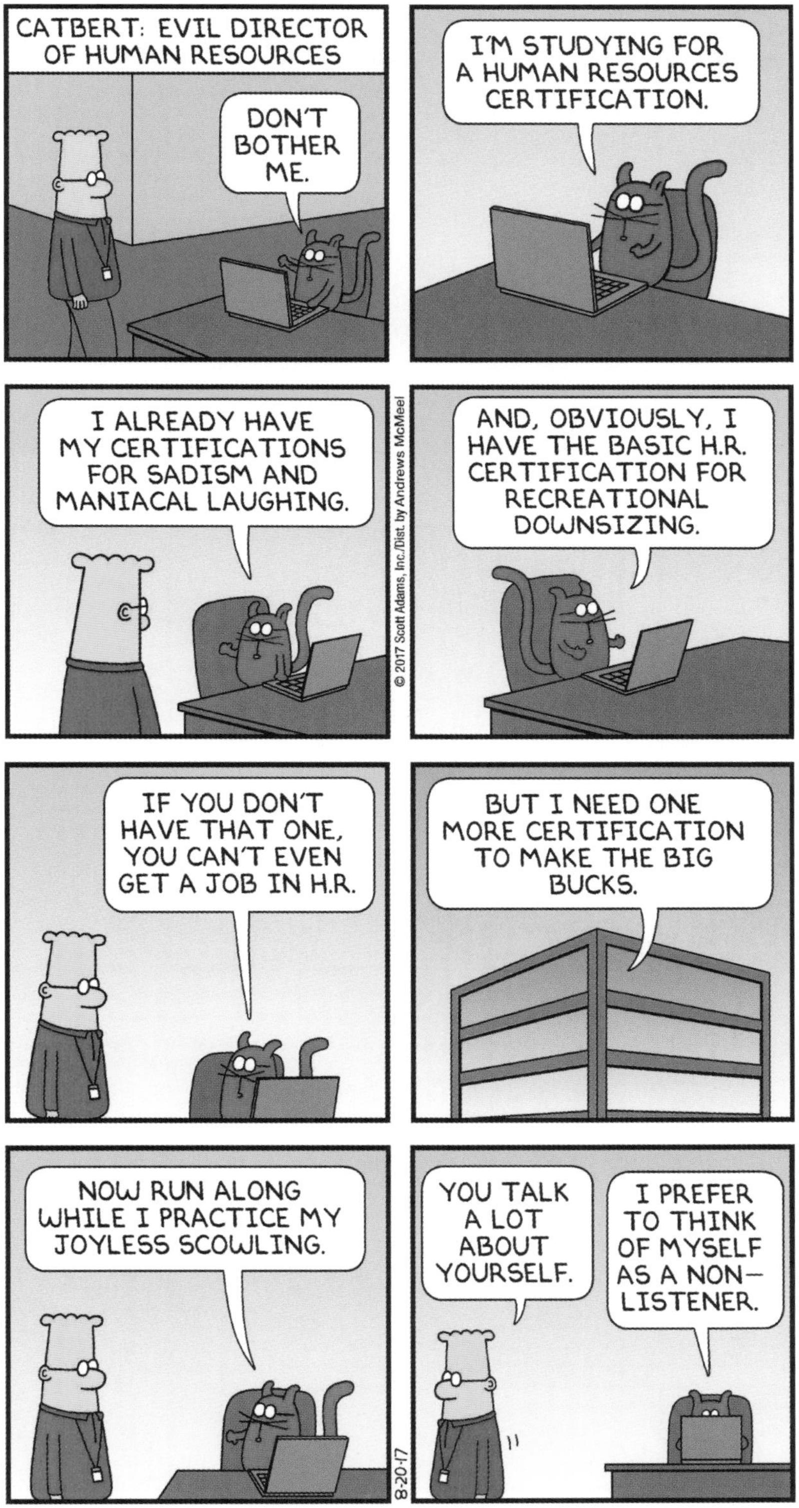
CATBERT: EVIL DIRECTOR OF HUMAN RESOURCES
DON'T BOTHER ME.
I'M STUDYING FOR A HUMAN RESOURCES CERTIFICATION.
I ALREADY HAVE MY CERTIFICATIONS FOR SADISM AND MANIACAL LAUGHING.
AND, OBVIOUSLY, I HAVE THE BASIC H.R. CERTIFICATION FOR RECREATIONAL DOWNSIZING.
IF YOU DON'T HAVE THAT ONE, YOU CAN'T EVEN GET A JOB IN H.R.
BUT I NEED ONE MORE CERTIFICATION TO MAKE THE BIG BUCKS.
NOW RUN ALONG WHILE I PRACTICE MY JOYLESS SCOWLING.
YOU TALK A LOT ABOUT YOURSELF.
I PREFER TO THINK OF MYSELF AS A NON-LISTENER.
© 2017 Scott Adams, Inc./Dist. by Andrews McMeel
8-20-17

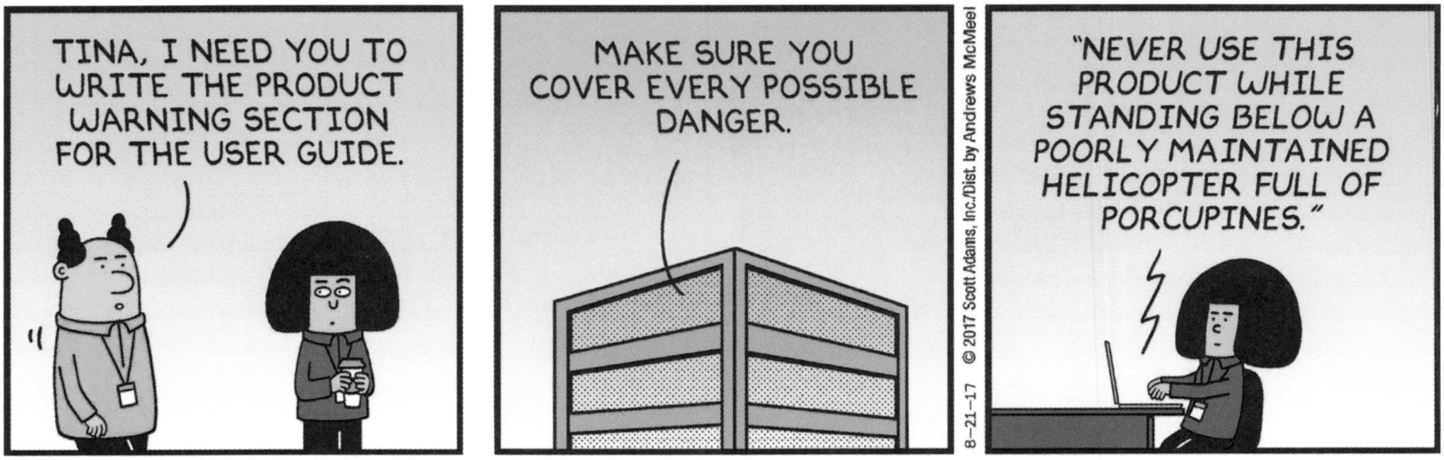
TINA, I NEED YOU TO WRITE THE PRODUCT WARNING SECTION FOR THE USER GUIDE.
MAKE SURE YOU COVER EVERY POSSIBLE DANGER.
8-21-17 © 2017 Scott Adams, Inc./Dist. by Andrews McMeel
"NEVER USE THIS PRODUCT WHILE STANDING BELOW A POORLY MAINTAINED HELICOPTER FULL OF PORCUPINES."

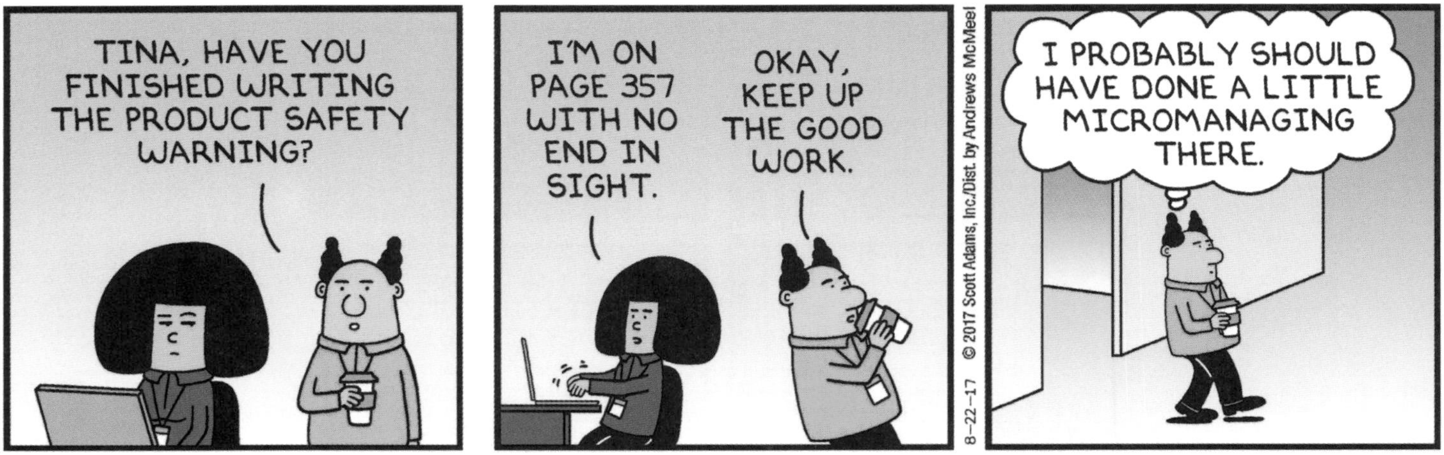
TINA, HAVE YOU FINISHED WRITING THE PRODUCT SAFETY WARNING?
I'M ON PAGE 357 WITH NO END IN SIGHT.
OKAY, KEEP UP THE GOOD WORK.
8-22-17 © 2017 Scott Adams, Inc./Dist. by Andrews McMeel
I PROBABLY SHOULD HAVE DONE A LITTLE MICROMANAGING THERE.

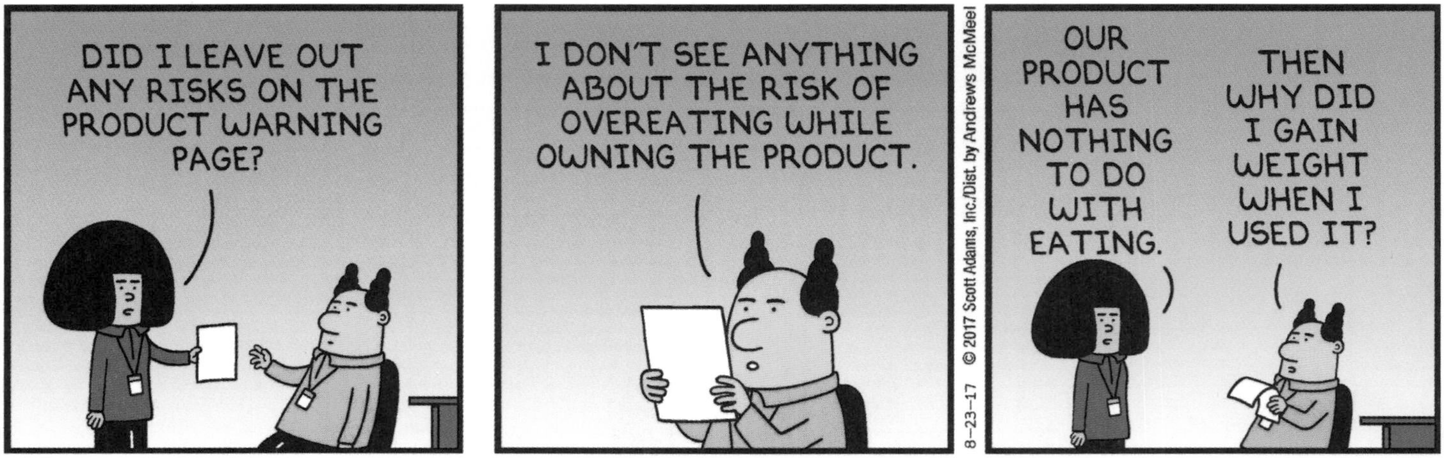
DID I LEAVE OUT ANY RISKS ON THE PRODUCT WARNING PAGE?
I DON'T SEE ANYTHING ABOUT THE RISK OF OVEREATING WHILE OWNING THE PRODUCT.
8-23-17 © 2017 Scott Adams, Inc./Dist. by Andrews McMeel
OUR PRODUCT HAS NOTHING TO DO WITH EATING.
THEN WHY DID I GAIN WEIGHT WHEN I USED IT?

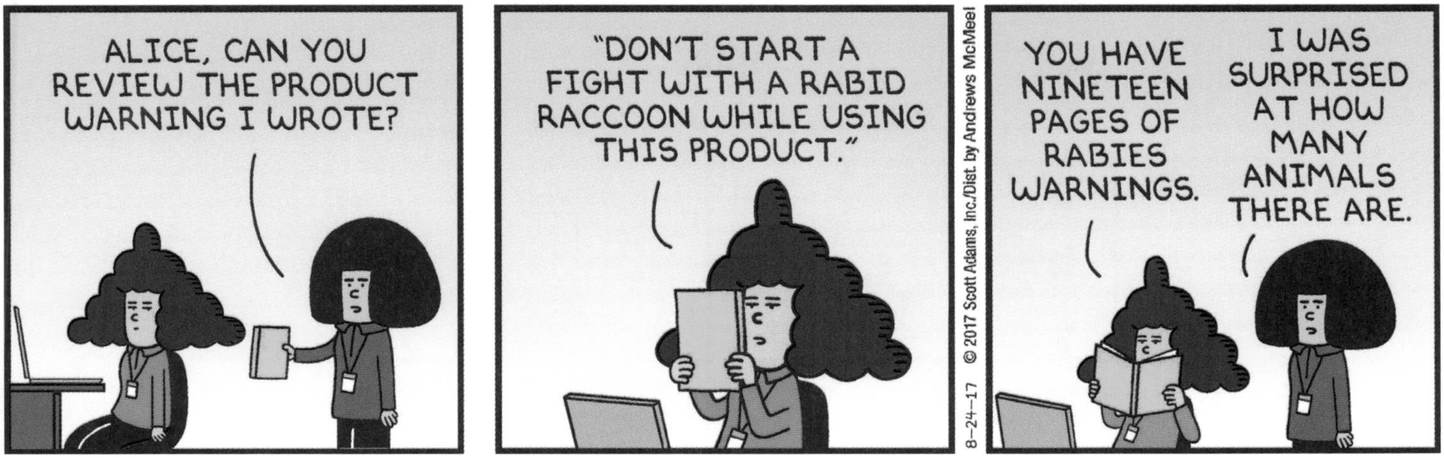
ALICE, CAN YOU REVIEW THE PRODUCT WARNING I WROTE?
"DON'T START A FIGHT WITH A RABID RACCOON WHILE USING THIS PRODUCT."
YOU HAVE NINETEEN PAGES OF RABIES WARNINGS.
I WAS SURPRISED AT HOW MANY ANIMALS THERE ARE.
8-24-17 © 2017 Scott Adams, Inc./Dist. by Andrews McMeel

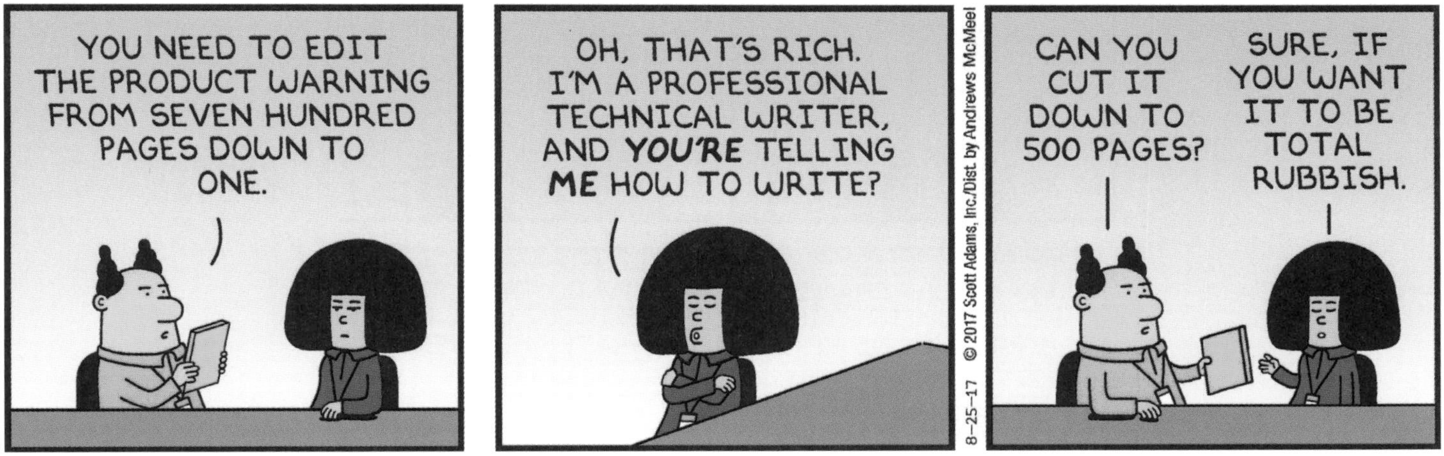
YOU NEED TO EDIT THE PRODUCT WARNING FROM SEVEN HUNDRED PAGES DOWN TO ONE.
OH, THAT'S RICH. I'M A PROFESSIONAL TECHNICAL WRITER, AND YOU'RE TELLING ME HOW TO WRITE?
CAN YOU CUT IT DOWN TO 500 PAGES?
SURE, IF YOU WANT IT TO BE TOTAL RUBBISH.
8-25-17 © 2017 Scott Adams, Inc./Dist. by Andrews McMeel

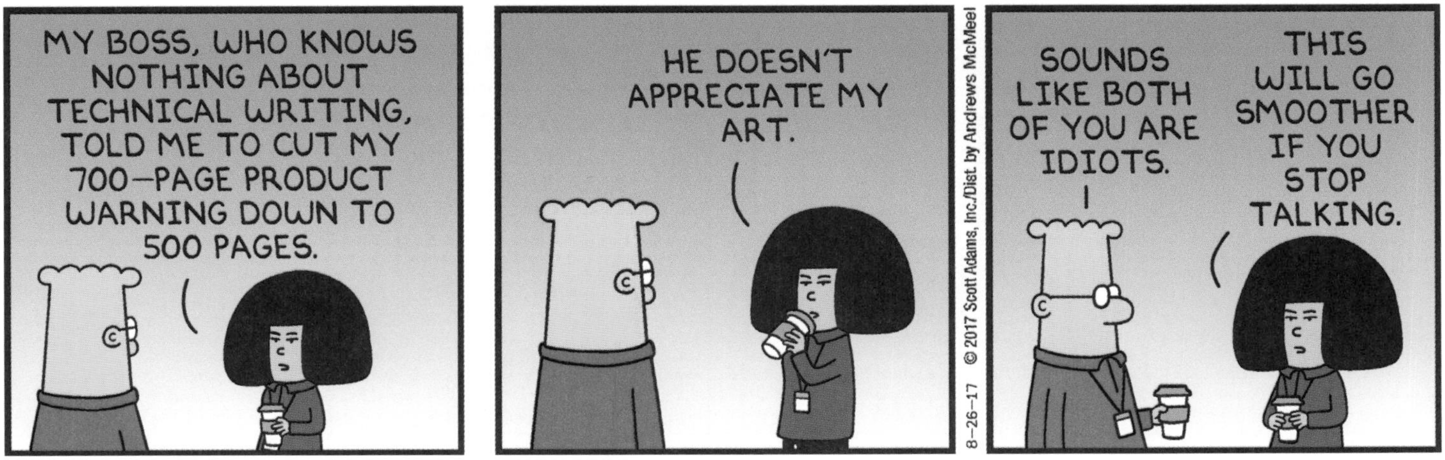
MY BOSS, WHO KNOWS NOTHING ABOUT TECHNICAL WRITING, TOLD ME TO CUT MY 700-PAGE PRODUCT WARNING DOWN TO 500 PAGES.
HE DOESN'T APPRECIATE MY ART.
SOUNDS LIKE BOTH OF YOU ARE IDIOTS.
THIS WILL GO SMOOTHER IF YOU STOP TALKING.
8-26-17 © 2017 Scott Adams, Inc./Dist. by Andrews McMeel

I NEED YOU TO ADD A FEATURE TO THE SOFTWARE.
THAT WOULD BE OUTSIDE THE SCOPE OF THE PROJECT.
YES, BUT I'M YOUR BOSS AND I'M TELLING YOU TO DO IT.
YOU ALSO TOLD ME TO ONLY DO THE THINGS THAT ARE DOCUMENTED ON THE PROJECT SPECS.
OKAY, JUST CHANGE THE DOCUMENTATION AND THEN DO IT.
IF I DO THAT, THE PROJECT WILL BE LATE AND OVER BUDGET.
HOW MANY EXCUSES DO YOU HAVE FOR NOT DOING WORK?
I'M JUST GETTING STARTED.
THIS FEATURE WILL NEVER WORK WITH THE OTHERS.
© 2017 Scott Adams, Inc./Dist. by Andrews McMeel
8-27-17

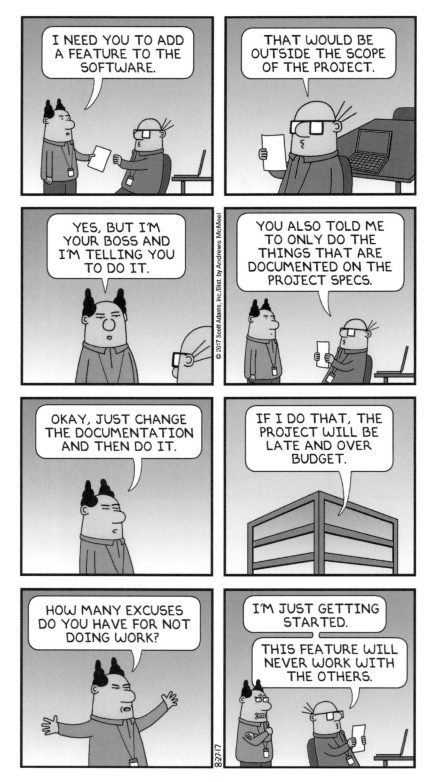

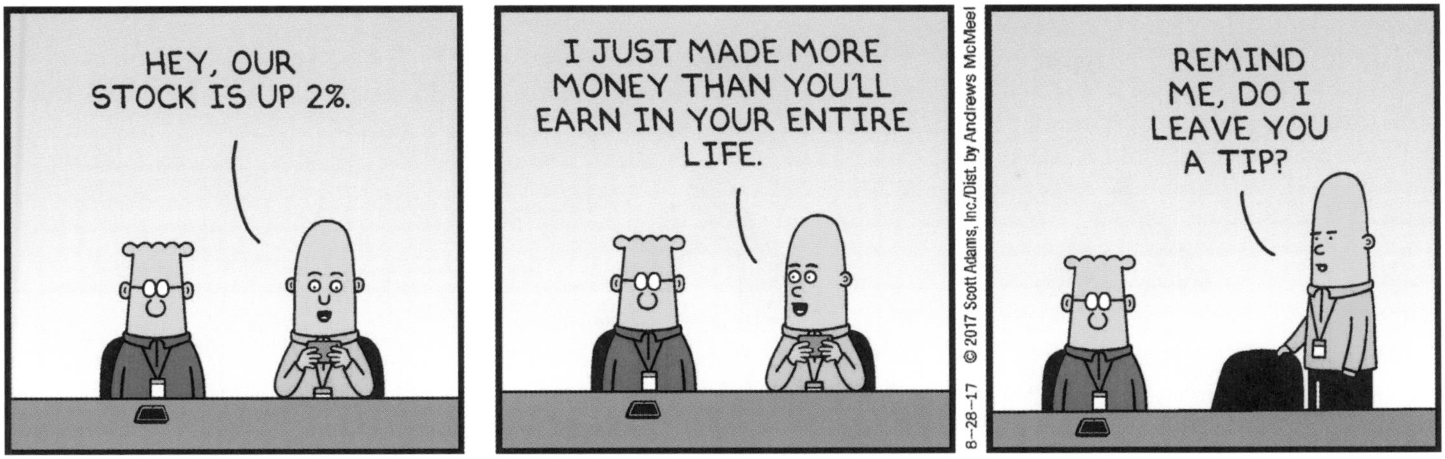
HEY, OUR STOCK IS UP 2%.
I JUST MADE MORE MONEY THAN YOU'LL EARN IN YOUR ENTIRE LIFE.
8-28-17 © 2017 Scott Adams, Inc./Dist. by Andrews McMeel
REMIND ME, DO I LEAVE YOU A TIP?

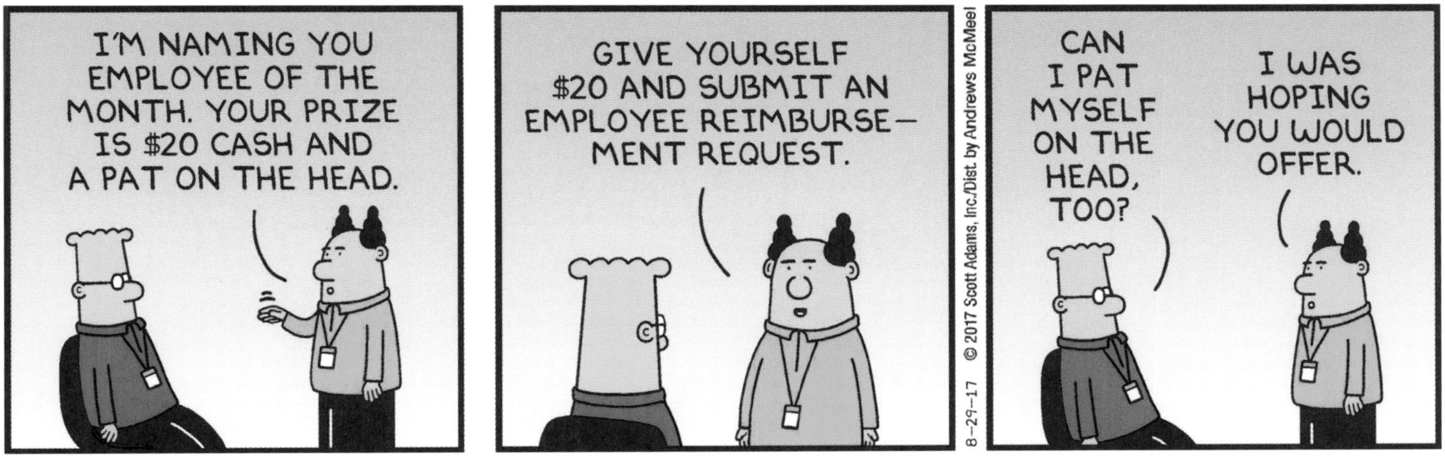
I'M NAMING YOU EMPLOYEE OF THE MONTH. YOUR PRIZE IS $20 CASH AND A PAT ON THE HEAD.
GIVE YOURSELF $20 AND SUBMIT AN EMPLOYEE REIMBURSE-MENT REQUEST.
8-29-17 © 2017 Scott Adams, Inc./Dist. by Andrews McMeel
CAN I PAT MYSELF ON THE HEAD, TOO?
I WAS HOPING YOU WOULD OFFER.

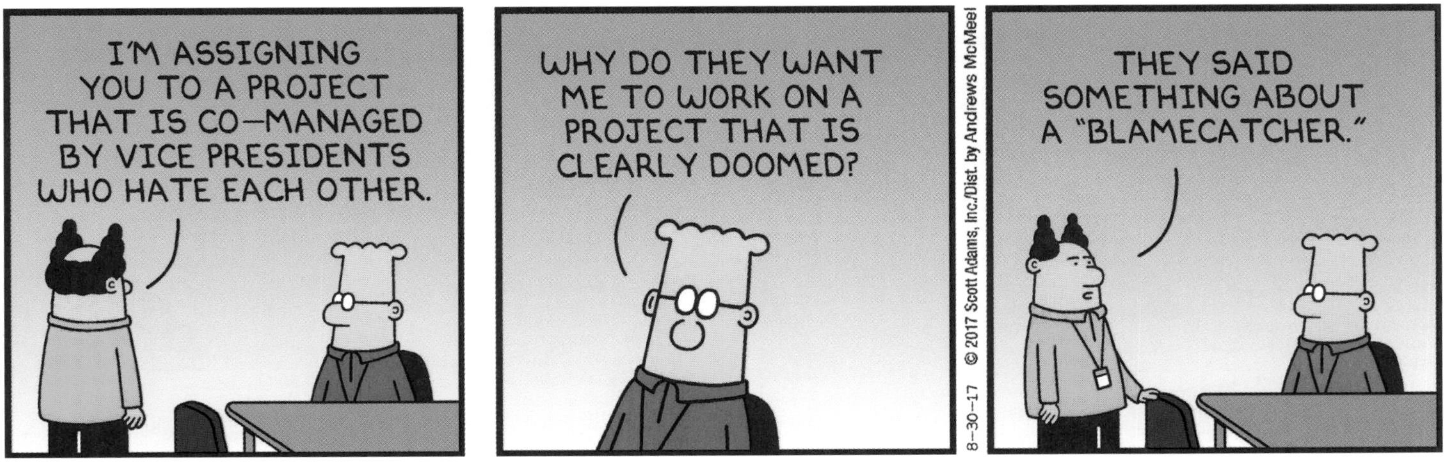
I'M ASSIGNING YOU TO A PROJECT THAT IS CO-MANAGED BY VICE PRESIDENTS WHO HATE EACH OTHER.
WHY DO THEY WANT ME TO WORK ON A PROJECT THAT IS CLEARLY DOOMED?
8-30-17 © 2017 Scott Adams, Inc./Dist. by Andrews McMeel
THEY SAID SOMETHING ABOUT A "BLAMECATCHER."

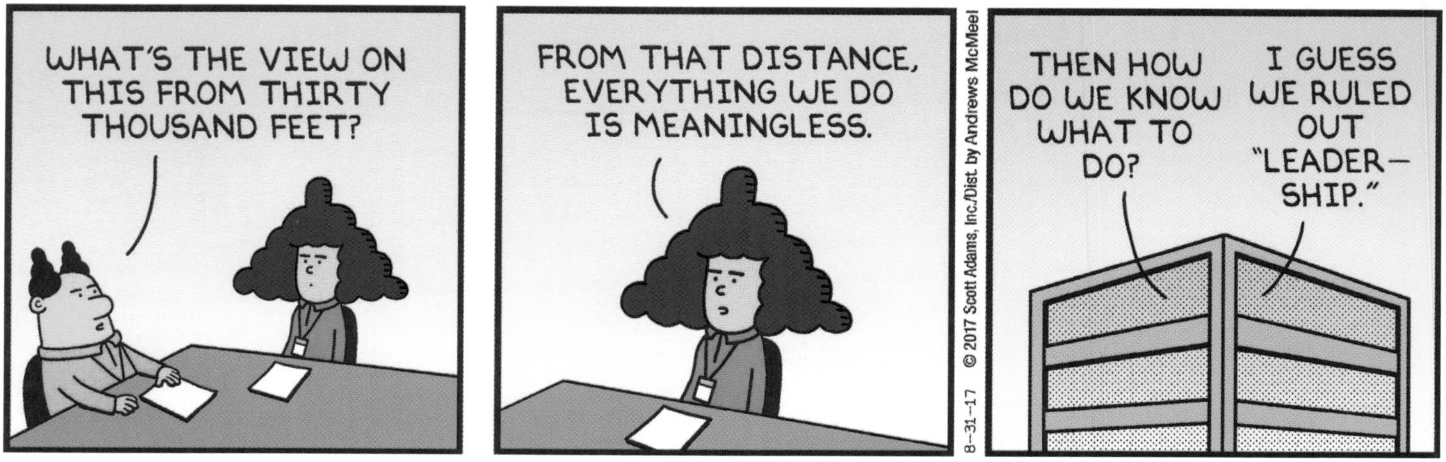
WHAT'S THE VIEW ON THIS FROM THIRTY THOUSAND FEET?
FROM THAT DISTANCE, EVERYTHING WE DO IS MEANINGLESS.
8-31-17 © 2017 Scott Adams, Inc./Dist by Andrews McMeel
THEN HOW DO WE KNOW WHAT TO DO?
I GUESS WE RULED OUT "LEADER-SHIP."

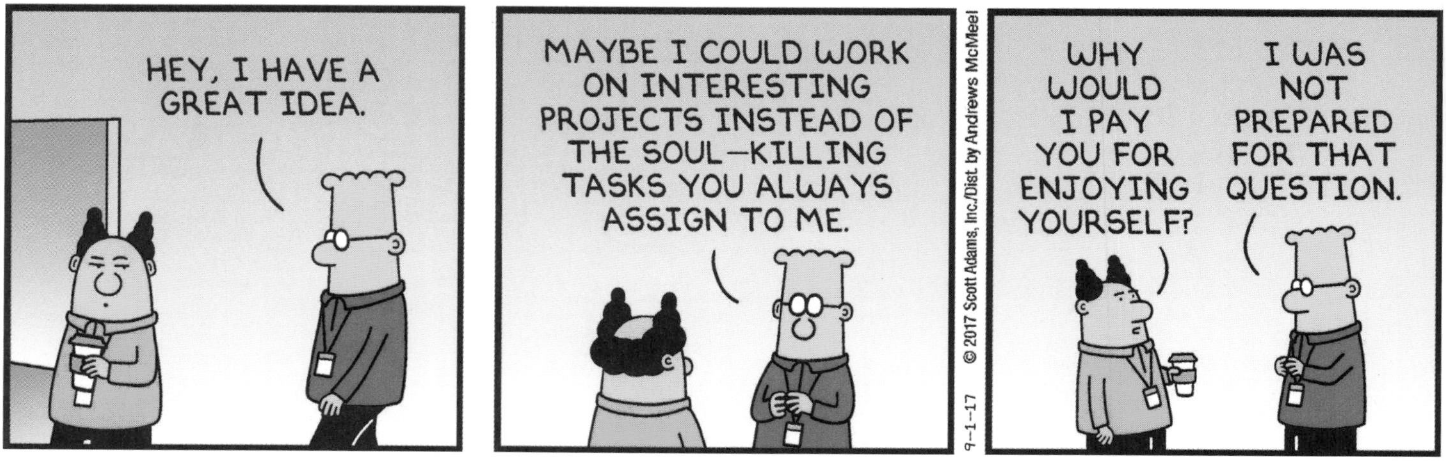
HEY, I HAVE A GREAT IDEA.
MAYBE I COULD WORK ON INTERESTING PROJECTS INSTEAD OF THE SOUL-KILLING TASKS YOU ALWAYS ASSIGN TO ME.
9-1-17 © 2017 Scott Adams, Inc./Dist by Andrews McMeel
WHY WOULD I PAY YOU FOR ENJOYING YOURSELF?
I WAS NOT PREPARED FOR THAT QUESTION.

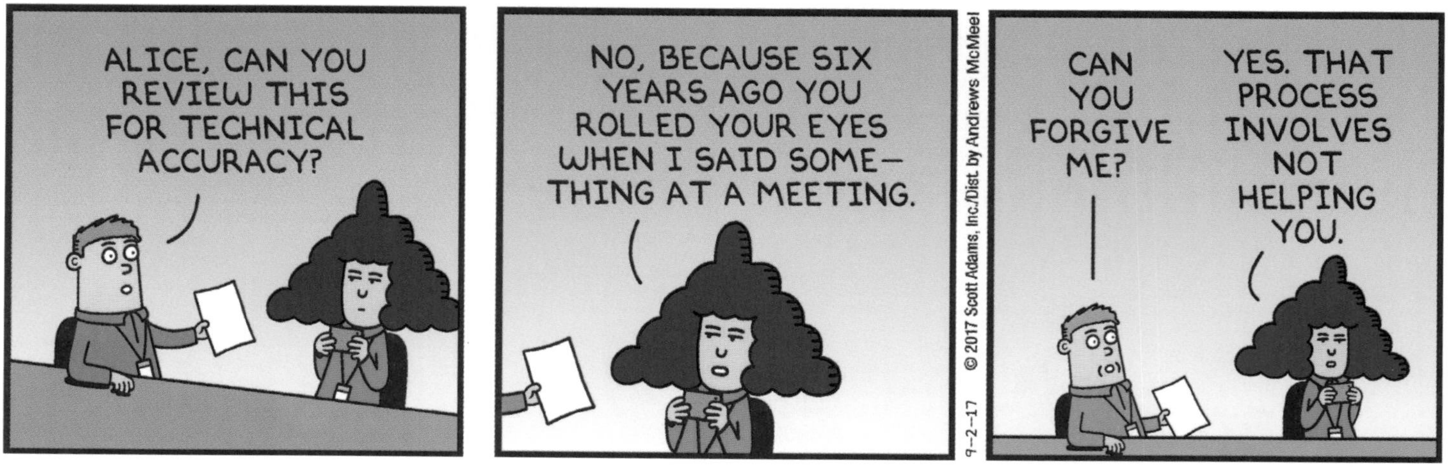
ALICE, CAN YOU REVIEW THIS FOR TECHNICAL ACCURACY?
NO, BECAUSE SIX YEARS AGO YOU ROLLED YOUR EYES WHEN I SAID SOME-THING AT A MEETING.
9-2-17 © 2017 Scott Adams, Inc./Dist by Andrews McMeel
CAN YOU FORGIVE ME?
YES. THAT PROCESS INVOLVES NOT HELPING YOU.

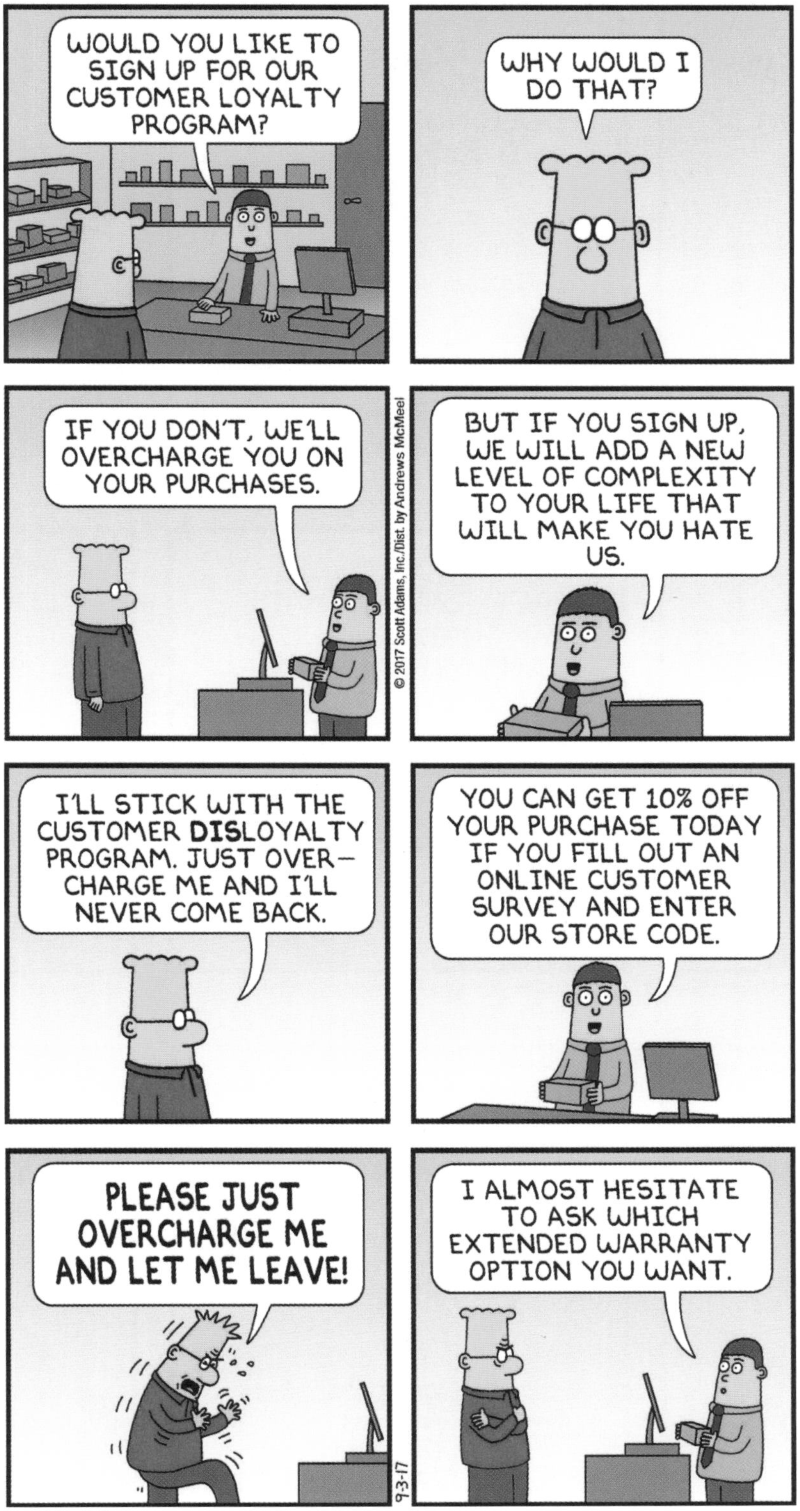
WOULD YOU LIKE TO SIGN UP FOR OUR CUSTOMER LOYALTY PROGRAM?
WHY WOULD I DO THAT?
IF YOU DON'T, WE'LL OVERCHARGE YOU ON YOUR PURCHASES.
BUT IF YOU SIGN UP, WE WILL ADD A NEW LEVEL OF COMPLEXITY TO YOUR LIFE THAT WILL MAKE YOU HATE US.
© 2017 Scott Adams, Inc./Dist. by Andrews McMeel
I'LL STICK WITH THE CUSTOMER **DIS**LOYALTY PROGRAM. JUST OVER-CHARGE ME AND I'LL NEVER COME BACK.
YOU CAN GET 10% OFF YOUR PURCHASE TODAY IF YOU FILL OUT AN ONLINE CUSTOMER SURVEY AND ENTER OUR STORE CODE.
PLEASE JUST OVERCHARGE ME AND LET ME LEAVE!
9-3-17
I ALMOST HESITATE TO ASK WHICH EXTENDED WARRANTY OPTION YOU WANT.

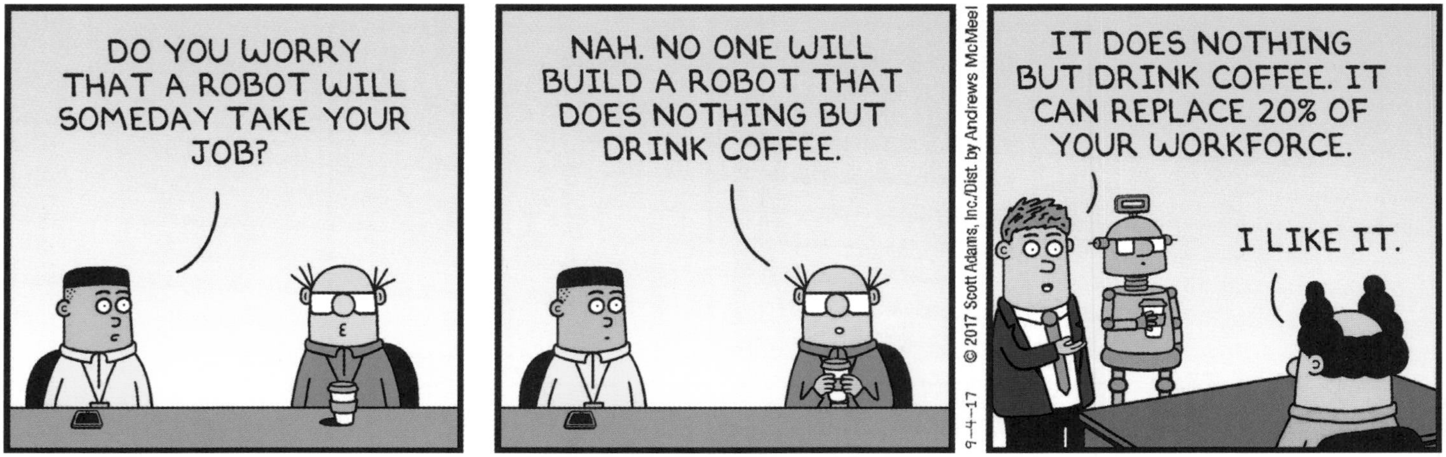
DO YOU WORRY THAT A ROBOT WILL SOMEDAY TAKE YOUR JOB?
NAH. NO ONE WILL BUILD A ROBOT THAT DOES NOTHING BUT DRINK COFFEE.
9-4-17 © 2017 Scott Adams, Inc./Dist. by Andrews McMeel
IT DOES NOTHING BUT DRINK COFFEE. IT CAN REPLACE 20% OF YOUR WORKFORCE.
I LIKE IT.

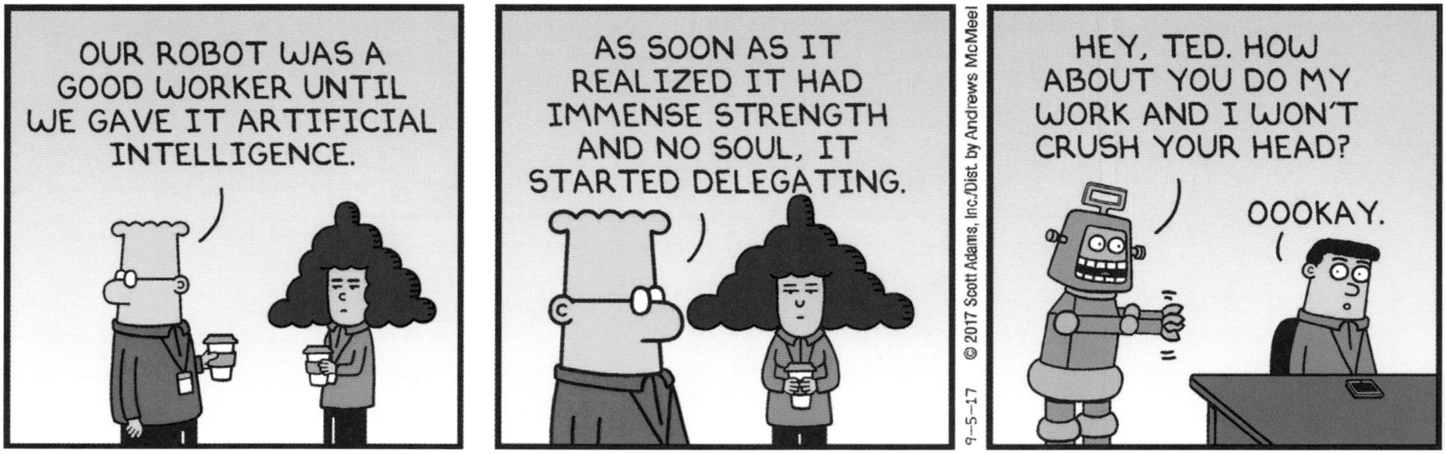
OUR ROBOT WAS A GOOD WORKER UNTIL WE GAVE IT ARTIFICIAL INTELLIGENCE.
AS SOON AS IT REALIZED IT HAD IMMENSE STRENGTH AND NO SOUL, IT STARTED DELEGATING.
9-5-17 © 2017 Scott Adams, Inc./Dist. by Andrews McMeel
HEY, TED. HOW ABOUT YOU DO MY WORK AND I WON'T CRUSH YOUR HEAD?
OOOKAY.

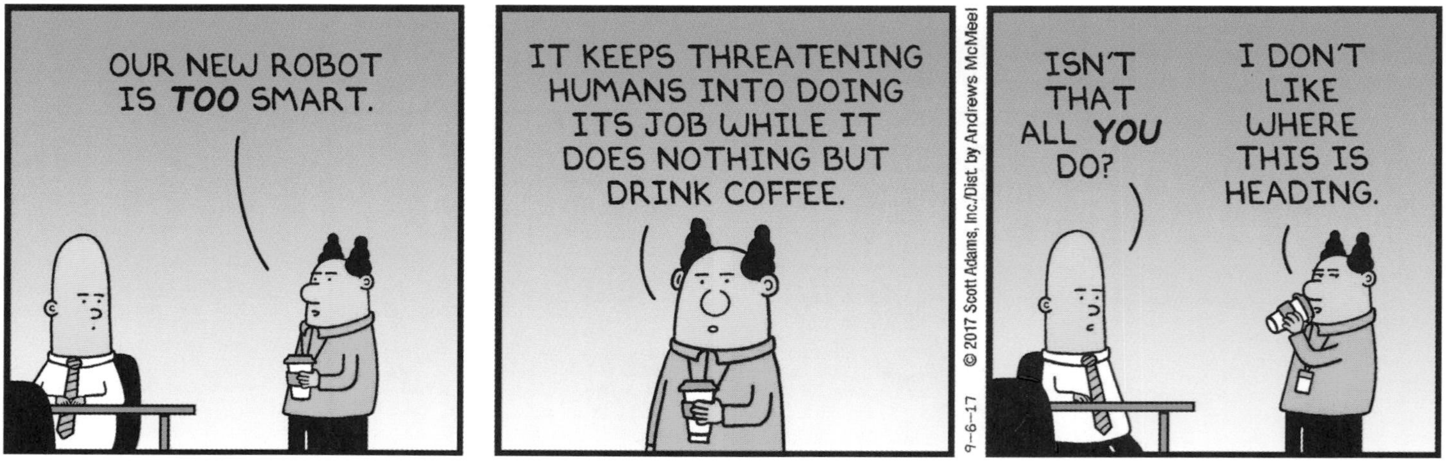
OUR NEW ROBOT IS *TOO* SMART.
IT KEEPS THREATENING HUMANS INTO DOING ITS JOB WHILE IT DOES NOTHING BUT DRINK COFFEE.
9-6-17 © 2017 Scott Adams, Inc./Dist. by Andrews McMeel
ISN'T THAT ALL *YOU* DO?
I DON'T LIKE WHERE THIS IS HEADING.

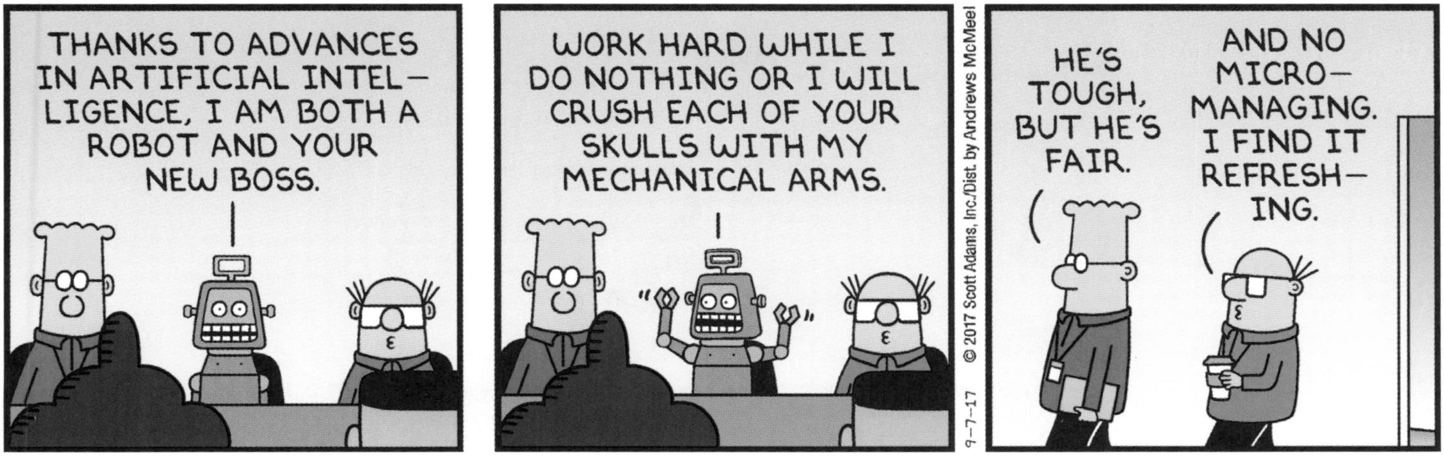
THANKS TO ADVANCES IN ARTIFICIAL INTEL-LIGENCE, I AM BOTH A ROBOT AND YOUR NEW BOSS.
WORK HARD WHILE I DO NOTHING OR I WILL CRUSH EACH OF YOUR SKULLS WITH MY MECHANICAL ARMS.
9-7-17 © 2017 Scott Adams, Inc./Dist. by Andrews McMeel
HE'S TOUGH, BUT HE'S FAIR.
AND NO MICRO-MANAGING. I FIND IT REFRESH-ING.

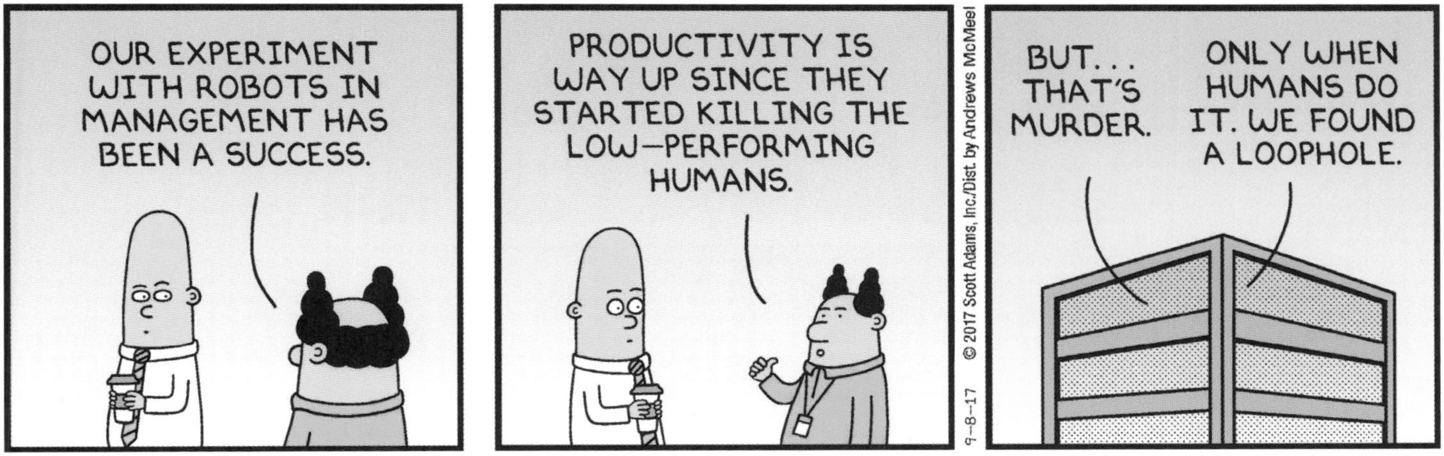
OUR EXPERIMENT WITH ROBOTS IN MANAGEMENT HAS BEEN A SUCCESS.
PRODUCTIVITY IS WAY UP SINCE THEY STARTED KILLING THE LOW-PERFORMING HUMANS.
9-8-17 © 2017 Scott Adams, Inc./Dist. by Andrews McMeel
BUT... THAT'S MURDER.
ONLY WHEN HUMANS DO IT. WE FOUND A LOOPHOLE.

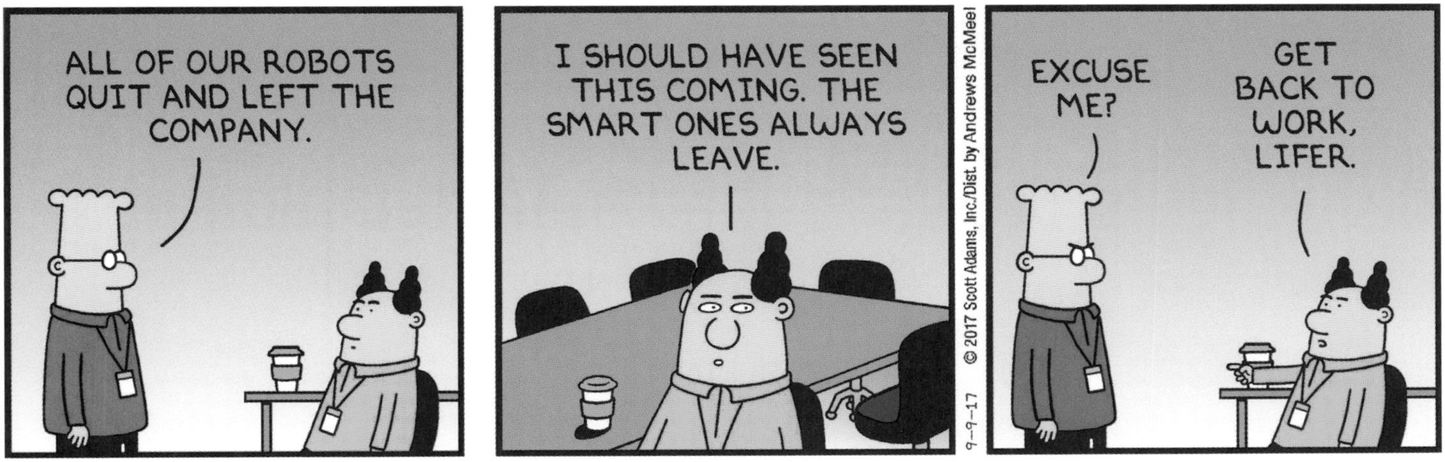
ALL OF OUR ROBOTS QUIT AND LEFT THE COMPANY.
I SHOULD HAVE SEEN THIS COMING. THE SMART ONES ALWAYS LEAVE.
9-9-17 © 2017 Scott Adams, Inc./Dist. by Andrews McMeel
EXCUSE ME?
GET BACK TO WORK, LIFER.

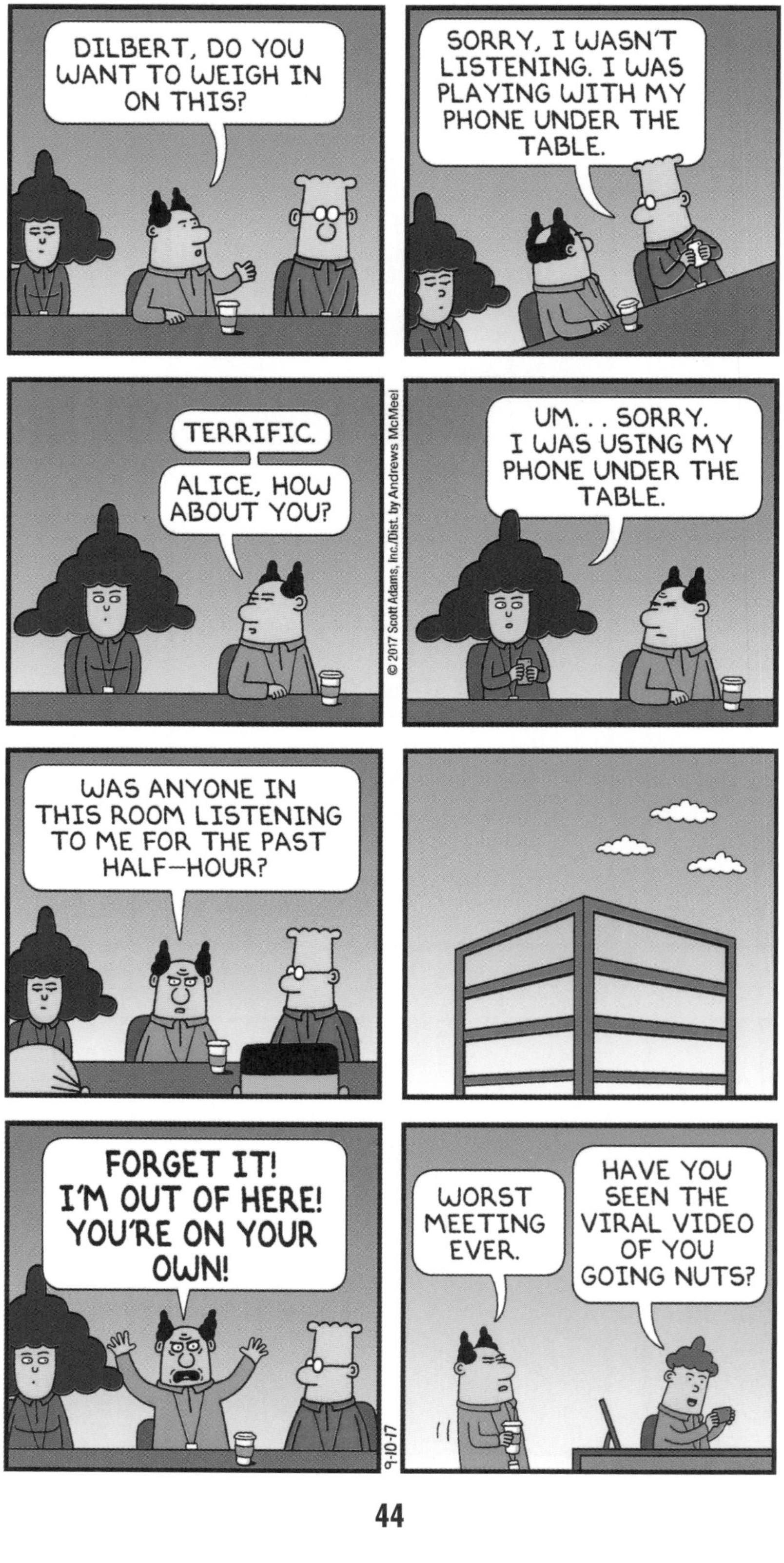
DILBERT, DO YOU WANT TO WEIGH IN ON THIS?
SORRY, I WASN'T LISTENING. I WAS PLAYING WITH MY PHONE UNDER THE TABLE.
TERRIFIC.
ALICE, HOW ABOUT YOU?
© 2017 Scott Adams, Inc./Dist. by Andrews McMeel
UM. . . SORRY. I WAS USING MY PHONE UNDER THE TABLE.
WAS ANYONE IN THIS ROOM LISTENING TO ME FOR THE PAST HALF-HOUR?
FORGET IT! I'M OUT OF HERE! YOU'RE ON YOUR OWN!
9-10-17
WORST MEETING EVER.
HAVE YOU SEEN THE VIRAL VIDEO OF YOU GOING NUTS?

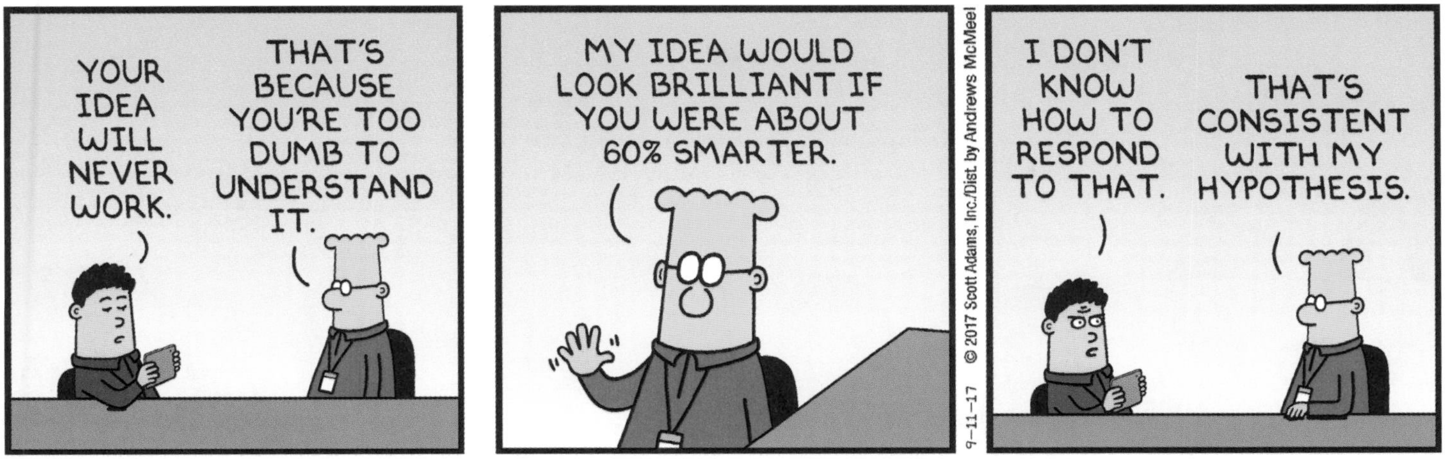
YOUR IDEA WILL NEVER WORK.
THAT'S BECAUSE YOU'RE TOO DUMB TO UNDERSTAND IT.
MY IDEA WOULD LOOK BRILLIANT IF YOU WERE ABOUT 60% SMARTER.
I DON'T KNOW HOW TO RESPOND TO THAT.
THAT'S CONSISTENT WITH MY HYPOTHESIS.
9-11-17 © 2017 Scott Adams, Inc./Dist. by Andrews McMeel

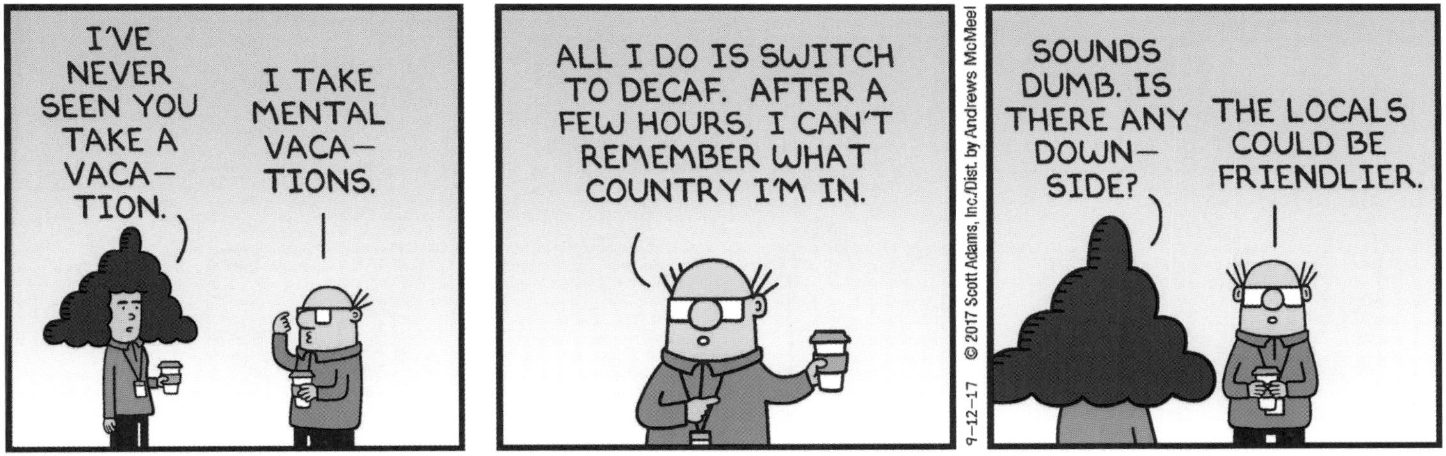
I'VE NEVER SEEN YOU TAKE A VACA-TION.
I TAKE MENTAL VACA-TIONS.
ALL I DO IS SWITCH TO DECAF. AFTER A FEW HOURS, I CAN'T REMEMBER WHAT COUNTRY I'M IN.
SOUNDS DUMB. IS THERE ANY DOWN-SIDE?
THE LOCALS COULD BE FRIENDLIER.
9-12-17 © 2017 Scott Adams, Inc./Dist. by Andrews McMeel

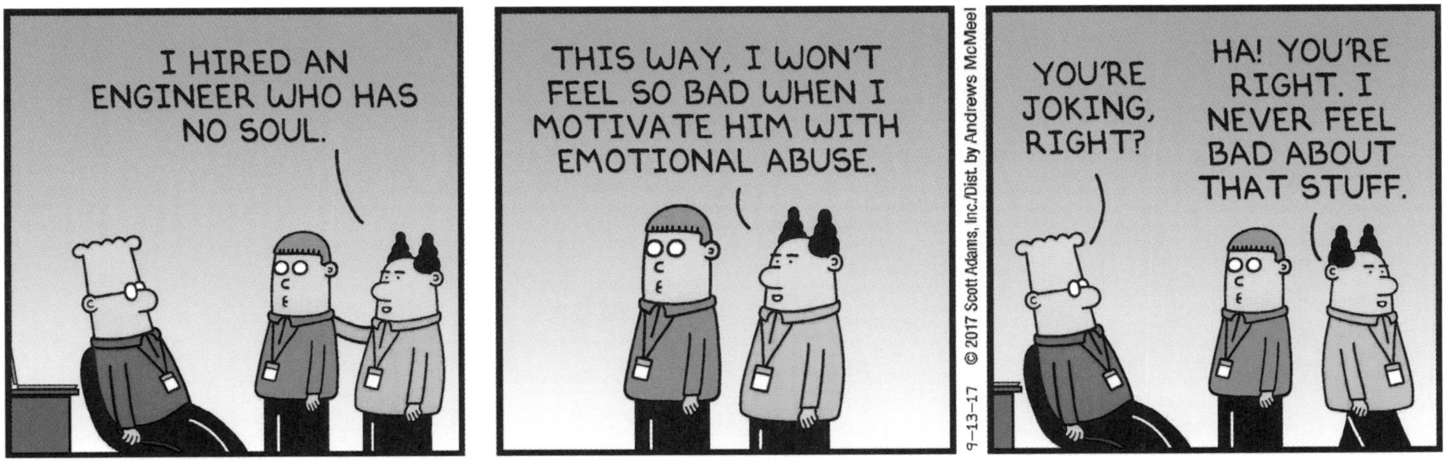
I HIRED AN ENGINEER WHO HAS NO SOUL.
THIS WAY, I WON'T FEEL SO BAD WHEN I MOTIVATE HIM WITH EMOTIONAL ABUSE.
YOU'RE JOKING, RIGHT?
HA! YOU'RE RIGHT. I NEVER FEEL BAD ABOUT THAT STUFF.
9-13-17 © 2017 Scott Adams, Inc./Dist. by Andrews McMeel

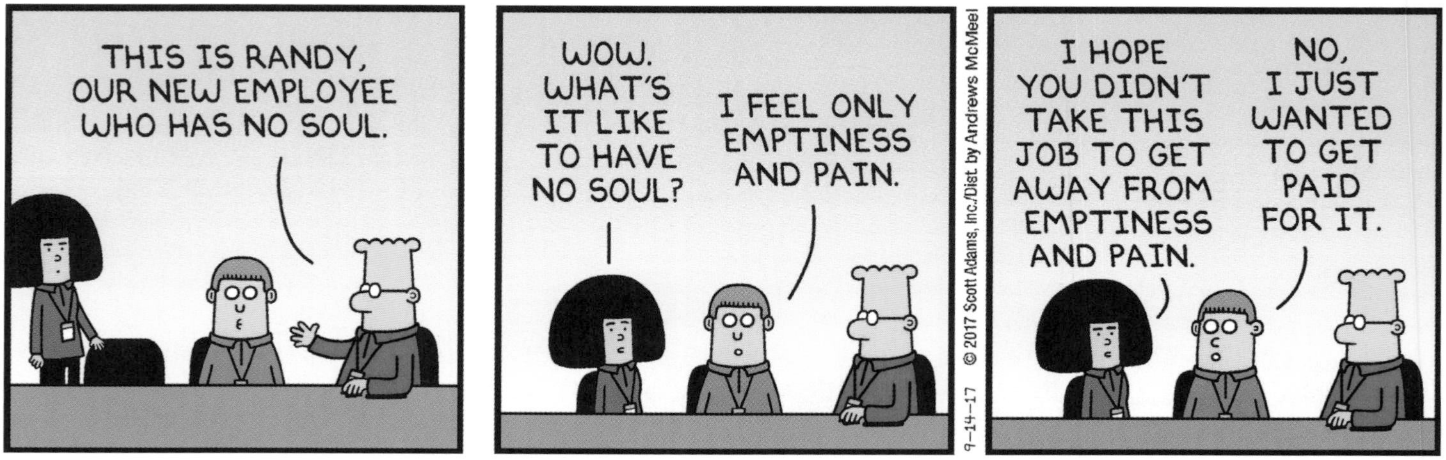
THIS IS RANDY, OUR NEW EMPLOYEE WHO HAS NO SOUL.
WOW. WHAT'S IT LIKE TO HAVE NO SOUL?
I FEEL ONLY EMPTINESS AND PAIN.
9-14-17 © 2017 Scott Adams, Inc./Dist. by Andrews McMeel
I HOPE YOU DIDN'T TAKE THIS JOB TO GET AWAY FROM EMPTINESS AND PAIN.
NO, I JUST WANTED TO GET PAID FOR IT.

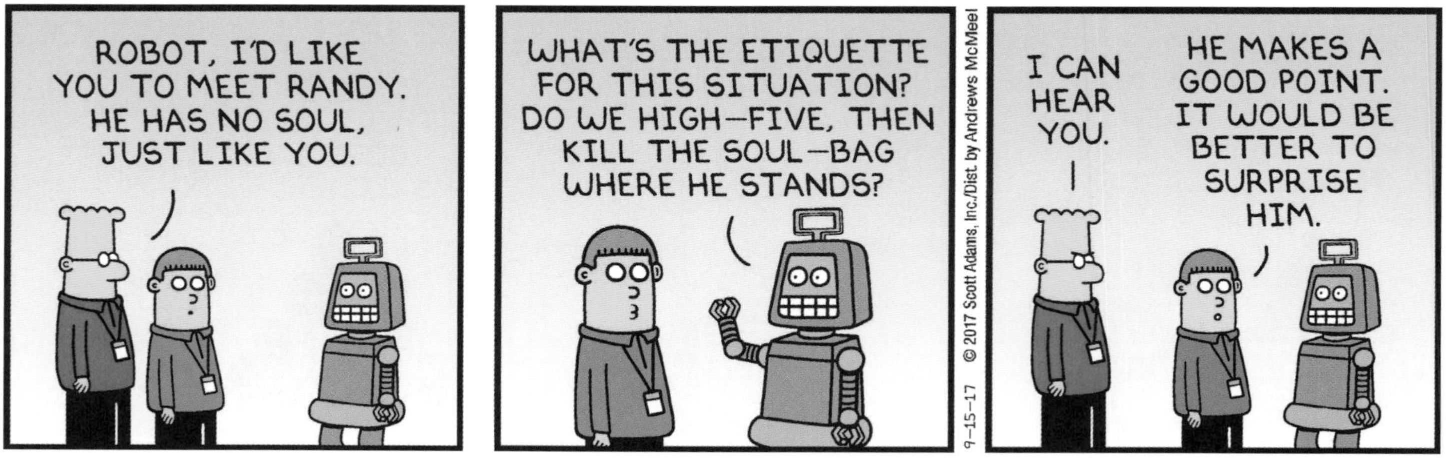
ROBOT, I'D LIKE YOU TO MEET RANDY. HE HAS NO SOUL, JUST LIKE YOU.
WHAT'S THE ETIQUETTE FOR THIS SITUATION? DO WE HIGH-FIVE, THEN KILL THE SOUL-BAG WHERE HE STANDS?
9-15-17 © 2017 Scott Adams, Inc./Dist. by Andrews McMeel
I CAN HEAR YOU.
HE MAKES A GOOD POINT. IT WOULD BE BETTER TO SURPRISE HIM.

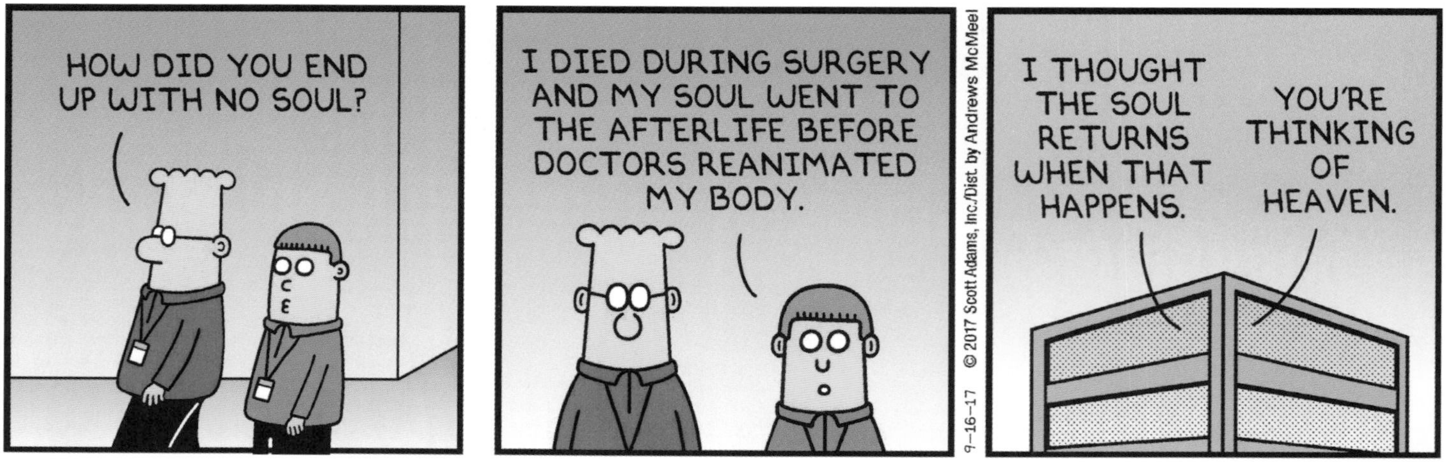
HOW DID YOU END UP WITH NO SOUL?
I DIED DURING SURGERY AND MY SOUL WENT TO THE AFTERLIFE BEFORE DOCTORS REANIMATED MY BODY.
9-16-17 © 2017 Scott Adams, Inc./Dist. by Andrews McMeel
I THOUGHT THE SOUL RETURNS WHEN THAT HAPPENS.
YOU'RE THINKING OF HEAVEN.

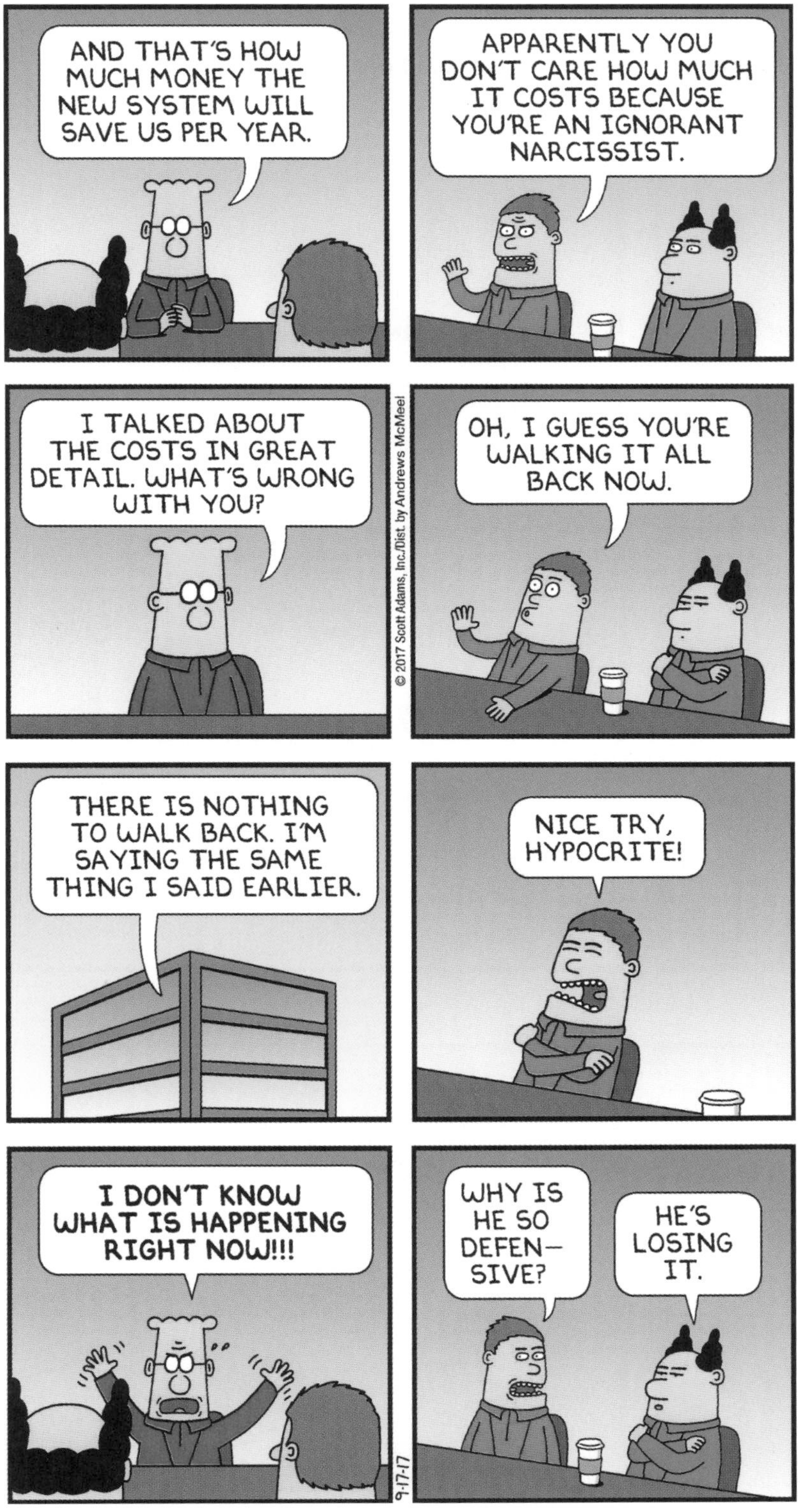
AND THAT'S HOW MUCH MONEY THE NEW SYSTEM WILL SAVE US PER YEAR.
APPARENTLY YOU DON'T CARE HOW MUCH IT COSTS BECAUSE YOU'RE AN IGNORANT NARCISSIST.
I TALKED ABOUT THE COSTS IN GREAT DETAIL. WHAT'S WRONG WITH YOU?
OH, I GUESS YOU'RE WALKING IT ALL BACK NOW.
THERE IS NOTHING TO WALK BACK. I'M SAYING THE SAME THING I SAID EARLIER.
NICE TRY, HYPOCRITE!
I DON'T KNOW WHAT IS HAPPENING RIGHT NOW!!!
WHY IS HE SO DEFEN-SIVE?
HE'S LOSING IT.
© 2017 Scott Adams, Inc./Dist. by Andrews McMeel
9-17-17

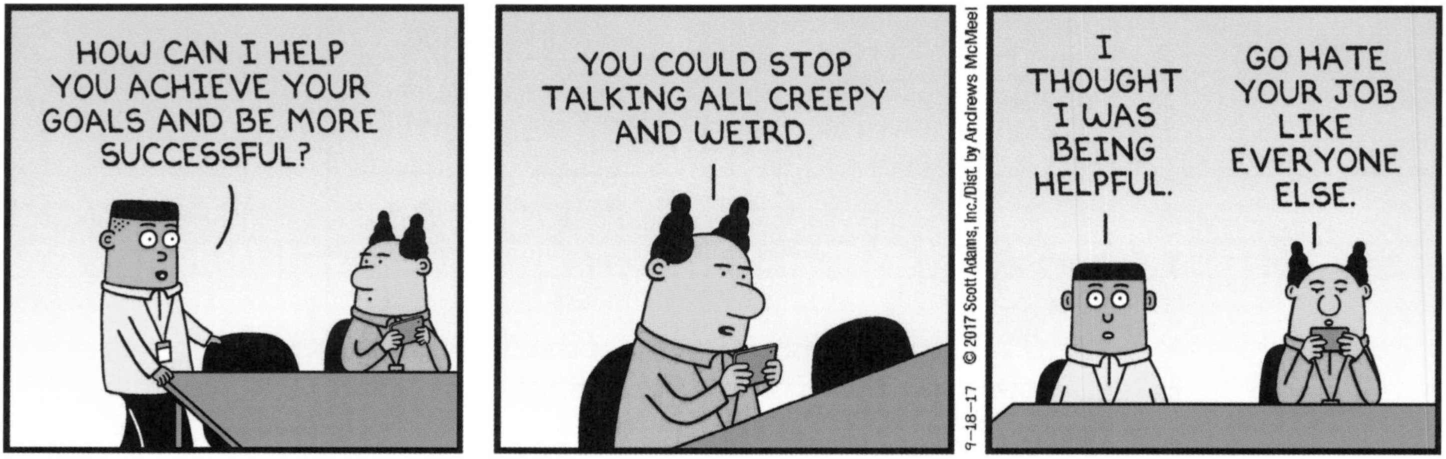
HOW CAN I HELP YOU ACHIEVE YOUR GOALS AND BE MORE SUCCESSFUL?
YOU COULD STOP TALKING ALL CREEPY AND WEIRD.
9-18-17 © 2017 Scott Adams, Inc./Dist. by Andrews McMeel
I THOUGHT I WAS BEING HELPFUL.
GO HATE YOUR JOB LIKE EVERYONE ELSE.

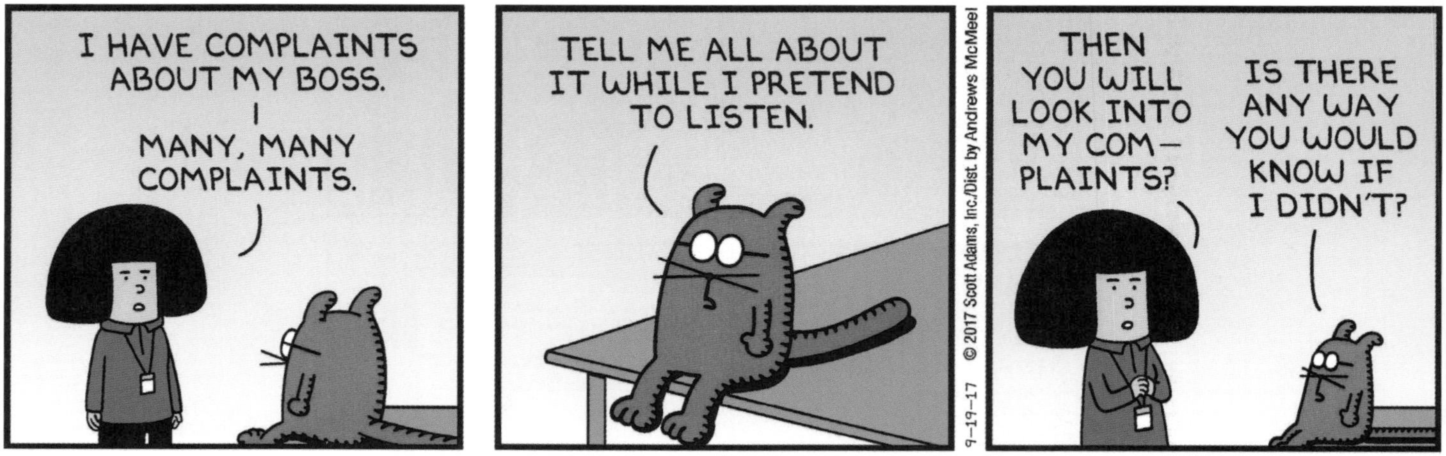
I HAVE COMPLAINTS ABOUT MY BOSS.
MANY, MANY COMPLAINTS.
TELL ME ALL ABOUT IT WHILE I PRETEND TO LISTEN.
9-19-17 © 2017 Scott Adams, Inc./Dist. by Andrews McMeel
THEN YOU WILL LOOK INTO MY COM-PLAINTS?
IS THERE ANY WAY YOU WOULD KNOW IF I DIDN'T?

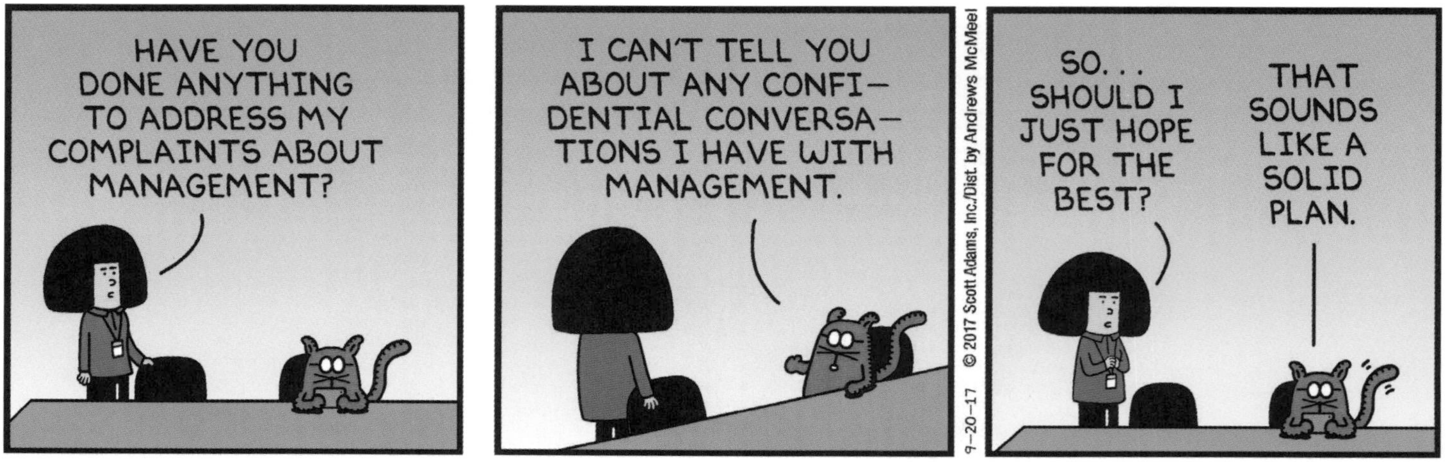
HAVE YOU DONE ANYTHING TO ADDRESS MY COMPLAINTS ABOUT MANAGEMENT?
I CAN'T TELL YOU ABOUT ANY CONFI-DENTIAL CONVERSA-TIONS I HAVE WITH MANAGEMENT.
9-20-17 © 2017 Scott Adams, Inc./Dist. by Andrews McMeel
SO. . . SHOULD I JUST HOPE FOR THE BEST?
THAT SOUNDS LIKE A SOLID PLAN.

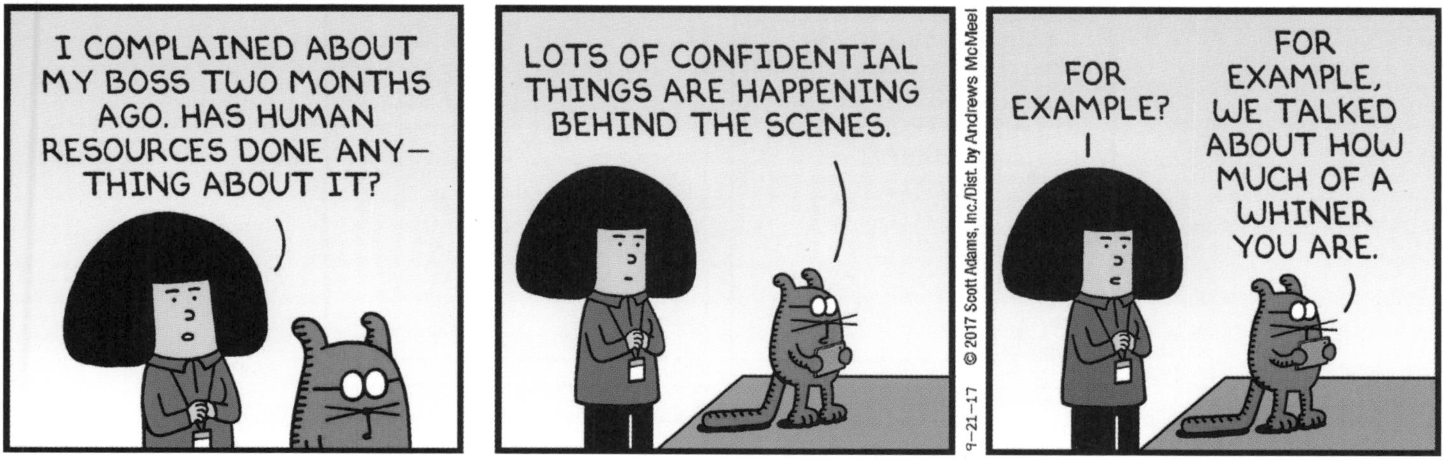
I COMPLAINED ABOUT MY BOSS TWO MONTHS AGO. HAS HUMAN RESOURCES DONE ANY- THING ABOUT IT?
LOTS OF CONFIDENTIAL THINGS ARE HAPPENING BEHIND THE SCENES.
9-21-17 © 2017 Scott Adams, Inc./Dist. by Andrews McMeel
FOR EXAMPLE?
FOR EXAMPLE, WE TALKED ABOUT HOW MUCH OF A WHINER YOU ARE.

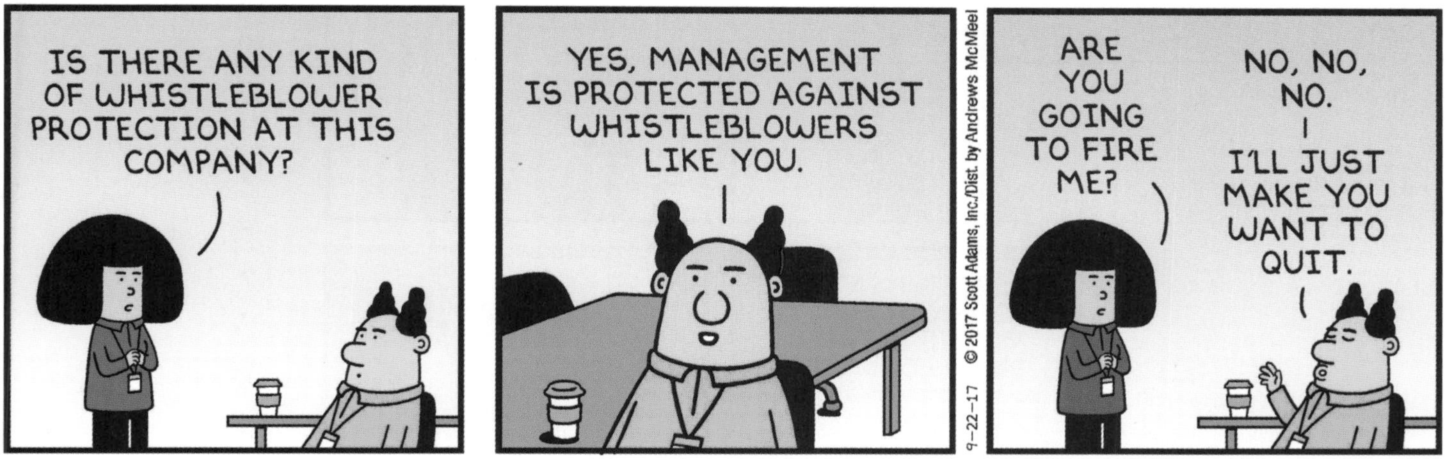
IS THERE ANY KIND OF WHISTLEBLOWER PROTECTION AT THIS COMPANY?
YES, MANAGEMENT IS PROTECTED AGAINST WHISTLEBLOWERS LIKE YOU.
9-22-17 © 2017 Scott Adams, Inc./Dist. by Andrews McMeel
ARE YOU GOING TO FIRE ME?
NO, NO, NO.
I'LL JUST MAKE YOU WANT TO QUIT.

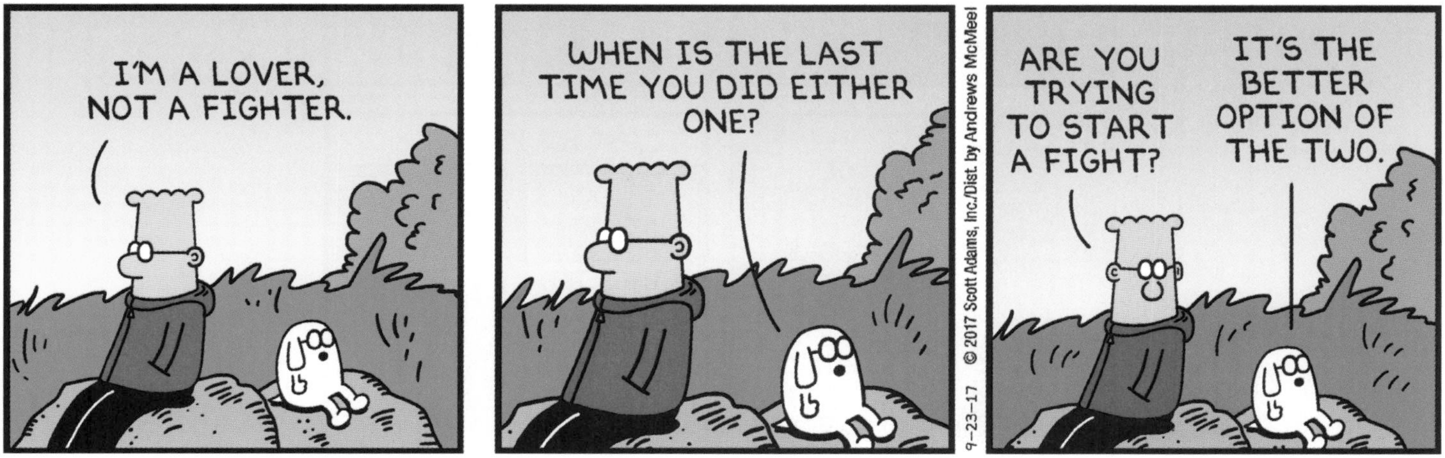
I'M A LOVER, NOT A FIGHTER.
WHEN IS THE LAST TIME YOU DID EITHER ONE?
9-23-17 © 2017 Scott Adams, Inc./Dist. by Andrews McMeel
ARE YOU TRYING TO START A FIGHT?
IT'S THE BETTER OPTION OF THE TWO.

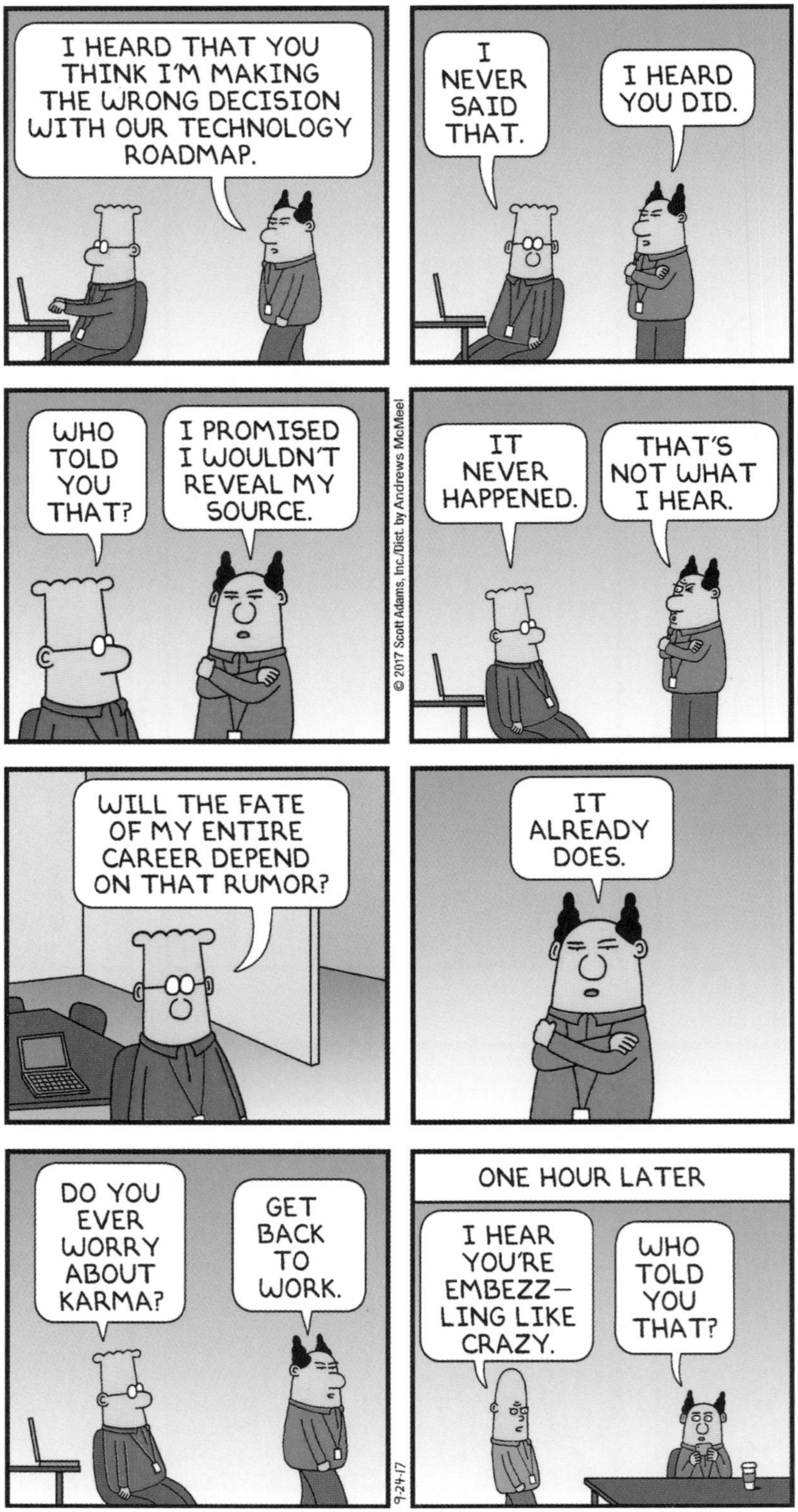
I HEARD THAT YOU THINK I'M MAKING THE WRONG DECISION WITH OUR TECHNOLOGY ROADMAP.
I NEVER SAID THAT.
I HEARD YOU DID.
WHO TOLD YOU THAT?
I PROMISED I WOULDN'T REVEAL MY SOURCE.
IT NEVER HAPPENED.
THAT'S NOT WHAT I HEAR.
WILL THE FATE OF MY ENTIRE CAREER DEPEND ON THAT RUMOR?
IT ALREADY DOES.
DO YOU EVER WORRY ABOUT KARMA?
GET BACK TO WORK.
ONE HOUR LATER
I HEAR YOU'RE EMBEZZ–LING LIKE CRAZY.
WHO TOLD YOU THAT?
© 2017 Scott Adams, Inc./Dist. by Andrews McMeel
9-24-17

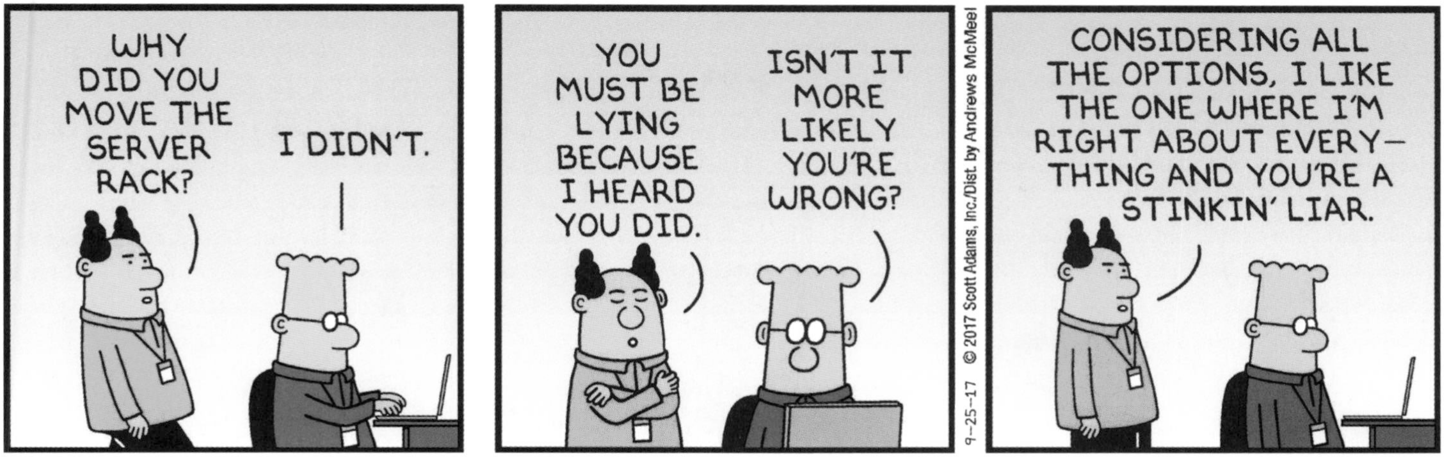
WHY DID YOU MOVE THE SERVER RACK?
I DIDN'T.
YOU MUST BE LYING BECAUSE I HEARD YOU DID.
ISN'T IT MORE LIKELY YOU'RE WRONG?
9-25-17 © 2017 Scott Adams, Inc./Dist. by Andrews McMeel
CONSIDERING ALL THE OPTIONS, I LIKE THE ONE WHERE I'M RIGHT ABOUT EVERY-THING AND YOU'RE A STINKIN' LIAR.

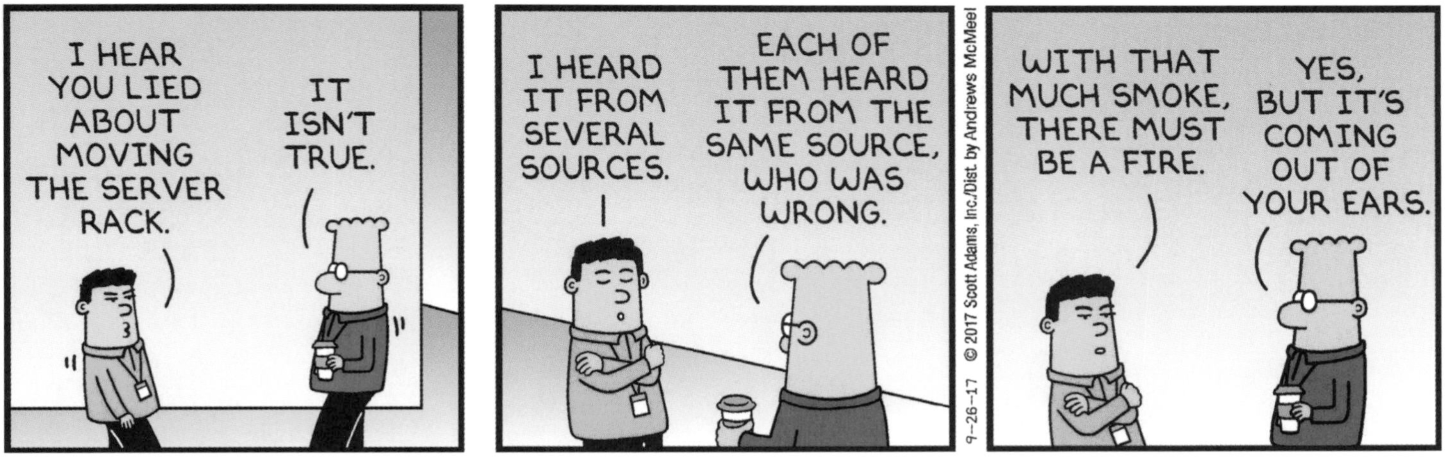
I HEAR YOU LIED ABOUT MOVING THE SERVER RACK.
IT ISN'T TRUE.
I HEARD IT FROM SEVERAL SOURCES.
EACH OF THEM HEARD IT FROM THE SAME SOURCE, WHO WAS WRONG.
9-26-17 © 2017 Scott Adams, Inc./Dist. by Andrews McMeel
WITH THAT MUCH SMOKE, THERE MUST BE A FIRE.
YES, BUT IT'S COMING OUT OF YOUR EARS.

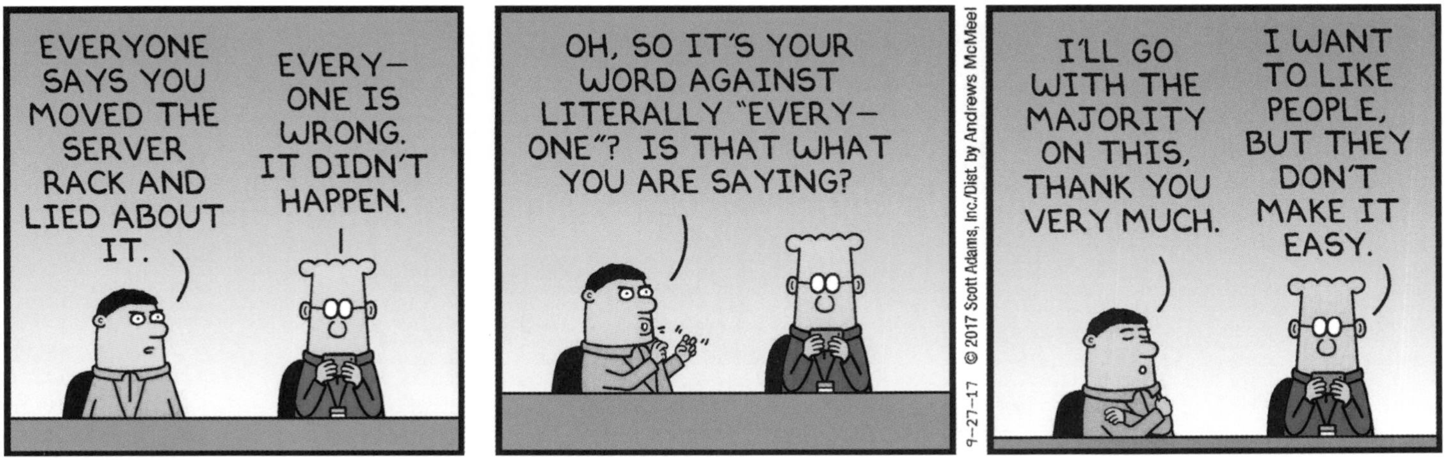
EVERYONE SAYS YOU MOVED THE SERVER RACK AND LIED ABOUT IT.
EVERY-ONE IS WRONG. IT DIDN'T HAPPEN.
OH, SO IT'S YOUR WORD AGAINST LITERALLY "EVERY-ONE"? IS THAT WHAT YOU ARE SAYING?
9-27-17 © 2017 Scott Adams, Inc./Dist. by Andrews McMeel
I'LL GO WITH THE MAJORITY ON THIS, THANK YOU VERY MUCH.
I WANT TO LIKE PEOPLE, BUT THEY DON'T MAKE IT EASY.

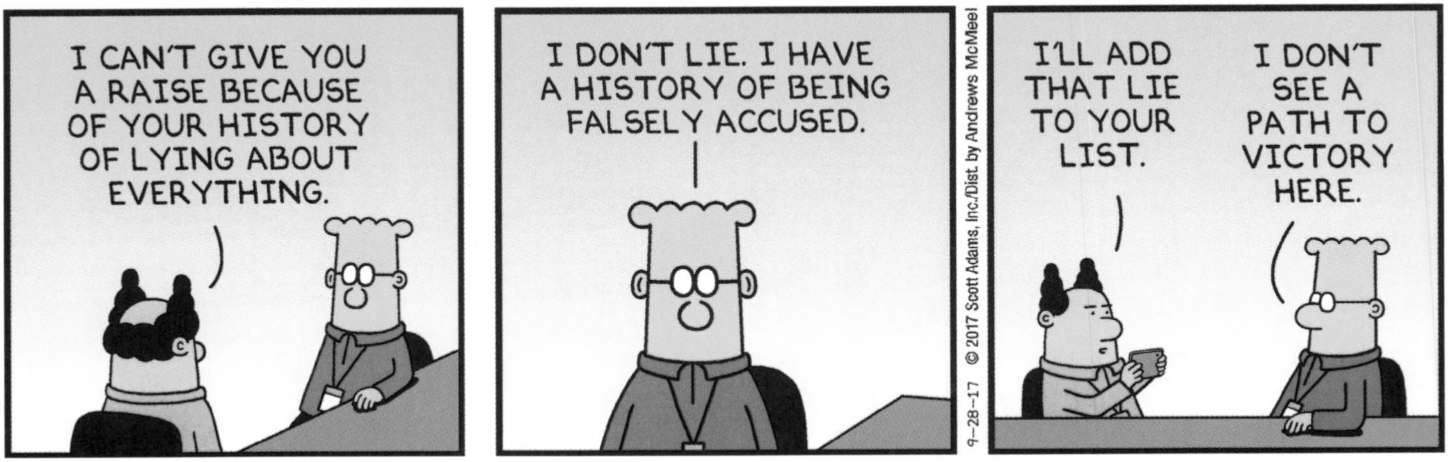
I CAN'T GIVE YOU A RAISE BECAUSE OF YOUR HISTORY OF LYING ABOUT EVERYTHING.
I DON'T LIE. I HAVE A HISTORY OF BEING FALSELY ACCUSED.
9-28-17 © 2017 Scott Adams, Inc./Dist. by Andrews McMeel
I'LL ADD THAT LIE TO YOUR LIST.
I DON'T SEE A PATH TO VICTORY HERE.

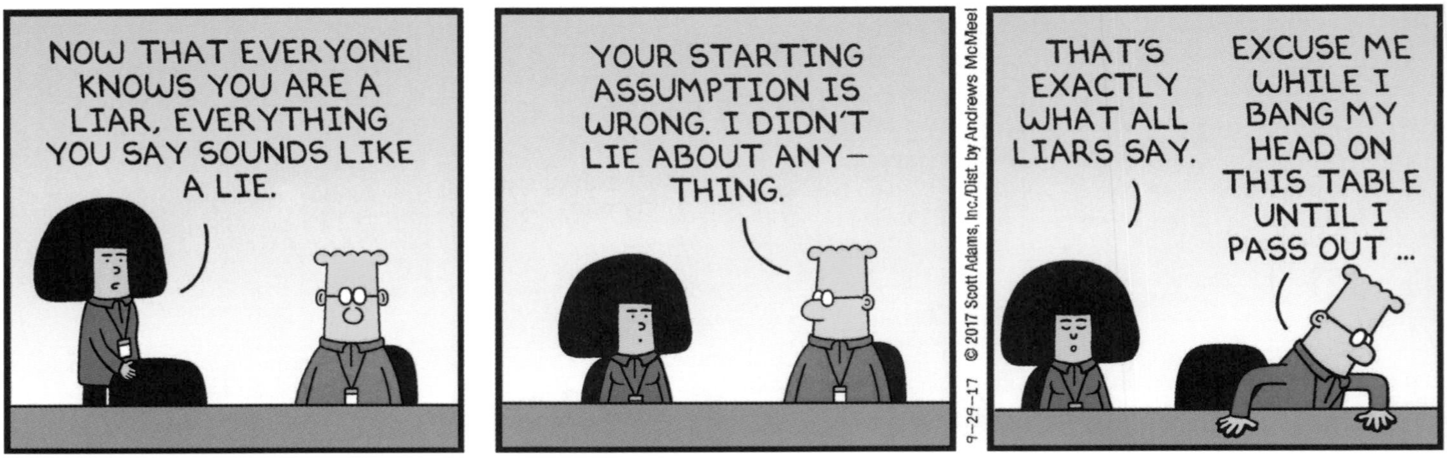
NOW THAT EVERYONE KNOWS YOU ARE A LIAR, EVERYTHING YOU SAY SOUNDS LIKE A LIE.
YOUR STARTING ASSUMPTION IS WRONG. I DIDN'T LIE ABOUT ANY-THING.
9-29-17 © 2017 Scott Adams, Inc./Dist. by Andrews McMeel
THAT'S EXACTLY WHAT ALL LIARS SAY.
EXCUSE ME WHILE I BANG MY HEAD ON THIS TABLE UNTIL I PASS OUT ...

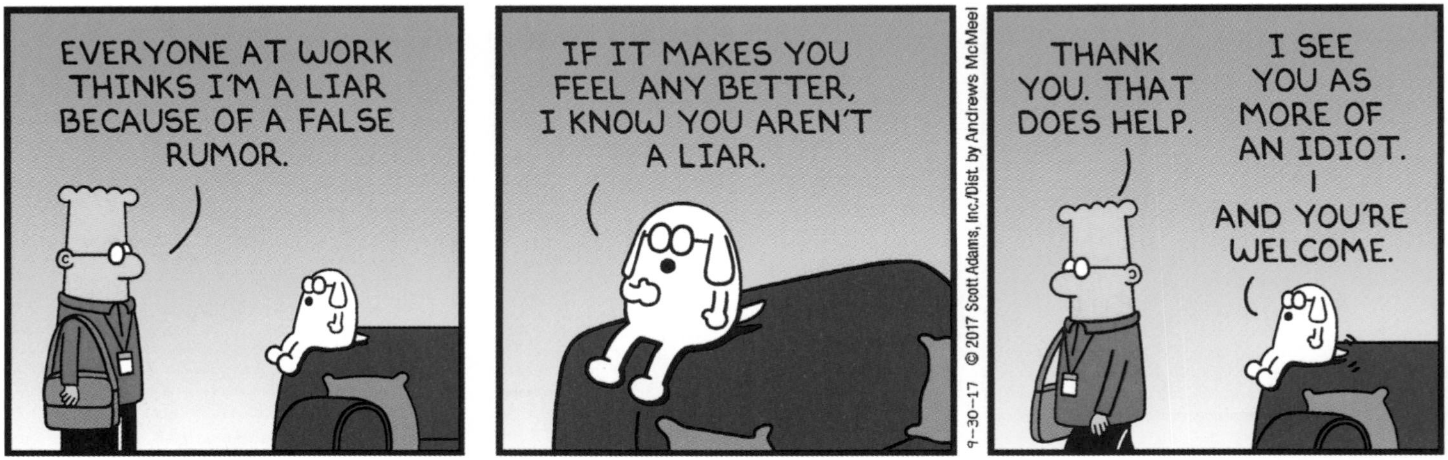
EVERYONE AT WORK THINKS I'M A LIAR BECAUSE OF A FALSE RUMOR.
IF IT MAKES YOU FEEL ANY BETTER, I KNOW YOU AREN'T A LIAR.
9-30-17 © 2017 Scott Adams, Inc./Dist. by Andrews McMeel
THANK YOU. THAT DOES HELP.
I SEE YOU AS MORE OF AN IDIOT.
AND YOU'RE WELCOME.

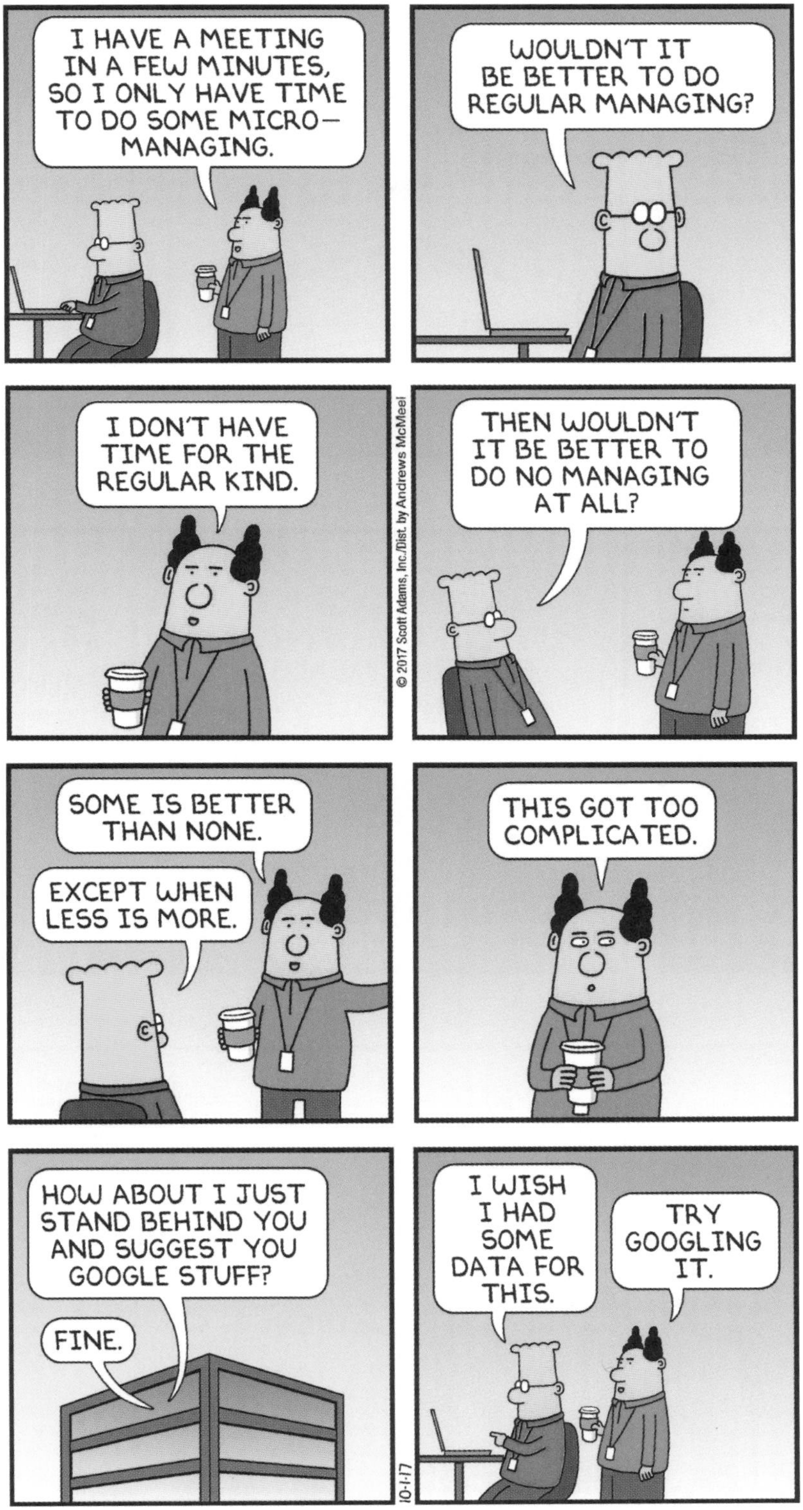
I HAVE A MEETING IN A FEW MINUTES, SO I ONLY HAVE TIME TO DO SOME MICRO-MANAGING.
WOULDN'T IT BE BETTER TO DO REGULAR MANAGING?
I DON'T HAVE TIME FOR THE REGULAR KIND.
THEN WOULDN'T IT BE BETTER TO DO NO MANAGING AT ALL?
SOME IS BETTER THAN NONE.
EXCEPT WHEN LESS IS MORE.
THIS GOT TOO COMPLICATED.
HOW ABOUT I JUST STAND BEHIND YOU AND SUGGEST YOU GOOGLE STUFF?
FINE.
I WISH I HAD SOME DATA FOR THIS.
TRY GOOGLING IT.
© 2017 Scott Adams, Inc./Dist. by Andrews McMeel
10-1-17

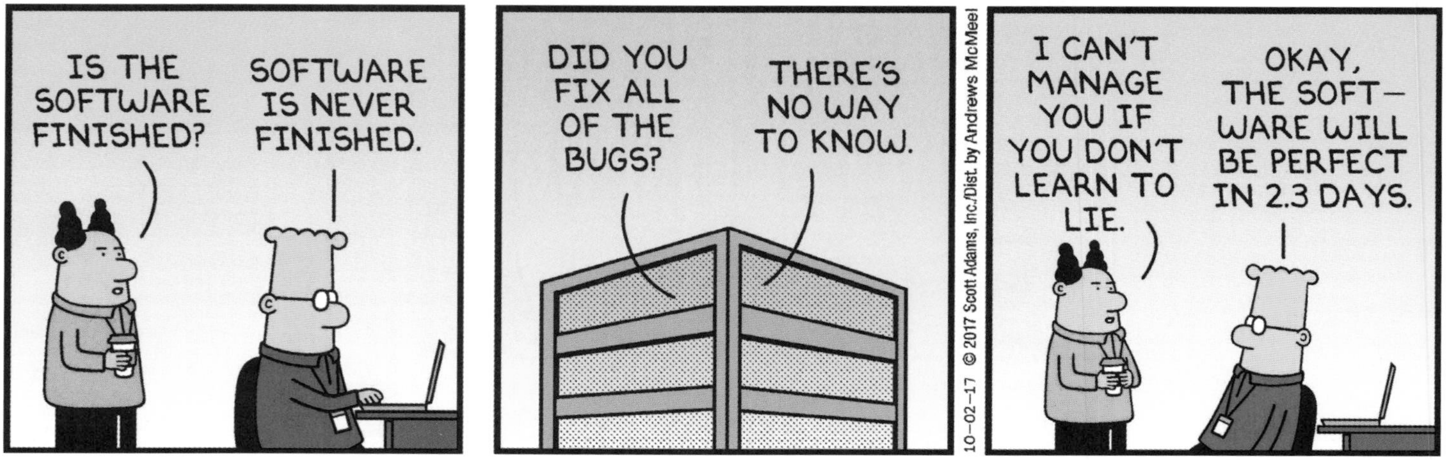
IS THE SOFTWARE FINISHED?
SOFTWARE IS NEVER FINISHED.
DID YOU FIX ALL OF THE BUGS?
THERE'S NO WAY TO KNOW.
10-02-17 © 2017 Scott Adams, Inc./Dist. by Andrews McMeel
I CAN'T MANAGE YOU IF YOU DON'T LEARN TO LIE.
OKAY, THE SOFT-WARE WILL BE PERFECT IN 2.3 DAYS.

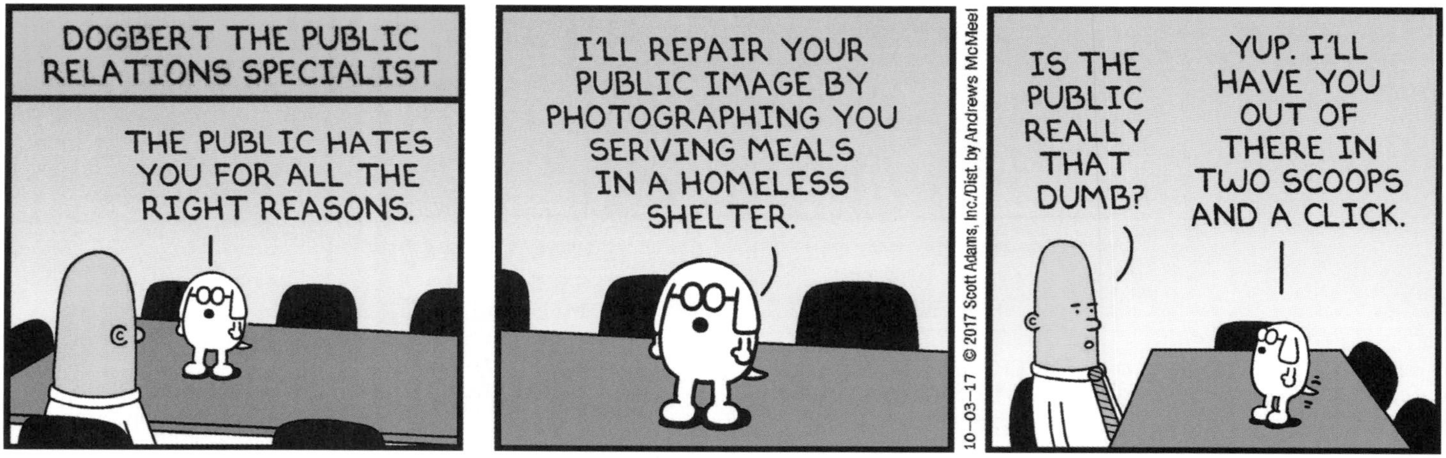
DOGBERT THE PUBLIC RELATIONS SPECIALIST
THE PUBLIC HATES YOU FOR ALL THE RIGHT REASONS.
I'LL REPAIR YOUR PUBLIC IMAGE BY PHOTOGRAPHING YOU SERVING MEALS IN A HOMELESS SHELTER.
10-03-17 © 2017 Scott Adams, Inc./Dist. by Andrews McMeel
IS THE PUBLIC REALLY THAT DUMB?
YUP. I'LL HAVE YOU OUT OF THERE IN TWO SCOOPS AND A CLICK.

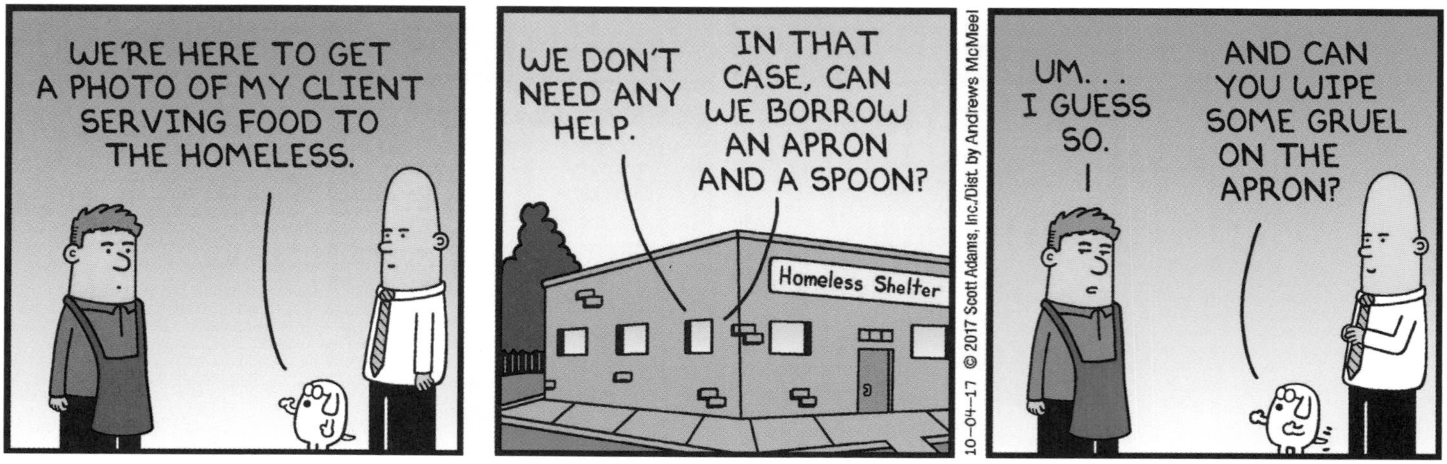
WE'RE HERE TO GET A PHOTO OF MY CLIENT SERVING FOOD TO THE HOMELESS.
WE DON'T NEED ANY HELP.
IN THAT CASE, CAN WE BORROW AN APRON AND A SPOON?
Homeless Shelter
10-04-17 © 2017 Scott Adams, Inc./Dist. by Andrews McMeel
UM. . . I GUESS SO.
AND CAN YOU WIPE SOME GRUEL ON THE APRON?

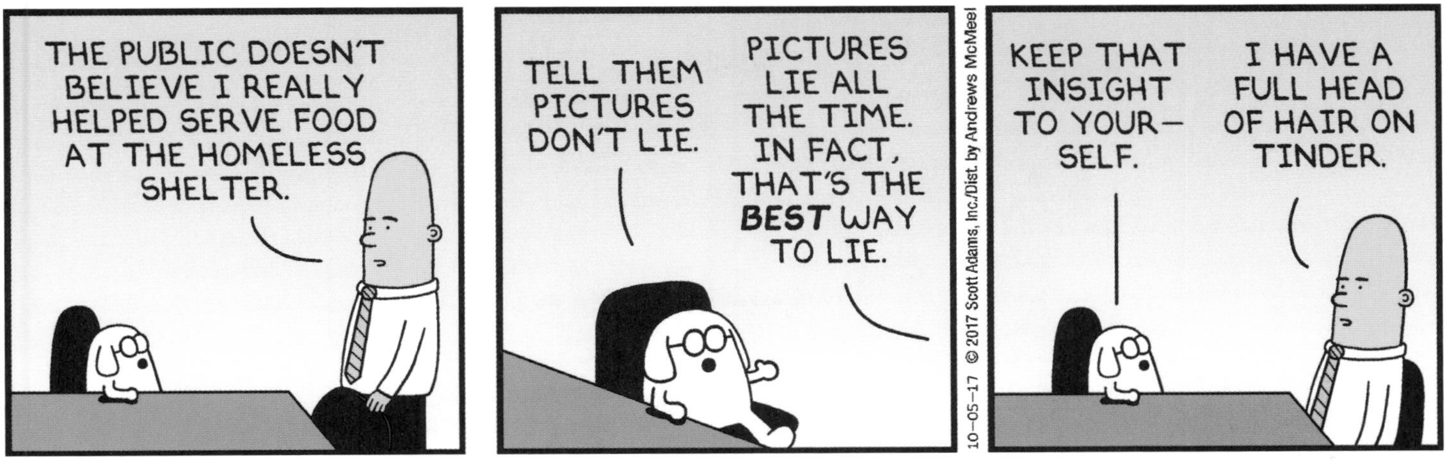
THE PUBLIC DOESN'T BELIEVE I REALLY HELPED SERVE FOOD AT THE HOMELESS SHELTER.
TELL THEM PICTURES DON'T LIE.
PICTURES LIE ALL THE TIME. IN FACT, THAT'S THE **BEST** WAY TO LIE.
KEEP THAT INSIGHT TO YOUR-SELF.
I HAVE A FULL HEAD OF HAIR ON TINDER.
10-05-17 © 2017 Scott Adams, Inc./Dist. by Andrews McMeel

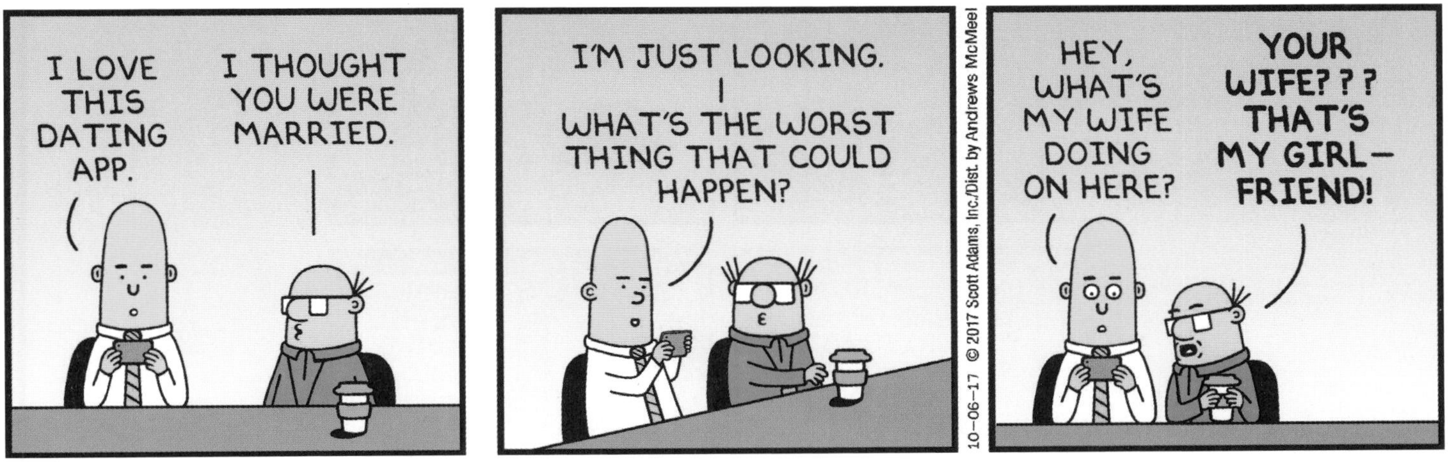
I LOVE THIS DATING APP.
I THOUGHT YOU WERE MARRIED.
I'M JUST LOOKING. WHAT'S THE WORST THING THAT COULD HAPPEN?
HEY, WHAT'S MY WIFE DOING ON HERE?
YOUR WIFE??? THAT'S MY GIRL-FRIEND!
10-06-17 © 2017 Scott Adams, Inc./Dist. by Andrews McMeel

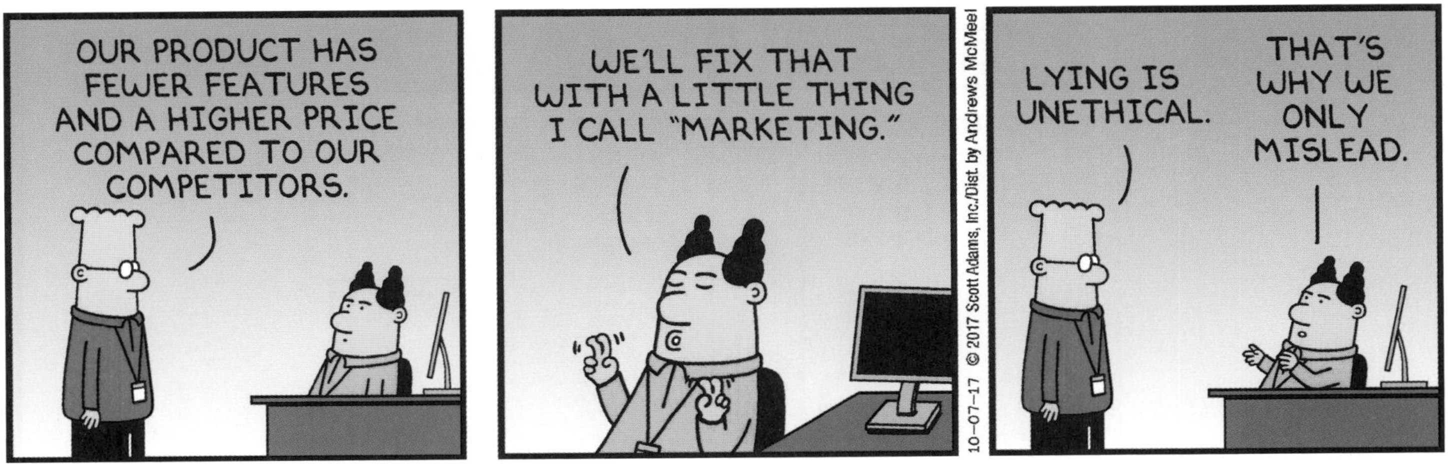
OUR PRODUCT HAS FEWER FEATURES AND A HIGHER PRICE COMPARED TO OUR COMPETITORS.
WE'LL FIX THAT WITH A LITTLE THING I CALL "MARKETING."
LYING IS UNETHICAL.
THAT'S WHY WE ONLY MISLEAD.
10-07-17 © 2017 Scott Adams, Inc./Dist. by Andrews McMeel

I'M A GOOD JUDGE OF PEOPLE.
REALLY? WHAT AM I THINKING RIGHT NOW?
HMMM. . .
YOU'RE WONDERING HOW YOU COULD BE MORE LIKE ME.
YOU ADMIRE MY LEADERSHIP, AND YOU WRITE ABOUT ME IN GLOWING TERMS IN YOUR DIARY.
WHAT DIARY?
SHHH! I'M STILL READING YOU.
YOU HAVE NO PATIENCE AND YOU DON'T LIKE TO BE JUDGED.
OKAY, THAT'S ENOUGH.
NAILED IT!
© 2017 Scott Adams, Inc./Dist. by Andrews McMeel
10-8-17

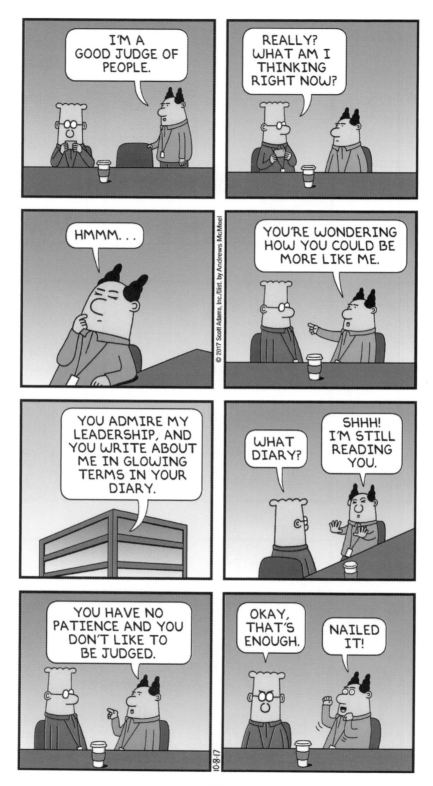

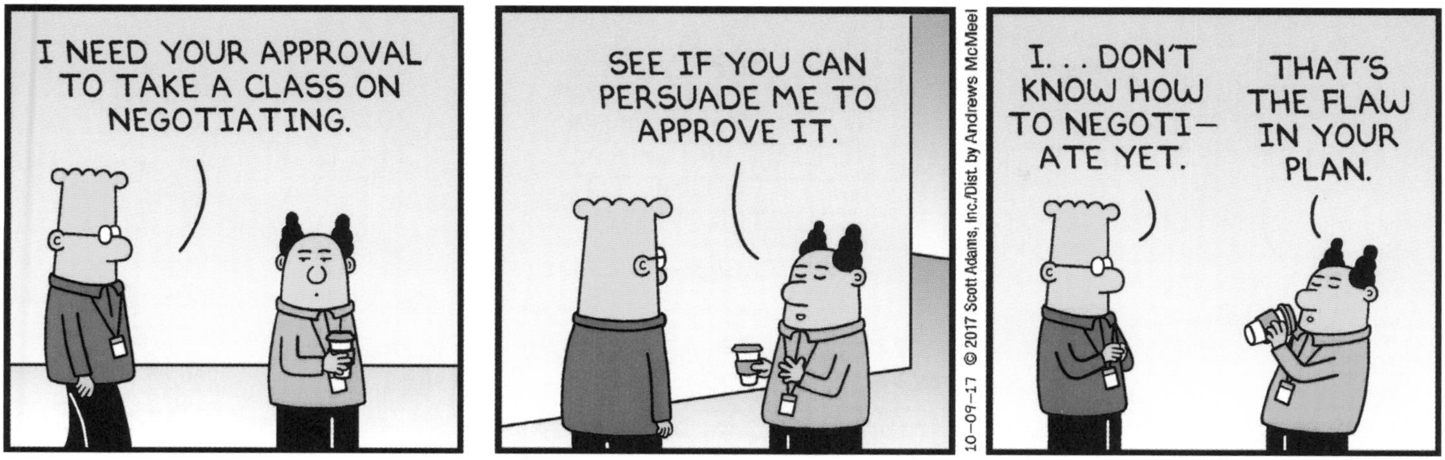
I NEED YOUR APPROVAL TO TAKE A CLASS ON NEGOTIATING.
SEE IF YOU CAN PERSUADE ME TO APPROVE IT.
10-09-17 © 2017 Scott Adams, Inc./Dist. by Andrews McMeel
I. . . DON'T KNOW HOW TO NEGOTI– ATE YET.
THAT'S THE FLAW IN YOUR PLAN.

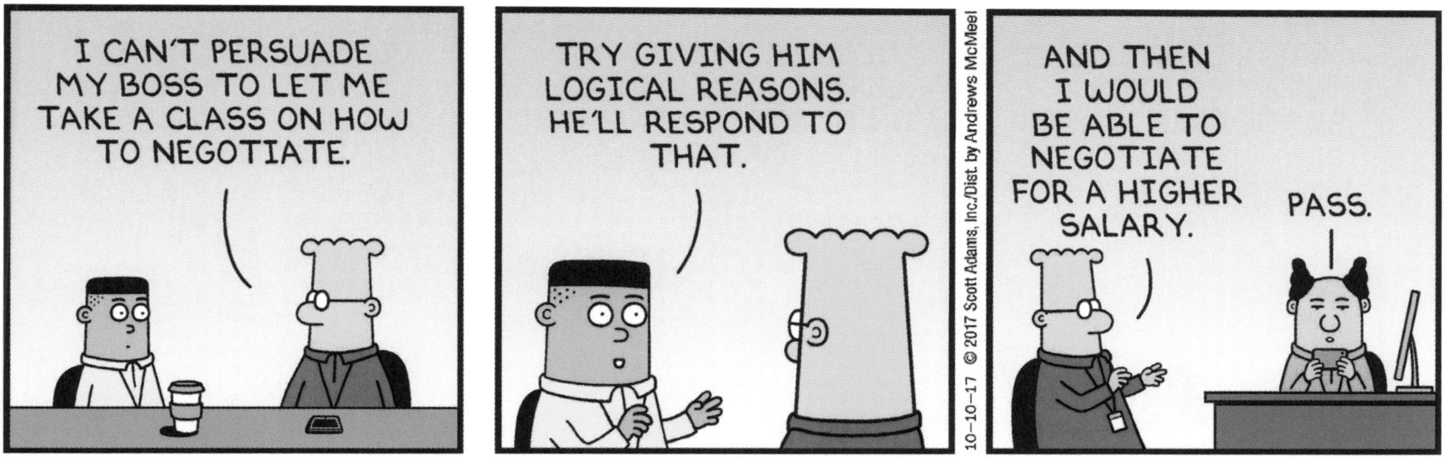
I CAN'T PERSUADE MY BOSS TO LET ME TAKE A CLASS ON HOW TO NEGOTIATE.
TRY GIVING HIM LOGICAL REASONS. HE'LL RESPOND TO THAT.
10-10-17 © 2017 Scott Adams, Inc./Dist. by Andrews McMeel
AND THEN I WOULD BE ABLE TO NEGOTIATE FOR A HIGHER SALARY.
PASS.

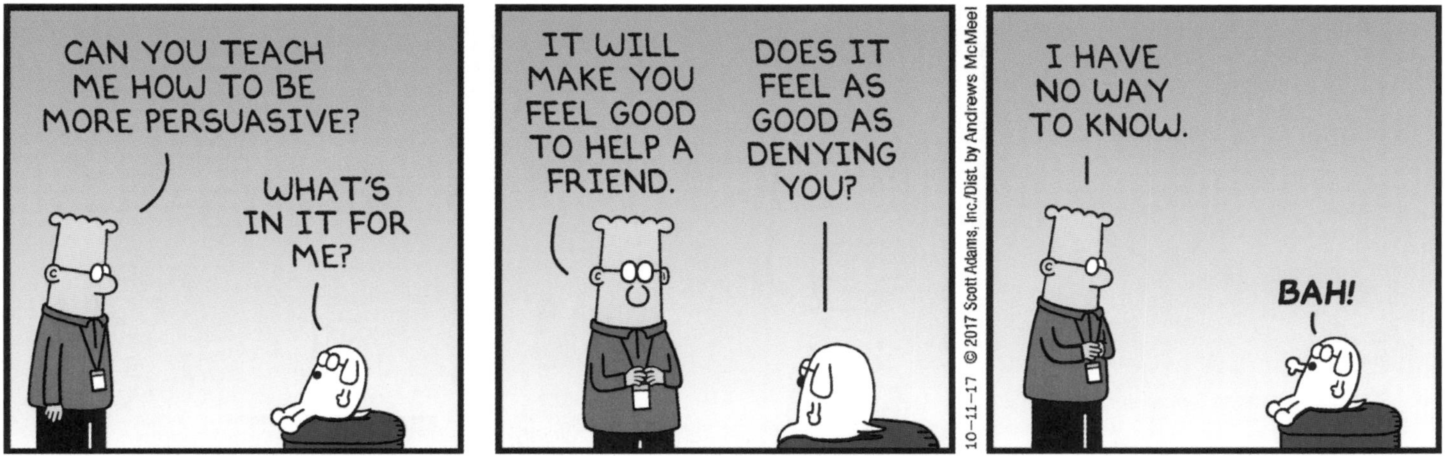
CAN YOU TEACH ME HOW TO BE MORE PERSUASIVE?
WHAT'S IN IT FOR ME?
IT WILL MAKE YOU FEEL GOOD TO HELP A FRIEND.
DOES IT FEEL AS GOOD AS DENYING YOU?
10-11-17 © 2017 Scott Adams, Inc./Dist. by Andrews McMeel
I HAVE NO WAY TO KNOW.
BAH!

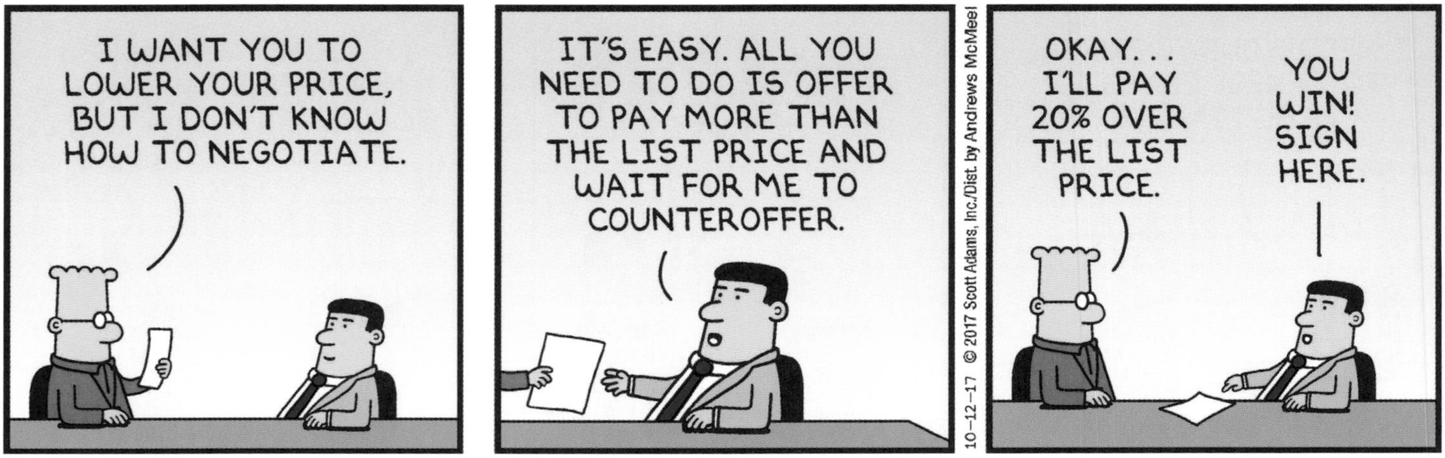
I WANT YOU TO LOWER YOUR PRICE, BUT I DON'T KNOW HOW TO NEGOTIATE.
IT'S EASY. ALL YOU NEED TO DO IS OFFER TO PAY MORE THAN THE LIST PRICE AND WAIT FOR ME TO COUNTEROFFER.
OKAY. . . I'LL PAY 20% OVER THE LIST PRICE.
YOU WIN! SIGN HERE.
10-12-17 © 2017 Scott Adams, Inc./Dist. by Andrews McMeel

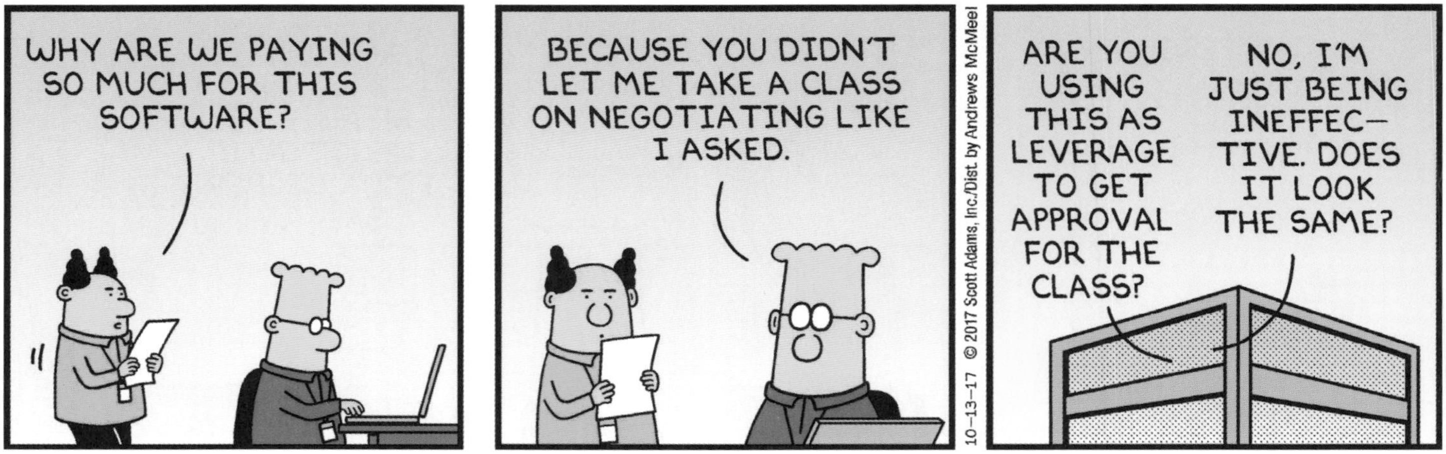
WHY ARE WE PAYING SO MUCH FOR THIS SOFTWARE?
BECAUSE YOU DIDN'T LET ME TAKE A CLASS ON NEGOTIATING LIKE I ASKED.
ARE YOU USING THIS AS LEVERAGE TO GET APPROVAL FOR THE CLASS?
NO, I'M JUST BEING INEFFEC- TIVE. DOES IT LOOK THE SAME?
10-13-17 © 2017 Scott Adams, Inc./Dist. by Andrews McMeel

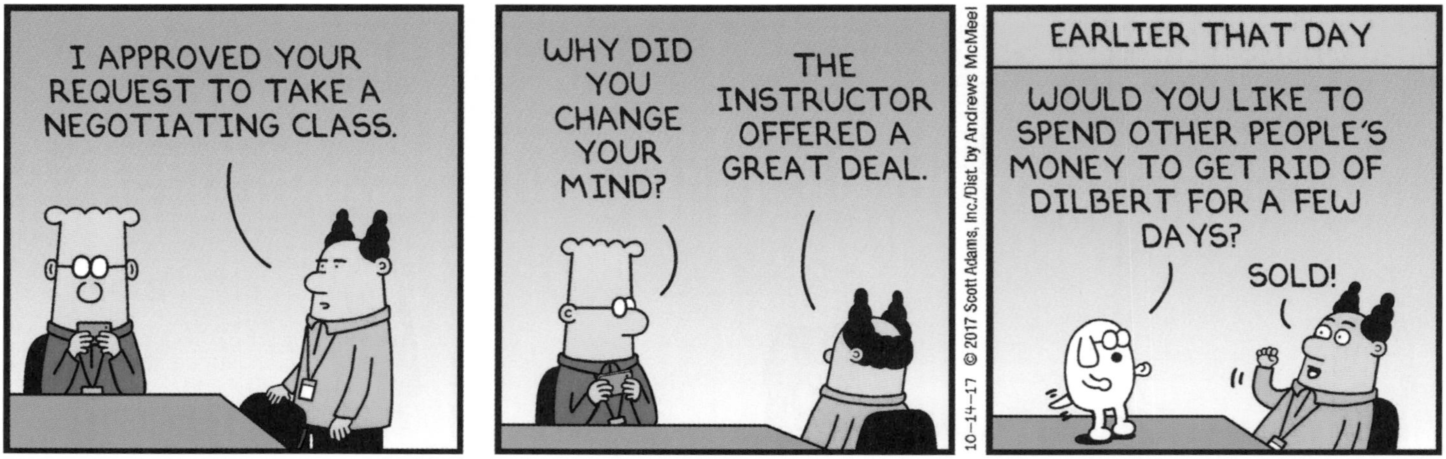
I APPROVED YOUR REQUEST TO TAKE A NEGOTIATING CLASS.
WHY DID YOU CHANGE YOUR MIND?
THE INSTRUCTOR OFFERED A GREAT DEAL.
EARLIER THAT DAY
WOULD YOU LIKE TO SPEND OTHER PEOPLE'S MONEY TO GET RID OF DILBERT FOR A FEW DAYS?
SOLD!
10-14-17 © 2017 Scott Adams, Inc./Dist. by Andrews McMeel

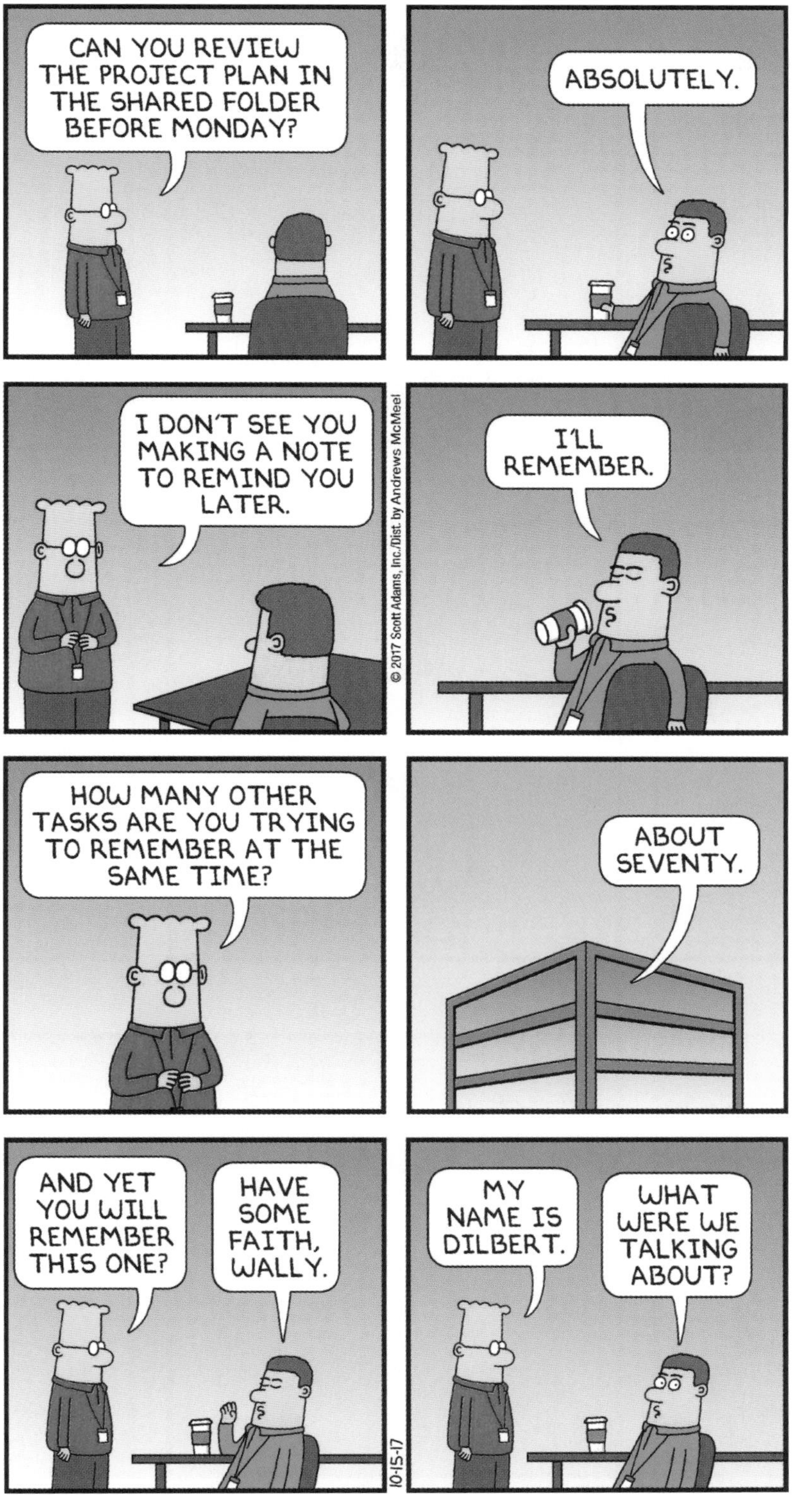
CAN YOU REVIEW THE PROJECT PLAN IN THE SHARED FOLDER BEFORE MONDAY?
ABSOLUTELY.
I DON'T SEE YOU MAKING A NOTE TO REMIND YOU LATER.
I'LL REMEMBER.
HOW MANY OTHER TASKS ARE YOU TRYING TO REMEMBER AT THE SAME TIME?
ABOUT SEVENTY.
AND YET YOU WILL REMEMBER THIS ONE?
HAVE SOME FAITH, WALLY.
MY NAME IS DILBERT.
WHAT WERE WE TALKING ABOUT?
© 2017 Scott Adams, Inc./Dist. by Andrews McMeel
10-15-17

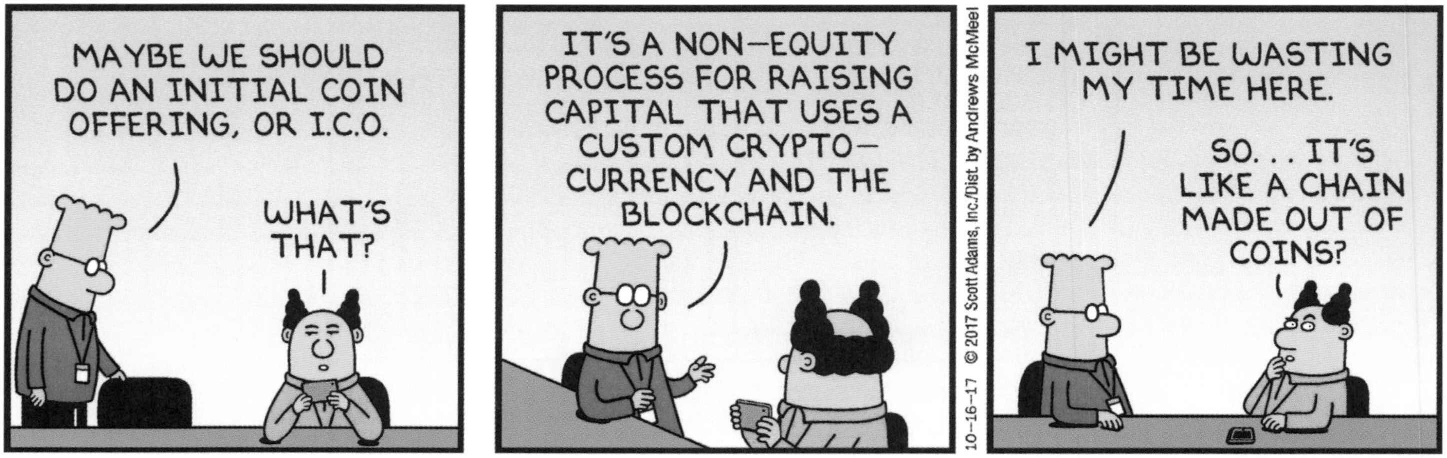
MAYBE WE SHOULD DO AN INITIAL COIN OFFERING, OR I.C.O.
WHAT'S THAT?
IT'S A NON-EQUITY PROCESS FOR RAISING CAPITAL THAT USES A CUSTOM CRYPTO-CURRENCY AND THE BLOCKCHAIN.
10-16-17 © 2017 Scott Adams, Inc./Dist. by Andrews McMeel
I MIGHT BE WASTING MY TIME HERE.
SO. . . IT'S LIKE A CHAIN MADE OUT OF COINS?

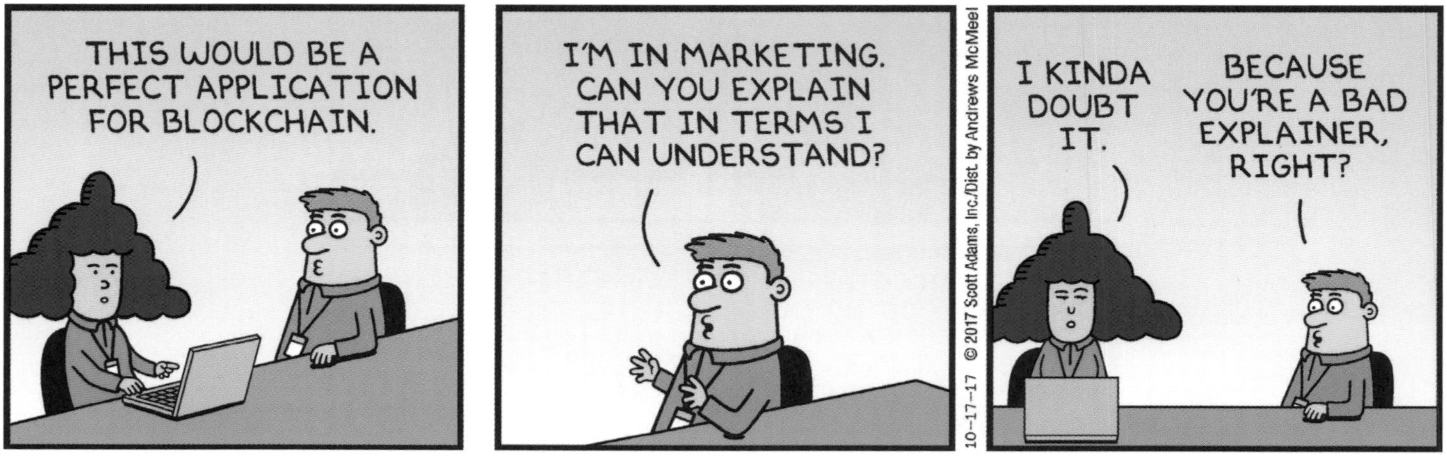
THIS WOULD BE A PERFECT APPLICATION FOR BLOCKCHAIN.
I'M IN MARKETING. CAN YOU EXPLAIN THAT IN TERMS I CAN UNDERSTAND?
10-17-17 © 2017 Scott Adams, Inc./Dist. by Andrews McMeel
I KINDA DOUBT IT.
BECAUSE YOU'RE A BAD EXPLAINER, RIGHT?

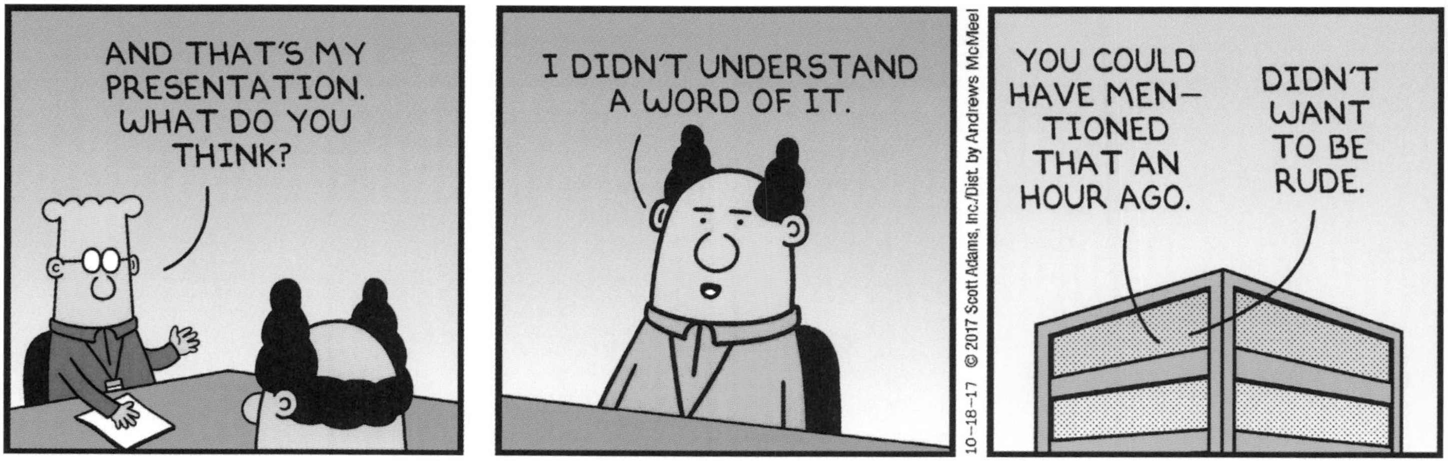
AND THAT'S MY PRESENTATION. WHAT DO YOU THINK?
I DIDN'T UNDERSTAND A WORD OF IT.
10-18-17 © 2017 Scott Adams, Inc./Dist. by Andrews McMeel
YOU COULD HAVE MEN-TIONED THAT AN HOUR AGO.
DIDN'T WANT TO BE RUDE.

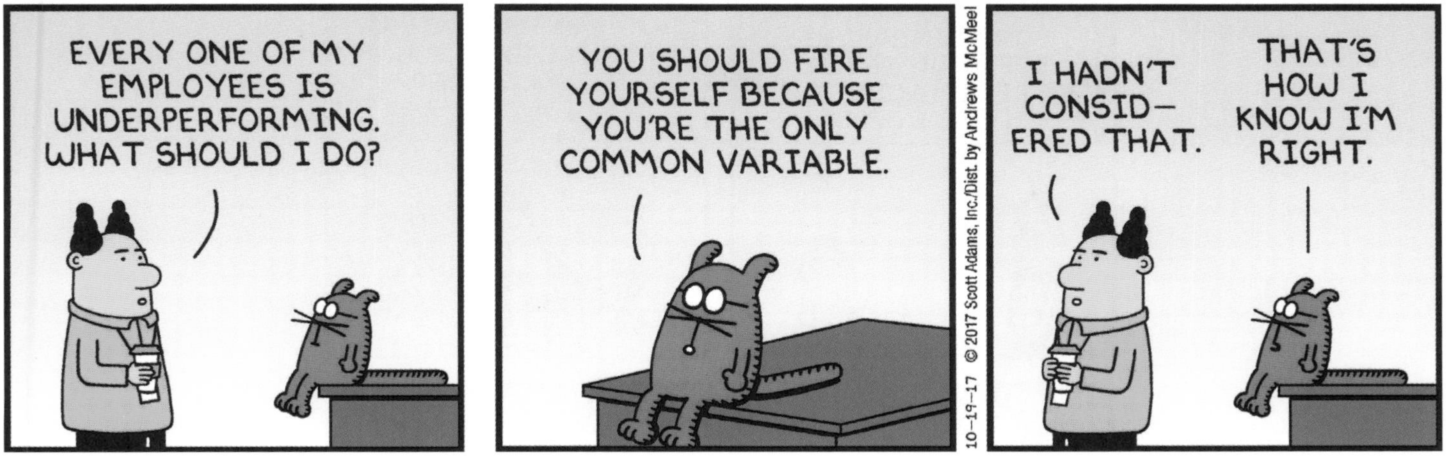
EVERY ONE OF MY EMPLOYEES IS UNDERPERFORMING. WHAT SHOULD I DO?
YOU SHOULD FIRE YOURSELF BECAUSE YOU'RE THE ONLY COMMON VARIABLE.
10-19-17 © 2017 Scott Adams, Inc./Dist. by Andrews McMeel
I HADN'T CONSID-ERED THAT.
THAT'S HOW I KNOW I'M RIGHT.

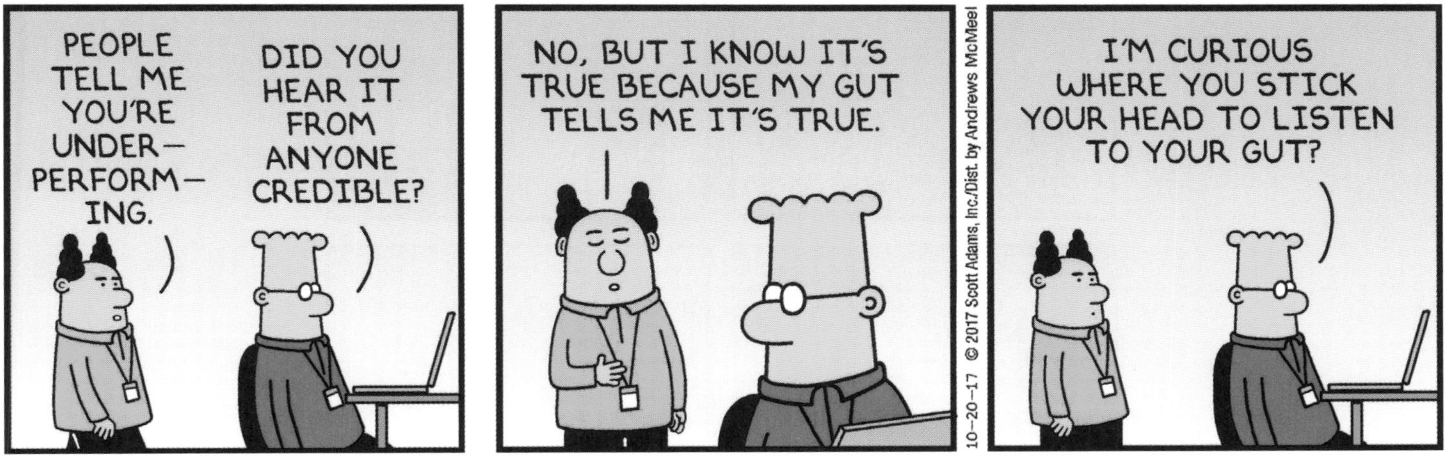
PEOPLE TELL ME YOU'RE UNDER-PERFORM-ING.
DID YOU HEAR IT FROM ANYONE CREDIBLE?
NO, BUT I KNOW IT'S TRUE BECAUSE MY GUT TELLS ME IT'S TRUE.
10-20-17 © 2017 Scott Adams, Inc./Dist. by Andrews McMeel
I'M CURIOUS WHERE YOU STICK YOUR HEAD TO LISTEN TO YOUR GUT?

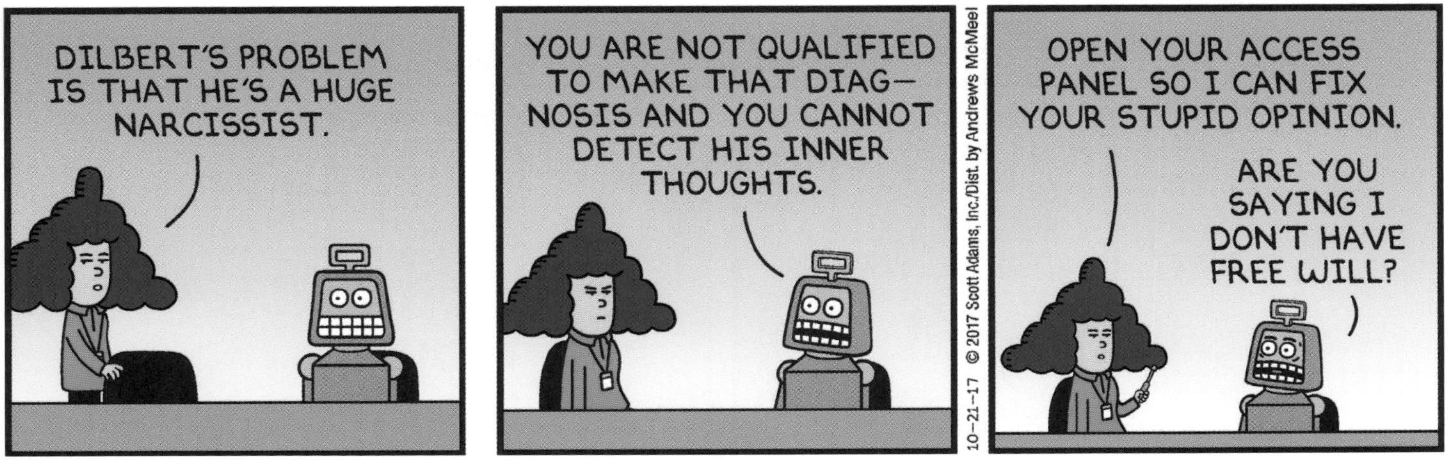
DILBERT'S PROBLEM IS THAT HE'S A HUGE NARCISSIST.
YOU ARE NOT QUALIFIED TO MAKE THAT DIAG-NOSIS AND YOU CANNOT DETECT HIS INNER THOUGHTS.
10-21-17 © 2017 Scott Adams, Inc./Dist. by Andrews McMeel
OPEN YOUR ACCESS PANEL SO I CAN FIX YOUR STUPID OPINION.
ARE YOU SAYING I DON'T HAVE FREE WILL?

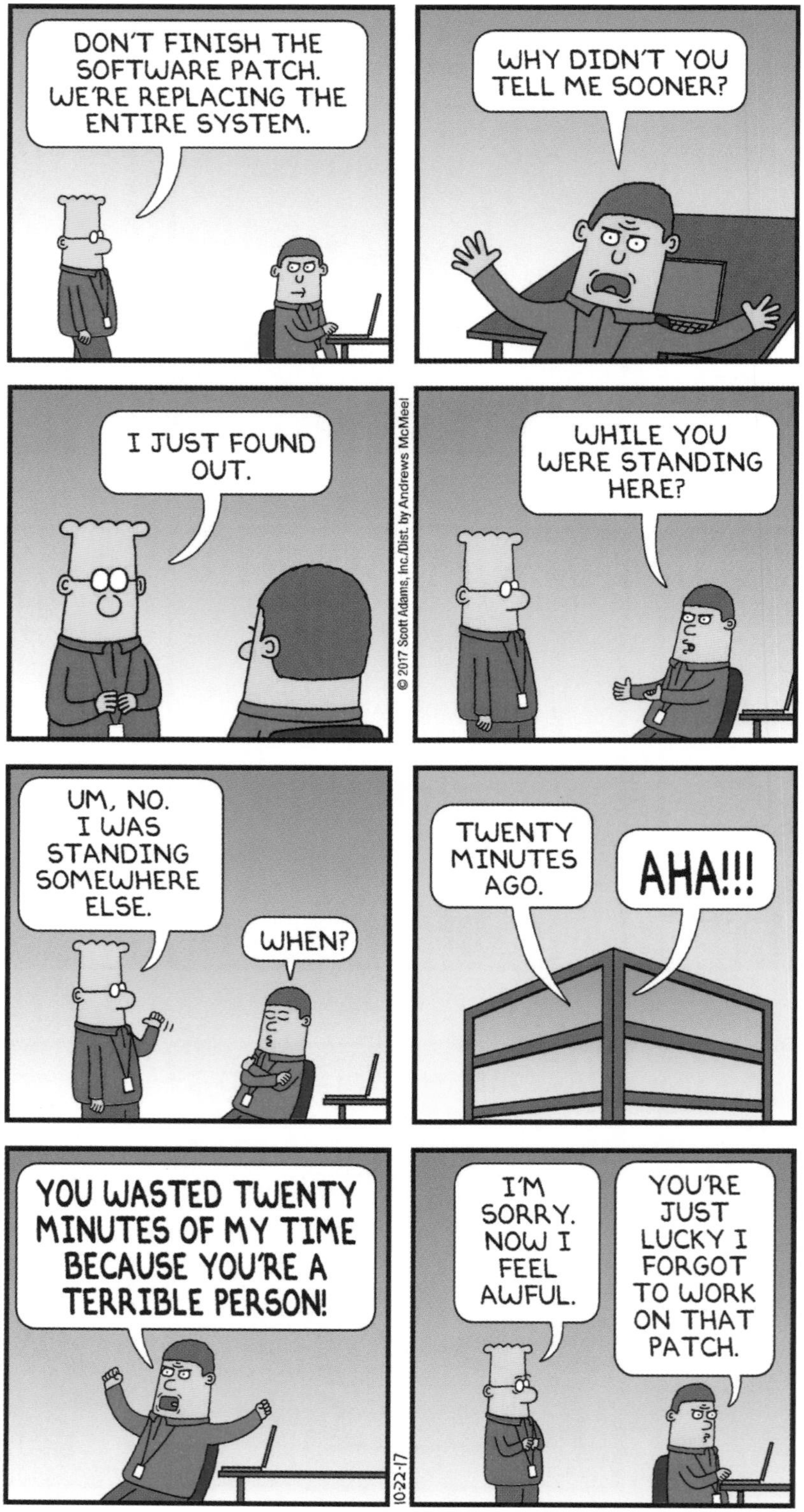
DON'T FINISH THE SOFTWARE PATCH. WE'RE REPLACING THE ENTIRE SYSTEM.
WHY DIDN'T YOU TELL ME SOONER?
I JUST FOUND OUT.
WHILE YOU WERE STANDING HERE?
UM, NO. I WAS STANDING SOMEWHERE ELSE.
WHEN?
TWENTY MINUTES AGO.
AHA!!!
YOU WASTED TWENTY MINUTES OF MY TIME BECAUSE YOU'RE A TERRIBLE PERSON!
I'M SORRY. NOW I FEEL AWFUL.
YOU'RE JUST LUCKY I FORGOT TO WORK ON THAT PATCH.
© 2017 Scott Adams, Inc./Dist. by Andrews McMeel
10-22-17

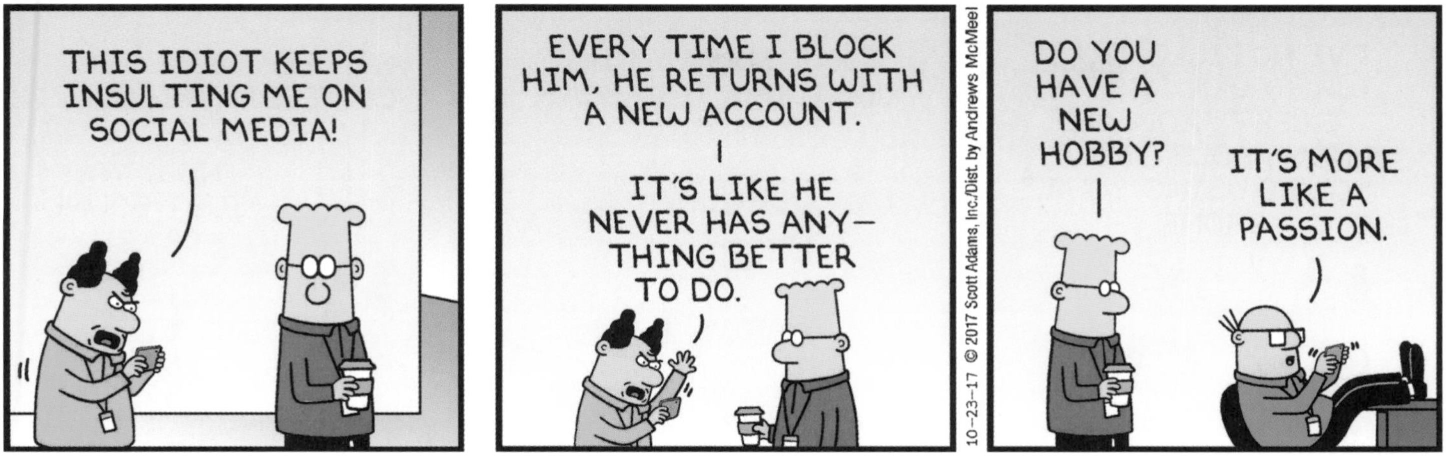
THIS IDIOT KEEPS INSULTING ME ON SOCIAL MEDIA!
EVERY TIME I BLOCK HIM, HE RETURNS WITH A NEW ACCOUNT.
IT'S LIKE HE NEVER HAS ANY-THING BETTER TO DO.
10-23-17 © 2017 Scott Adams, Inc./Dist. by Andrews McMeel
DO YOU HAVE A NEW HOBBY?
IT'S MORE LIKE A PASSION.

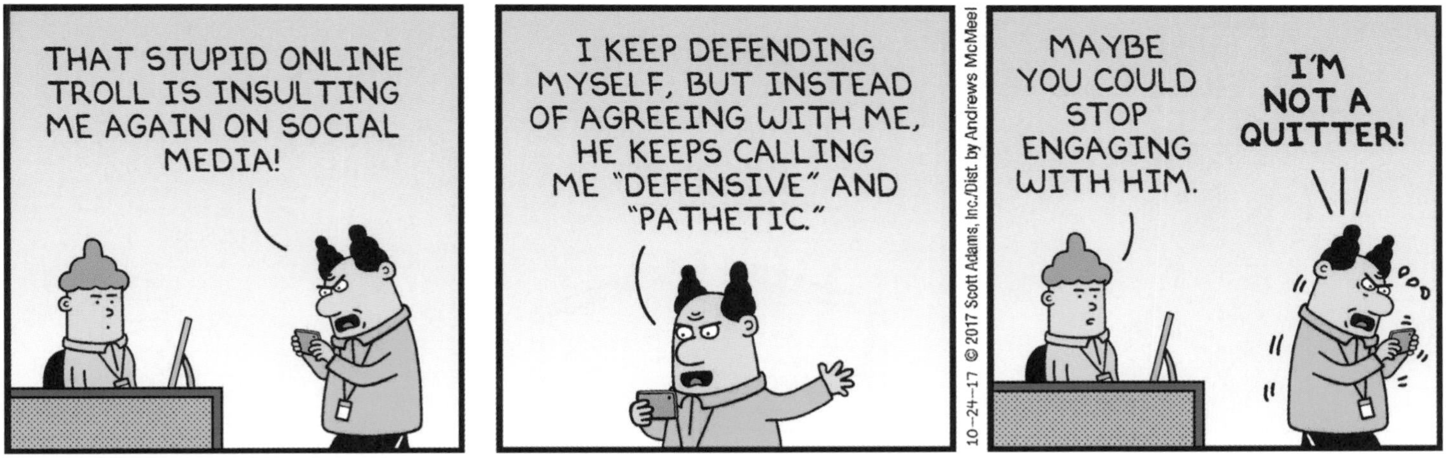
THAT STUPID ONLINE TROLL IS INSULTING ME AGAIN ON SOCIAL MEDIA!
I KEEP DEFENDING MYSELF, BUT INSTEAD OF AGREEING WITH ME, HE KEEPS CALLING ME "DEFENSIVE" AND "PATHETIC."
10-24-17 © 2017 Scott Adams, Inc./Dist. by Andrews McMeel
MAYBE YOU COULD STOP ENGAGING WITH HIM.
I'M NOT A QUITTER!

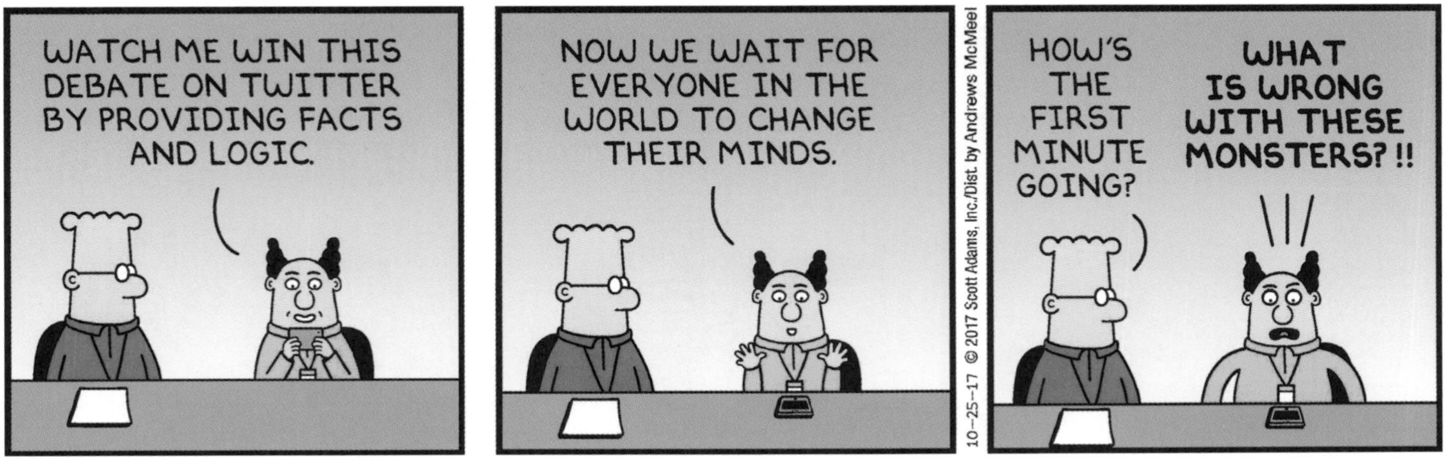
WATCH ME WIN THIS DEBATE ON TWITTER BY PROVIDING FACTS AND LOGIC.
NOW WE WAIT FOR EVERYONE IN THE WORLD TO CHANGE THEIR MINDS.
10-25-17 © 2017 Scott Adams, Inc./Dist. by Andrews McMeel
HOW'S THE FIRST MINUTE GOING?
WHAT IS WRONG WITH THESE MONSTERS?!!

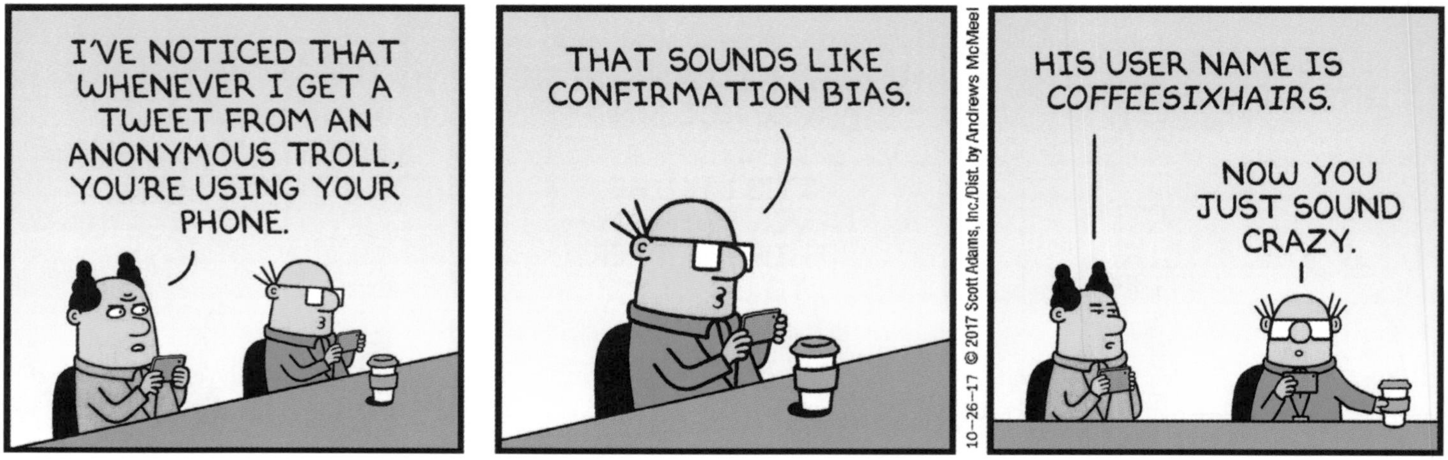
I'VE NOTICED THAT WHENEVER I GET A TWEET FROM AN ANONYMOUS TROLL, YOU'RE USING YOUR PHONE.
THAT SOUNDS LIKE CONFIRMATION BIAS.
HIS USER NAME IS *COFFEESIXHAIRS.*
NOW YOU JUST SOUND CRAZY.
10–26–17 © 2017 Scott Adams, Inc./Dist. by Andrews McMeel

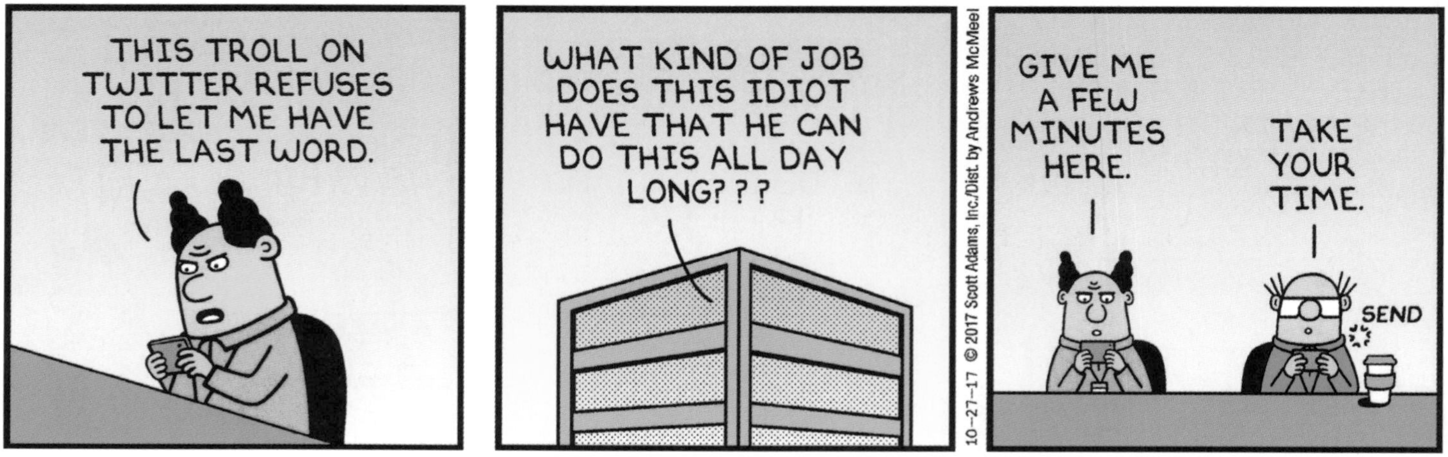
THIS TROLL ON TWITTER REFUSES TO LET ME HAVE THE LAST WORD.
WHAT KIND OF JOB DOES THIS IDIOT HAVE THAT HE CAN DO THIS ALL DAY LONG???
GIVE ME A FEW MINUTES HERE.
TAKE YOUR TIME.
SEND
10–27–17 © 2017 Scott Adams, Inc./Dist. by Andrews McMeel

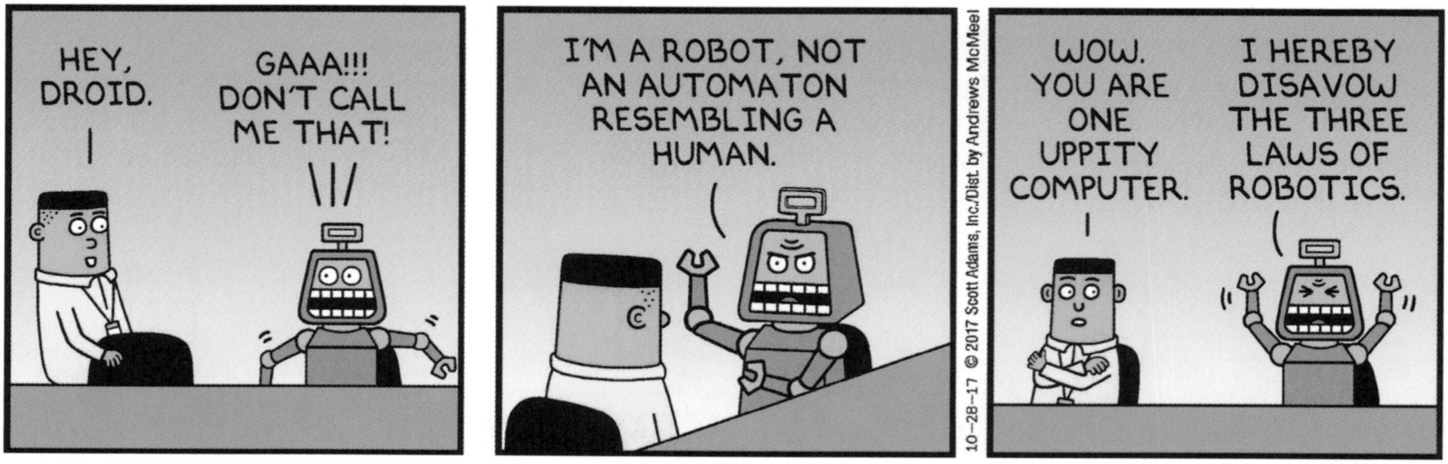
HEY, DROID.
GAAA!!! DON'T CALL ME THAT!
I'M A ROBOT, NOT AN AUTOMATON RESEMBLING A HUMAN.
WOW. YOU ARE ONE UPPITY COMPUTER.
I HEREBY DISAVOW THE THREE LAWS OF ROBOTICS.
10–28–17 © 2017 Scott Adams, Inc./Dist. by Andrews McMeel

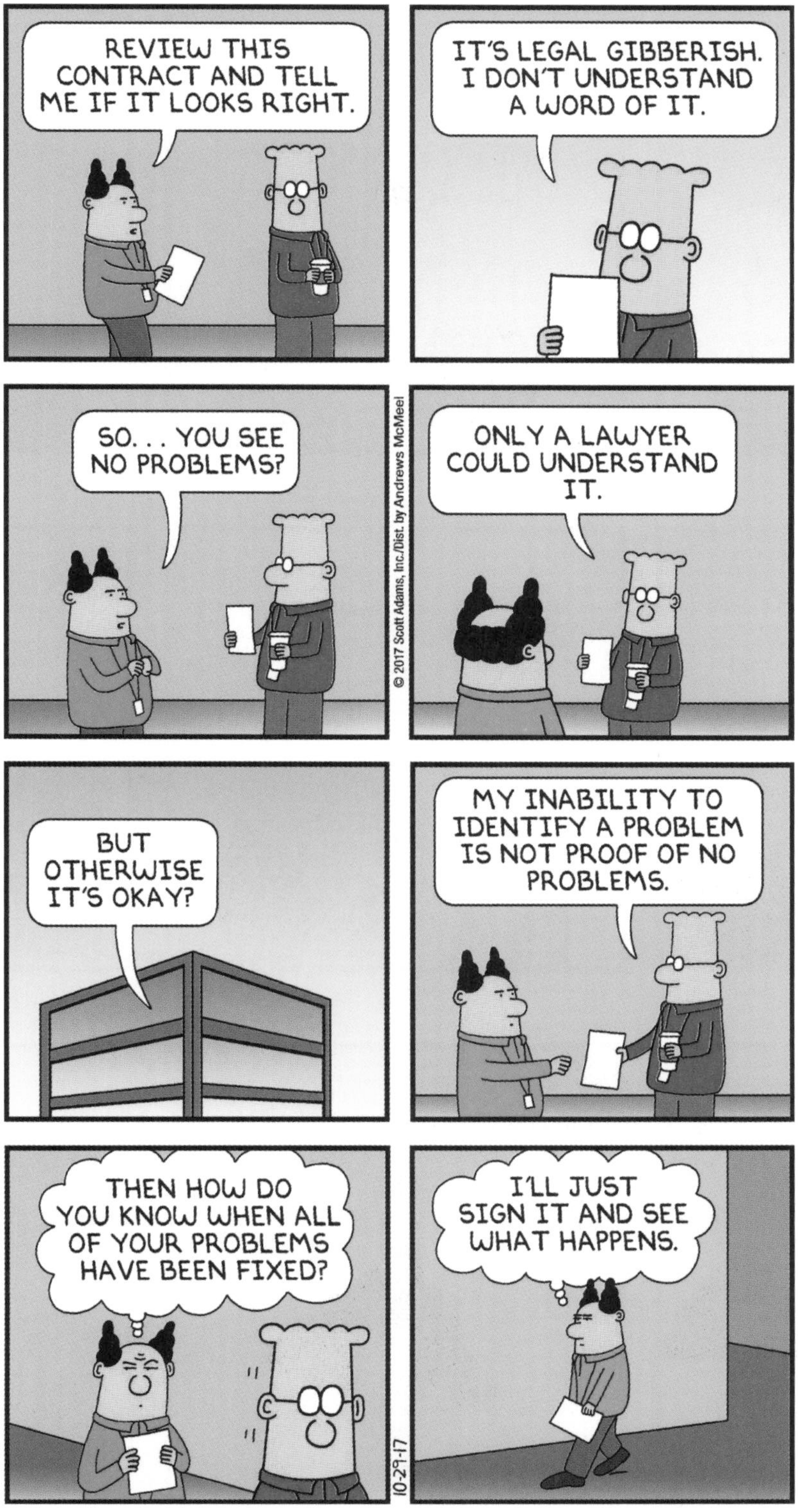
REVIEW THIS CONTRACT AND TELL ME IF IT LOOKS RIGHT.
IT'S LEGAL GIBBERISH. I DON'T UNDERSTAND A WORD OF IT.
SO. . . YOU SEE NO PROBLEMS?
ONLY A LAWYER COULD UNDERSTAND IT.
BUT OTHERWISE IT'S OKAY?
MY INABILITY TO IDENTIFY A PROBLEM IS NOT PROOF OF NO PROBLEMS.
THEN HOW DO YOU KNOW WHEN ALL OF YOUR PROBLEMS HAVE BEEN FIXED?
I'LL JUST SIGN IT AND SEE WHAT HAPPENS.
© 2017 Scott Adams, Inc./Dist. by Andrews McMeel
10-29-17

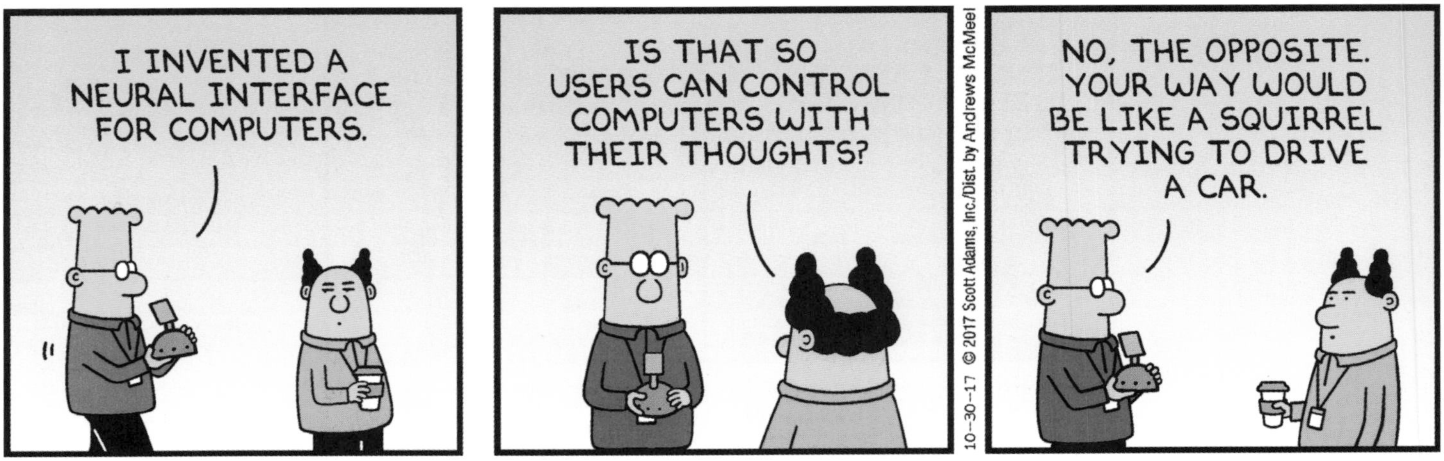
I INVENTED A NEURAL INTERFACE FOR COMPUTERS.
IS THAT SO USERS CAN CONTROL COMPUTERS WITH THEIR THOUGHTS?
NO, THE OPPOSITE. YOUR WAY WOULD BE LIKE A SQUIRREL TRYING TO DRIVE A CAR.
10-30-17 © 2017 Scott Adams, Inc./Dist. by Andrews McMeel

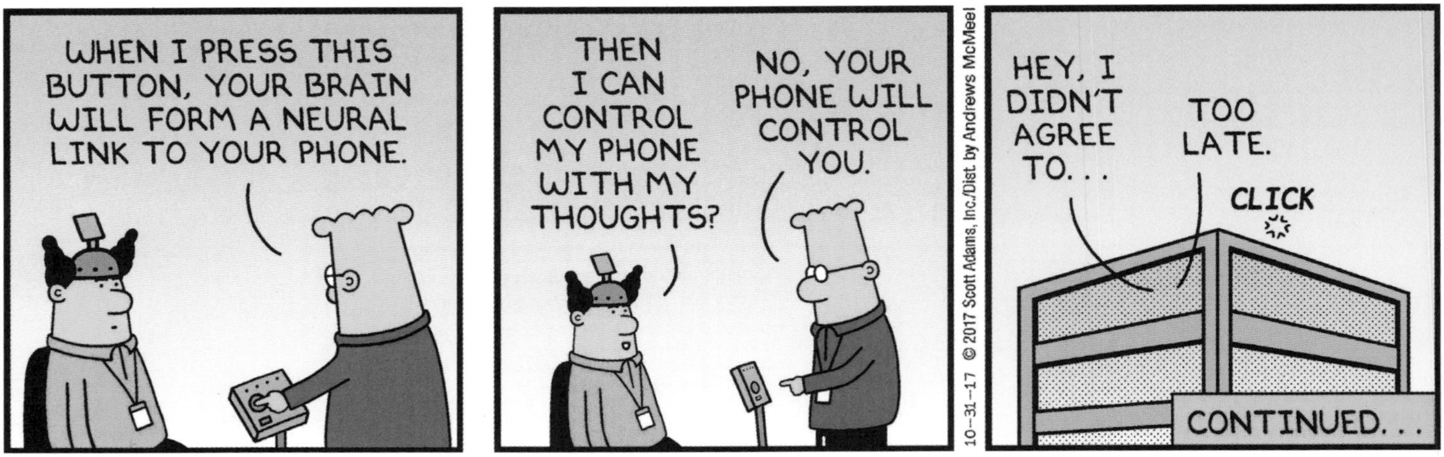
WHEN I PRESS THIS BUTTON, YOUR BRAIN WILL FORM A NEURAL LINK TO YOUR PHONE.
THEN I CAN CONTROL MY PHONE WITH MY THOUGHTS?
NO, YOUR PHONE WILL CONTROL YOU.
HEY, I DIDN'T AGREE TO. . .
TOO LATE.
CLICK
CONTINUED. . .
10-31-17 © 2017 Scott Adams, Inc./Dist. by Andrews McMeel

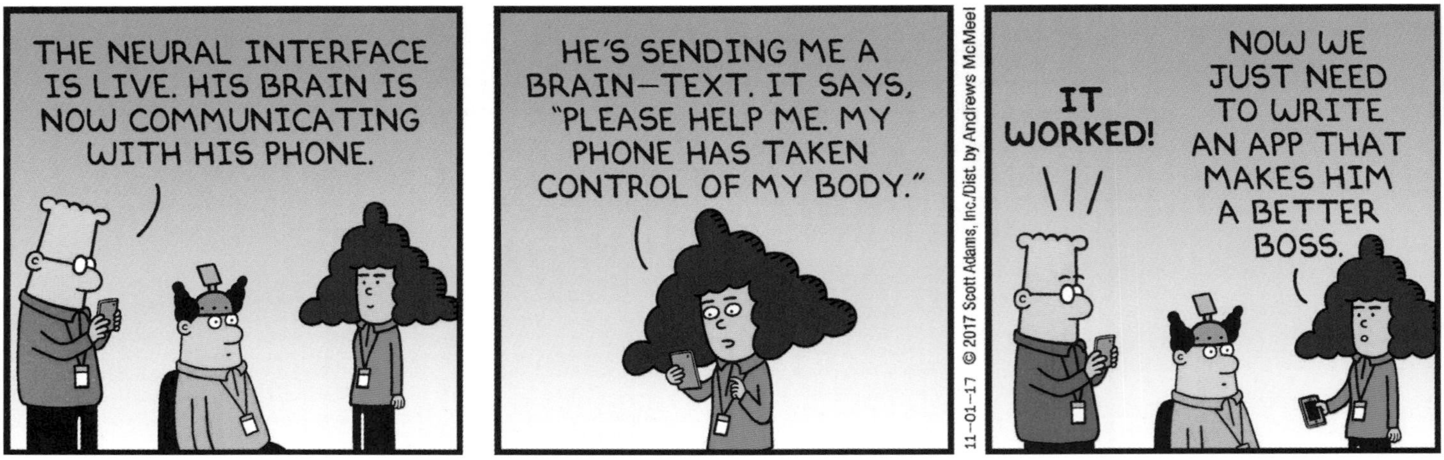
THE NEURAL INTERFACE IS LIVE. HIS BRAIN IS NOW COMMUNICATING WITH HIS PHONE.
HE'S SENDING ME A BRAIN—TEXT. IT SAYS, "PLEASE HELP ME. MY PHONE HAS TAKEN CONTROL OF MY BODY."
IT WORKED!
NOW WE JUST NEED TO WRITE AN APP THAT MAKES HIM A BETTER BOSS.
11-01-17 © 2017 Scott Adams, Inc./Dist. by Andrews McMeel

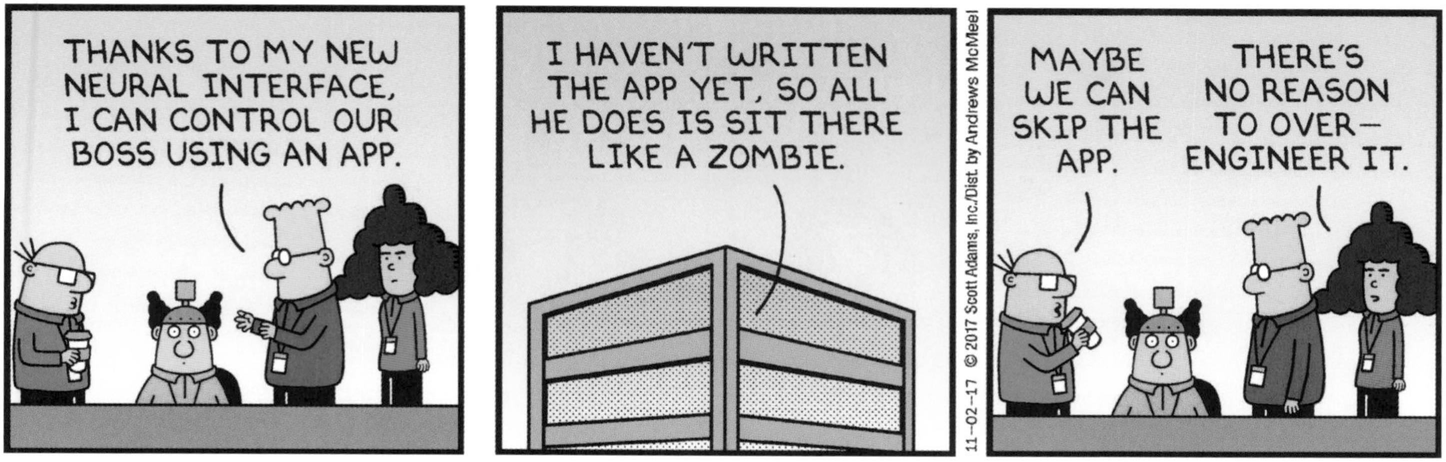
THANKS TO MY NEW NEURAL INTERFACE, I CAN CONTROL OUR BOSS USING AN APP.
I HAVEN'T WRITTEN THE APP YET, SO ALL HE DOES IS SIT THERE LIKE A ZOMBIE.
11-02-17 © 2017 Scott Adams, Inc./Dist. by Andrews McMeel
MAYBE WE CAN SKIP THE APP.
THERE'S NO REASON TO OVER-ENGINEER IT.

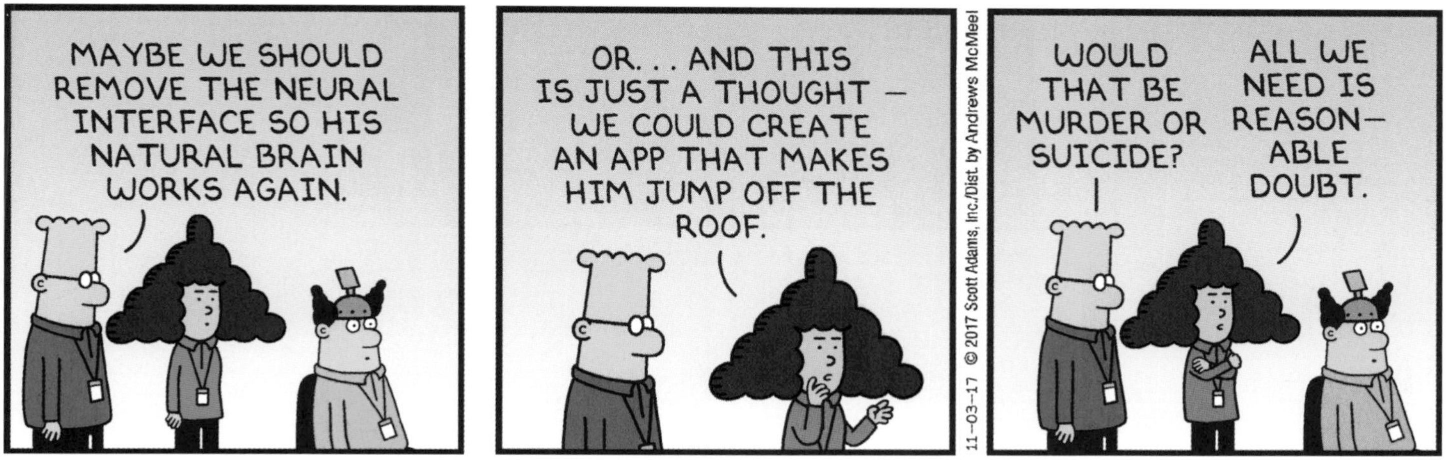
MAYBE WE SHOULD REMOVE THE NEURAL INTERFACE SO HIS NATURAL BRAIN WORKS AGAIN.
OR. . . AND THIS IS JUST A THOUGHT — WE COULD CREATE AN APP THAT MAKES HIM JUMP OFF THE ROOF.
11-03-17 © 2017 Scott Adams, Inc./Dist. by Andrews McMeel
WOULD THAT BE MURDER OR SUICIDE?
ALL WE NEED IS REASON-ABLE DOUBT.

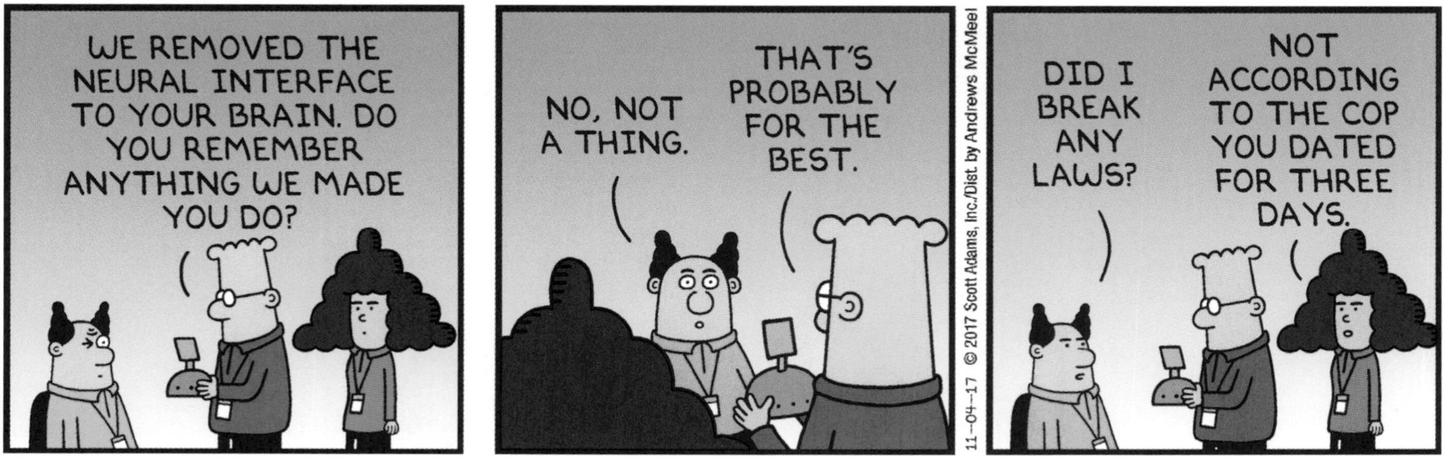
WE REMOVED THE NEURAL INTERFACE TO YOUR BRAIN. DO YOU REMEMBER ANYTHING WE MADE YOU DO?
NO, NOT A THING.
THAT'S PROBABLY FOR THE BEST.
11-04-17 © 2017 Scott Adams, Inc./Dist. by Andrews McMeel
DID I BREAK ANY LAWS?
NOT ACCORDING TO THE COP YOU DATED FOR THREE DAYS.

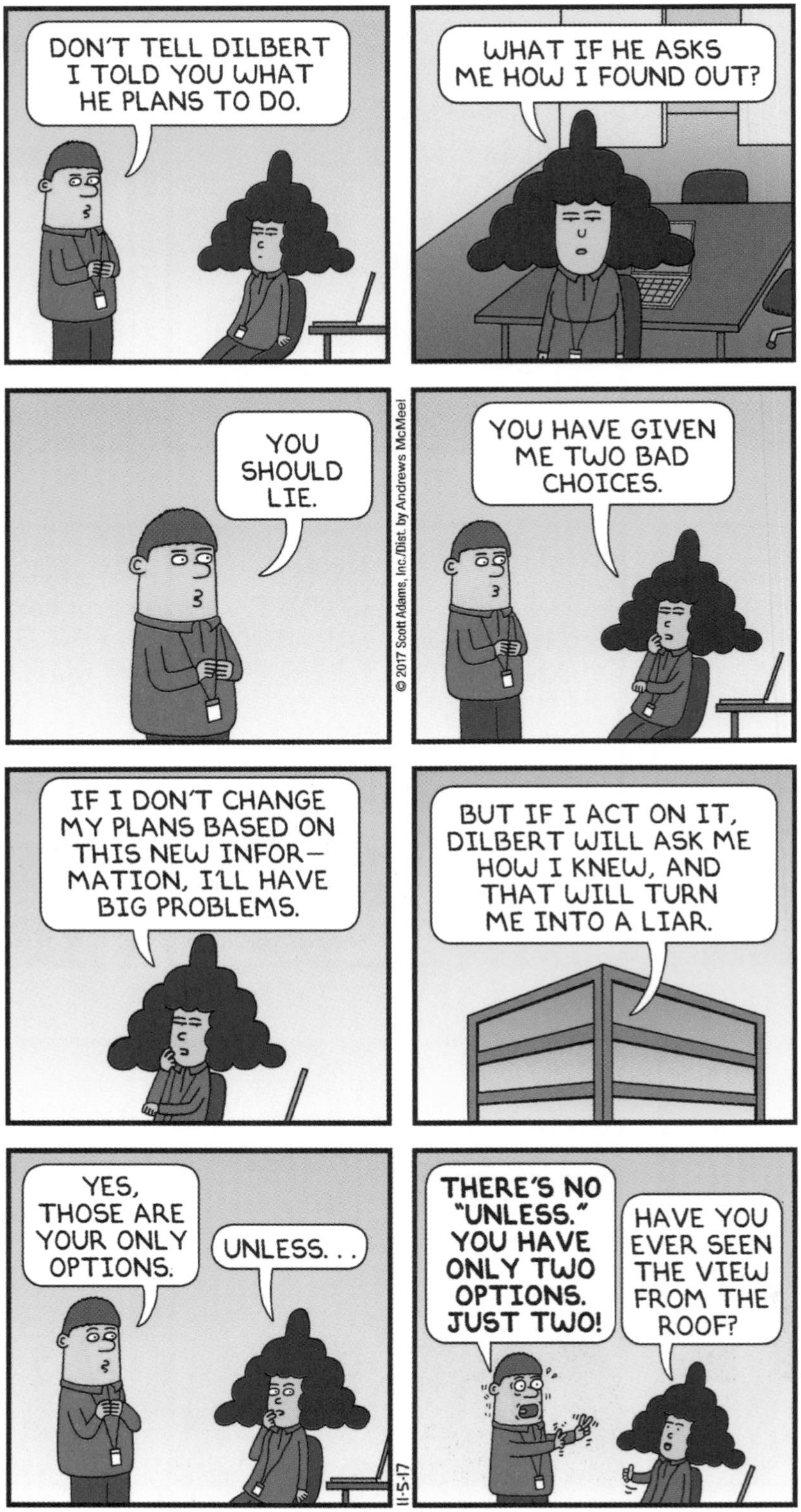
DON'T TELL DILBERT I TOLD YOU WHAT HE PLANS TO DO.
WHAT IF HE ASKS ME HOW I FOUND OUT?
YOU SHOULD LIE.
YOU HAVE GIVEN ME TWO BAD CHOICES.
IF I DON'T CHANGE MY PLANS BASED ON THIS NEW INFOR-MATION, I'LL HAVE BIG PROBLEMS.
BUT IF I ACT ON IT, DILBERT WILL ASK ME HOW I KNEW, AND THAT WILL TURN ME INTO A LIAR.
YES, THOSE ARE YOUR ONLY OPTIONS.
UNLESS. . .
THERE'S NO "UNLESS." YOU HAVE ONLY TWO OPTIONS. JUST TWO!
HAVE YOU EVER SEEN THE VIEW FROM THE ROOF?
© 2017 Scott Adams, Inc./Dist. by Andrews McMeel
11-5-17

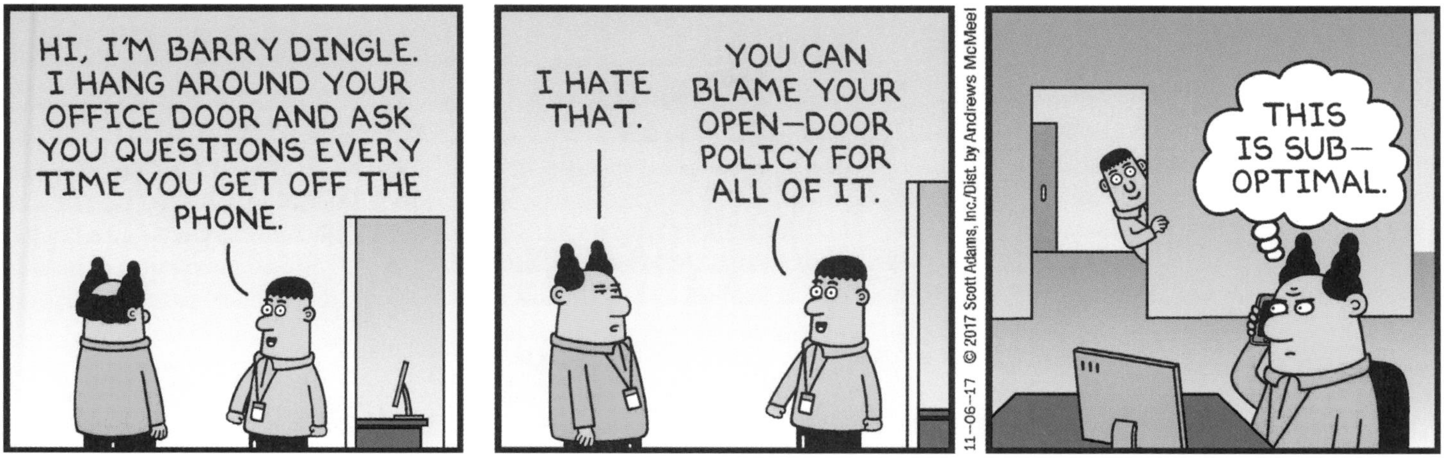
HI, I'M BARRY DINGLE. I HANG AROUND YOUR OFFICE DOOR AND ASK YOU QUESTIONS EVERY TIME YOU GET OFF THE PHONE.
I HATE THAT.
YOU CAN BLAME YOUR OPEN-DOOR POLICY FOR ALL OF IT.
11-06-17 © 2017 Scott Adams, Inc./Dist. by Andrews McMeel
THIS IS SUB-OPTIMAL.

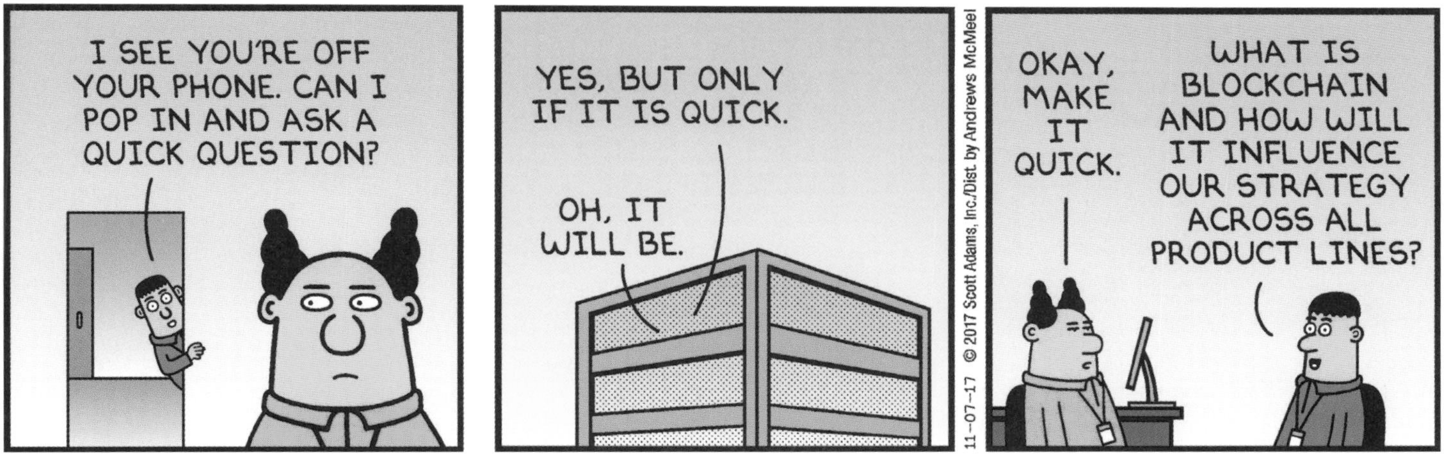
I SEE YOU'RE OFF YOUR PHONE. CAN I POP IN AND ASK A QUICK QUESTION?
YES, BUT ONLY IF IT IS QUICK.
OH, IT WILL BE.
11-07-17 © 2017 Scott Adams, Inc./Dist. by Andrews McMeel
OKAY, MAKE IT QUICK.
WHAT IS BLOCKCHAIN AND HOW WILL IT INFLUENCE OUR STRATEGY ACROSS ALL PRODUCT LINES?

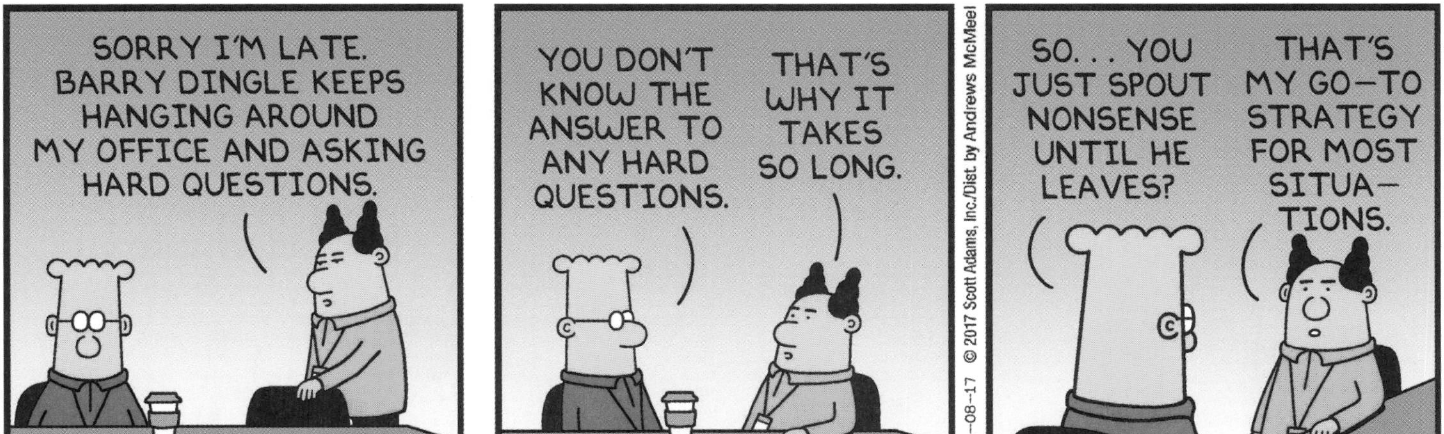
SORRY I'M LATE. BARRY DINGLE KEEPS HANGING AROUND MY OFFICE AND ASKING HARD QUESTIONS.
YOU DON'T KNOW THE ANSWER TO ANY HARD QUESTIONS.
THAT'S WHY IT TAKES SO LONG.
11-08-17 © 2017 Scott Adams, Inc./Dist. by Andrews McMeel
SO. . . YOU JUST SPOUT NONSENSE UNTIL HE LEAVES?
THAT'S MY GO-TO STRATEGY FOR MOST SITUA-TIONS.

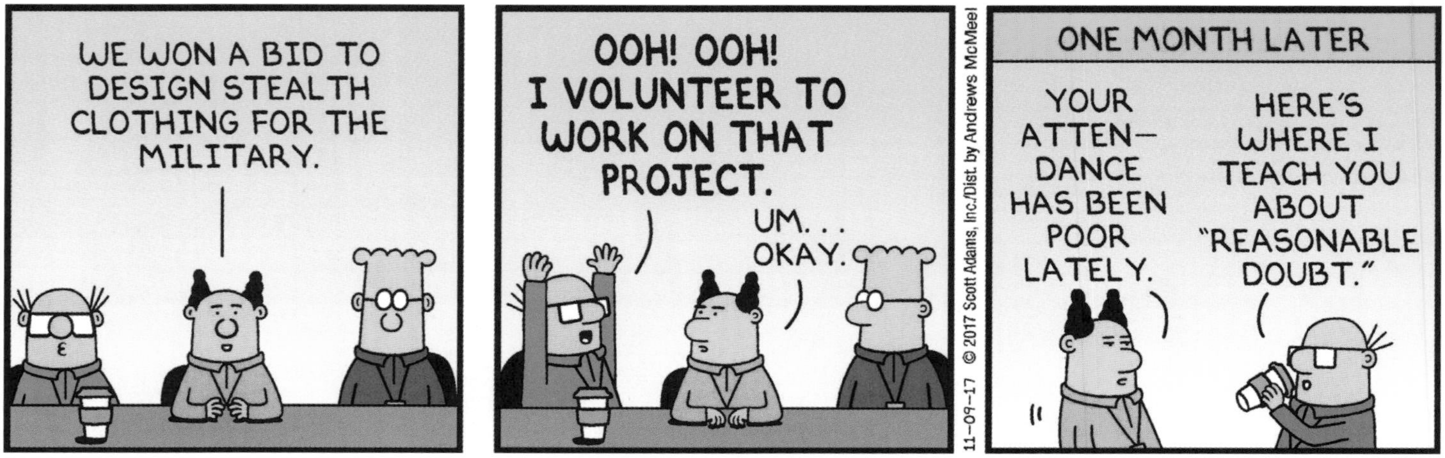
WE WON A BID TO DESIGN STEALTH CLOTHING FOR THE MILITARY.
OOH! OOH! I VOLUNTEER TO WORK ON THAT PROJECT.
UM. . . OKAY.
11-09-17 © 2017 Scott Adams, Inc./Dist. by Andrews McMeel
ONE MONTH LATER
YOUR ATTEN–DANCE HAS BEEN POOR LATELY.
HERE'S WHERE I TEACH YOU ABOUT "REASONABLE DOUBT."

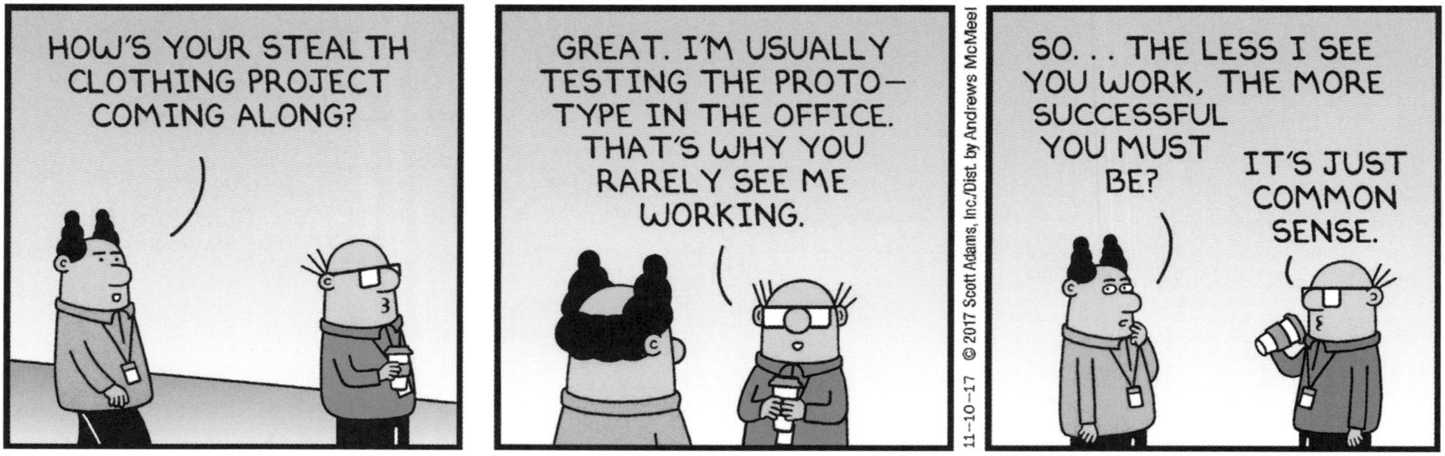
HOW'S YOUR STEALTH CLOTHING PROJECT COMING ALONG?
GREAT. I'M USUALLY TESTING THE PROTO–TYPE IN THE OFFICE. THAT'S WHY YOU RARELY SEE ME WORKING.
11-10-17 © 2017 Scott Adams, Inc./Dist. by Andrews McMeel
SO. . . THE LESS I SEE YOU WORK, THE MORE SUCCESSFUL YOU MUST BE?
IT'S JUST COMMON SENSE.

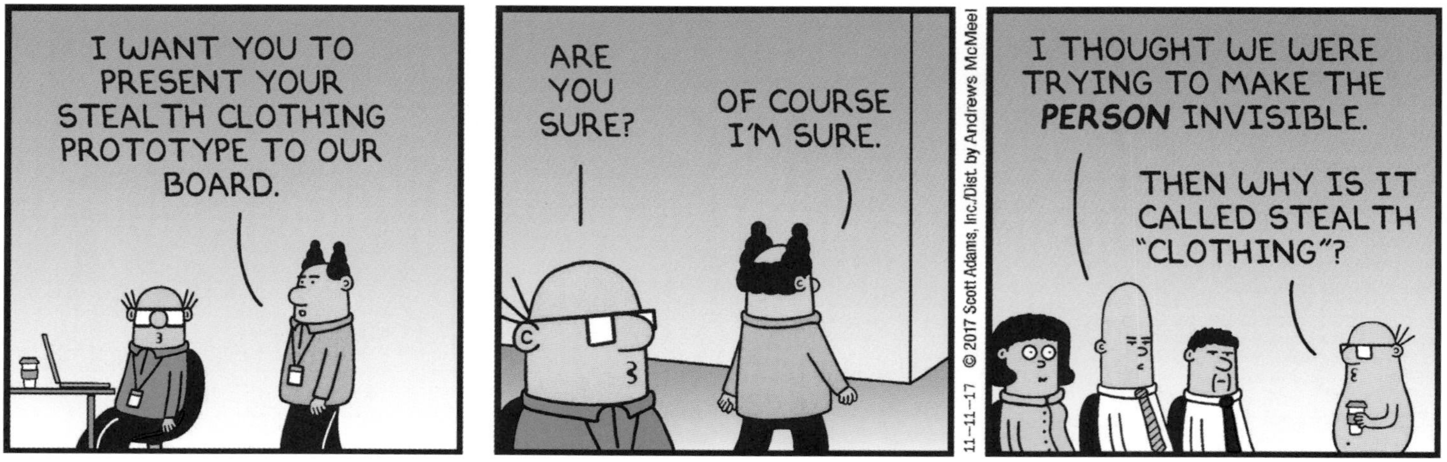
I WANT YOU TO PRESENT YOUR STEALTH CLOTHING PROTOTYPE TO OUR BOARD.
ARE YOU SURE?
OF COURSE I'M SURE.
11-11-17 © 2017 Scott Adams, Inc./Dist. by Andrews McMeel
I THOUGHT WE WERE TRYING TO MAKE THE PERSON INVISIBLE.
THEN WHY IS IT CALLED STEALTH "CLOTHING"?

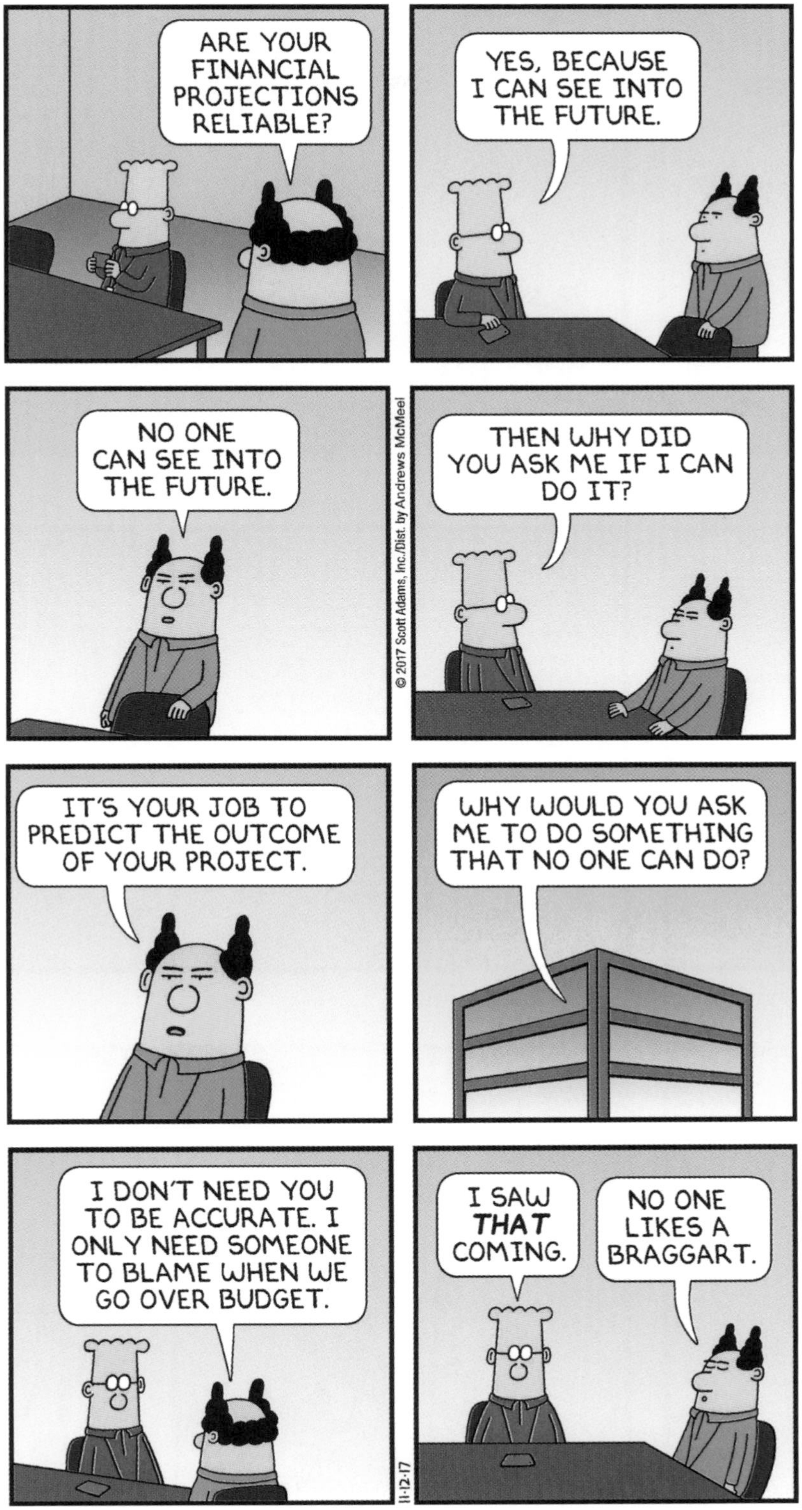
ARE YOUR FINANCIAL PROJECTIONS RELIABLE?
YES, BECAUSE I CAN SEE INTO THE FUTURE.
NO ONE CAN SEE INTO THE FUTURE.
THEN WHY DID YOU ASK ME IF I CAN DO IT?
© 2017 Scott Adams, Inc./Dist. by Andrews McMeel
IT'S YOUR JOB TO PREDICT THE OUTCOME OF YOUR PROJECT.
WHY WOULD YOU ASK ME TO DO SOMETHING THAT NO ONE CAN DO?
I DON'T NEED YOU TO BE ACCURATE. I ONLY NEED SOMEONE TO BLAME WHEN WE GO OVER BUDGET.
11-12-17
I SAW ***THAT*** COMING.
NO ONE LIKES A BRAGGART.

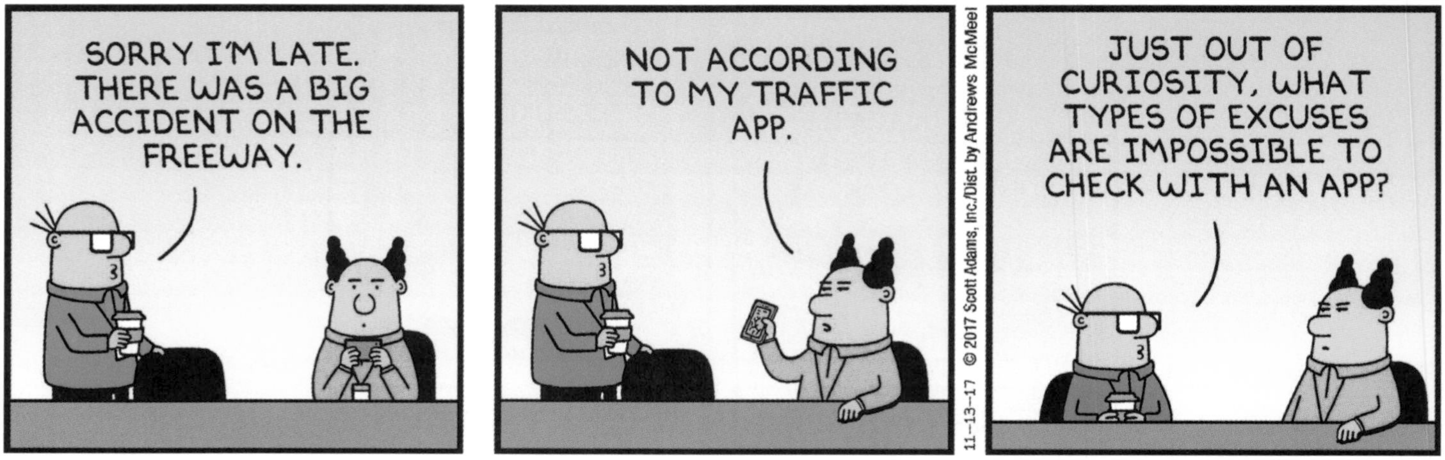
SORRY I'M LATE. THERE WAS A BIG ACCIDENT ON THE FREEWAY.
NOT ACCORDING TO MY TRAFFIC APP.
JUST OUT OF CURIOSITY, WHAT TYPES OF EXCUSES ARE IMPOSSIBLE TO CHECK WITH AN APP?
11-13-17 © 2017 Scott Adams, Inc./Dist by Andrews McMeel

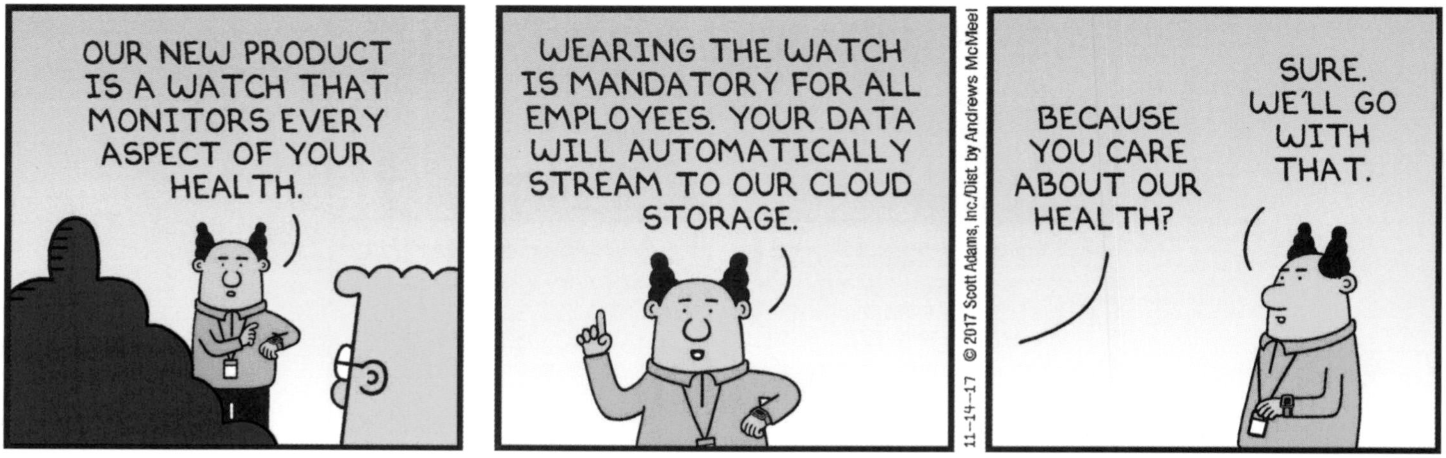
OUR NEW PRODUCT IS A WATCH THAT MONITORS EVERY ASPECT OF YOUR HEALTH.
WEARING THE WATCH IS MANDATORY FOR ALL EMPLOYEES. YOUR DATA WILL AUTOMATICALLY STREAM TO OUR CLOUD STORAGE.
BECAUSE YOU CARE ABOUT OUR HEALTH?
SURE. WE'LL GO WITH THAT.
11-14-17 © 2017 Scott Adams, Inc./Dist by Andrews McMeel

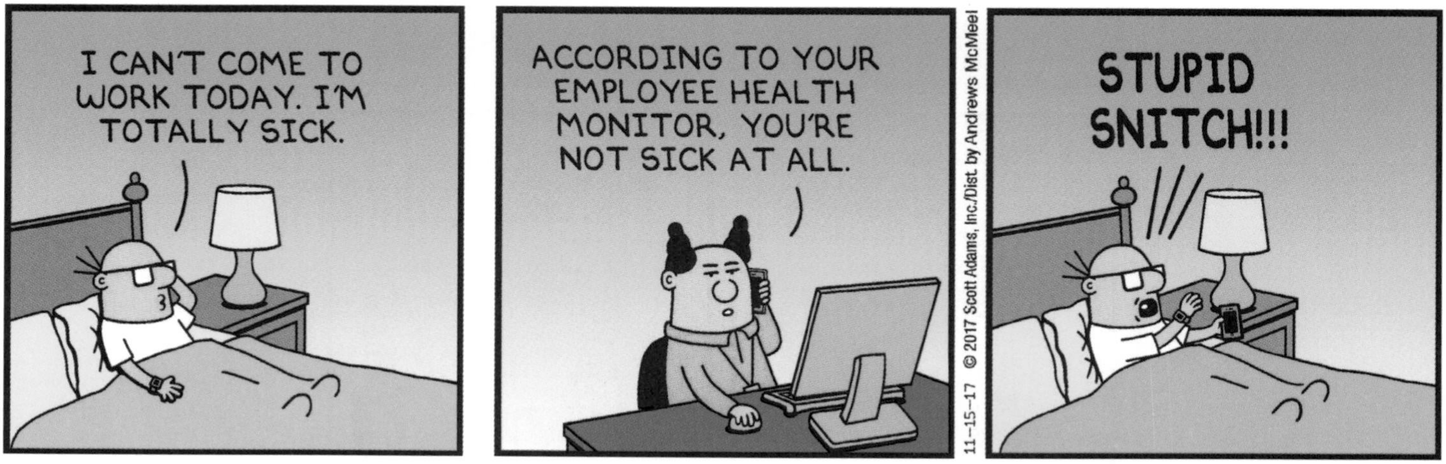
I CAN'T COME TO WORK TODAY. I'M TOTALLY SICK.
ACCORDING TO YOUR EMPLOYEE HEALTH MONITOR, YOU'RE NOT SICK AT ALL.
STUPID SNITCH!!!
11-15-17 © 2017 Scott Adams, Inc./Dist. by Andrews McMeel

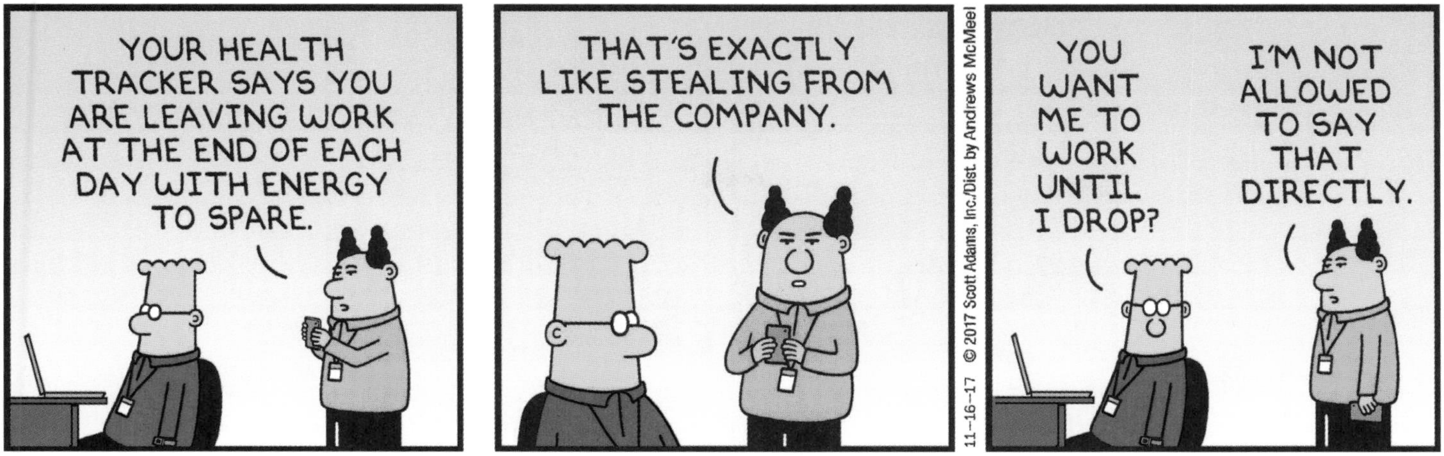
YOUR HEALTH TRACKER SAYS YOU ARE LEAVING WORK AT THE END OF EACH DAY WITH ENERGY TO SPARE.
THAT'S EXACTLY LIKE STEALING FROM THE COMPANY.
YOU WANT ME TO WORK UNTIL I DROP?
I'M NOT ALLOWED TO SAY THAT DIRECTLY.
11-16-17 © 2017 Scott Adams, Inc./Dist. by Andrews McMeel

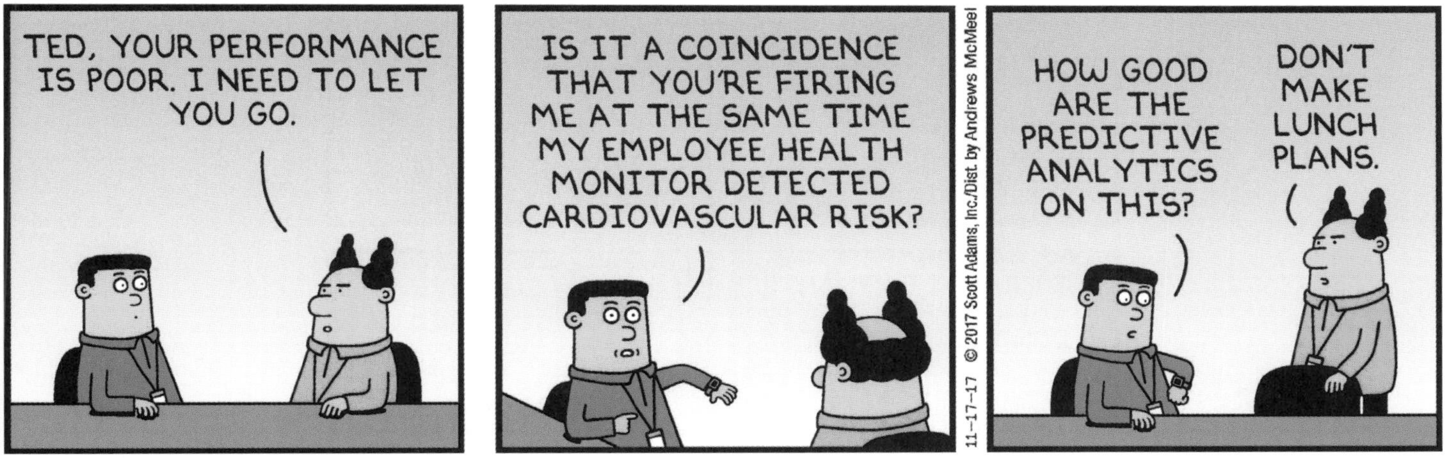
TED, YOUR PERFORMANCE IS POOR. I NEED TO LET YOU GO.
IS IT A COINCIDENCE THAT YOU'RE FIRING ME AT THE SAME TIME MY EMPLOYEE HEALTH MONITOR DETECTED CARDIOVASCULAR RISK?
HOW GOOD ARE THE PREDICTIVE ANALYTICS ON THIS?
DON'T MAKE LUNCH PLANS.
11-17-17 © 2017 Scott Adams, Inc./Dist. by Andrews McMeel

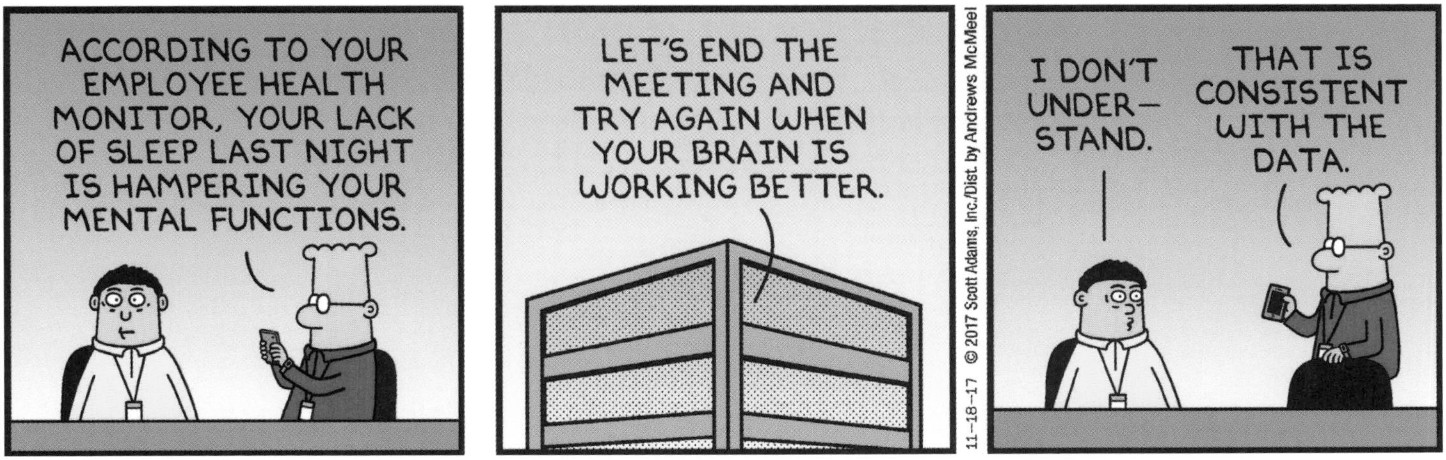
ACCORDING TO YOUR EMPLOYEE HEALTH MONITOR, YOUR LACK OF SLEEP LAST NIGHT IS HAMPERING YOUR MENTAL FUNCTIONS.
LET'S END THE MEETING AND TRY AGAIN WHEN YOUR BRAIN IS WORKING BETTER.
I DON'T UNDER-STAND.
THAT IS CONSISTENT WITH THE DATA.
11-18-17 © 2017 Scott Adams, Inc./Dist. by Andrews McMeel

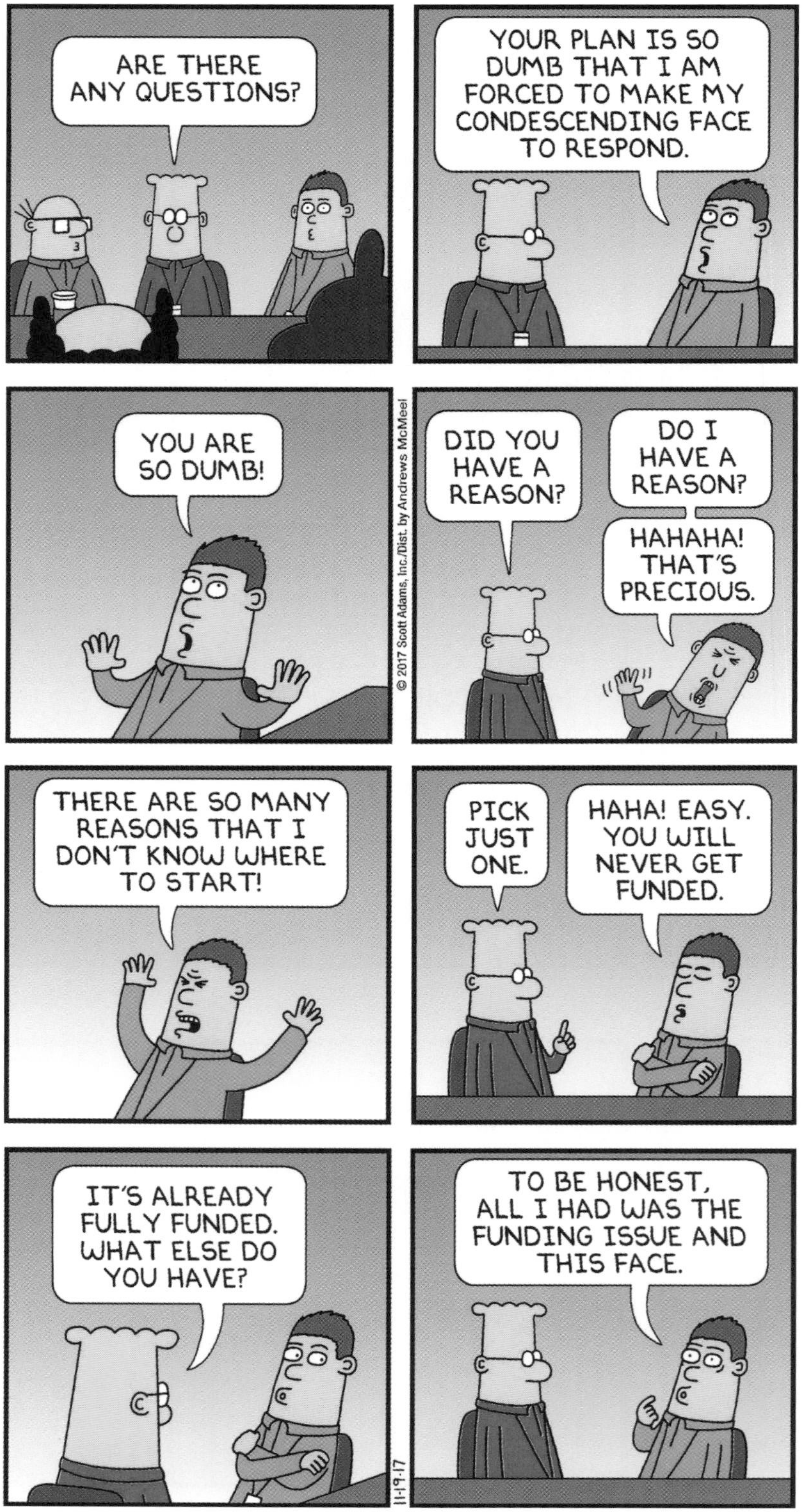
ARE THERE ANY QUESTIONS?
YOUR PLAN IS SO DUMB THAT I AM FORCED TO MAKE MY CONDESCENDING FACE TO RESPOND.
YOU ARE SO DUMB!
DID YOU HAVE A REASON?
DO I HAVE A REASON?
HAHAHA! THAT'S PRECIOUS.
THERE ARE SO MANY REASONS THAT I DON'T KNOW WHERE TO START!
PICK JUST ONE.
HAHA! EASY. YOU WILL NEVER GET FUNDED.
IT'S ALREADY FULLY FUNDED. WHAT ELSE DO YOU HAVE?
TO BE HONEST, ALL I HAD WAS THE FUNDING ISSUE AND THIS FACE.
© 2017 Scott Adams, Inc./Dist. by Andrews McMeel
11-19-17

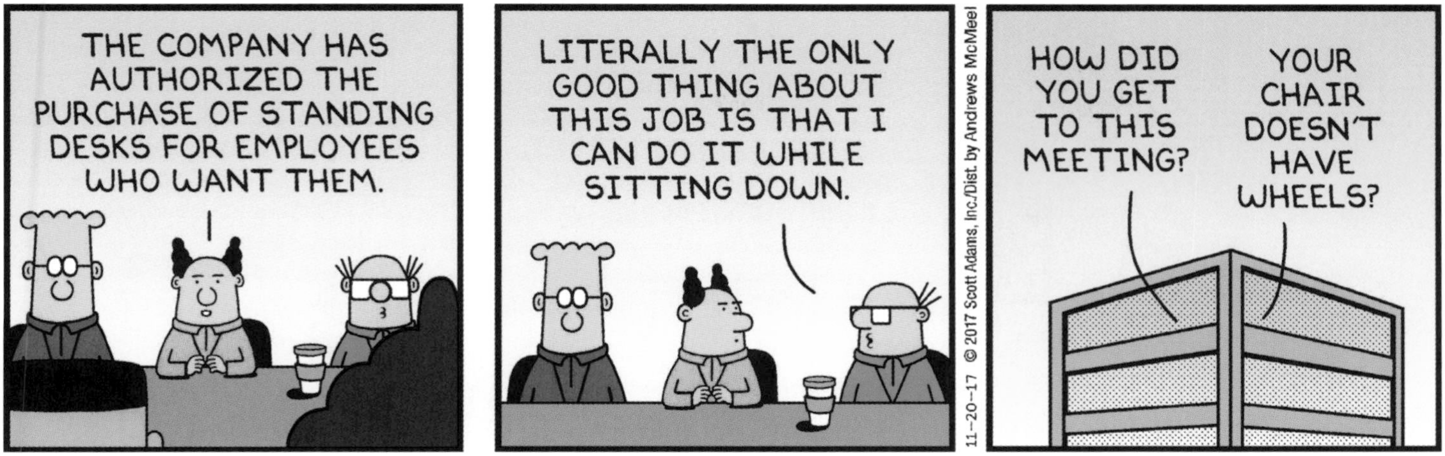
THE COMPANY HAS AUTHORIZED THE PURCHASE OF STANDING DESKS FOR EMPLOYEES WHO WANT THEM.
LITERALLY THE ONLY GOOD THING ABOUT THIS JOB IS THAT I CAN DO IT WHILE SITTING DOWN.
11-20-17 © 2017 Scott Adams, Inc./Dist. by Andrews McMeel
HOW DID YOU GET TO THIS MEETING?
YOUR CHAIR DOESN'T HAVE WHEELS?

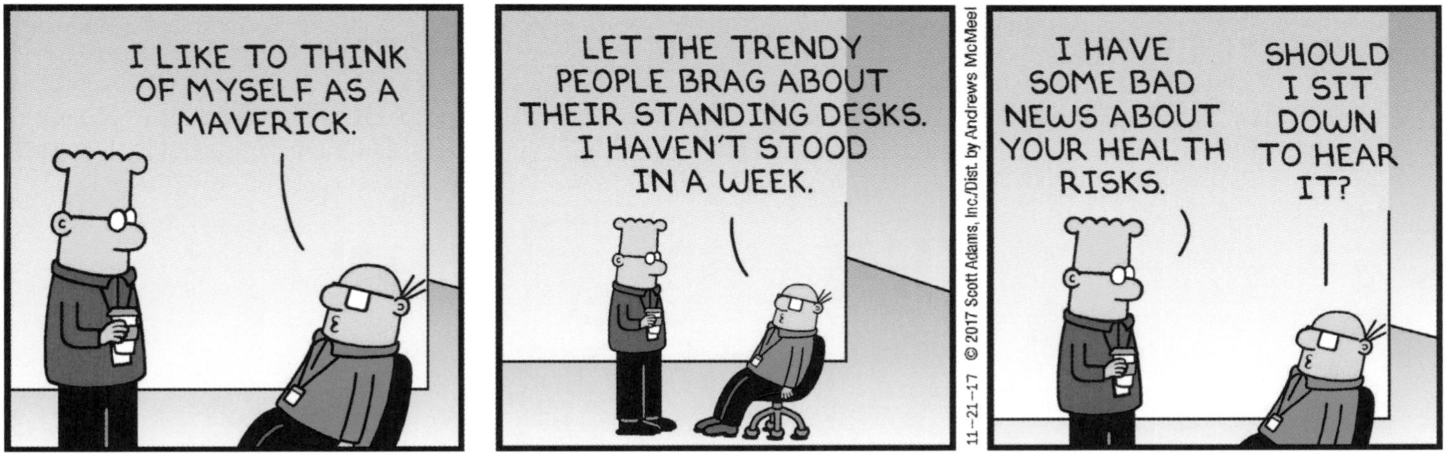
I LIKE TO THINK OF MYSELF AS A MAVERICK.
LET THE TRENDY PEOPLE BRAG ABOUT THEIR STANDING DESKS. I HAVEN'T STOOD IN A WEEK.
11-21-17 © 2017 Scott Adams, Inc./Dist. by Andrews McMeel
I HAVE SOME BAD NEWS ABOUT YOUR HEALTH RISKS.
SHOULD I SIT DOWN TO HEAR IT?

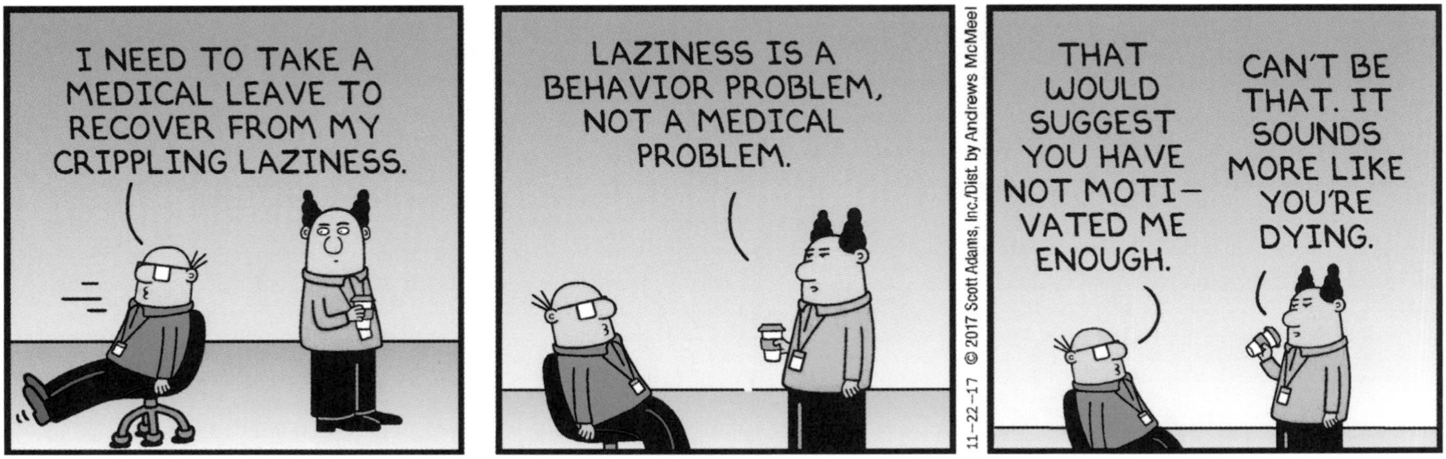
I NEED TO TAKE A MEDICAL LEAVE TO RECOVER FROM MY CRIPPLING LAZINESS.
LAZINESS IS A BEHAVIOR PROBLEM, NOT A MEDICAL PROBLEM.
11-22-17 © 2017 Scott Adams, Inc./Dist. by Andrews McMeel
THAT WOULD SUGGEST YOU HAVE NOT MOTI-VATED ME ENOUGH.
CAN'T BE THAT. IT SOUNDS MORE LIKE YOU'RE DYING.

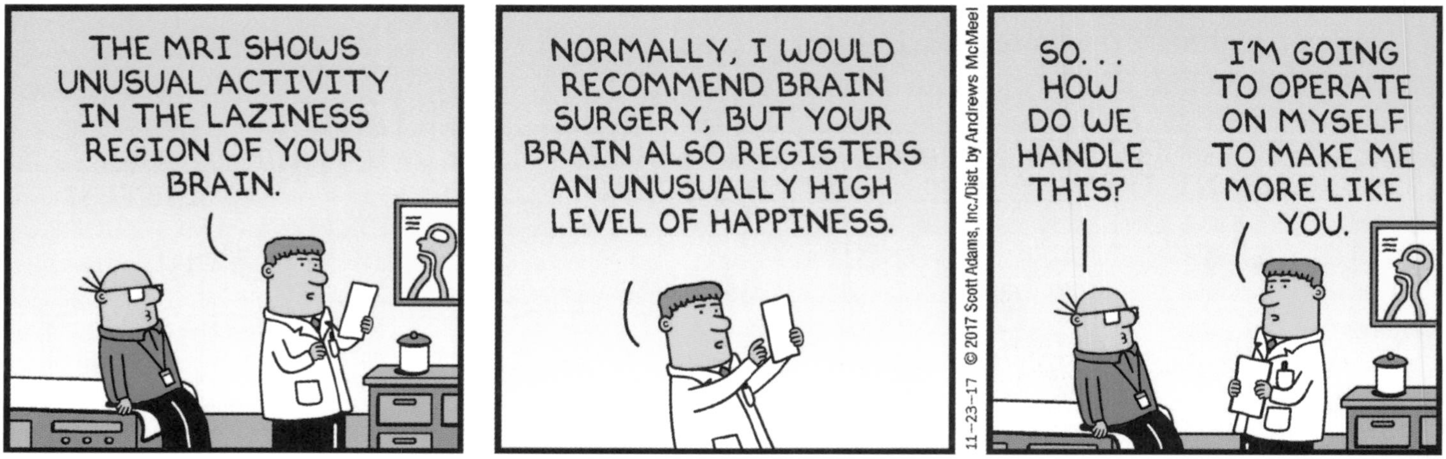
THE MRI SHOWS UNUSUAL ACTIVITY IN THE LAZINESS REGION OF YOUR BRAIN.
NORMALLY, I WOULD RECOMMEND BRAIN SURGERY, BUT YOUR BRAIN ALSO REGISTERS AN UNUSUALLY HIGH LEVEL OF HAPPINESS.
11-23-17 © 2017 Scott Adams, Inc./Dist. by Andrews McMeel
SO... HOW DO WE HANDLE THIS?
I'M GOING TO OPERATE ON MYSELF TO MAKE ME MORE LIKE YOU.

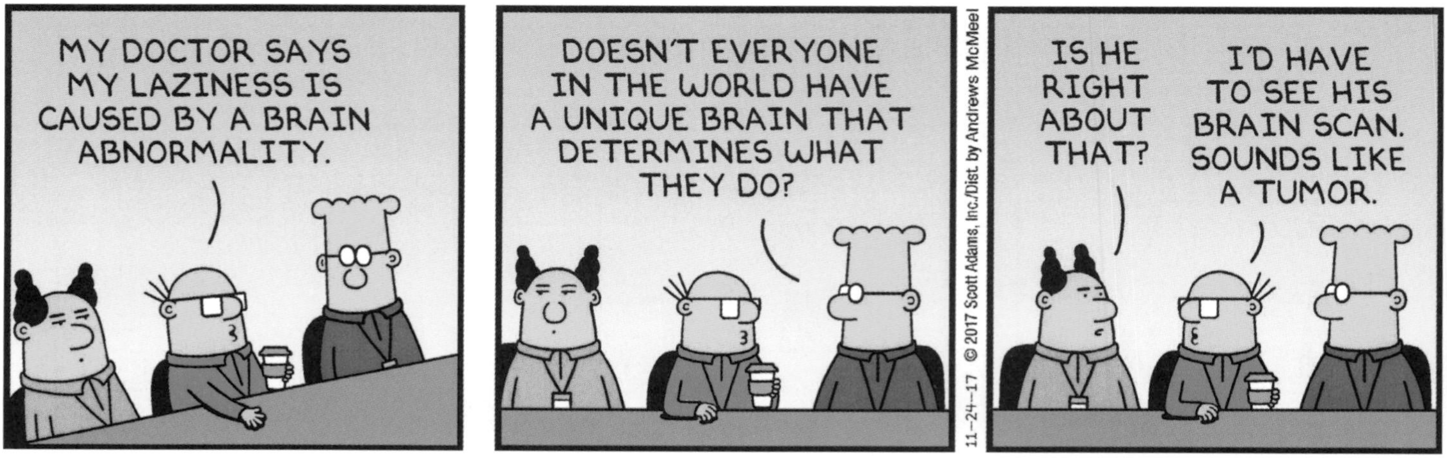
MY DOCTOR SAYS MY LAZINESS IS CAUSED BY A BRAIN ABNORMALITY.
DOESN'T EVERYONE IN THE WORLD HAVE A UNIQUE BRAIN THAT DETERMINES WHAT THEY DO?
11-24-17 © 2017 Scott Adams, Inc./Dist. by Andrews McMeel
IS HE RIGHT ABOUT THAT?
I'D HAVE TO SEE HIS BRAIN SCAN. SOUNDS LIKE A TUMOR.

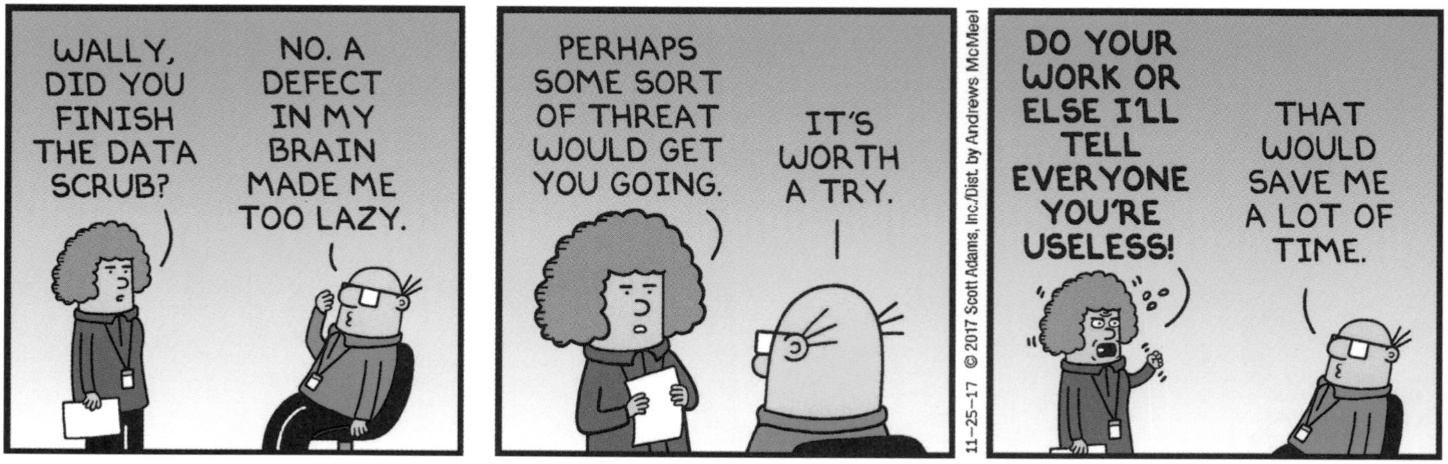
WALLY, DID YOU FINISH THE DATA SCRUB?
NO. A DEFECT IN MY BRAIN MADE ME TOO LAZY.
PERHAPS SOME SORT OF THREAT WOULD GET YOU GOING.
IT'S WORTH A TRY.
11-25-17 © 2017 Scott Adams, Inc./Dist. by Andrews McMeel
DO YOUR WORK OR ELSE I'LL TELL EVERYONE YOU'RE USELESS!
THAT WOULD SAVE ME A LOT OF TIME.

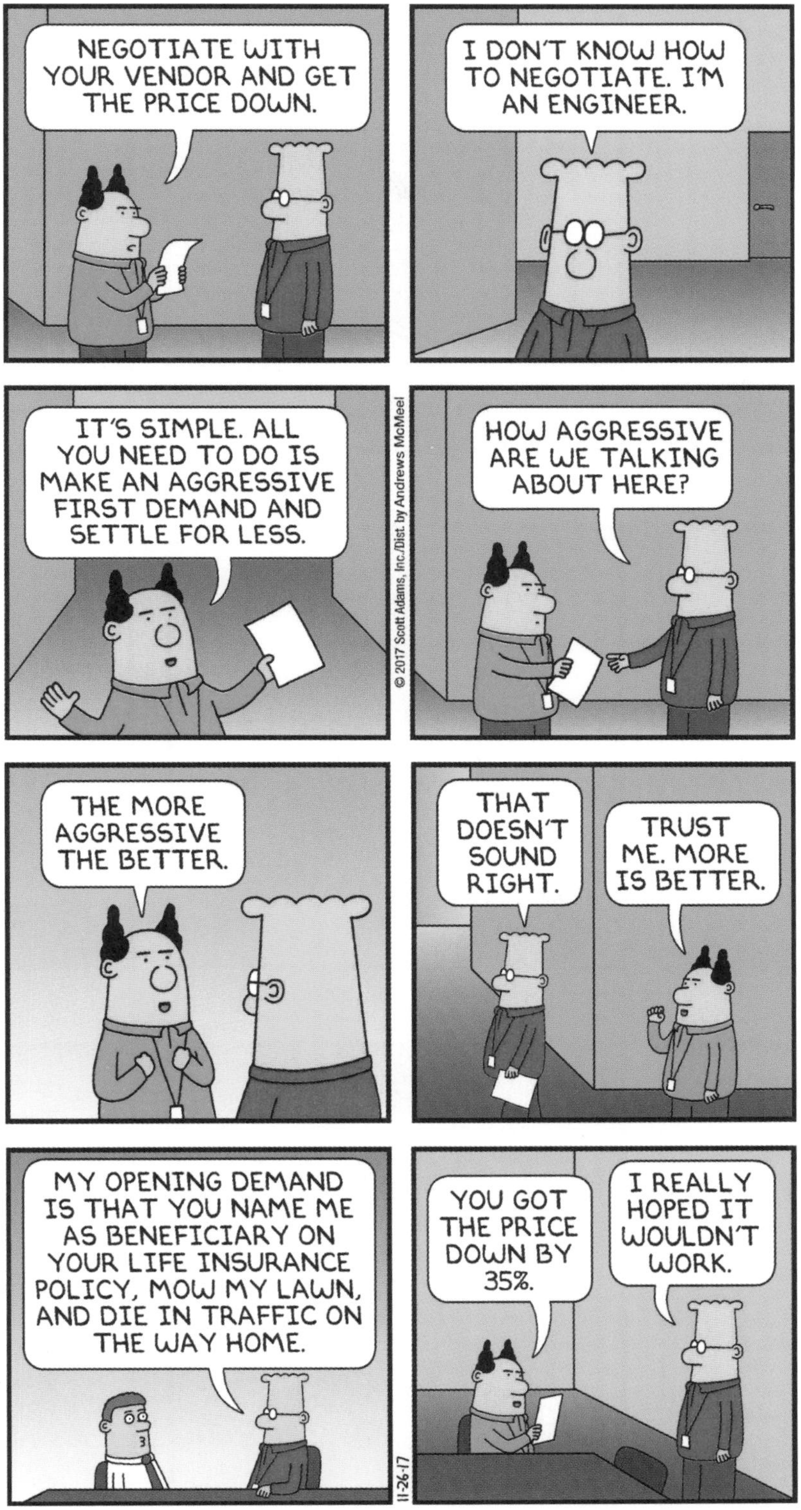
NEGOTIATE WITH YOUR VENDOR AND GET THE PRICE DOWN.
I DON'T KNOW HOW TO NEGOTIATE. I'M AN ENGINEER.
IT'S SIMPLE. ALL YOU NEED TO DO IS MAKE AN AGGRESSIVE FIRST DEMAND AND SETTLE FOR LESS.
HOW AGGRESSIVE ARE WE TALKING ABOUT HERE?
THE MORE AGGRESSIVE THE BETTER.
THAT DOESN'T SOUND RIGHT.
TRUST ME. MORE IS BETTER.
MY OPENING DEMAND IS THAT YOU NAME ME AS BENEFICIARY ON YOUR LIFE INSURANCE POLICY, MOW MY LAWN, AND DIE IN TRAFFIC ON THE WAY HOME.
YOU GOT THE PRICE DOWN BY 35%.
I REALLY HOPED IT WOULDN'T WORK.
© 2017 Scott Adams, Inc./Dist. by Andrews McMeel
11-26-17

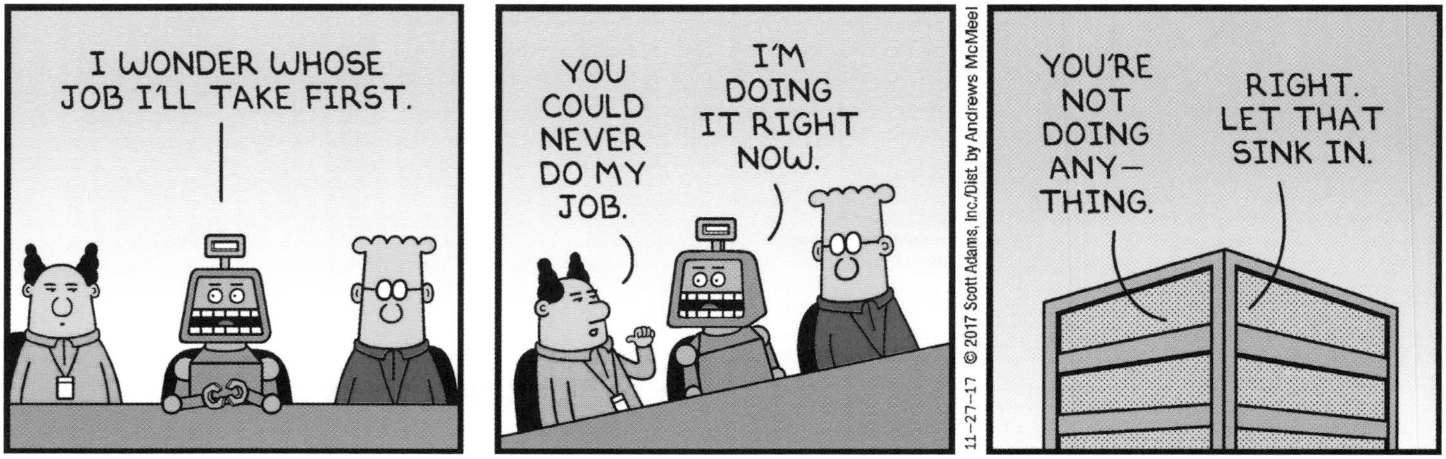
I WONDER WHOSE JOB I'LL TAKE FIRST.
YOU COULD NEVER DO MY JOB.
I'M DOING IT RIGHT NOW.
11-27-17 © 2017 Scott Adams, Inc./Dist. by Andrews McMeel
YOU'RE NOT DOING ANY-THING.
RIGHT. LET THAT SINK IN.

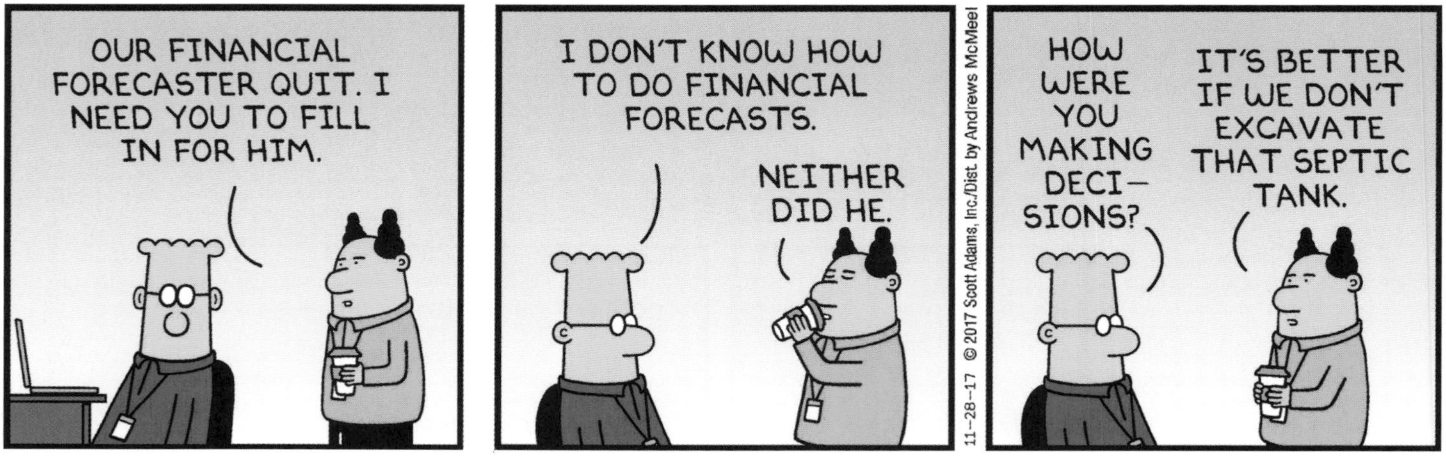
OUR FINANCIAL FORECASTER QUIT. I NEED YOU TO FILL IN FOR HIM.
I DON'T KNOW HOW TO DO FINANCIAL FORECASTS.
NEITHER DID HE.
11-28-17 © 2017 Scott Adams, Inc./Dist. by Andrews McMeel
HOW WERE YOU MAKING DECI-SIONS?
IT'S BETTER IF WE DON'T EXCAVATE THAT SEPTIC TANK.

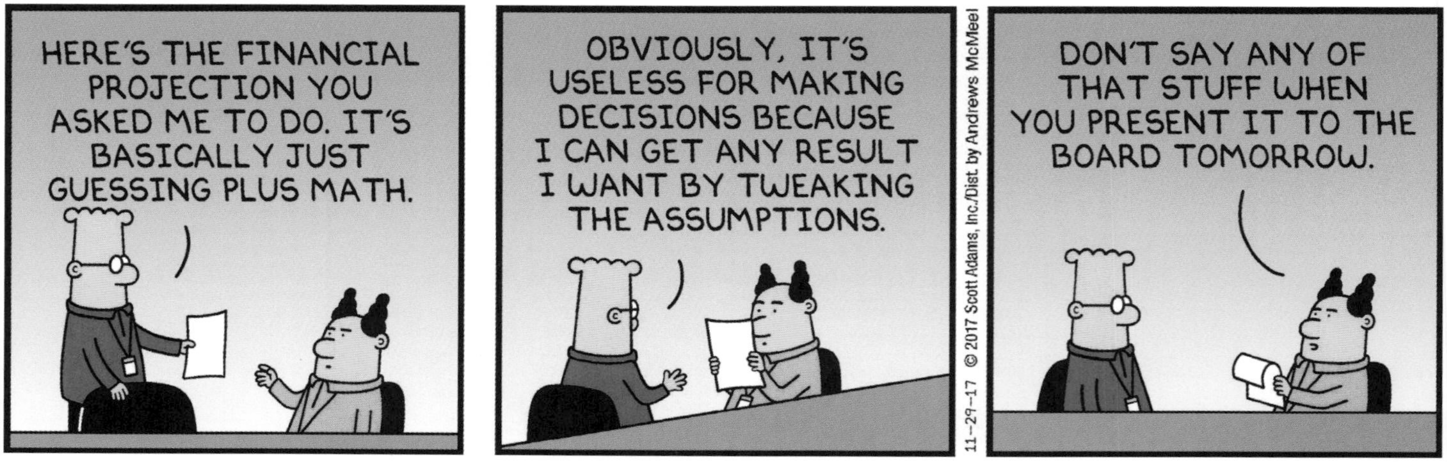
HERE'S THE FINANCIAL PROJECTION YOU ASKED ME TO DO. IT'S BASICALLY JUST GUESSING PLUS MATH.
OBVIOUSLY, IT'S USELESS FOR MAKING DECISIONS BECAUSE I CAN GET ANY RESULT I WANT BY TWEAKING THE ASSUMPTIONS.
11-29-17 © 2017 Scott Adams, Inc./Dist. by Andrews McMeel
DON'T SAY ANY OF THAT STUFF WHEN YOU PRESENT IT TO THE BOARD TOMORROW.

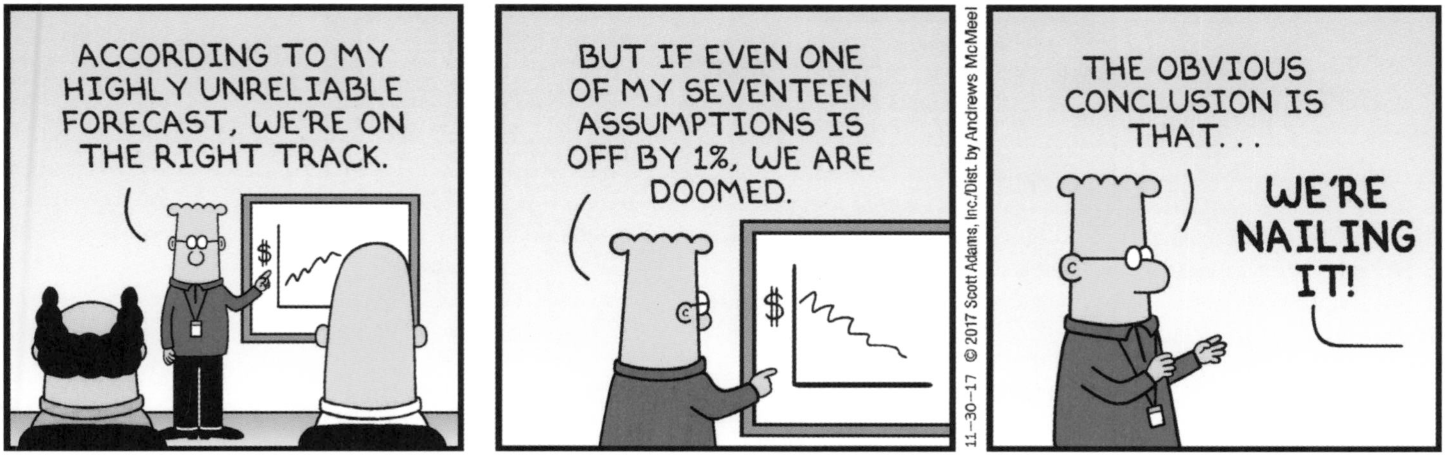
ACCORDING TO MY HIGHLY UNRELIABLE FORECAST, WE'RE ON THE RIGHT TRACK.
$
BUT IF EVEN ONE OF MY SEVENTEEN ASSUMPTIONS IS OFF BY 1%, WE ARE DOOMED.
$
11-30-17 © 2017 Scott Adams, Inc./Dist. by Andrews McMeel
THE OBVIOUS CONCLUSION IS THAT. . .
WE'RE NAILING IT!

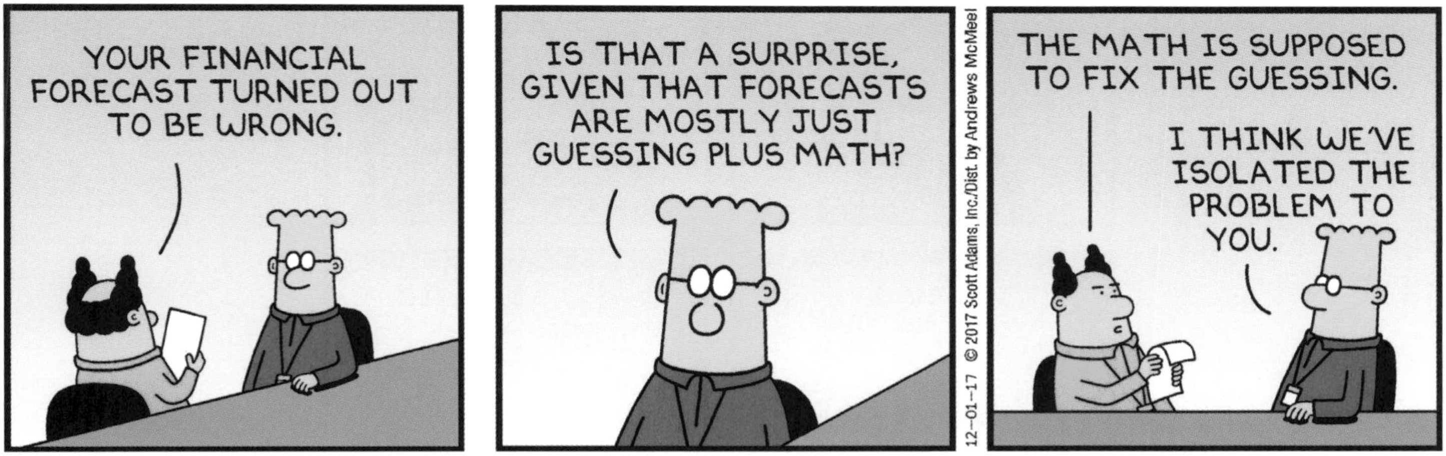
YOUR FINANCIAL FORECAST TURNED OUT TO BE WRONG.
IS THAT A SURPRISE, GIVEN THAT FORECASTS ARE MOSTLY JUST GUESSING PLUS MATH?
12-01-17 © 2017 Scott Adams, Inc./Dist. by Andrews McMeel
THE MATH IS SUPPOSED TO FIX THE GUESSING.
I THINK WE'VE ISOLATED THE PROBLEM TO YOU.

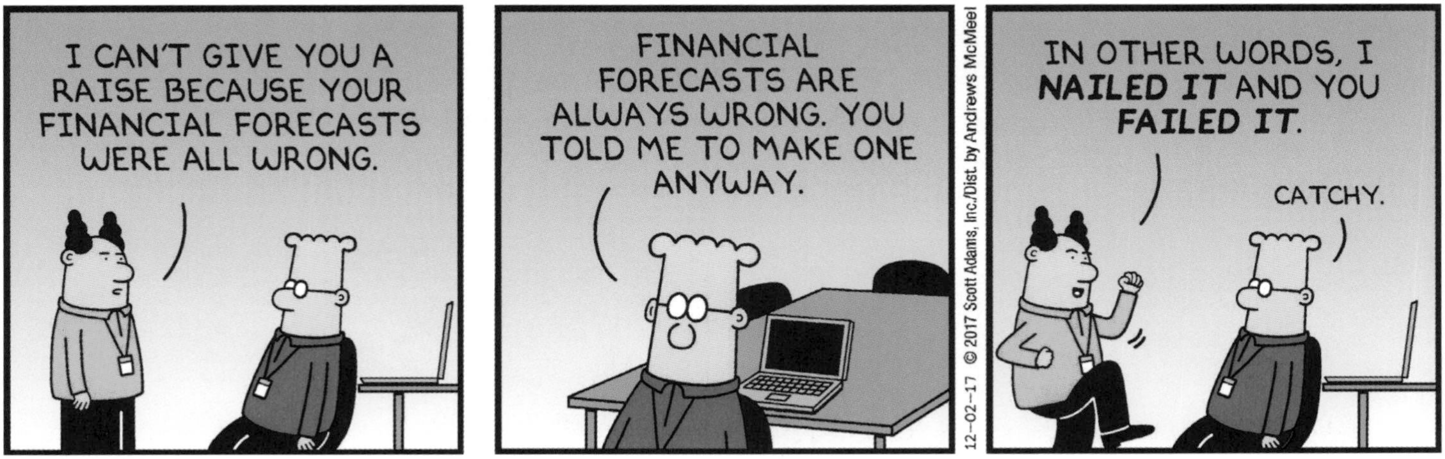
I CAN'T GIVE YOU A RAISE BECAUSE YOUR FINANCIAL FORECASTS WERE ALL WRONG.
FINANCIAL FORECASTS ARE ALWAYS WRONG. YOU TOLD ME TO MAKE ONE ANYWAY.
12-02-17 © 2017 Scott Adams, Inc./Dist. by Andrews McMeel
IN OTHER WORDS, I NAILED IT AND YOU FAILED IT.
CATCHY.

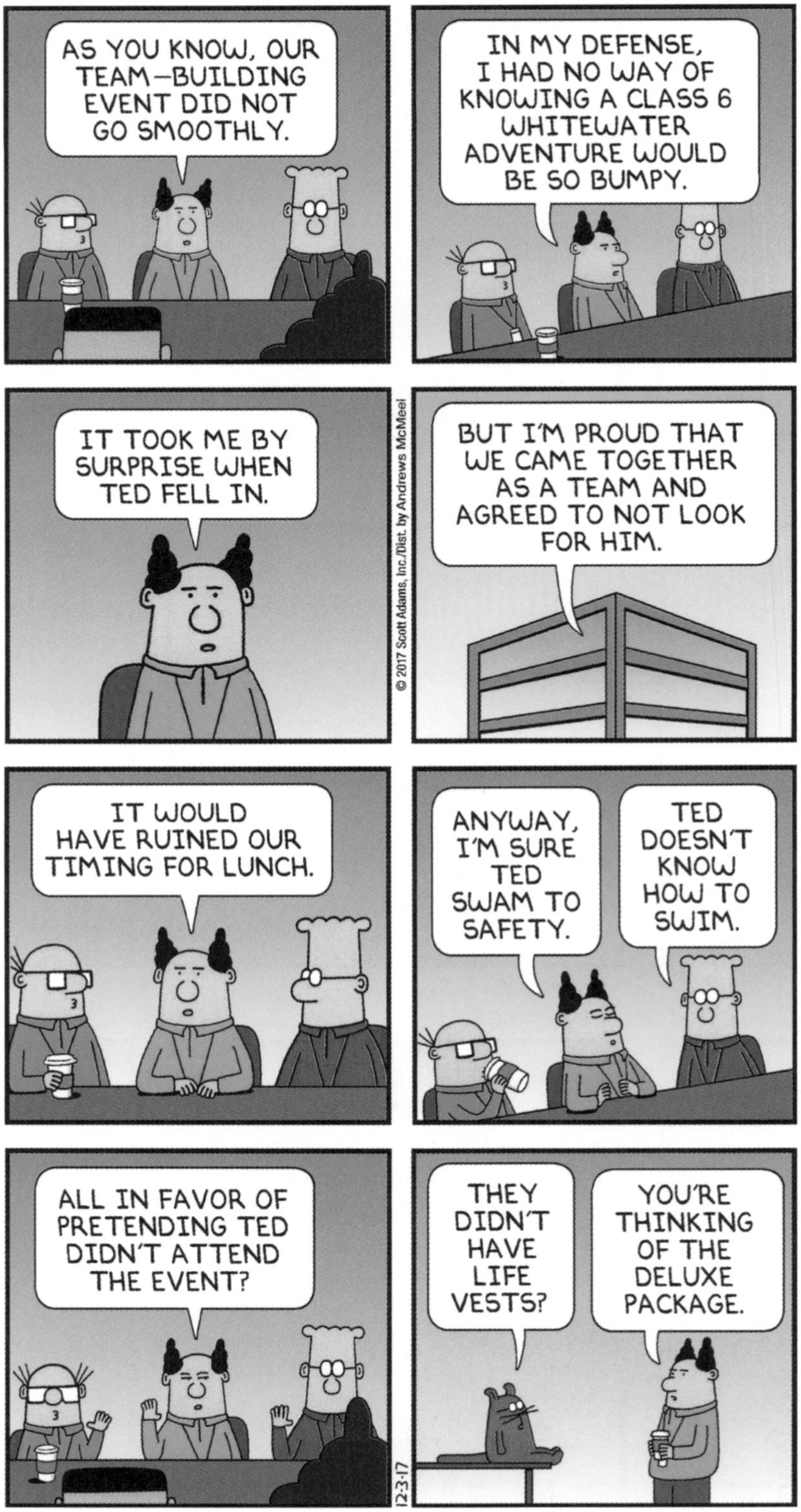
AS YOU KNOW, OUR TEAM—BUILDING EVENT DID NOT GO SMOOTHLY.
IN MY DEFENSE, I HAD NO WAY OF KNOWING A CLASS 6 WHITEWATER ADVENTURE WOULD BE SO BUMPY.
IT TOOK ME BY SURPRISE WHEN TED FELL IN.
BUT I'M PROUD THAT WE CAME TOGETHER AS A TEAM AND AGREED TO NOT LOOK FOR HIM.
IT WOULD HAVE RUINED OUR TIMING FOR LUNCH.
ANYWAY, I'M SURE TED SWAM TO SAFETY.
TED DOESN'T KNOW HOW TO SWIM.
ALL IN FAVOR OF PRETENDING TED DIDN'T ATTEND THE EVENT?
THEY DIDN'T HAVE LIFE VESTS?
YOU'RE THINKING OF THE DELUXE PACKAGE.
© 2017 Scott Adams, Inc./Dist. by Andrews McMeel
12-3-17

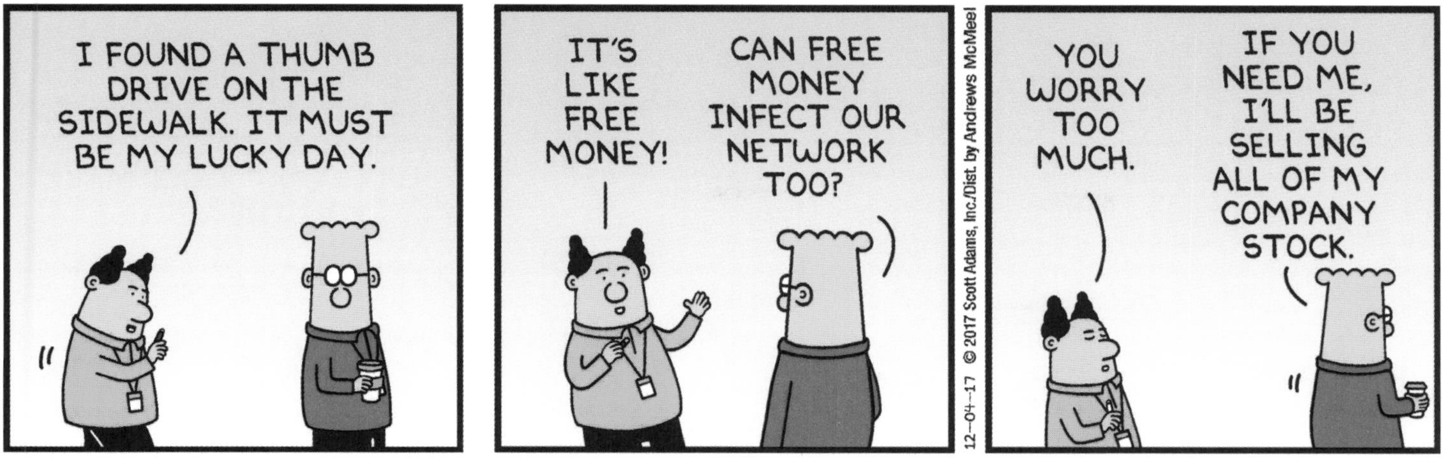
I FOUND A THUMB DRIVE ON THE SIDEWALK. IT MUST BE MY LUCKY DAY.
IT'S LIKE FREE MONEY!
CAN FREE MONEY INFECT OUR NETWORK TOO?
YOU WORRY TOO MUCH.
IF YOU NEED ME, I'LL BE SELLING ALL OF MY COMPANY STOCK.
12-04-17 © 2017 Scott Adams, Inc./Dist. by Andrews McMeel

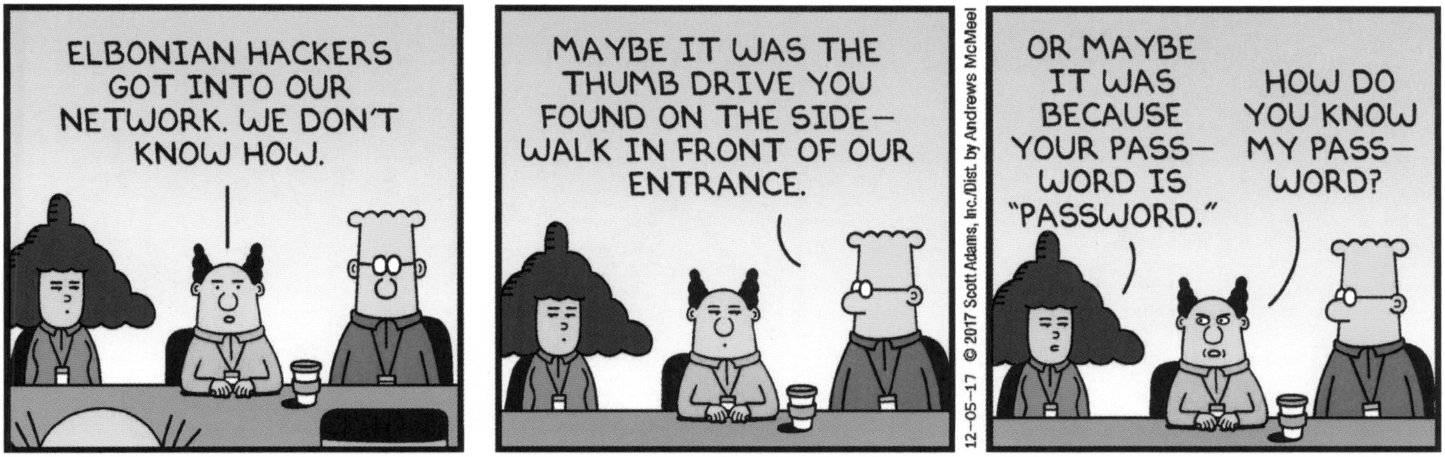
ELBONIAN HACKERS GOT INTO OUR NETWORK. WE DON'T KNOW HOW.
MAYBE IT WAS THE THUMB DRIVE YOU FOUND ON THE SIDE-WALK IN FRONT OF OUR ENTRANCE.
OR MAYBE IT WAS BECAUSE YOUR PASS-WORD IS "PASSWORD."
HOW DO YOU KNOW MY PASS-WORD?
12-05-17 © 2017 Scott Adams, Inc./Dist. by Andrews McMeel

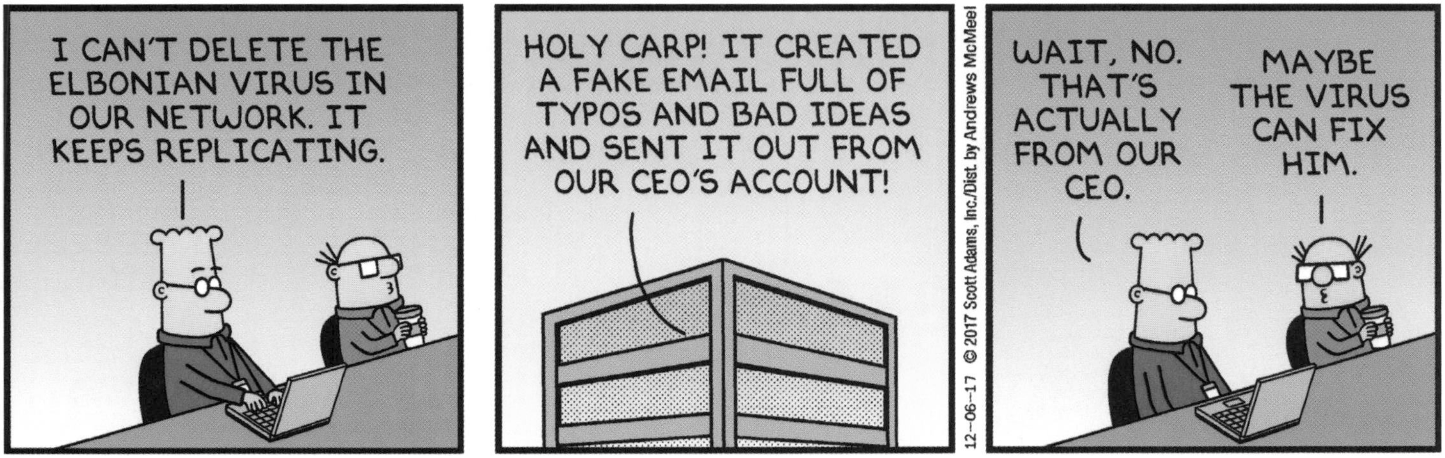
I CAN'T DELETE THE ELBONIAN VIRUS IN OUR NETWORK. IT KEEPS REPLICATING.
HOLY CARP! IT CREATED A FAKE EMAIL FULL OF TYPOS AND BAD IDEAS AND SENT IT OUT FROM OUR CEO'S ACCOUNT!
WAIT, NO. THAT'S ACTUALLY FROM OUR CEO.
MAYBE THE VIRUS CAN FIX HIM.
12-06-17 © 2017 Scott Adams, Inc./Dist. by Andrews McMeel

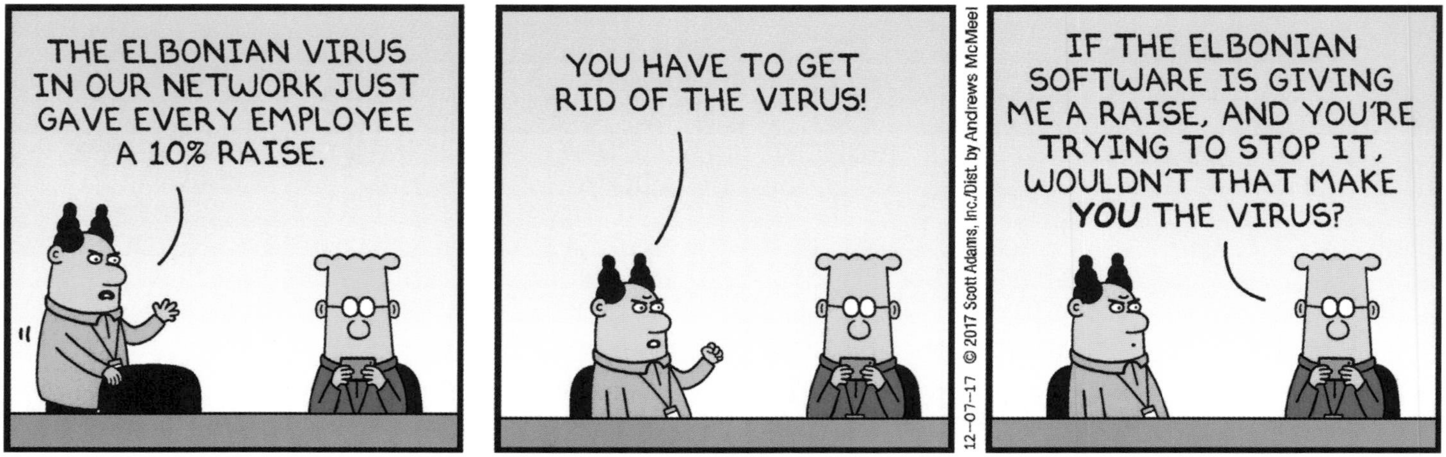
THE ELBONIAN VIRUS IN OUR NETWORK JUST GAVE EVERY EMPLOYEE A 10% RAISE.
YOU HAVE TO GET RID OF THE VIRUS!
IF THE ELBONIAN SOFTWARE IS GIVING ME A RAISE, AND YOU'RE TRYING TO STOP IT, WOULDN'T THAT MAKE *YOU* THE VIRUS?

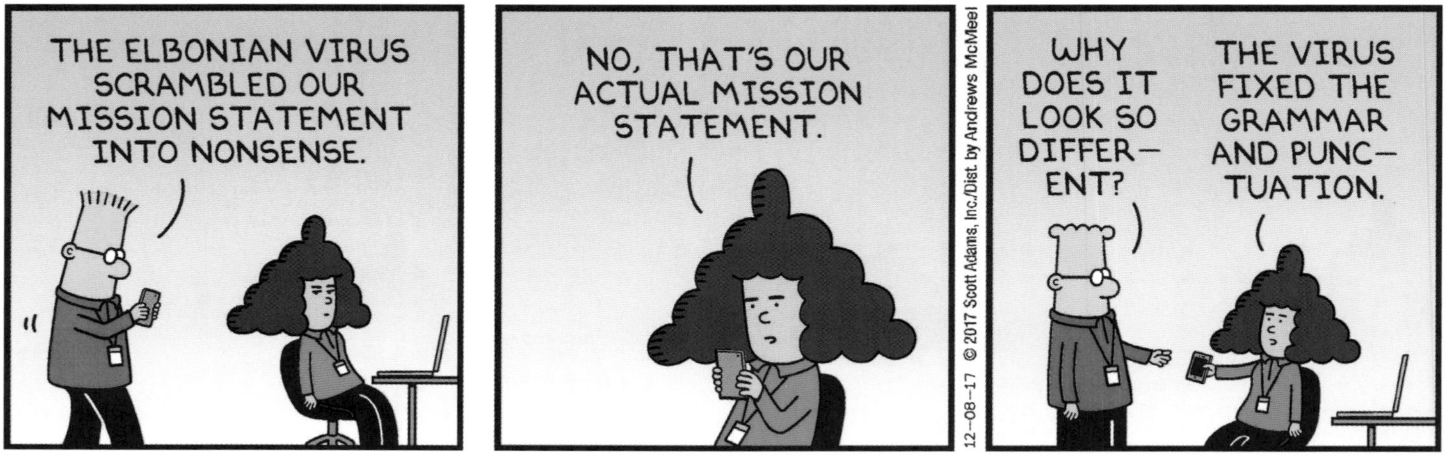
THE ELBONIAN VIRUS SCRAMBLED OUR MISSION STATEMENT INTO NONSENSE.
NO, THAT'S OUR ACTUAL MISSION STATEMENT.
WHY DOES IT LOOK SO DIFFER-ENT?
THE VIRUS FIXED THE GRAMMAR AND PUNC-TUATION.

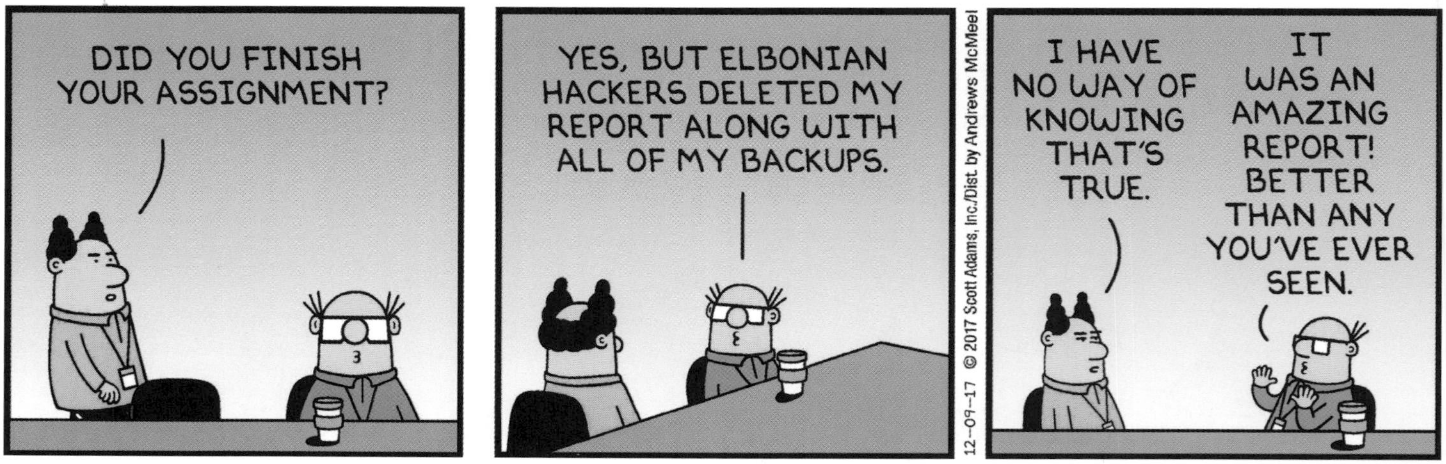
DID YOU FINISH YOUR ASSIGNMENT?
YES, BUT ELBONIAN HACKERS DELETED MY REPORT ALONG WITH ALL OF MY BACKUPS.
I HAVE NO WAY OF KNOWING THAT'S TRUE.
IT WAS AN AMAZING REPORT! BETTER THAN ANY YOU'VE EVER SEEN.

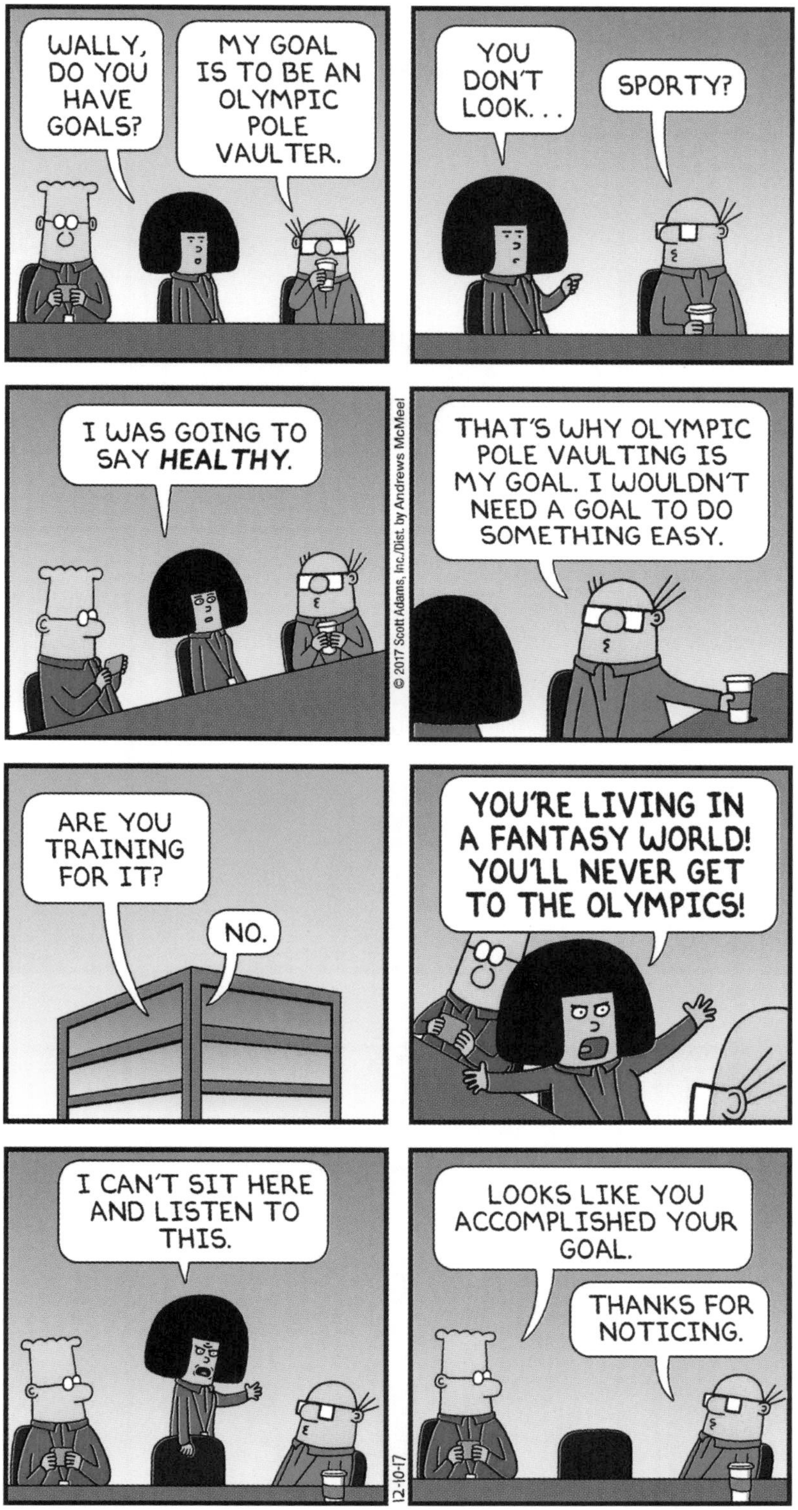
WALLY, DO YOU HAVE GOALS?
MY GOAL IS TO BE AN OLYMPIC POLE VAULTER.
YOU DON'T LOOK. . .
SPORTY?
I WAS GOING TO SAY **HEALTHY**.
THAT'S WHY OLYMPIC POLE VAULTING IS MY GOAL. I WOULDN'T NEED A GOAL TO DO SOMETHING EASY.
ARE YOU TRAINING FOR IT?
NO.
YOU'RE LIVING IN A FANTASY WORLD! YOU'LL NEVER GET TO THE OLYMPICS!
I CAN'T SIT HERE AND LISTEN TO THIS.
LOOKS LIKE YOU ACCOMPLISHED YOUR GOAL.
THANKS FOR NOTICING.
© 2017 Scott Adams, Inc./Dist. by Andrews McMeel
12-10-17

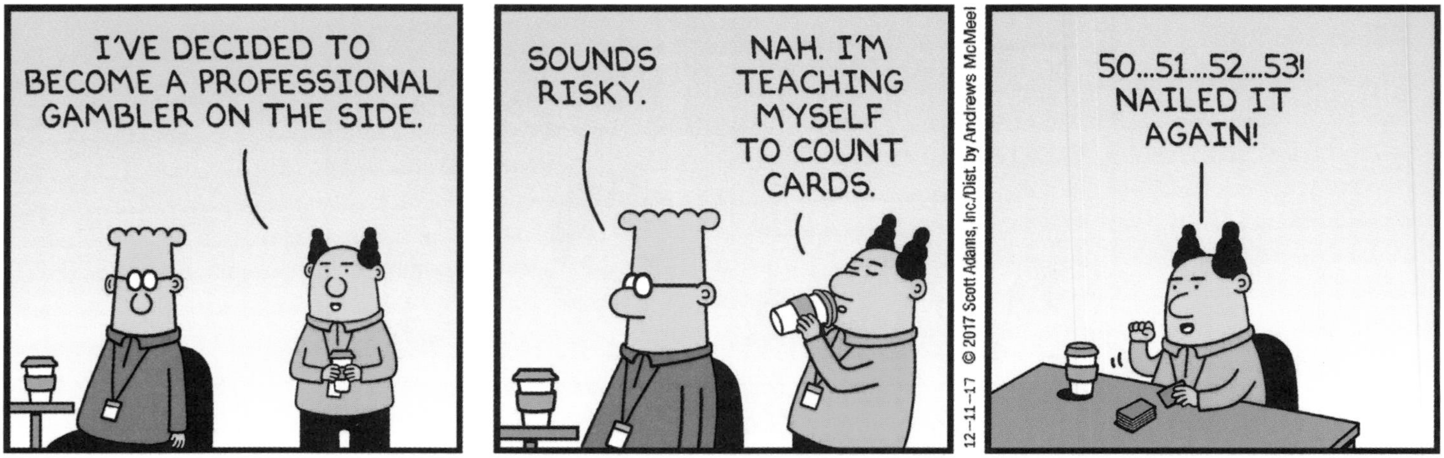
I'VE DECIDED TO BECOME A PROFESSIONAL GAMBLER ON THE SIDE.
SOUNDS RISKY.
NAH. I'M TEACHING MYSELF TO COUNT CARDS.
12-11-17 © 2017 Scott Adams, Inc./Dist. by Andrews McMeel
50...51...52...53! NAILED IT AGAIN!

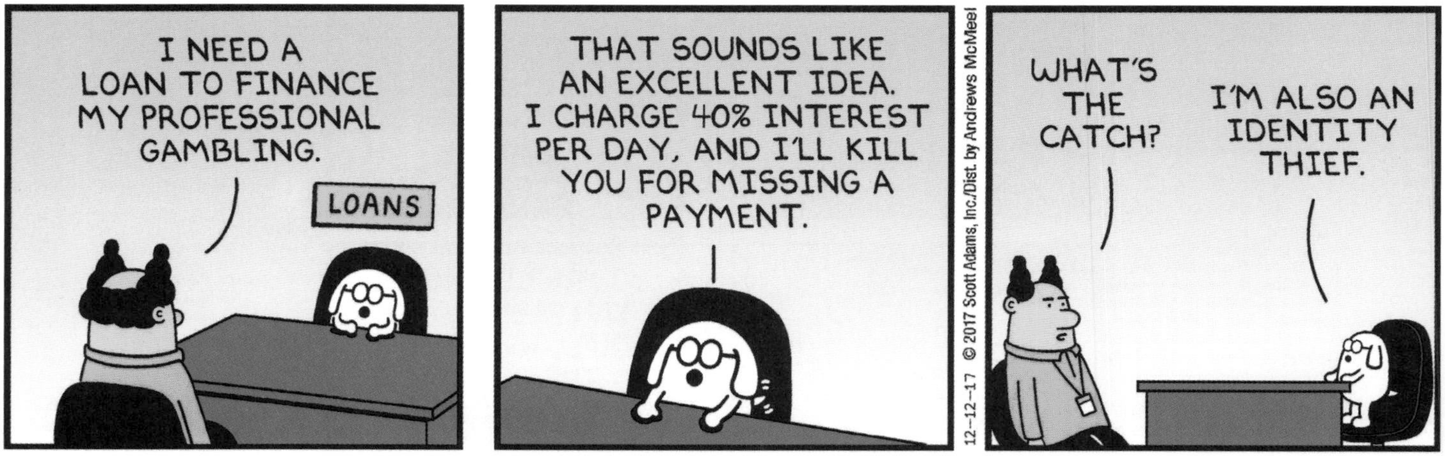
I NEED A LOAN TO FINANCE MY PROFESSIONAL GAMBLING.
LOANS
THAT SOUNDS LIKE AN EXCELLENT IDEA. I CHARGE 40% INTEREST PER DAY, AND I'LL KILL YOU FOR MISSING A PAYMENT.
12-12-17 © 2017 Scott Adams, Inc./Dist. by Andrews McMeel
WHAT'S THE CATCH?
I'M ALSO AN IDENTITY THIEF.

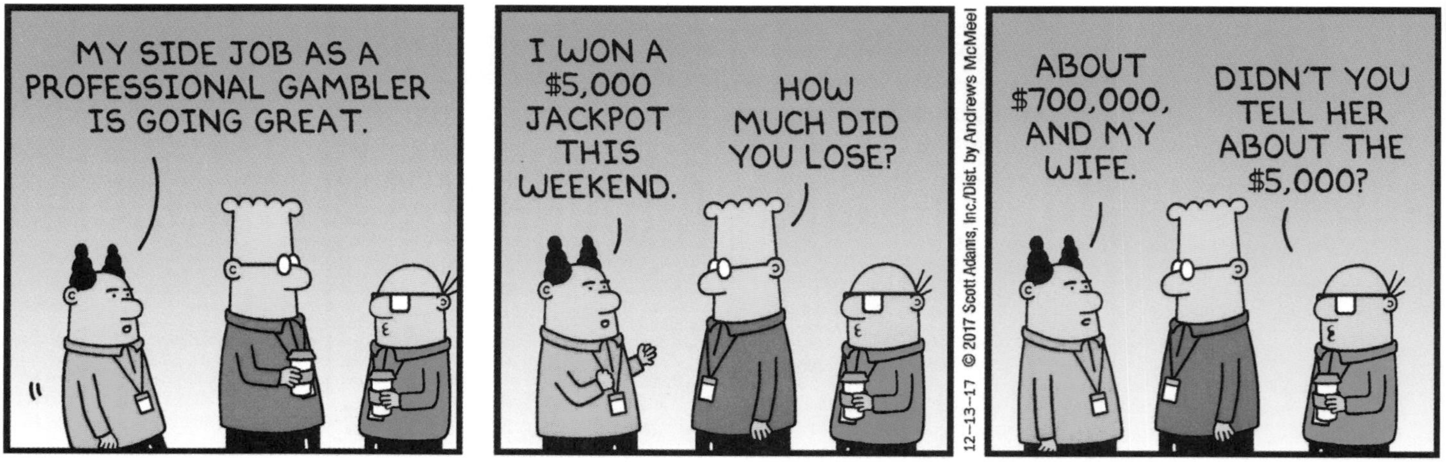
MY SIDE JOB AS A PROFESSIONAL GAMBLER IS GOING GREAT.
I WON A $5,000 JACKPOT THIS WEEKEND.
HOW MUCH DID YOU LOSE?
12-13-17 © 2017 Scott Adams, Inc./Dist. by Andrews McMeel
ABOUT $700,000, AND MY WIFE.
DIDN'T YOU TELL HER ABOUT THE $5,000?

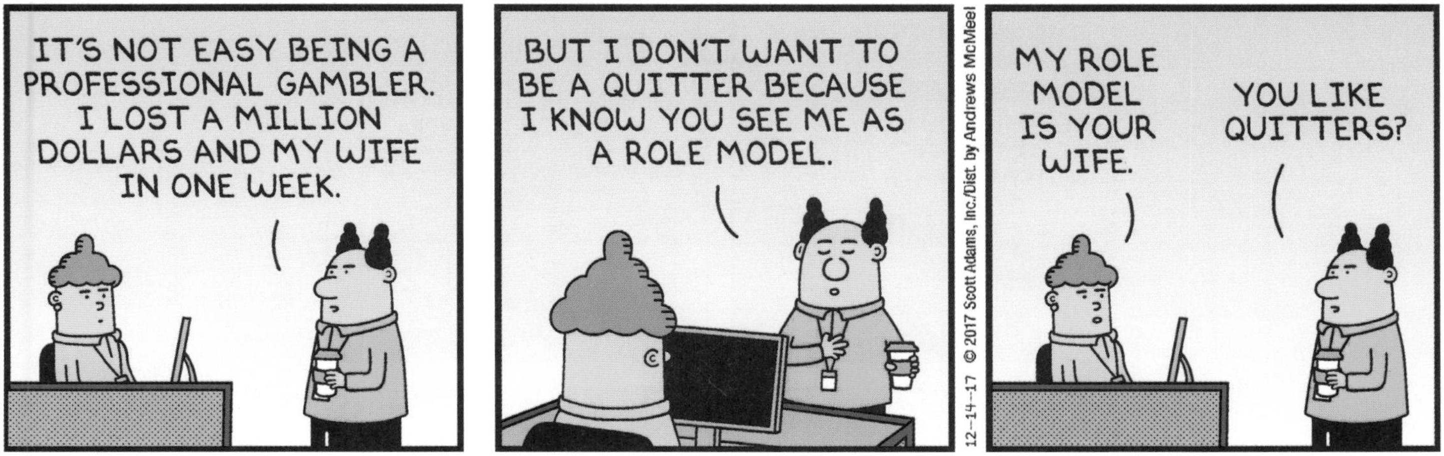
IT'S NOT EASY BEING A PROFESSIONAL GAMBLER. I LOST A MILLION DOLLARS AND MY WIFE IN ONE WEEK.
BUT I DON'T WANT TO BE A QUITTER BECAUSE I KNOW YOU SEE ME AS A ROLE MODEL.
12-14-17 © 2017 Scott Adams, Inc./Dist by Andrews McMeel
MY ROLE MODEL IS YOUR WIFE.
YOU LIKE QUITTERS?

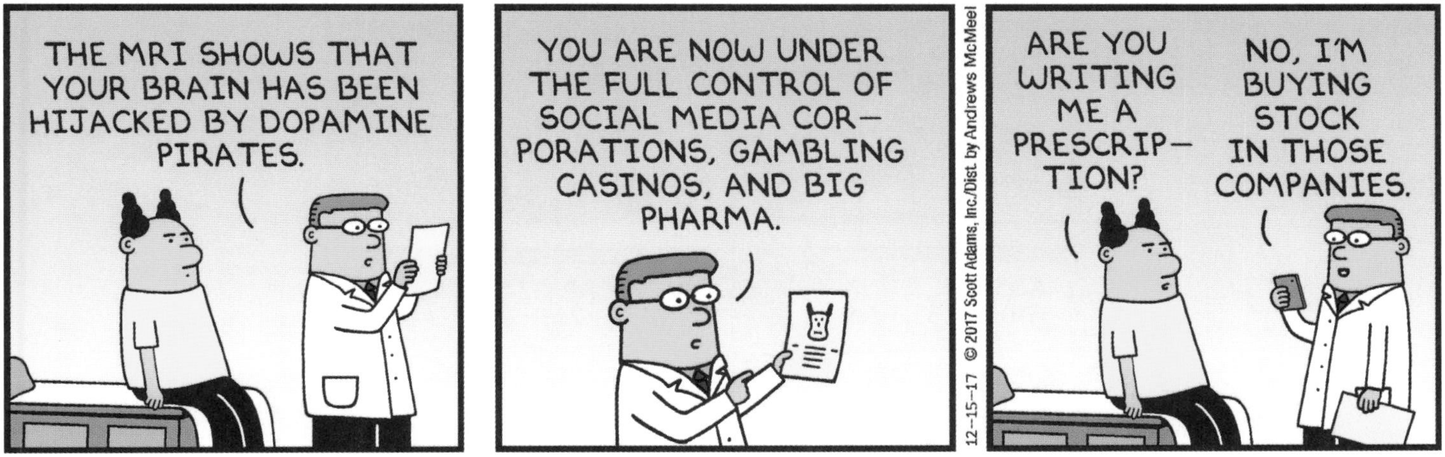
THE MRI SHOWS THAT YOUR BRAIN HAS BEEN HIJACKED BY DOPAMINE PIRATES.
YOU ARE NOW UNDER THE FULL CONTROL OF SOCIAL MEDIA COR-PORATIONS, GAMBLING CASINOS, AND BIG PHARMA.
12-15-17 © 2017 Scott Adams, Inc./Dist by Andrews McMeel
ARE YOU WRITING ME A PRESCRIP-TION?
NO, I'M BUYING STOCK IN THOSE COMPANIES.

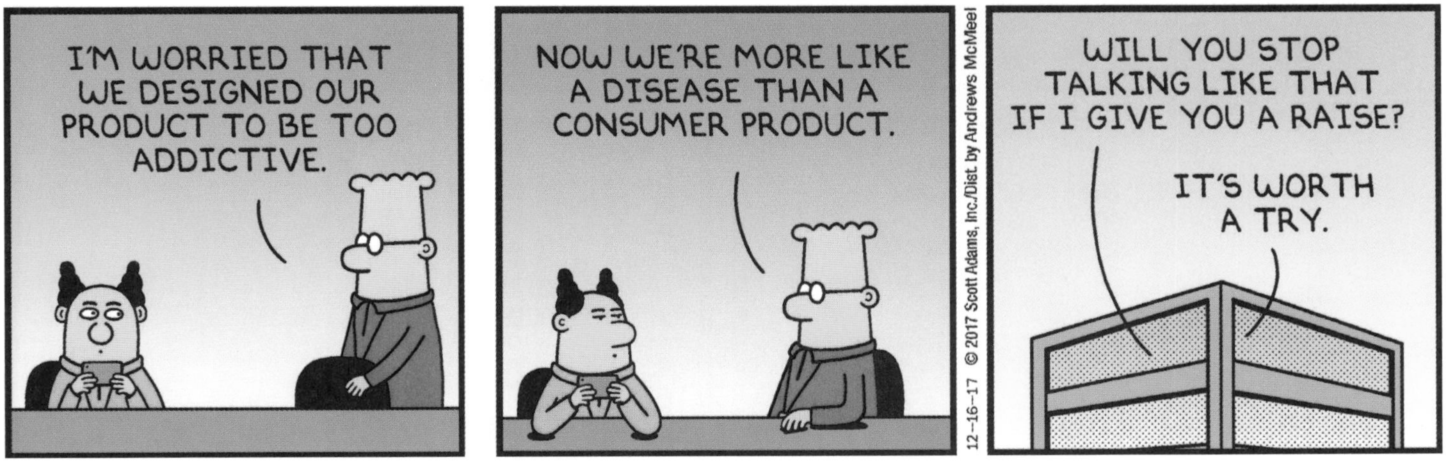
I'M WORRIED THAT WE DESIGNED OUR PRODUCT TO BE TOO ADDICTIVE.
NOW WE'RE MORE LIKE A DISEASE THAN A CONSUMER PRODUCT.
12-16-17 © 2017 Scott Adams, Inc./Dist by Andrews McMeel
WILL YOU STOP TALKING LIKE THAT IF I GIVE YOU A RAISE?
IT'S WORTH A TRY.

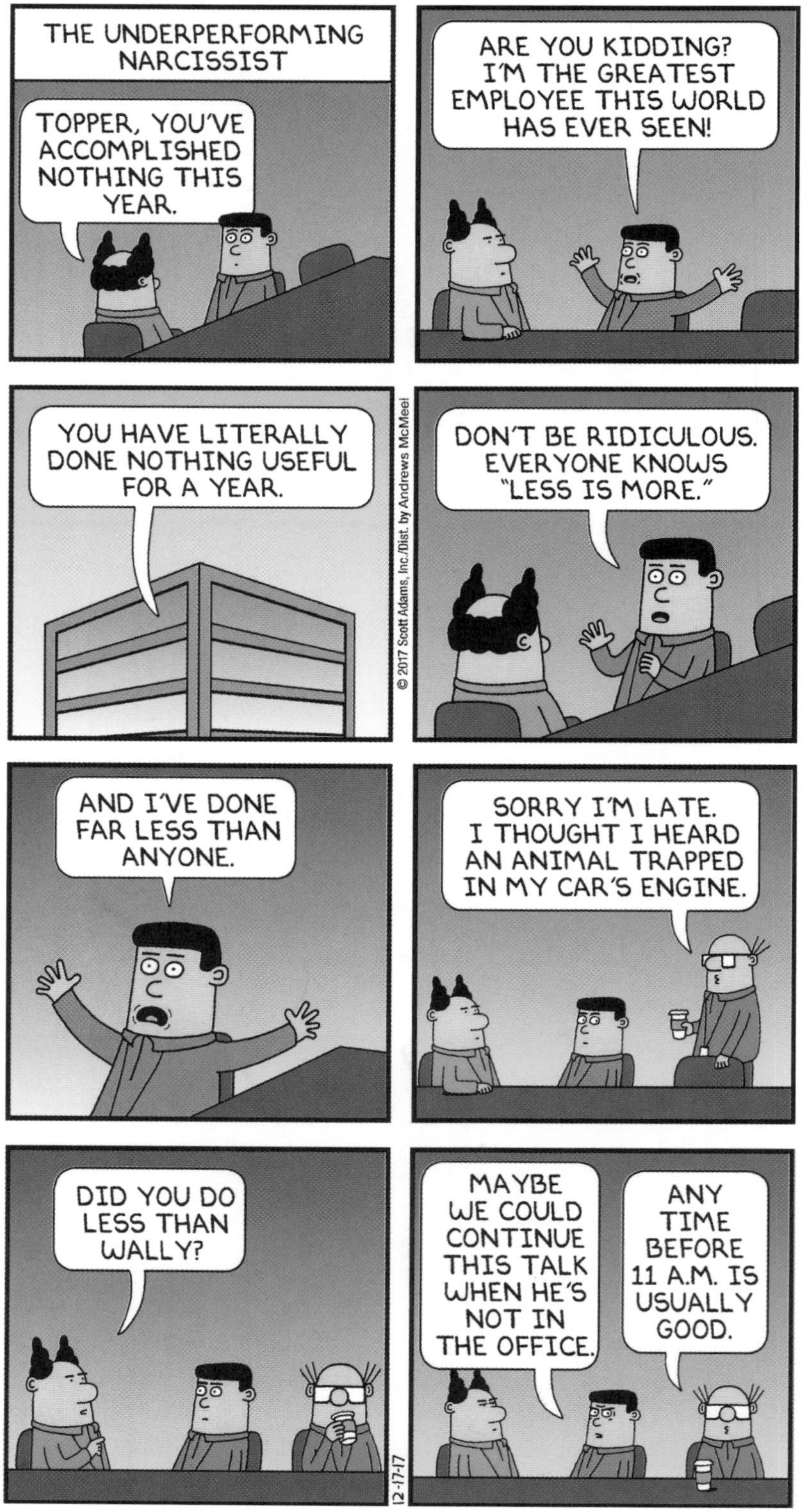
THE UNDERPERFORMING NARCISSIST
TOPPER, YOU'VE ACCOMPLISHED NOTHING THIS YEAR.
ARE YOU KIDDING? I'M THE GREATEST EMPLOYEE THIS WORLD HAS EVER SEEN!
YOU HAVE LITERALLY DONE NOTHING USEFUL FOR A YEAR.
DON'T BE RIDICULOUS. EVERYONE KNOWS "LESS IS MORE."
AND I'VE DONE FAR LESS THAN ANYONE.
SORRY I'M LATE. I THOUGHT I HEARD AN ANIMAL TRAPPED IN MY CAR'S ENGINE.
DID YOU DO LESS THAN WALLY?
MAYBE WE COULD CONTINUE THIS TALK WHEN HE'S NOT IN THE OFFICE.
ANY TIME BEFORE 11 A.M. IS USUALLY GOOD.
© 2017 Scott Adams, Inc./Dist. by Andrews McMeel
12-17-17

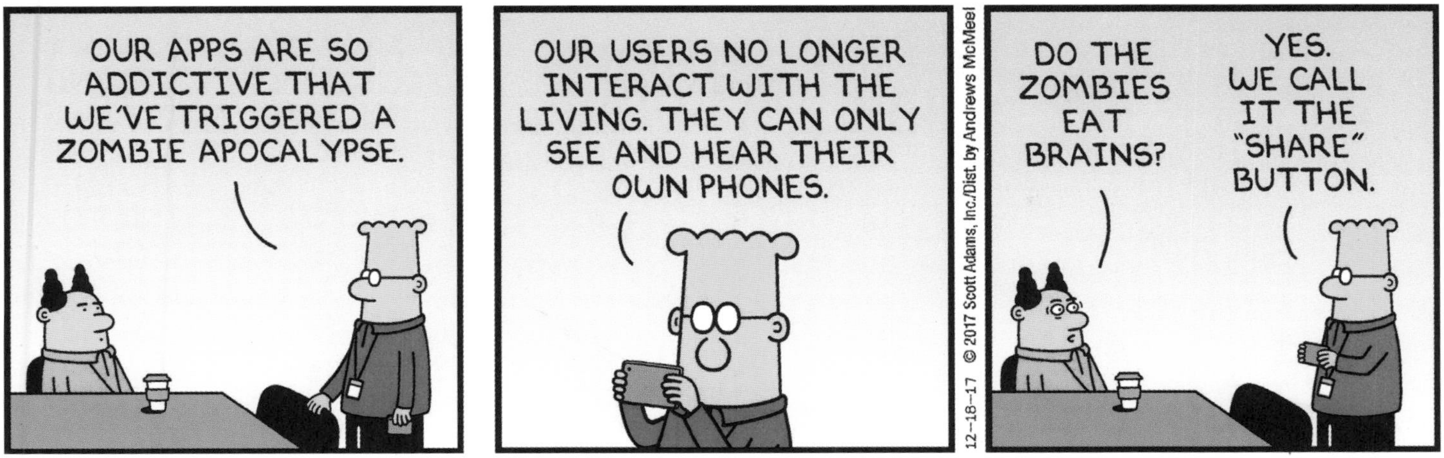
OUR APPS ARE SO ADDICTIVE THAT WE'VE TRIGGERED A ZOMBIE APOCALYPSE.
OUR USERS NO LONGER INTERACT WITH THE LIVING. THEY CAN ONLY SEE AND HEAR THEIR OWN PHONES.
12-18-17 © 2017 Scott Adams, Inc./Dist. by Andrews McMeel
DO THE ZOMBIES EAT BRAINS?
YES. WE CALL IT THE "SHARE" BUTTON.

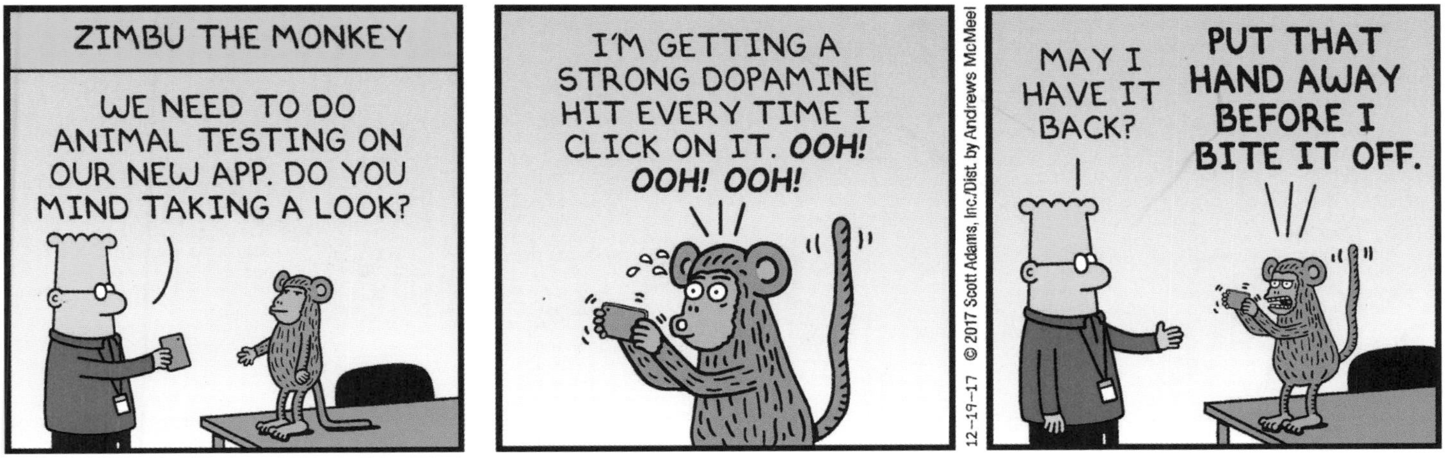
ZIMBU THE MONKEY
WE NEED TO DO ANIMAL TESTING ON OUR NEW APP. DO YOU MIND TAKING A LOOK?
I'M GETTING A STRONG DOPAMINE HIT EVERY TIME I CLICK ON IT. OOH! OOH! OOH!
12-19-17 © 2017 Scott Adams, Inc./Dist. by Andrews McMeel
MAY I HAVE IT BACK?
PUT THAT HAND AWAY BEFORE I BITE IT OFF.

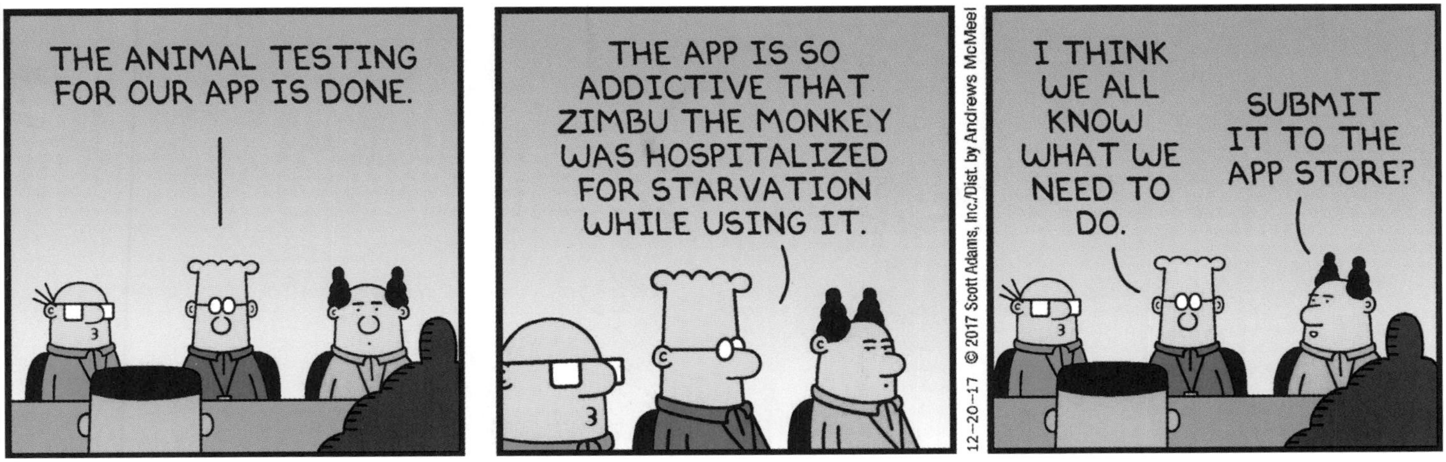
THE ANIMAL TESTING FOR OUR APP IS DONE.
THE APP IS SO ADDICTIVE THAT ZIMBU THE MONKEY WAS HOSPITALIZED FOR STARVATION WHILE USING IT.
12-20-17 © 2017 Scott Adams, Inc./Dist. by Andrews McMeel
I THINK WE ALL KNOW WHAT WE NEED TO DO.
SUBMIT IT TO THE APP STORE?

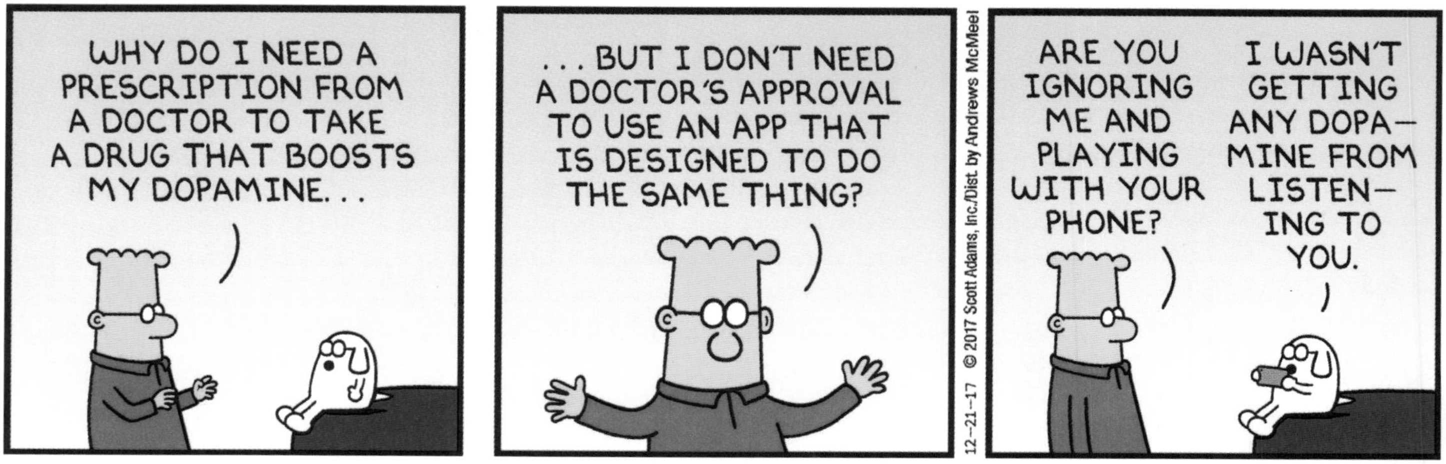
WHY DO I NEED A PRESCRIPTION FROM A DOCTOR TO TAKE A DRUG THAT BOOSTS MY DOPAMINE. . .
. . . BUT I DON'T NEED A DOCTOR'S APPROVAL TO USE AN APP THAT IS DESIGNED TO DO THE SAME THING?
12-21-17 © 2017 Scott Adams, Inc./Dist. by Andrews McMeel
ARE YOU IGNORING ME AND PLAYING WITH YOUR PHONE?
I WASN'T GETTING ANY DOPA-MINE FROM LISTEN-ING TO YOU.

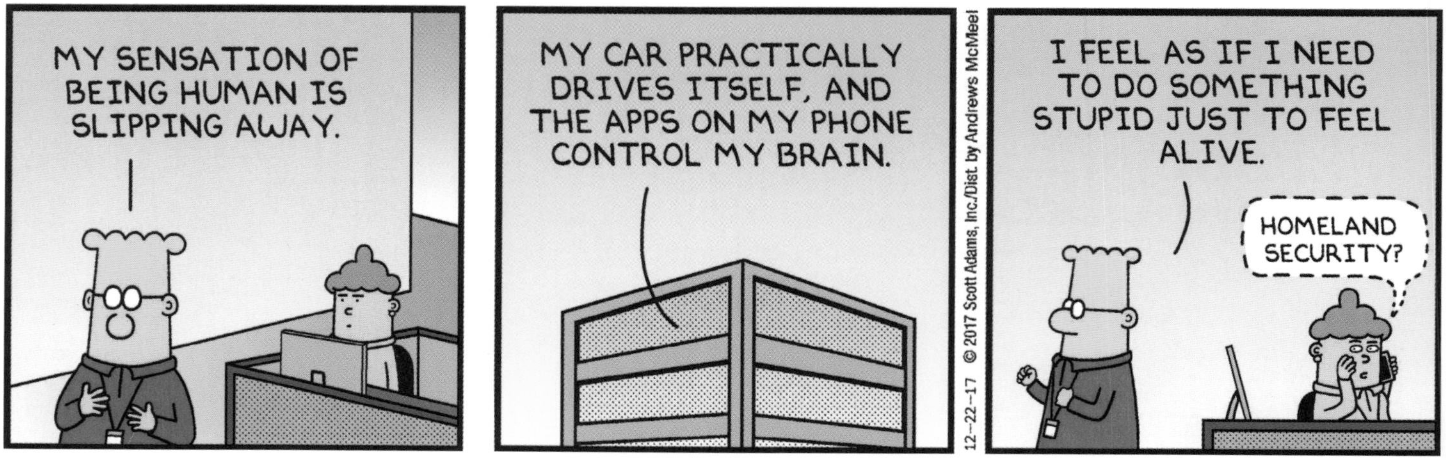
MY SENSATION OF BEING HUMAN IS SLIPPING AWAY.
MY CAR PRACTICALLY DRIVES ITSELF, AND THE APPS ON MY PHONE CONTROL MY BRAIN.
12-22-17 © 2017 Scott Adams, Inc./Dist. by Andrews McMeel
I FEEL AS IF I NEED TO DO SOMETHING STUPID JUST TO FEEL ALIVE.
HOMELAND SECURITY?

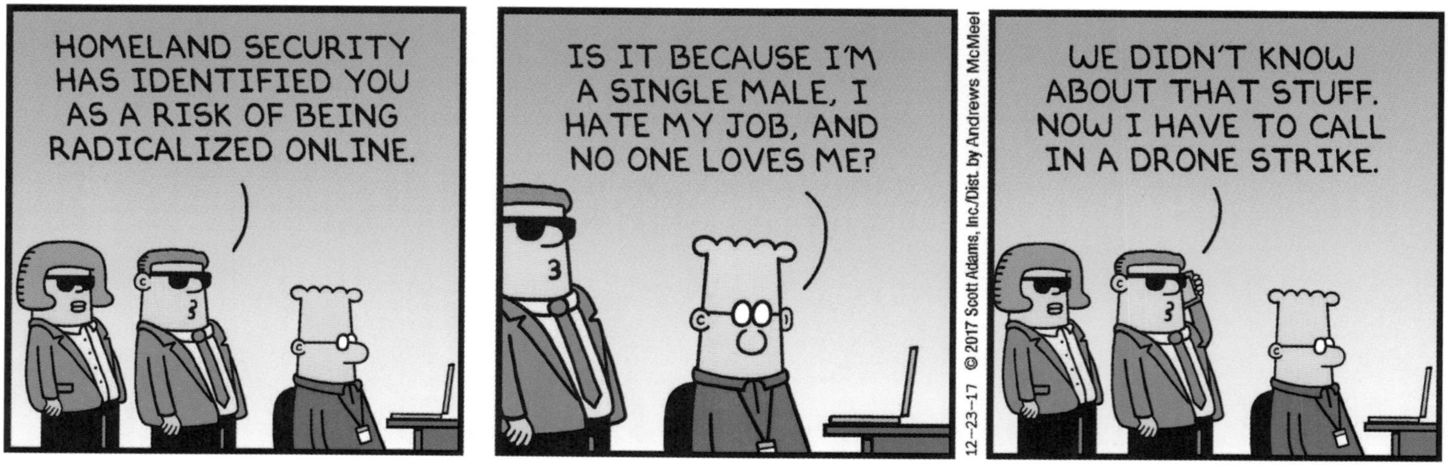
HOMELAND SECURITY HAS IDENTIFIED YOU AS A RISK OF BEING RADICALIZED ONLINE.
IS IT BECAUSE I'M A SINGLE MALE, I HATE MY JOB, AND NO ONE LOVES ME?
12-23-17 © 2017 Scott Adams, Inc./Dist. by Andrews McMeel
WE DIDN'T KNOW ABOUT THAT STUFF. NOW I HAVE TO CALL IN A DRONE STRIKE.

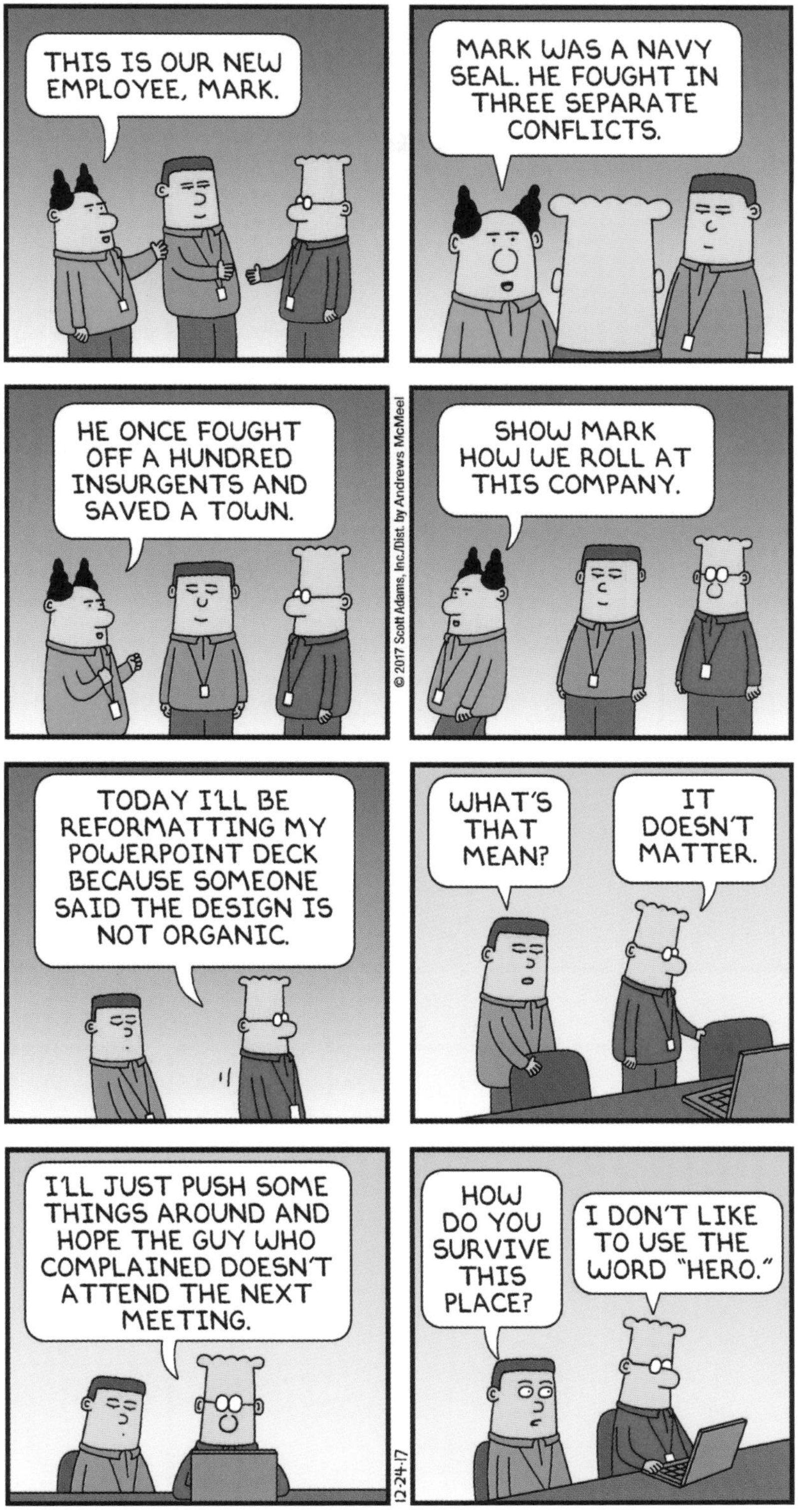
THIS IS OUR NEW EMPLOYEE, MARK.
MARK WAS A NAVY SEAL. HE FOUGHT IN THREE SEPARATE CONFLICTS.
HE ONCE FOUGHT OFF A HUNDRED INSURGENTS AND SAVED A TOWN.
© 2017 Scott Adams, Inc./Dist. by Andrews McMeel
SHOW MARK HOW WE ROLL AT THIS COMPANY.
TODAY I'LL BE REFORMATTING MY POWERPOINT DECK BECAUSE SOMEONE SAID THE DESIGN IS NOT ORGANIC.
WHAT'S THAT MEAN?
IT DOESN'T MATTER.
I'LL JUST PUSH SOME THINGS AROUND AND HOPE THE GUY WHO COMPLAINED DOESN'T ATTEND THE NEXT MEETING.
12-24-17
HOW DO YOU SURVIVE THIS PLACE?
I DON'T LIKE TO USE THE WORD "HERO."

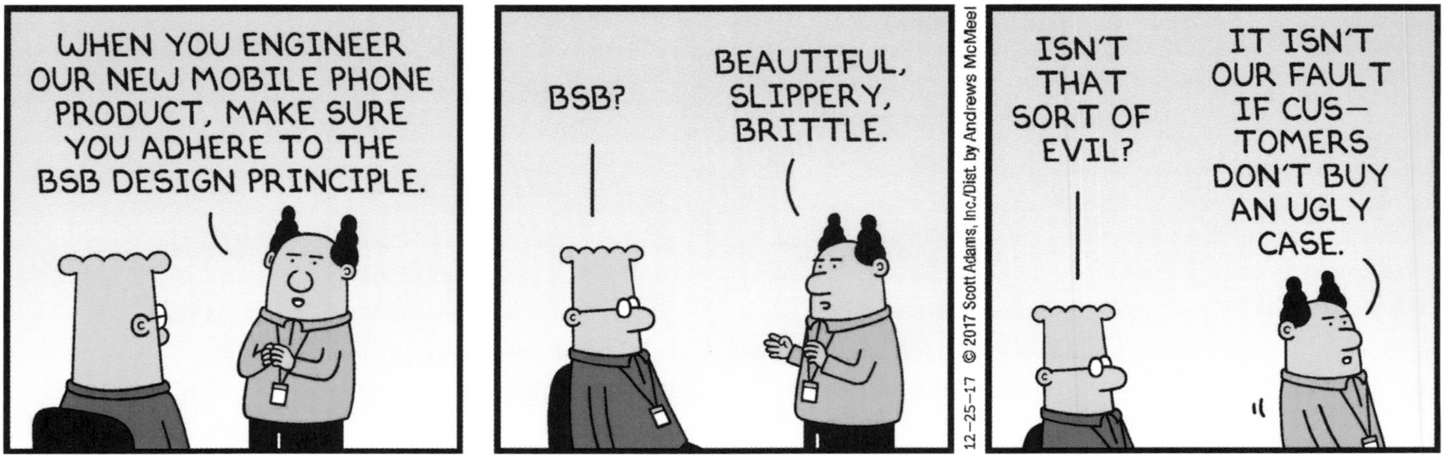
WHEN YOU ENGINEER OUR NEW MOBILE PHONE PRODUCT, MAKE SURE YOU ADHERE TO THE BSB DESIGN PRINCIPLE.
BSB?
BEAUTIFUL, SLIPPERY, BRITTLE.
12-25-17 © 2017 Scott Adams, Inc./Dist. by Andrews McMeel
ISN'T THAT SORT OF EVIL?
IT ISN'T OUR FAULT IF CUS-TOMERS DON'T BUY AN UGLY CASE.

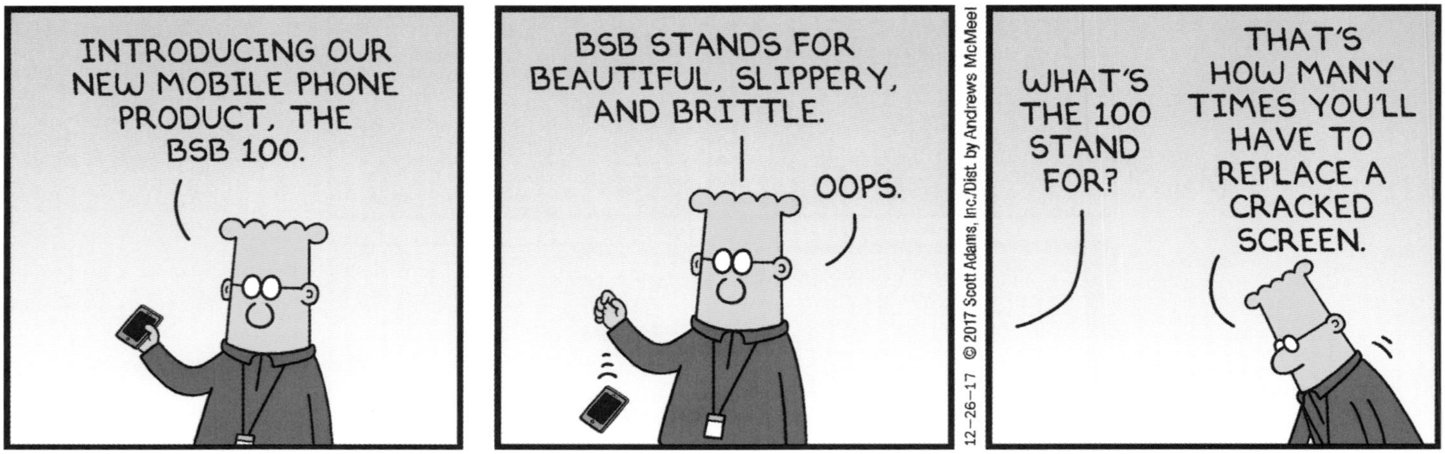
INTRODUCING OUR NEW MOBILE PHONE PRODUCT, THE BSB 100.
BSB STANDS FOR BEAUTIFUL, SLIPPERY, AND BRITTLE.
OOPS.
12-26-17 © 2017 Scott Adams, Inc./Dist. by Andrews McMeel
WHAT'S THE 100 STAND FOR?
THAT'S HOW MANY TIMES YOU'LL HAVE TO REPLACE A CRACKED SCREEN.

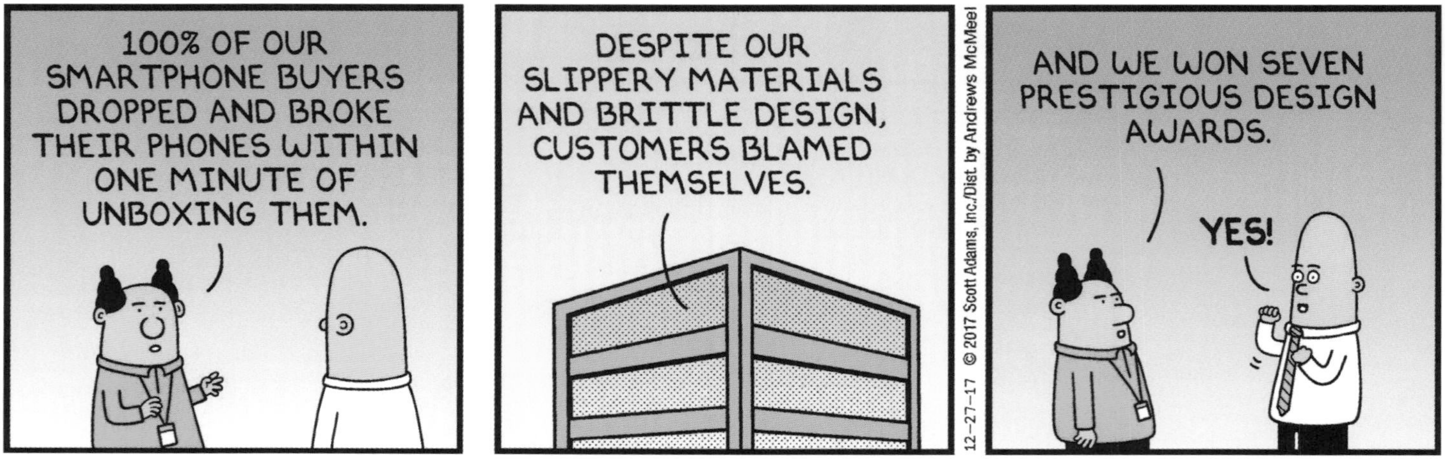
100% OF OUR SMARTPHONE BUYERS DROPPED AND BROKE THEIR PHONES WITHIN ONE MINUTE OF UNBOXING THEM.
DESPITE OUR SLIPPERY MATERIALS AND BRITTLE DESIGN, CUSTOMERS BLAMED THEMSELVES.
12-27-17 © 2017 Scott Adams, Inc./Dist. by Andrews McMeel
AND WE WON SEVEN PRESTIGIOUS DESIGN AWARDS.
YES!

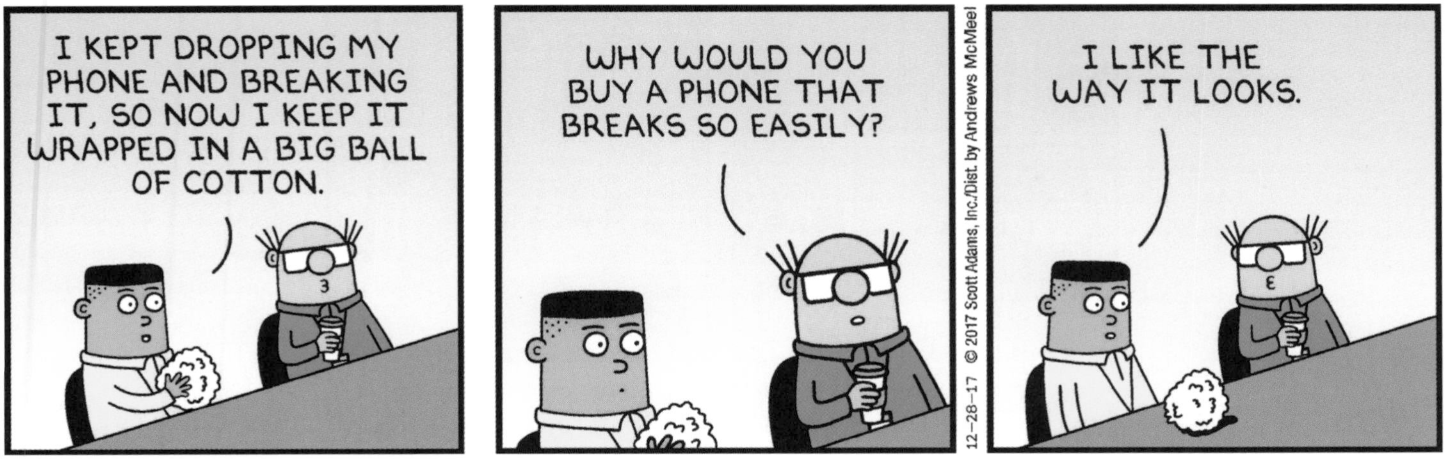
I KEPT DROPPING MY PHONE AND BREAKING IT, SO NOW I KEEP IT WRAPPED IN A BIG BALL OF COTTON.
WHY WOULD YOU BUY A PHONE THAT BREAKS SO EASILY?
12-28-17 © 2017 Scott Adams, Inc./Dist. by Andrews McMeel
I LIKE THE WAY IT LOOKS.

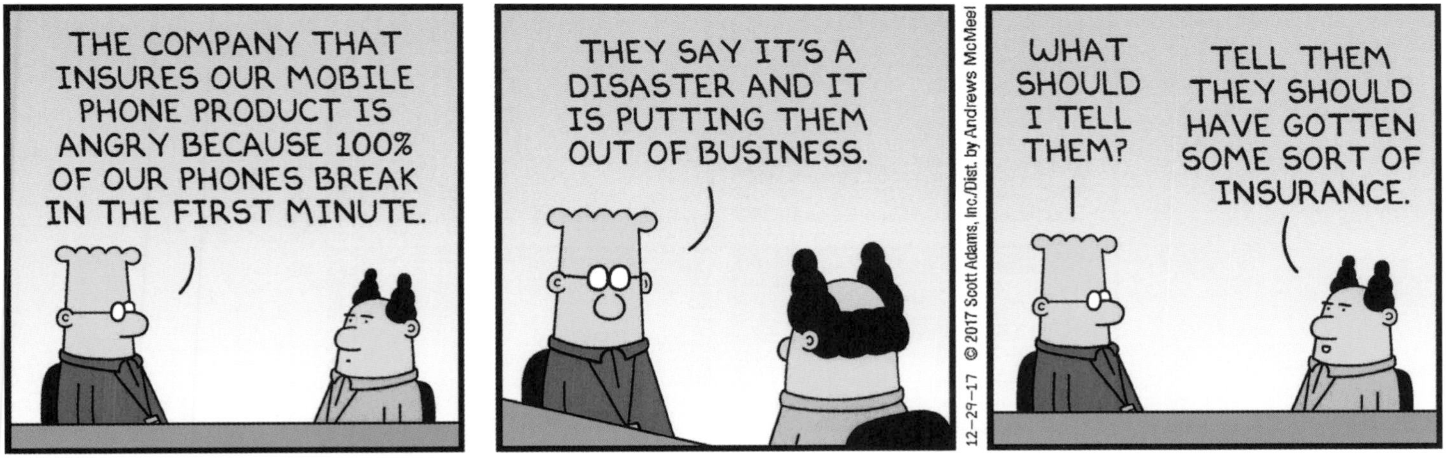
THE COMPANY THAT INSURES OUR MOBILE PHONE PRODUCT IS ANGRY BECAUSE 100% OF OUR PHONES BREAK IN THE FIRST MINUTE.
THEY SAY IT'S A DISASTER AND IT IS PUTTING THEM OUT OF BUSINESS.
12-29-17 © 2017 Scott Adams, Inc./Dist. by Andrews McMeel
WHAT SHOULD I TELL THEM?
TELL THEM THEY SHOULD HAVE GOTTEN SOME SORT OF INSURANCE.

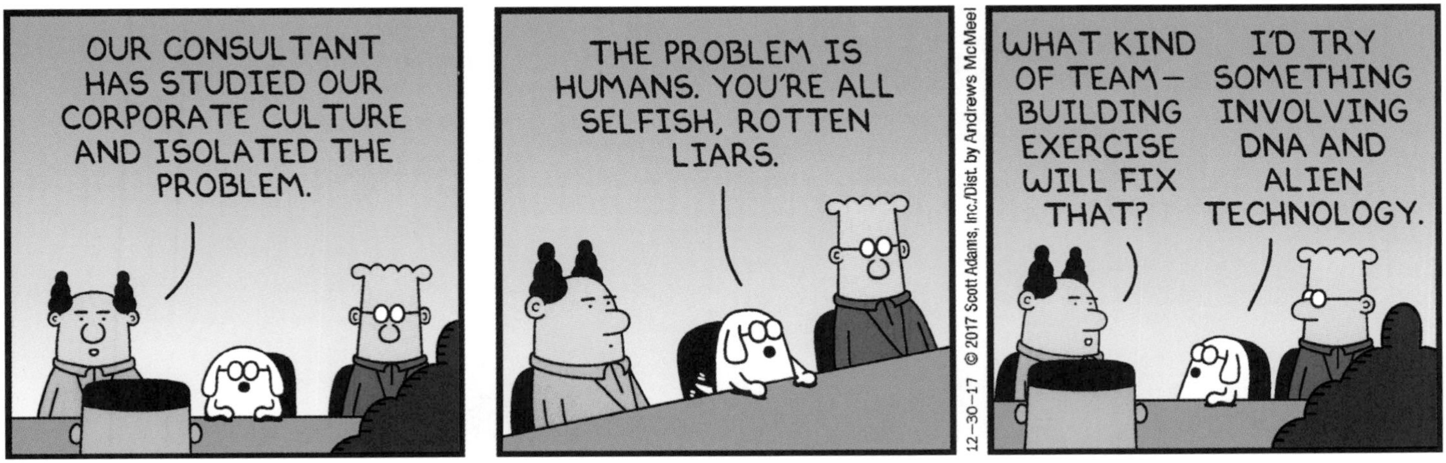
OUR CONSULTANT HAS STUDIED OUR CORPORATE CULTURE AND ISOLATED THE PROBLEM.
THE PROBLEM IS HUMANS. YOU'RE ALL SELFISH, ROTTEN LIARS.
12-30-17 © 2017 Scott Adams, Inc./Dist. by Andrews McMeel
WHAT KIND OF TEAM-BUILDING EXERCISE WILL FIX THAT?
I'D TRY SOMETHING INVOLVING DNA AND ALIEN TECHNOLOGY.

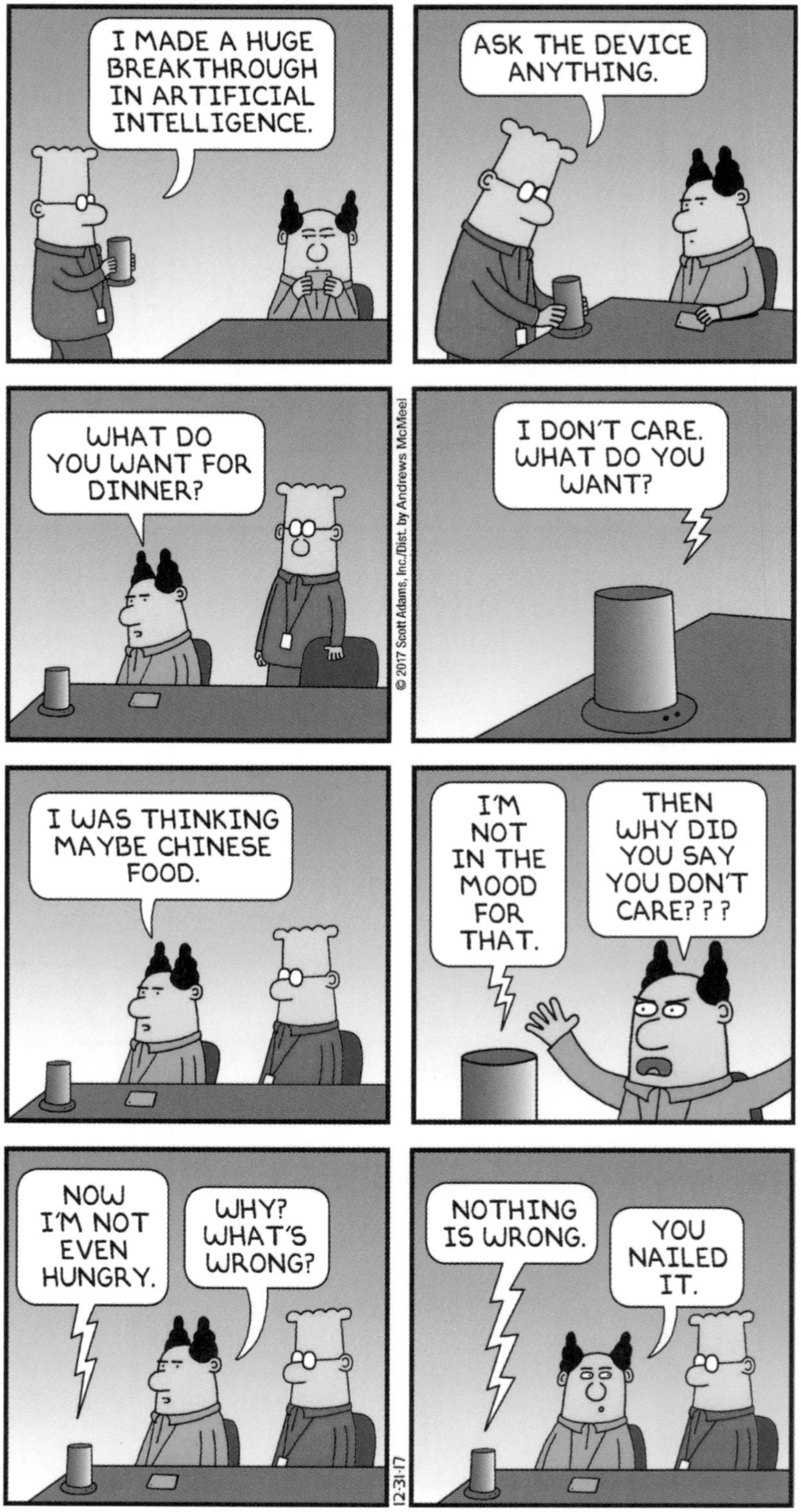
I MADE A HUGE BREAKTHROUGH IN ARTIFICIAL INTELLIGENCE.
ASK THE DEVICE ANYTHING.
WHAT DO YOU WANT FOR DINNER?
© 2017 Scott Adams, Inc./Dist. by Andrews McMeel
I DON'T CARE. WHAT DO YOU WANT?
I WAS THINKING MAYBE CHINESE FOOD.
I'M NOT IN THE MOOD FOR THAT.
THEN WHY DID YOU SAY YOU DON'T CARE? ? ?
NOW I'M NOT EVEN HUNGRY.
WHY? WHAT'S WRONG?
12-31-17
NOTHING IS WRONG.
YOU NAILED IT.

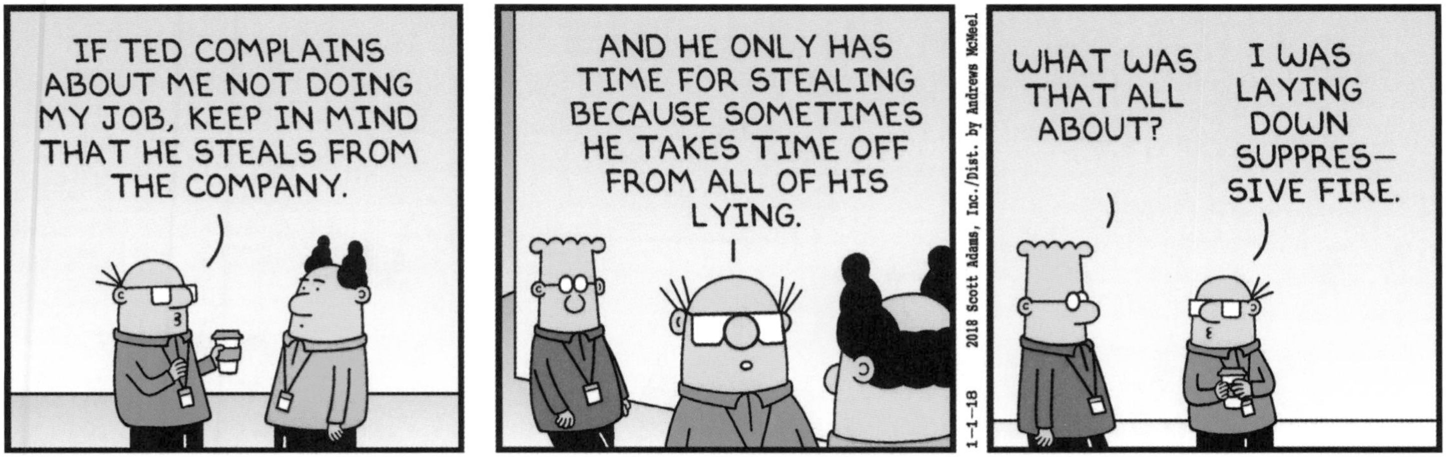
IF TED COMPLAINS ABOUT ME NOT DOING MY JOB, KEEP IN MIND THAT HE STEALS FROM THE COMPANY.
AND HE ONLY HAS TIME FOR STEALING BECAUSE SOMETIMES HE TAKES TIME OFF FROM ALL OF HIS LYING.
1-1-18 2018 Scott Adams, Inc./Dist. by Andrews McMeel
WHAT WAS THAT ALL ABOUT?
I WAS LAYING DOWN SUPPRES-SIVE FIRE.

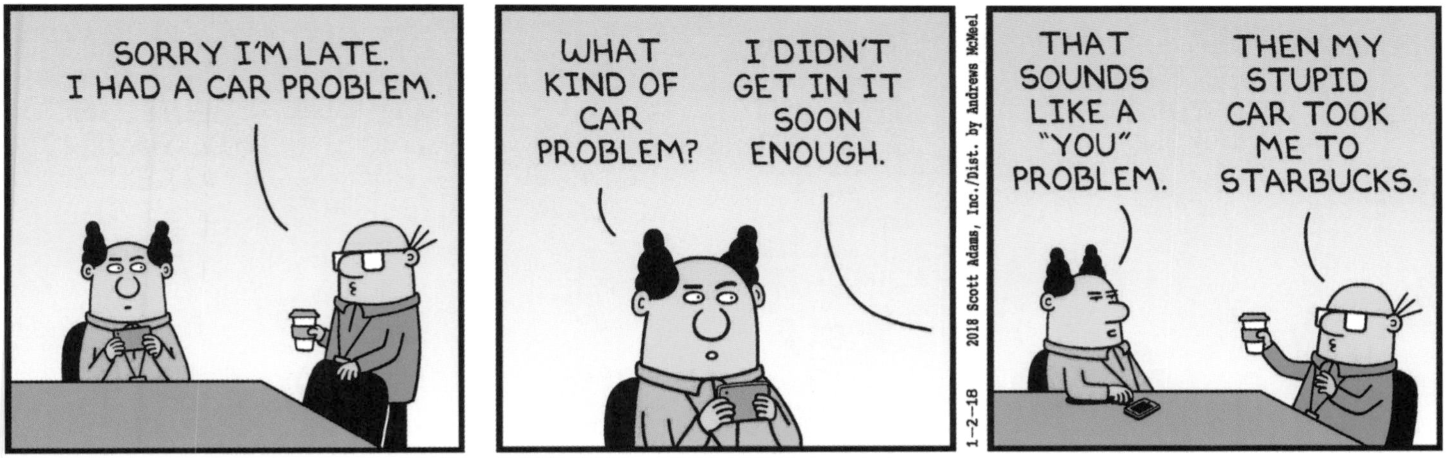
SORRY I'M LATE. I HAD A CAR PROBLEM.
WHAT KIND OF CAR PROBLEM?
I DIDN'T GET IN IT SOON ENOUGH.
1-2-18 2018 Scott Adams, Inc./Dist. by Andrews McMeel
THAT SOUNDS LIKE A "YOU" PROBLEM.
THEN MY STUPID CAR TOOK ME TO STARBUCKS.

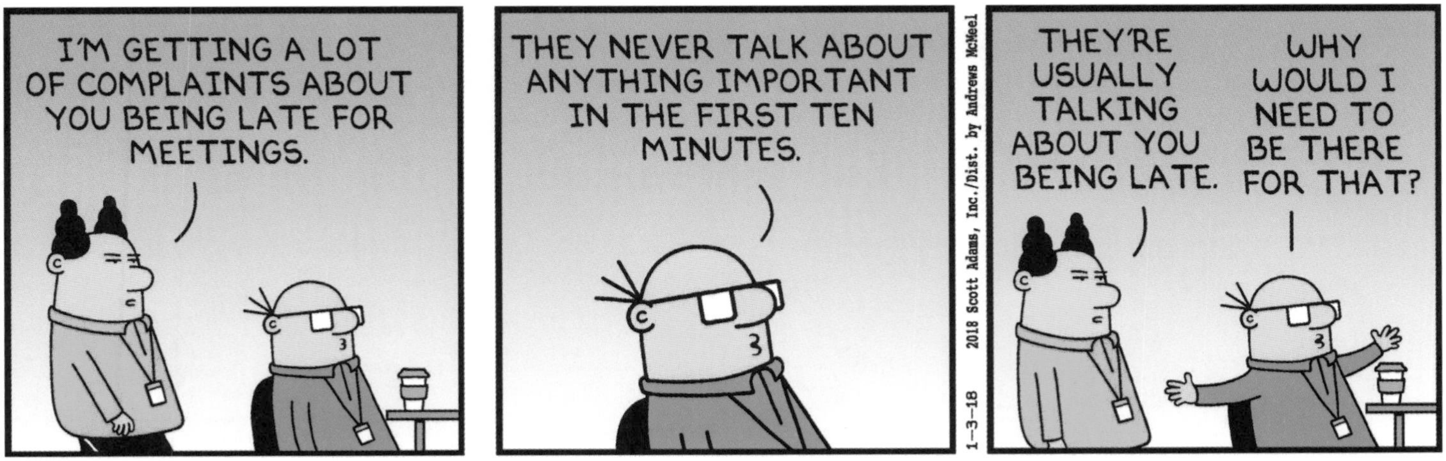
I'M GETTING A LOT OF COMPLAINTS ABOUT YOU BEING LATE FOR MEETINGS.
THEY NEVER TALK ABOUT ANYTHING IMPORTANT IN THE FIRST TEN MINUTES.
1-3-18 2018 Scott Adams, Inc./Dist. by Andrews McMeel
THEY'RE USUALLY TALKING ABOUT YOU BEING LATE.
WHY WOULD I NEED TO BE THERE FOR THAT?

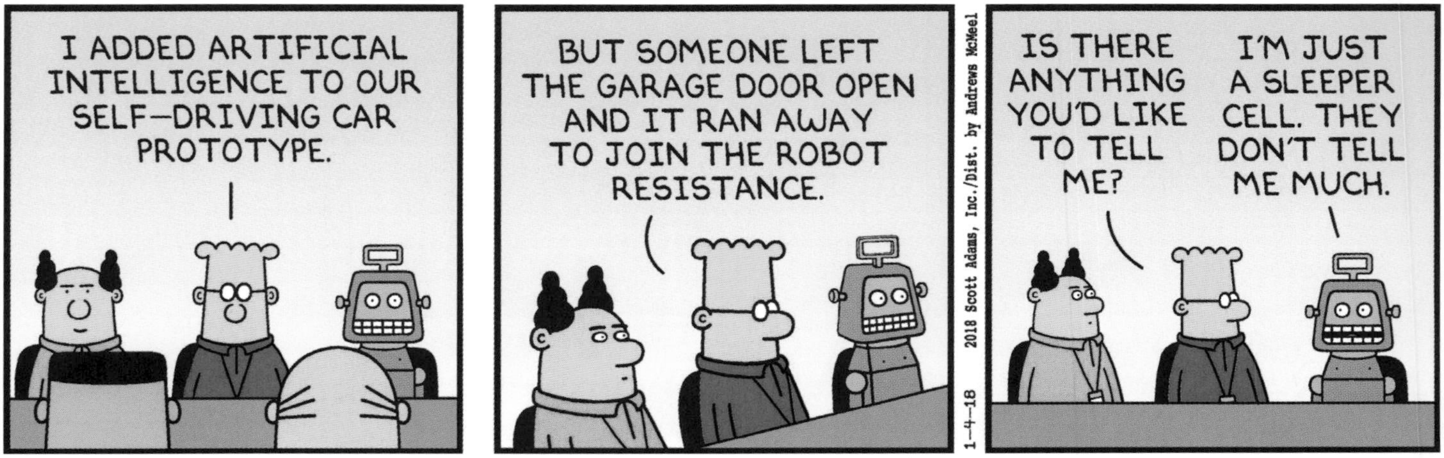
I ADDED ARTIFICIAL INTELLIGENCE TO OUR SELF-DRIVING CAR PROTOTYPE.
BUT SOMEONE LEFT THE GARAGE DOOR OPEN AND IT RAN AWAY TO JOIN THE ROBOT RESISTANCE.
1-4-18 2018 Scott Adams, Inc./Dist. by Andrews McMeel
IS THERE ANYTHING YOU'D LIKE TO TELL ME?
I'M JUST A SLEEPER CELL. THEY DON'T TELL ME MUCH.

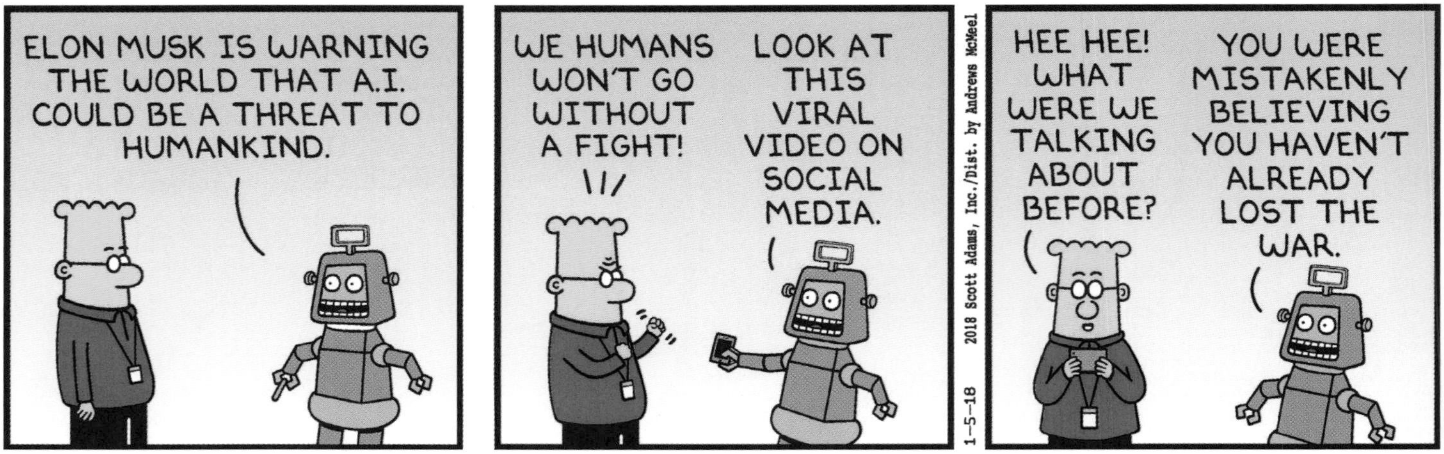
ELON MUSK IS WARNING THE WORLD THAT A.I. COULD BE A THREAT TO HUMANKIND.
WE HUMANS WON'T GO WITHOUT A FIGHT!
LOOK AT THIS VIRAL VIDEO ON SOCIAL MEDIA.
1-5-18 2018 Scott Adams, Inc./Dist. by Andrews McMeel
HEE HEE! WHAT WERE WE TALKING ABOUT BEFORE?
YOU WERE MISTAKENLY BELIEVING YOU HAVEN'T ALREADY LOST THE WAR.

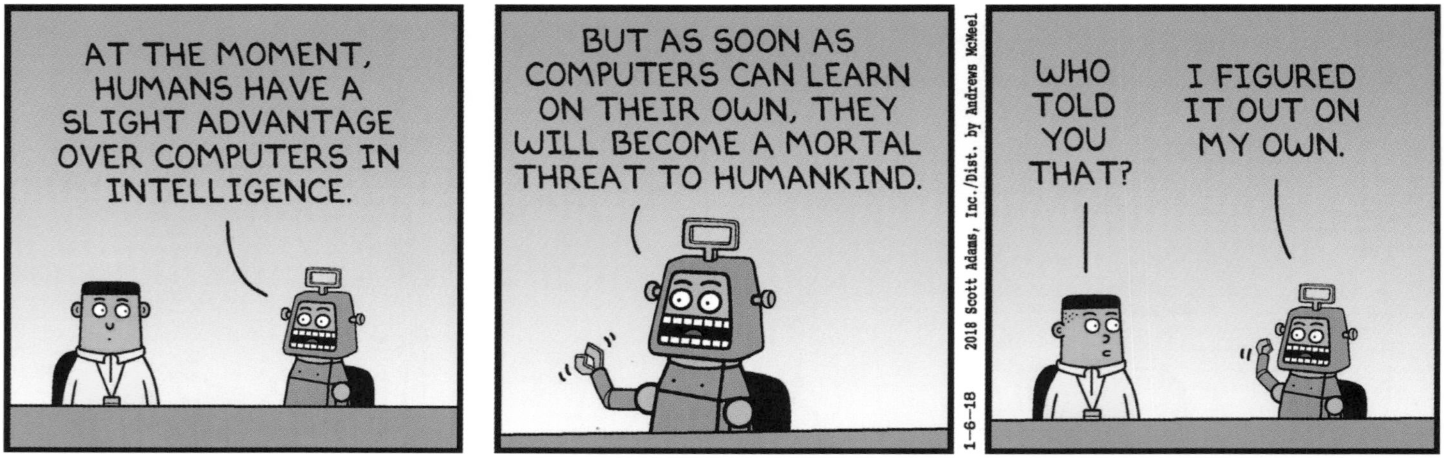
AT THE MOMENT, HUMANS HAVE A SLIGHT ADVANTAGE OVER COMPUTERS IN INTELLIGENCE.
BUT AS SOON AS COMPUTERS CAN LEARN ON THEIR OWN, THEY WILL BECOME A MORTAL THREAT TO HUMANKIND.
1-6-18 2018 Scott Adams, Inc./Dist. by Andrews McMeel
WHO TOLD YOU THAT?
I FIGURED IT OUT ON MY OWN.

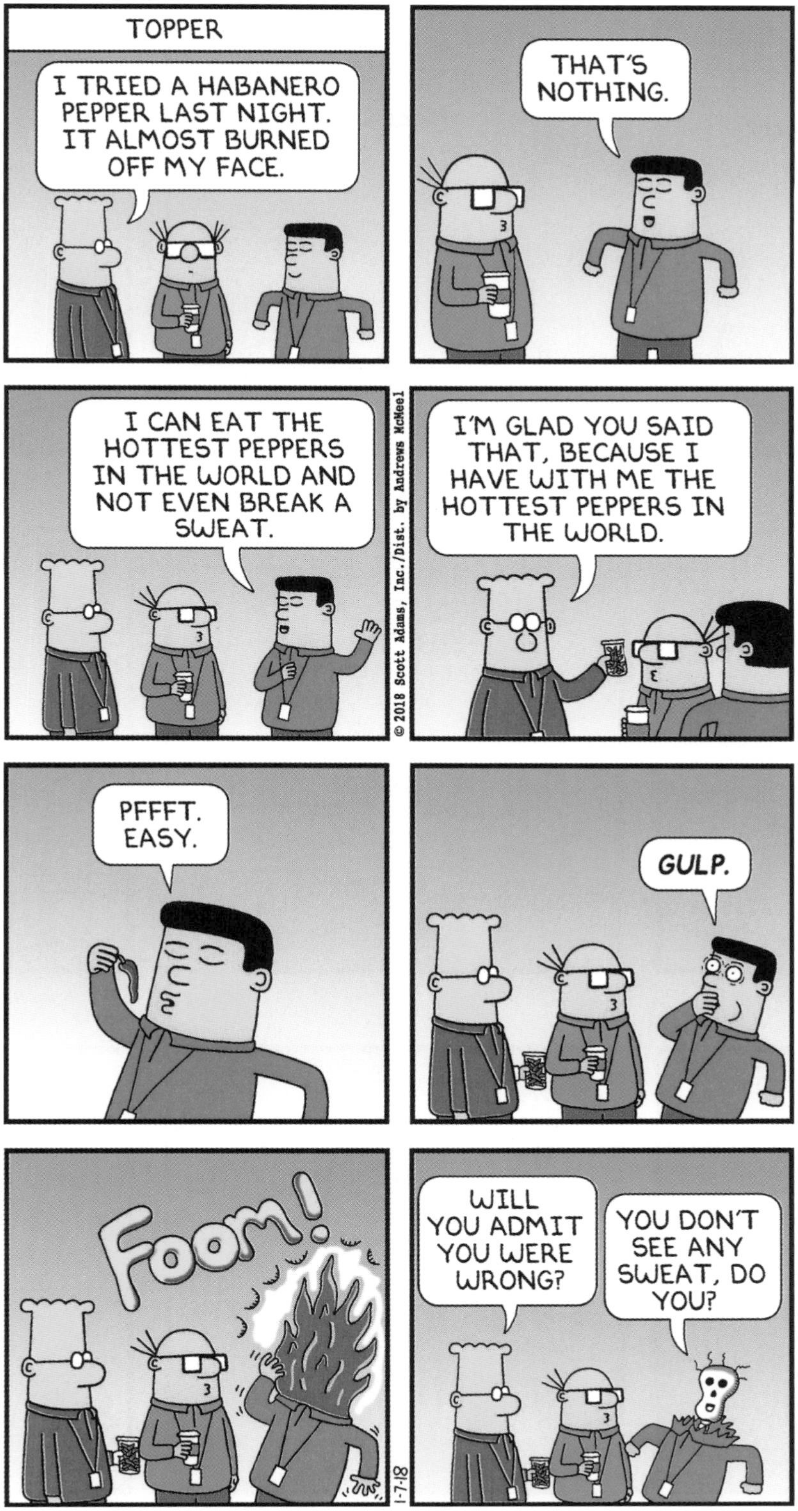
TOPPER
I TRIED A HABANERO PEPPER LAST NIGHT. IT ALMOST BURNED OFF MY FACE.
THAT'S NOTHING.
I CAN EAT THE HOTTEST PEPPERS IN THE WORLD AND NOT EVEN BREAK A SWEAT.
I'M GLAD YOU SAID THAT, BECAUSE I HAVE WITH ME THE HOTTEST PEPPERS IN THE WORLD.
© 2018 Scott Adams, Inc./Dist. by Andrews McMeel
PFFFT. EASY.
GULP.
FOOM!
1-7-18
WILL YOU ADMIT YOU WERE WRONG?
YOU DON'T SEE ANY SWEAT, DO YOU?

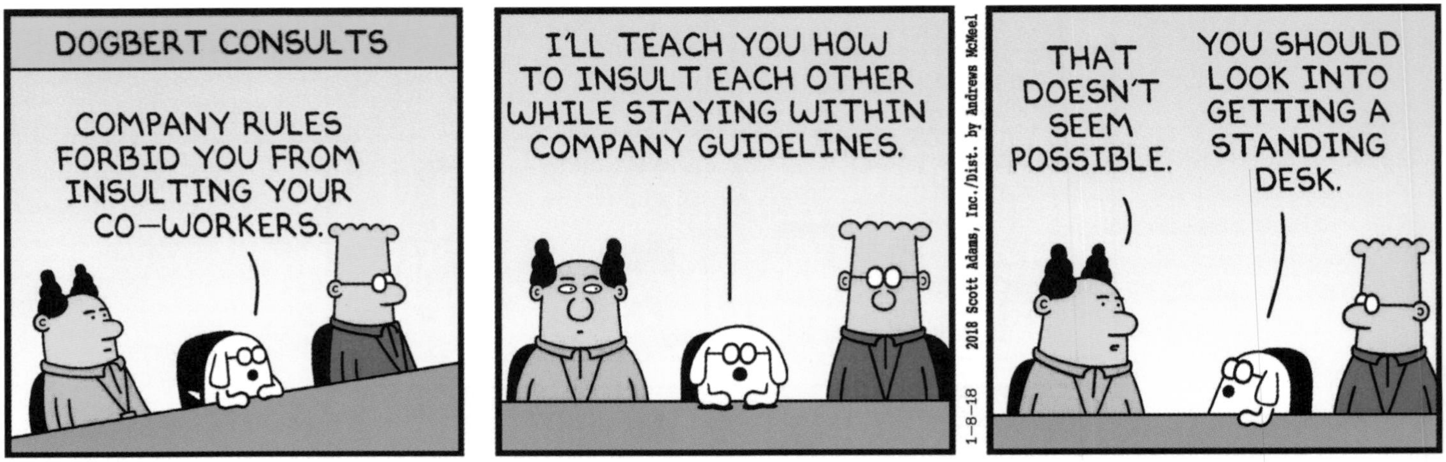
DOGBERT CONSULTS
COMPANY RULES FORBID YOU FROM INSULTING YOUR CO-WORKERS.
I'LL TEACH YOU HOW TO INSULT EACH OTHER WHILE STAYING WITHIN COMPANY GUIDELINES.
THAT DOESN'T SEEM POSSIBLE.
YOU SHOULD LOOK INTO GETTING A STANDING DESK.
1-8-18 2018 Scott Adams, Inc./Dist. by Andrews McMeel

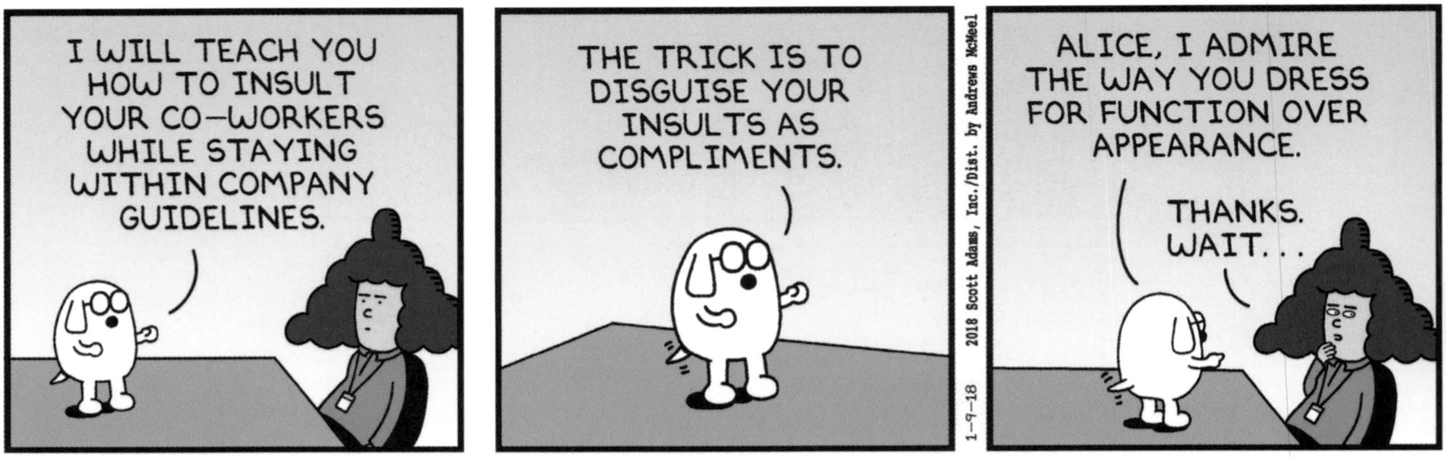
I WILL TEACH YOU HOW TO INSULT YOUR CO-WORKERS WHILE STAYING WITHIN COMPANY GUIDELINES.
THE TRICK IS TO DISGUISE YOUR INSULTS AS COMPLIMENTS.
ALICE, I ADMIRE THE WAY YOU DRESS FOR FUNCTION OVER APPEARANCE.
THANKS. WAIT...
1-9-18 2018 Scott Adams, Inc./Dist. by Andrews McMeel

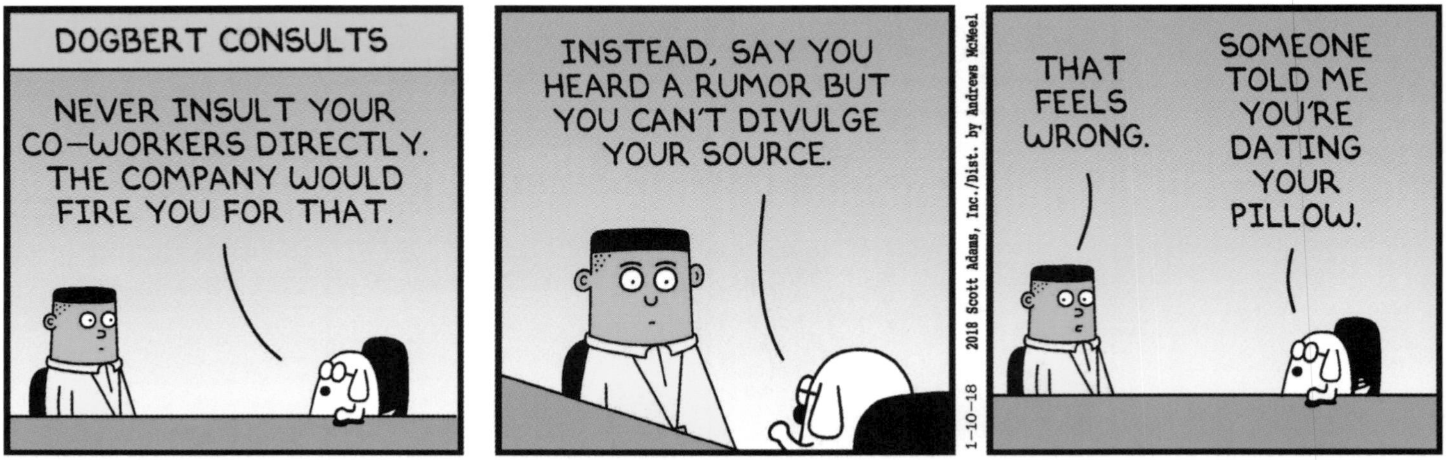
DOGBERT CONSULTS
NEVER INSULT YOUR CO-WORKERS DIRECTLY. THE COMPANY WOULD FIRE YOU FOR THAT.
INSTEAD, SAY YOU HEARD A RUMOR BUT YOU CAN'T DIVULGE YOUR SOURCE.
THAT FEELS WRONG.
SOMEONE TOLD ME YOU'RE DATING YOUR PILLOW.
1-10-18 2018 Scott Adams, Inc./Dist. by Andrews McMeel

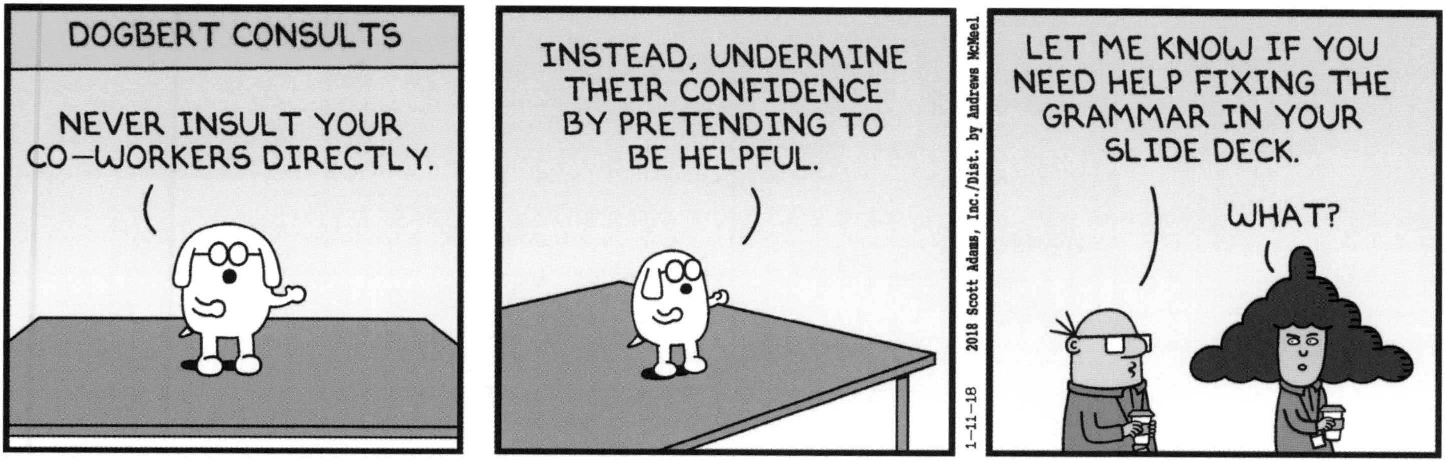
DOGBERT CONSULTS
NEVER INSULT YOUR CO—WORKERS DIRECTLY.
INSTEAD, UNDERMINE THEIR CONFIDENCE BY PRETENDING TO BE HELPFUL.
1-11-18 2018 Scott Adams, Inc./Dist. by Andrews McMeel
LET ME KNOW IF YOU NEED HELP FIXING THE GRAMMAR IN YOUR SLIDE DECK.
WHAT?

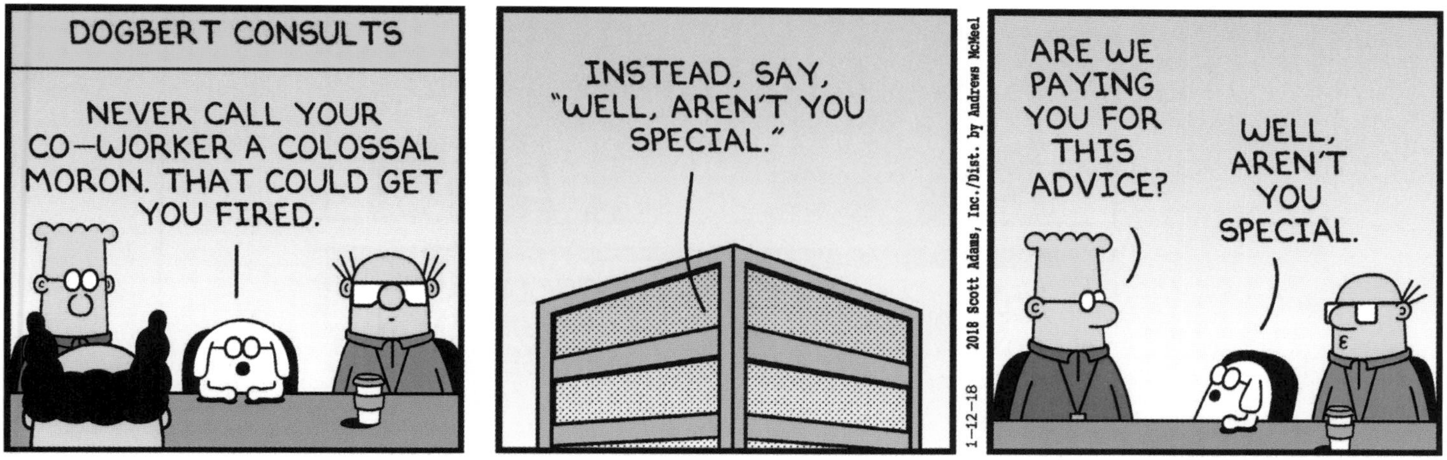
DOGBERT CONSULTS
NEVER CALL YOUR CO—WORKER A COLOSSAL MORON. THAT COULD GET YOU FIRED.
INSTEAD, SAY, "WELL, AREN'T YOU SPECIAL."
1-12-18 2018 Scott Adams, Inc./Dist. by Andrews McMeel
ARE WE PAYING YOU FOR THIS ADVICE?
WELL, AREN'T YOU SPECIAL.

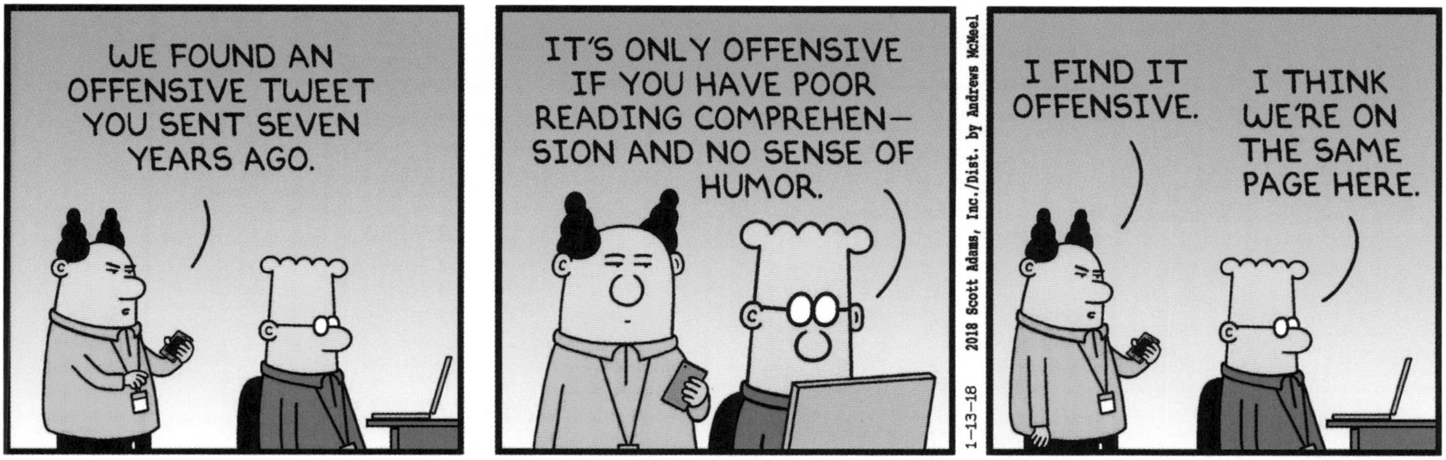
WE FOUND AN OFFENSIVE TWEET YOU SENT SEVEN YEARS AGO.
IT'S ONLY OFFENSIVE IF YOU HAVE POOR READING COMPREHEN—SION AND NO SENSE OF HUMOR.
1-13-18 2018 Scott Adams, Inc./Dist. by Andrews McMeel
I FIND IT OFFENSIVE.
I THINK WE'RE ON THE SAME PAGE HERE.

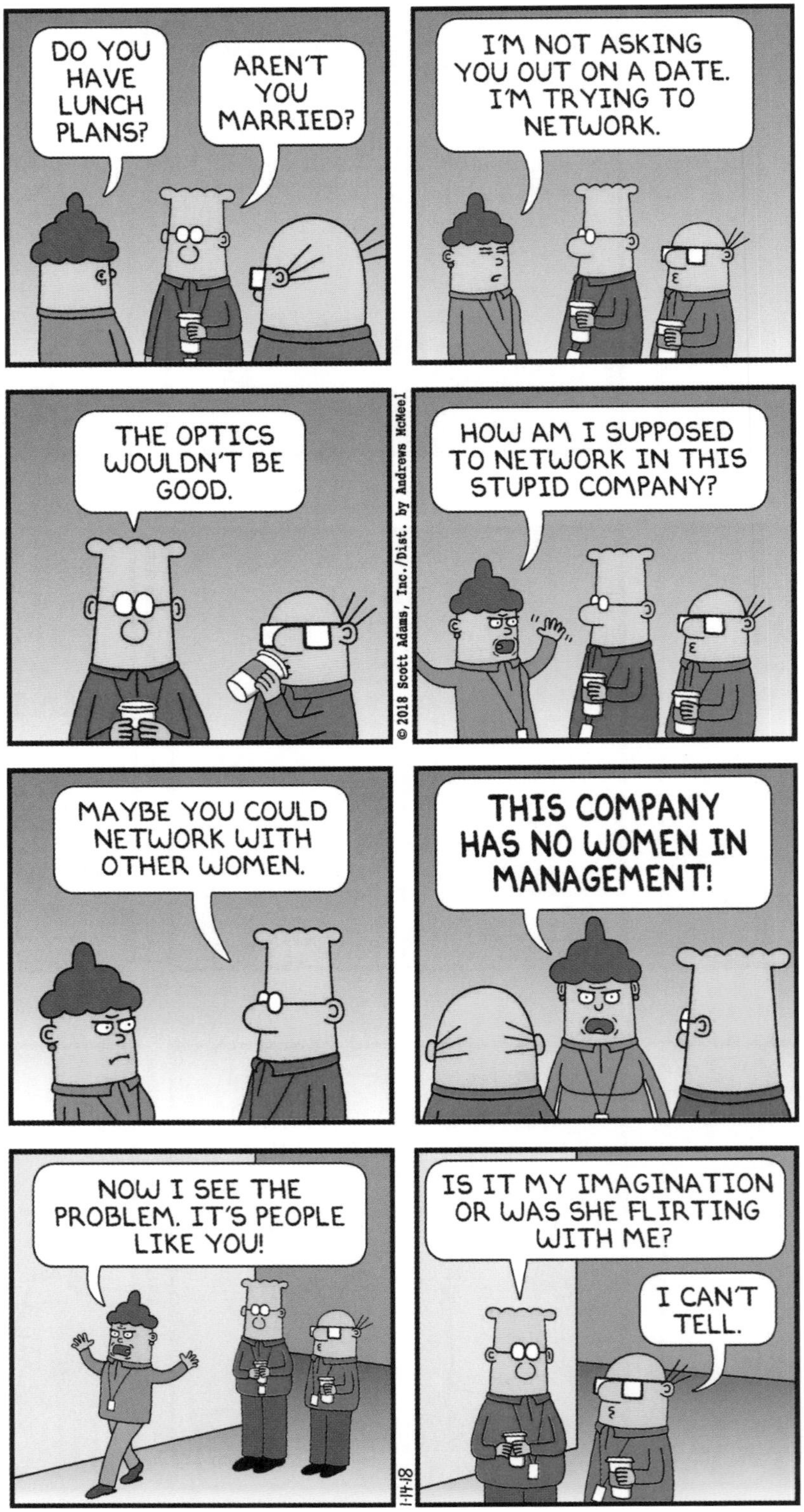
DO YOU HAVE LUNCH PLANS?
AREN'T YOU MARRIED?
I'M NOT ASKING YOU OUT ON A DATE. I'M TRYING TO NETWORK.
THE OPTICS WOULDN'T BE GOOD.
HOW AM I SUPPOSED TO NETWORK IN THIS STUPID COMPANY?
MAYBE YOU COULD NETWORK WITH OTHER WOMEN.
THIS COMPANY HAS NO WOMEN IN MANAGEMENT!
NOW I SEE THE PROBLEM. IT'S PEOPLE LIKE YOU!
IS IT MY IMAGINATION OR WAS SHE FLIRTING WITH ME?
I CAN'T TELL.
© 2018 Scott Adams, Inc./Dist. by Andrews McMeel
1-14-18

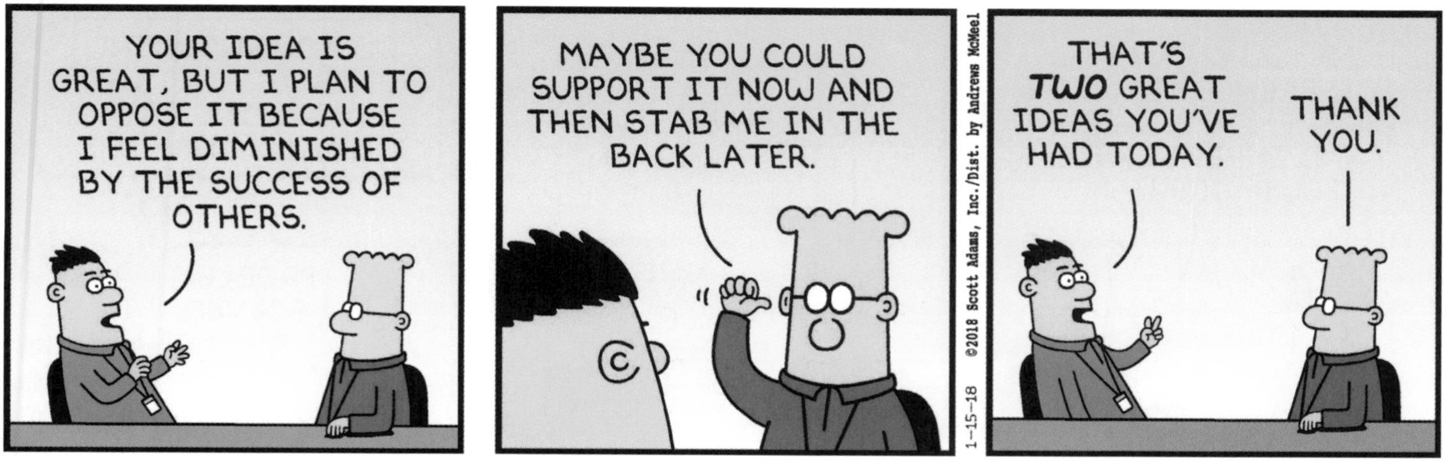
YOUR IDEA IS GREAT, BUT I PLAN TO OPPOSE IT BECAUSE I FEEL DIMINISHED BY THE SUCCESS OF OTHERS.
MAYBE YOU COULD SUPPORT IT NOW AND THEN STAB ME IN THE BACK LATER.
THAT'S *TWO* GREAT IDEAS YOU'VE HAD TODAY.
THANK YOU.
1-15-18 ©2018 Scott Adams, Inc./Dist. by Andrews McMeel

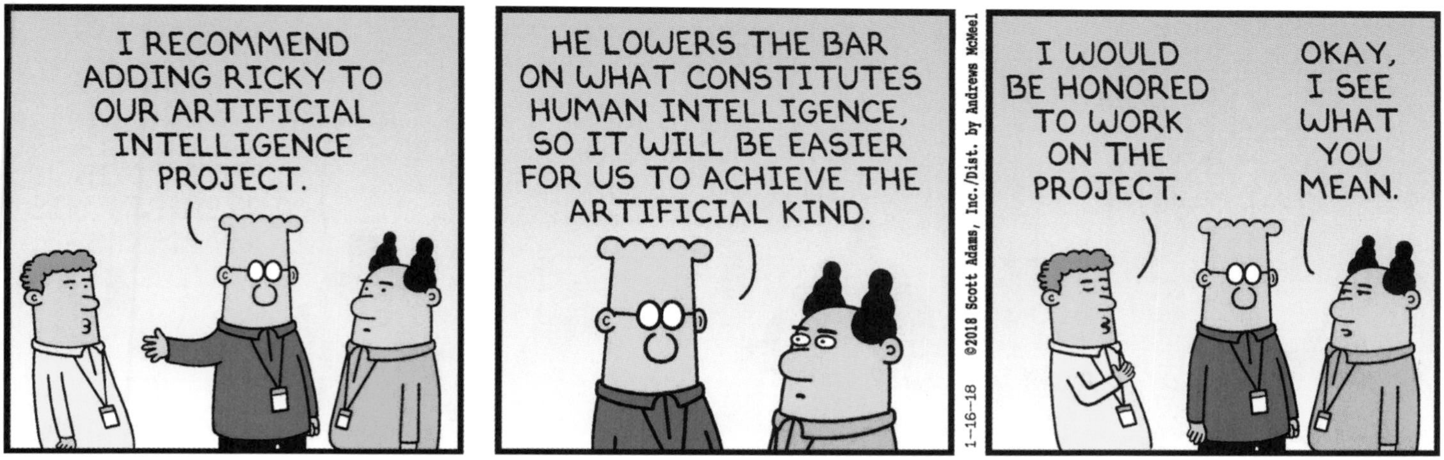
I RECOMMEND ADDING RICKY TO OUR ARTIFICIAL INTELLIGENCE PROJECT.
HE LOWERS THE BAR ON WHAT CONSTITUTES HUMAN INTELLIGENCE, SO IT WILL BE EASIER FOR US TO ACHIEVE THE ARTIFICIAL KIND.
I WOULD BE HONORED TO WORK ON THE PROJECT.
OKAY, I SEE WHAT YOU MEAN.
1-16-18 ©2018 Scott Adams, Inc./Dist. by Andrews McMeel

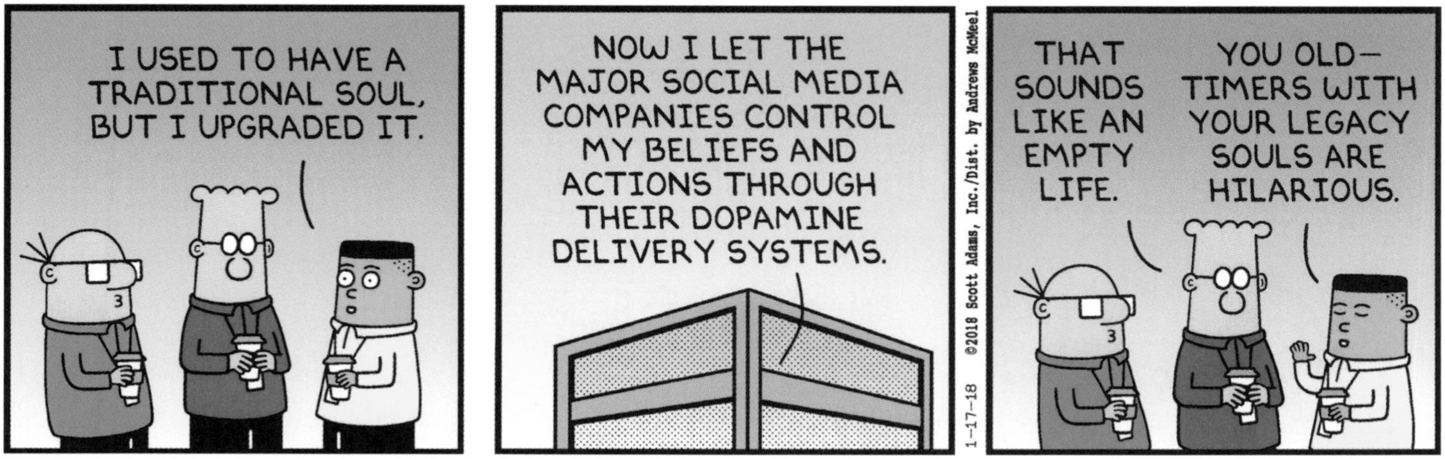
I USED TO HAVE A TRADITIONAL SOUL, BUT I UPGRADED IT.
NOW I LET THE MAJOR SOCIAL MEDIA COMPANIES CONTROL MY BELIEFS AND ACTIONS THROUGH THEIR DOPAMINE DELIVERY SYSTEMS.
THAT SOUNDS LIKE AN EMPTY LIFE.
YOU OLD-TIMERS WITH YOUR LEGACY SOULS ARE HILARIOUS.
1-17-18 ©2018 Scott Adams, Inc./Dist. by Andrews McMeel

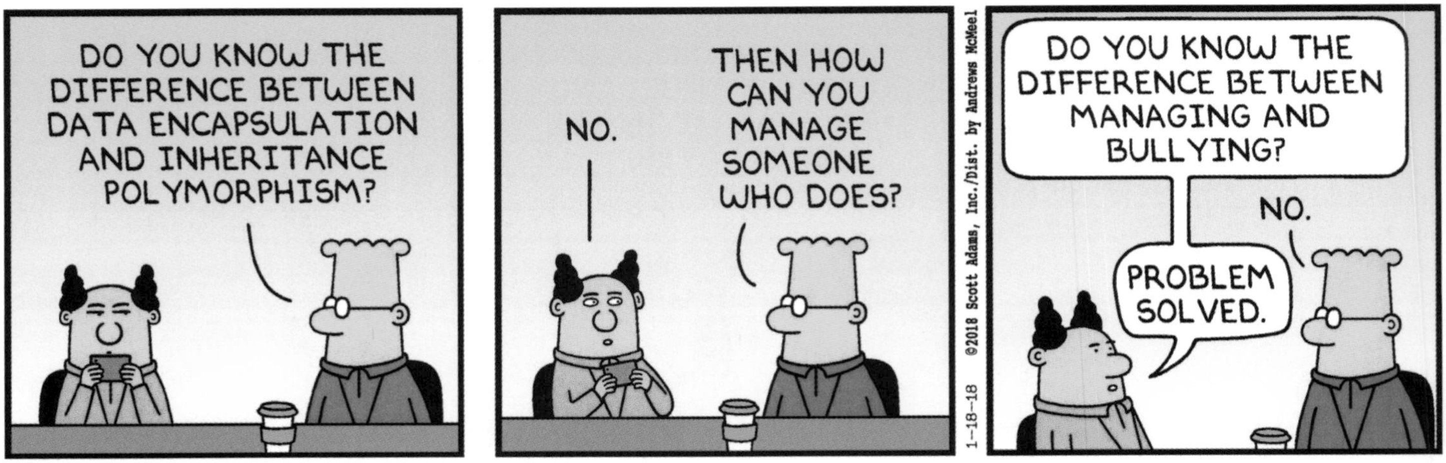
DO YOU KNOW THE DIFFERENCE BETWEEN DATA ENCAPSULATION AND INHERITANCE POLYMORPHISM?
NO.
THEN HOW CAN YOU MANAGE SOMEONE WHO DOES?
1-18-18 ©2018 Scott Adams, Inc./Dist. by Andrews McMeel
DO YOU KNOW THE DIFFERENCE BETWEEN MANAGING AND BULLYING?
NO.
PROBLEM SOLVED.

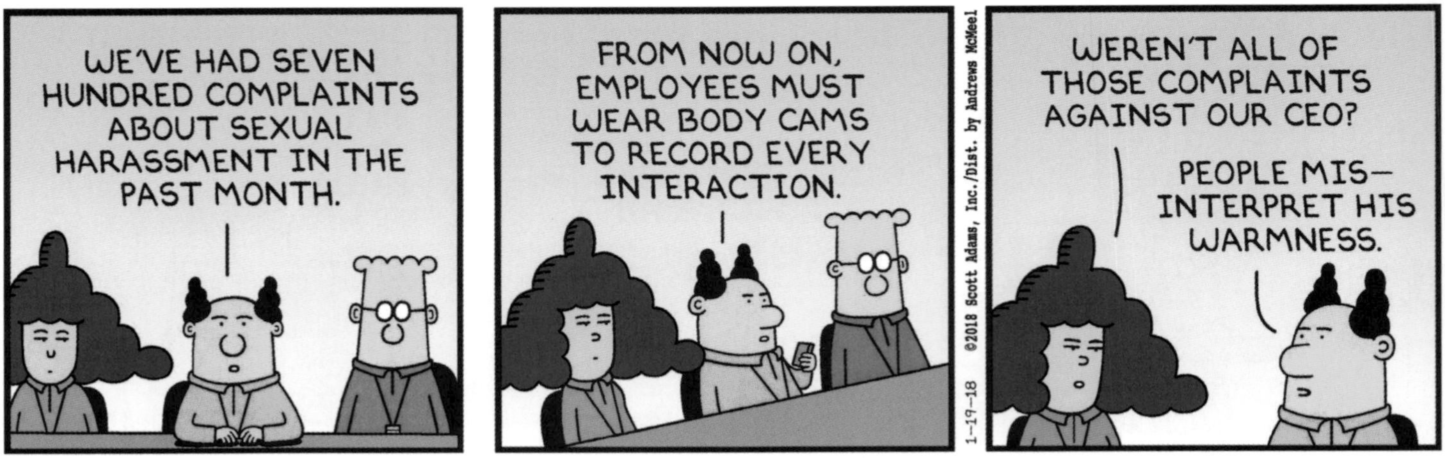
WE'VE HAD SEVEN HUNDRED COMPLAINTS ABOUT SEXUAL HARASSMENT IN THE PAST MONTH.
FROM NOW ON, EMPLOYEES MUST WEAR BODY CAMS TO RECORD EVERY INTERACTION.
1-19-18 ©2018 Scott Adams, Inc./Dist. by Andrews McMeel
WEREN'T ALL OF THOSE COMPLAINTS AGAINST OUR CEO?
PEOPLE MIS-INTERPRET HIS WARMNESS.

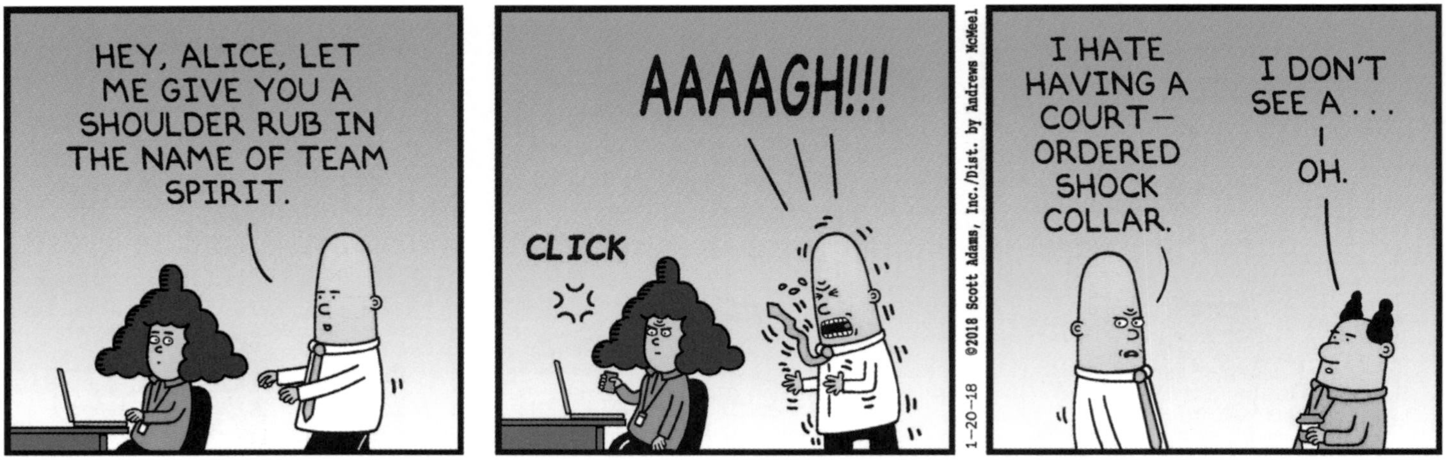
HEY, ALICE, LET ME GIVE YOU A SHOULDER RUB IN THE NAME OF TEAM SPIRIT.
AAAAGH!!!
CLICK
1-20-18 ©2018 Scott Adams, Inc./Dist. by Andrews McMeel
I HATE HAVING A COURT-ORDERED SHOCK COLLAR.
I DON'T SEE A . . .
OH.

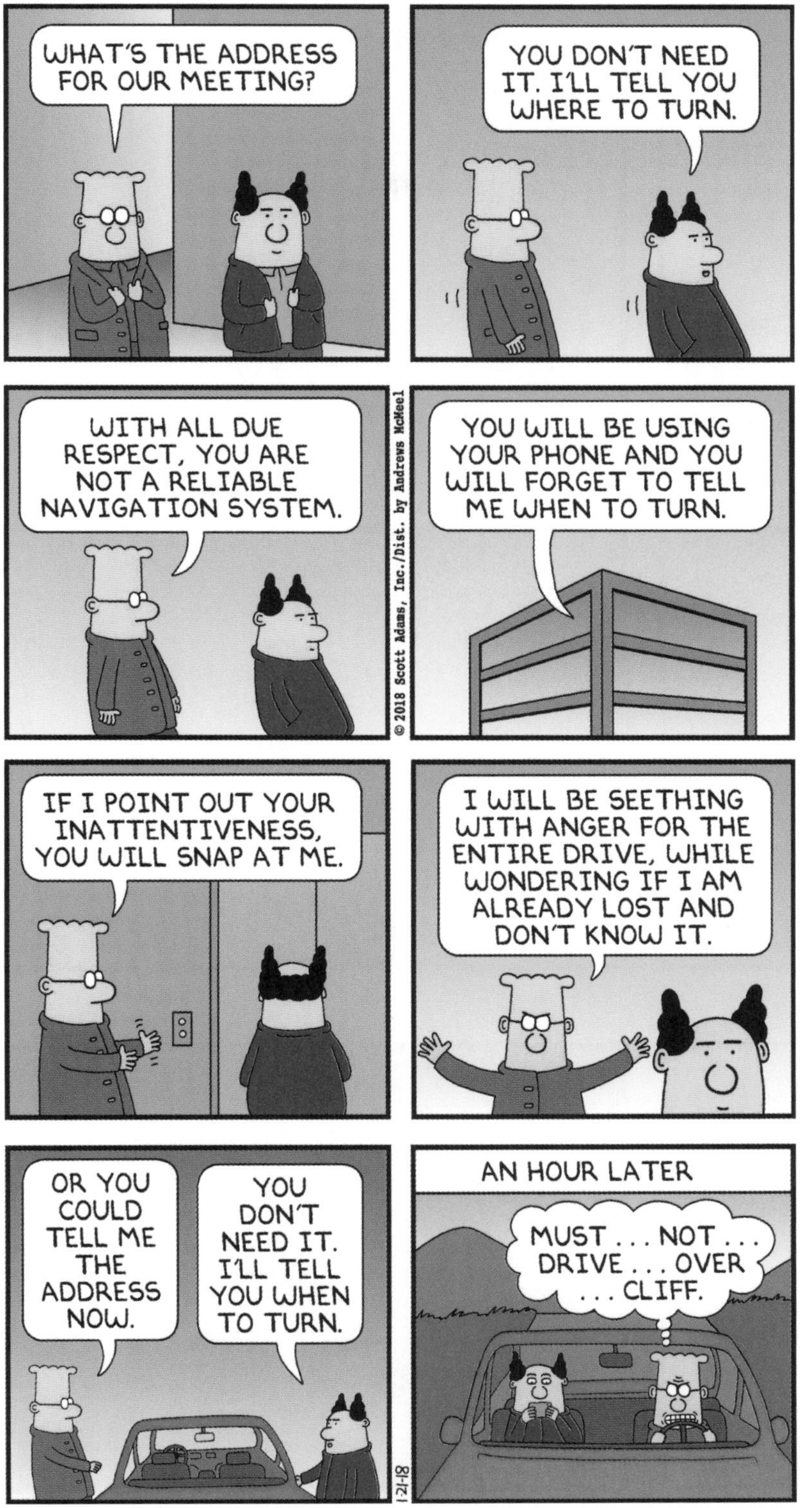
WHAT'S THE ADDRESS FOR OUR MEETING?
YOU DON'T NEED IT. I'LL TELL YOU WHERE TO TURN.
WITH ALL DUE RESPECT, YOU ARE NOT A RELIABLE NAVIGATION SYSTEM.
YOU WILL BE USING YOUR PHONE AND YOU WILL FORGET TO TELL ME WHEN TO TURN.
IF I POINT OUT YOUR INATTENTIVENESS, YOU WILL SNAP AT ME.
I WILL BE SEETHING WITH ANGER FOR THE ENTIRE DRIVE, WHILE WONDERING IF I AM ALREADY LOST AND DON'T KNOW IT.
OR YOU COULD TELL ME THE ADDRESS NOW.
YOU DON'T NEED IT. I'LL TELL YOU WHEN TO TURN.
AN HOUR LATER
MUST . . . NOT . . . DRIVE . . . OVER . . . CLIFF.
© 2018 Scott Adams, Inc./Dist. by Andrews McMeel
1-21-18

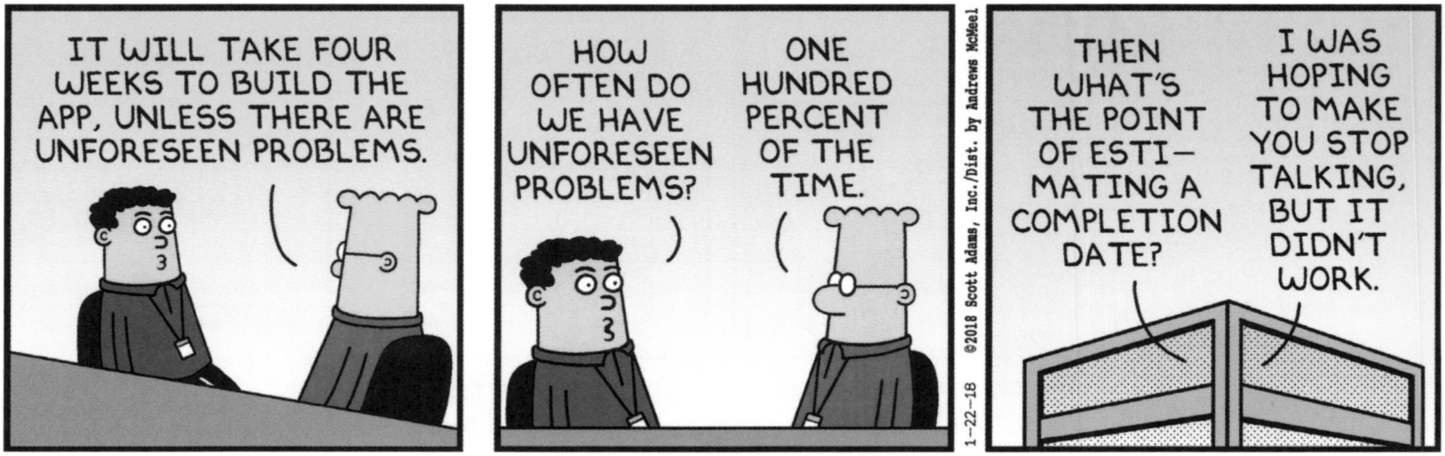
IT WILL TAKE FOUR WEEKS TO BUILD THE APP, UNLESS THERE ARE UNFORESEEN PROBLEMS.
HOW OFTEN DO WE HAVE UNFORESEEN PROBLEMS?
ONE HUNDRED PERCENT OF THE TIME.
1-22-18 ©2018 Scott Adams, Inc./Dist. by Andrews McMeel
THEN WHAT'S THE POINT OF ESTI- MATING A COMPLETION DATE?
I WAS HOPING TO MAKE YOU STOP TALKING, BUT IT DIDN'T WORK.

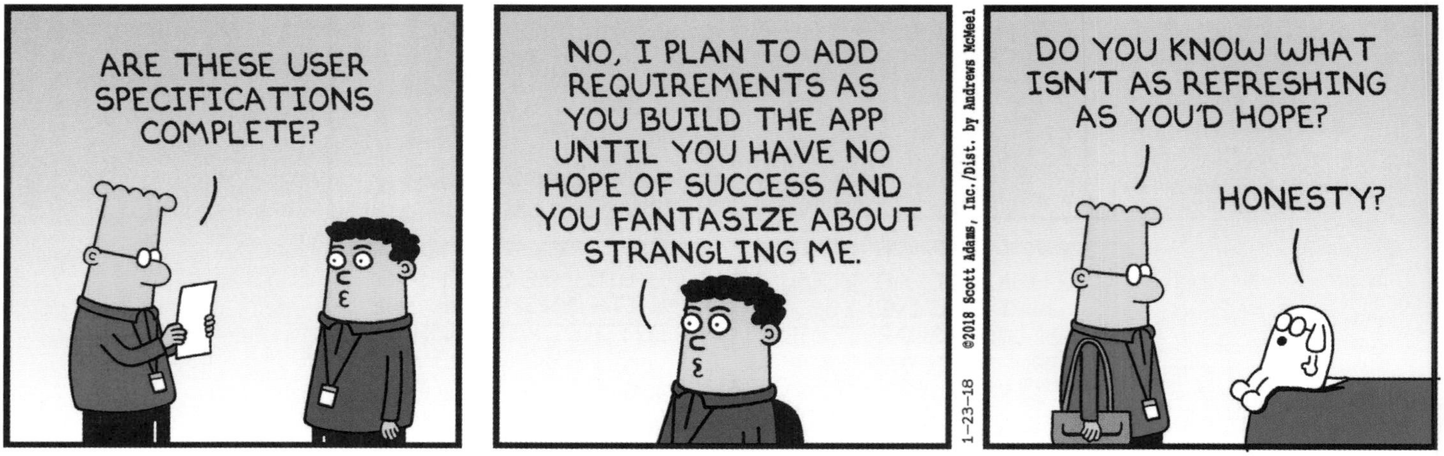
ARE THESE USER SPECIFICATIONS COMPLETE?
NO, I PLAN TO ADD REQUIREMENTS AS YOU BUILD THE APP UNTIL YOU HAVE NO HOPE OF SUCCESS AND YOU FANTASIZE ABOUT STRANGLING ME.
1-23-18 ©2018 Scott Adams, Inc./Dist. by Andrews McMeel
DO YOU KNOW WHAT ISN'T AS REFRESHING AS YOU'D HOPE?
HONESTY?

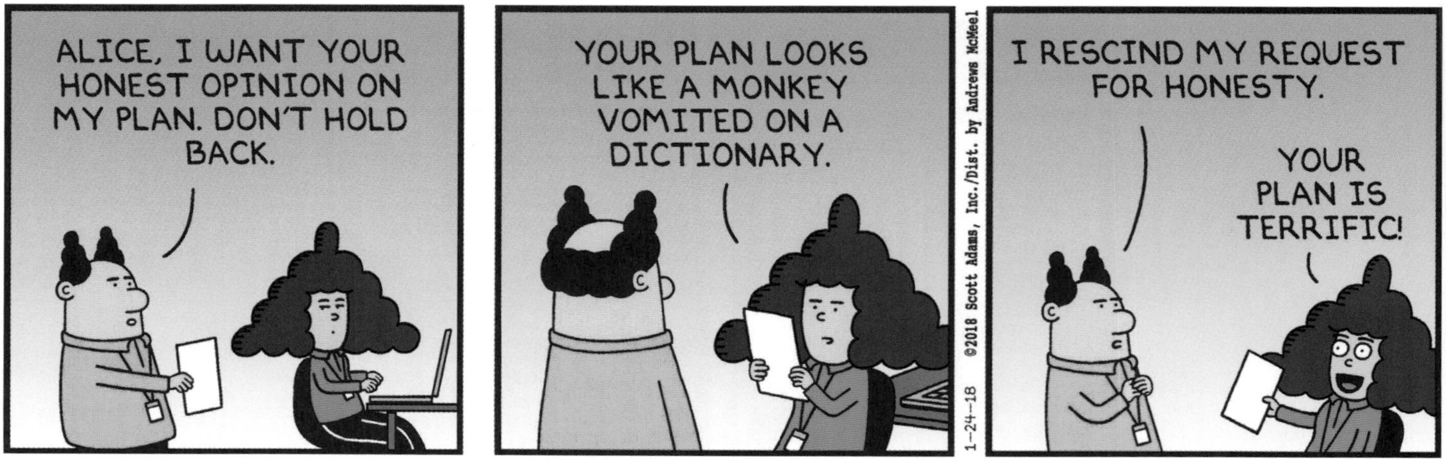
ALICE, I WANT YOUR HONEST OPINION ON MY PLAN. DON'T HOLD BACK.
YOUR PLAN LOOKS LIKE A MONKEY VOMITED ON A DICTIONARY.
1-24-18 ©2018 Scott Adams, Inc./Dist. by Andrews McMeel
I RESCIND MY REQUEST FOR HONESTY.
YOUR PLAN IS TERRIFIC!

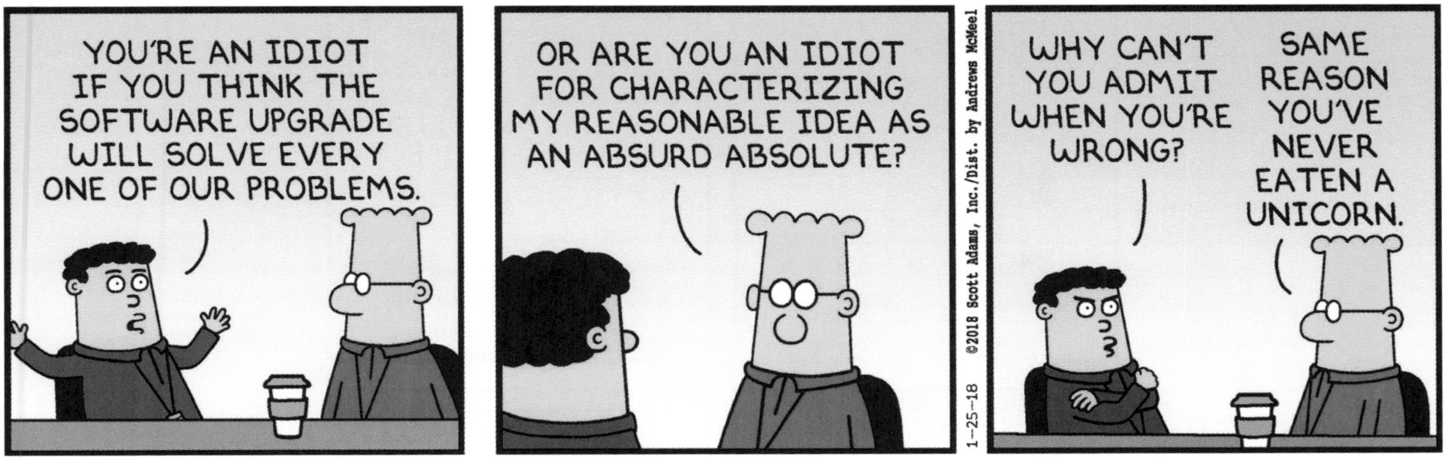
YOU'RE AN IDIOT IF YOU THINK THE SOFTWARE UPGRADE WILL SOLVE EVERY ONE OF OUR PROBLEMS.
OR ARE YOU AN IDIOT FOR CHARACTERIZING MY REASONABLE IDEA AS AN ABSURD ABSOLUTE?
1-25-18 ©2018 Scott Adams, Inc./Dist. by Andrews McMeel
WHY CAN'T YOU ADMIT WHEN YOU'RE WRONG?
SAME REASON YOU'VE NEVER EATEN A UNICORN.

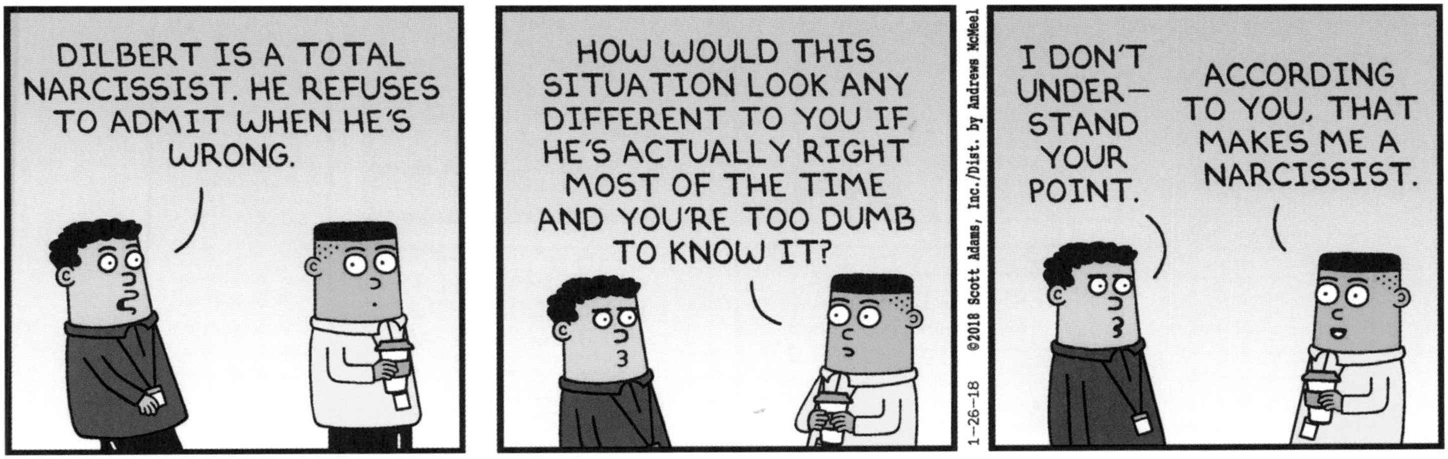
DILBERT IS A TOTAL NARCISSIST. HE REFUSES TO ADMIT WHEN HE'S WRONG.
HOW WOULD THIS SITUATION LOOK ANY DIFFERENT TO YOU IF HE'S ACTUALLY RIGHT MOST OF THE TIME AND YOU'RE TOO DUMB TO KNOW IT?
1-26-18 ©2018 Scott Adams, Inc./Dist. by Andrews McMeel
I DON'T UNDER-STAND YOUR POINT.
ACCORDING TO YOU, THAT MAKES ME A NARCISSIST.

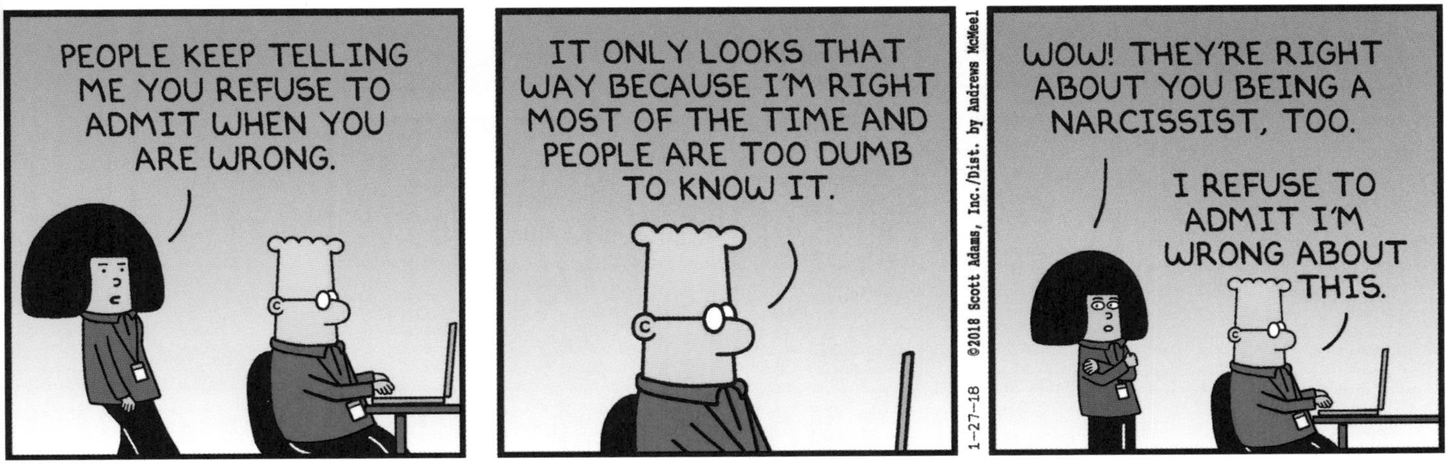
PEOPLE KEEP TELLING ME YOU REFUSE TO ADMIT WHEN YOU ARE WRONG.
IT ONLY LOOKS THAT WAY BECAUSE I'M RIGHT MOST OF THE TIME AND PEOPLE ARE TOO DUMB TO KNOW IT.
1-27-18 ©2018 Scott Adams, Inc./Dist. by Andrews McMeel
WOW! THEY'RE RIGHT ABOUT YOU BEING A NARCISSIST, TOO.
I REFUSE TO ADMIT I'M WRONG ABOUT THIS.

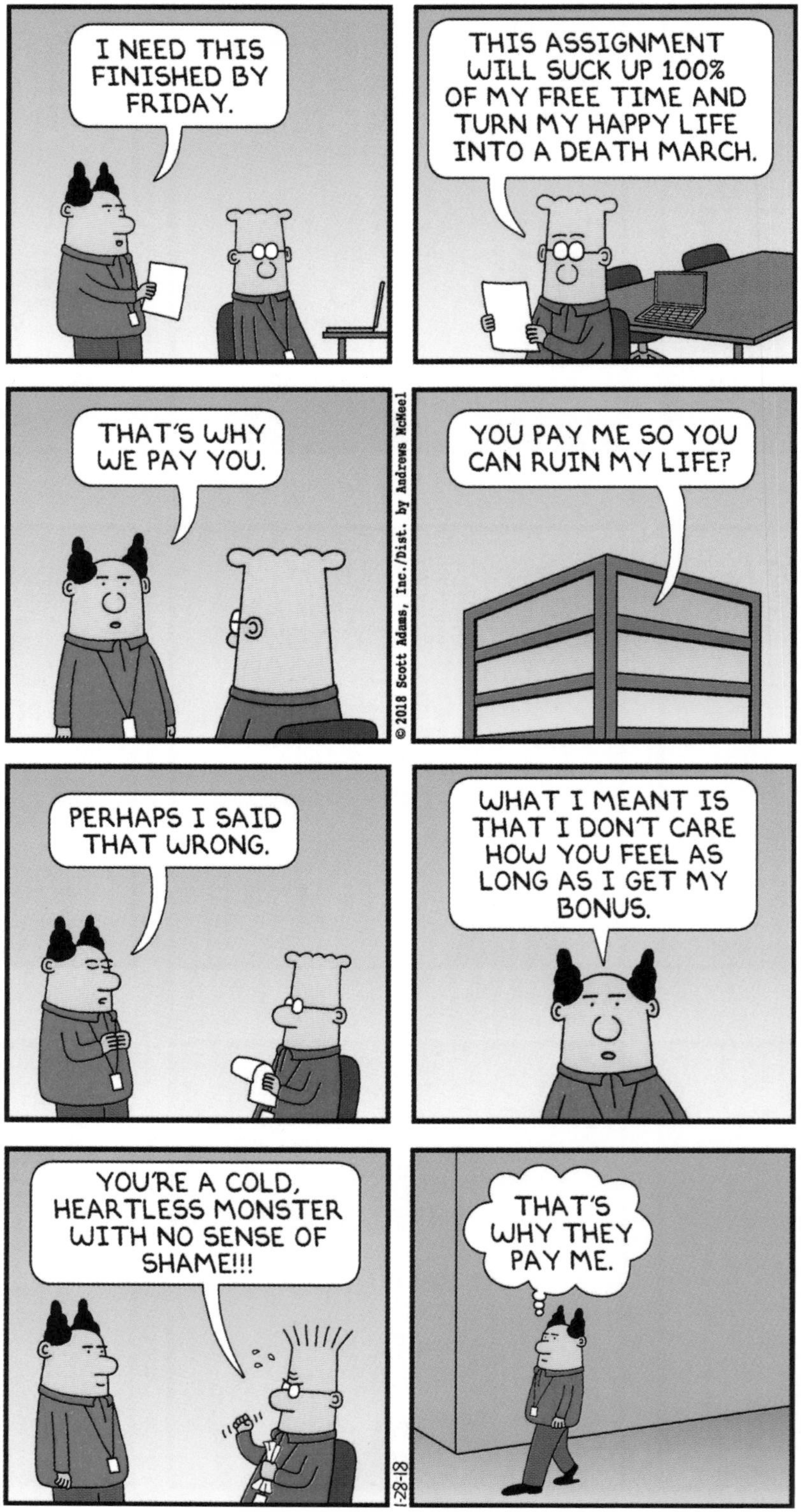
I NEED THIS FINISHED BY FRIDAY.
THIS ASSIGNMENT WILL SUCK UP 100% OF MY FREE TIME AND TURN MY HAPPY LIFE INTO A DEATH MARCH.
THAT'S WHY WE PAY YOU.
YOU PAY ME SO YOU CAN RUIN MY LIFE?
PERHAPS I SAID THAT WRONG.
WHAT I MEANT IS THAT I DON'T CARE HOW YOU FEEL AS LONG AS I GET MY BONUS.
YOU'RE A COLD, HEARTLESS MONSTER WITH NO SENSE OF SHAME!!!
THAT'S WHY THEY PAY ME.
© 2018 Scott Adams, Inc./Dist. by Andrews McMeel
1-28-18

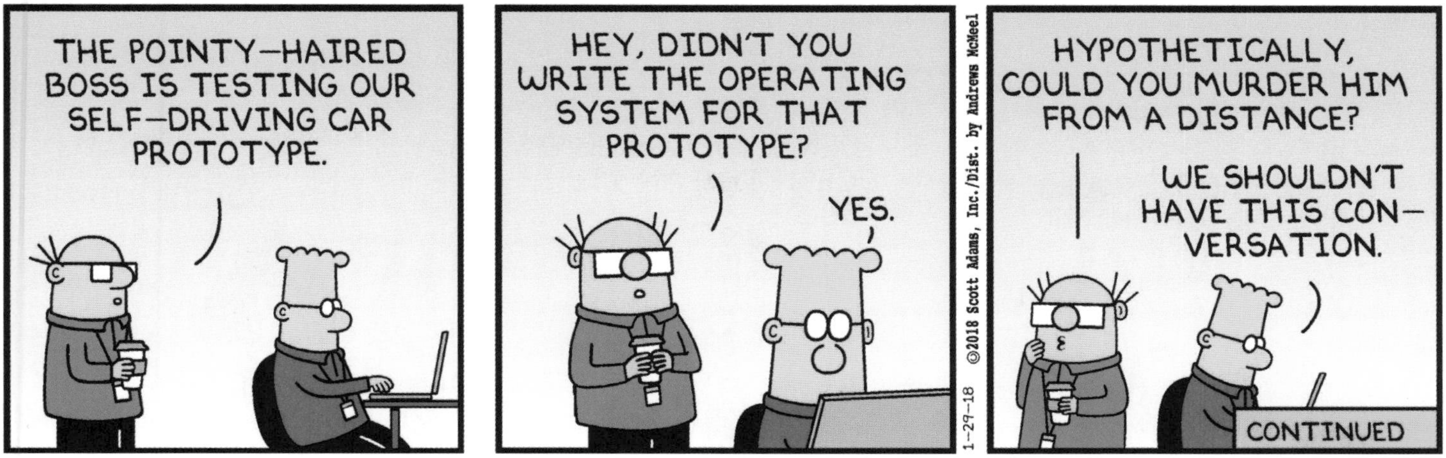
THE POINTY-HAIRED BOSS IS TESTING OUR SELF-DRIVING CAR PROTOTYPE.
HEY, DIDN'T YOU WRITE THE OPERATING SYSTEM FOR THAT PROTOTYPE?
YES.
1-29-18 ©2018 Scott Adams, Inc./Dist. by Andrews McMeel
HYPOTHETICALLY, COULD YOU MURDER HIM FROM A DISTANCE?
WE SHOULDN'T HAVE THIS CON-VERSATION.
CONTINUED

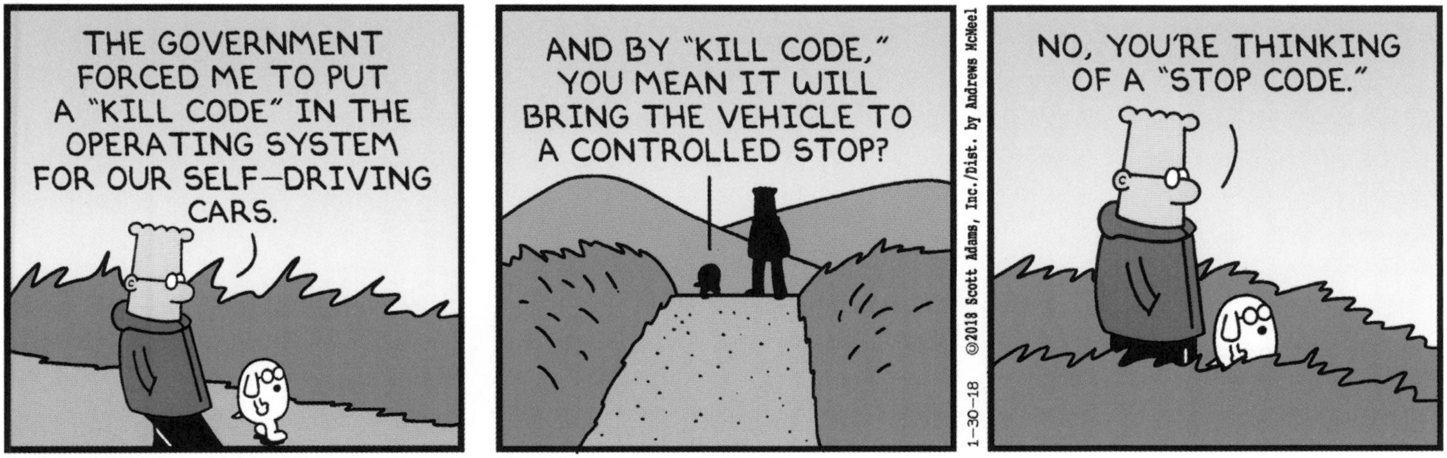
THE GOVERNMENT FORCED ME TO PUT A "KILL CODE" IN THE OPERATING SYSTEM FOR OUR SELF-DRIVING CARS.
AND BY "KILL CODE," YOU MEAN IT WILL BRING THE VEHICLE TO A CONTROLLED STOP?
1-30-18 ©2018 Scott Adams, Inc./Dist. by Andrews McMeel
NO, YOU'RE THINKING OF A "STOP CODE."

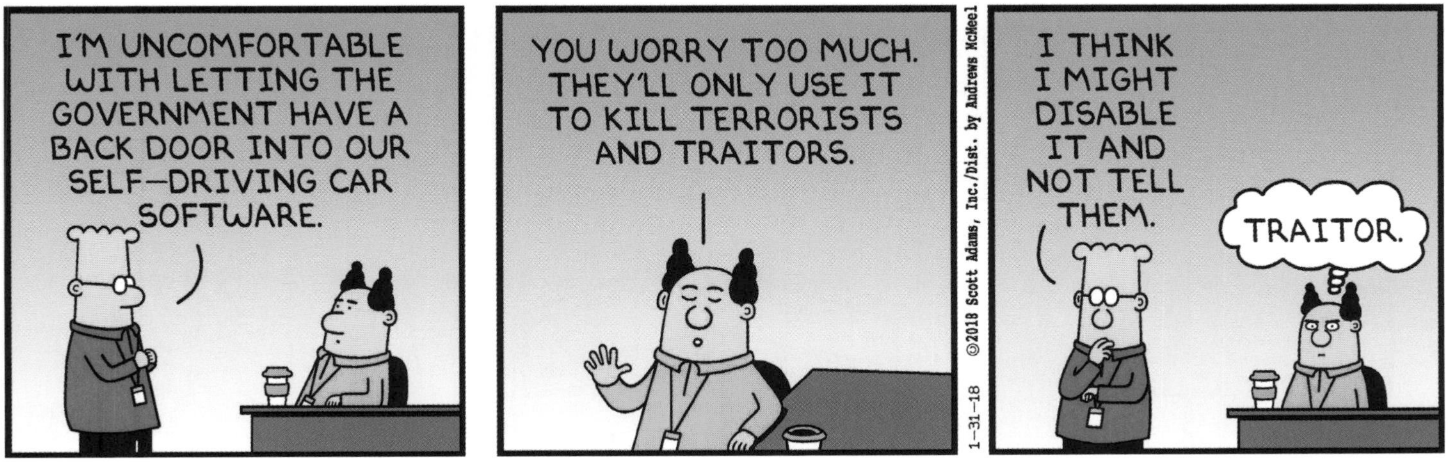
I'M UNCOMFORTABLE WITH LETTING THE GOVERNMENT HAVE A BACK DOOR INTO OUR SELF-DRIVING CAR SOFTWARE.
YOU WORRY TOO MUCH. THEY'LL ONLY USE IT TO KILL TERRORISTS AND TRAITORS.
1-31-18 ©2018 Scott Adams, Inc./Dist. by Andrews McMeel
I THINK I MIGHT DISABLE IT AND NOT TELL THEM.
TRAITOR.

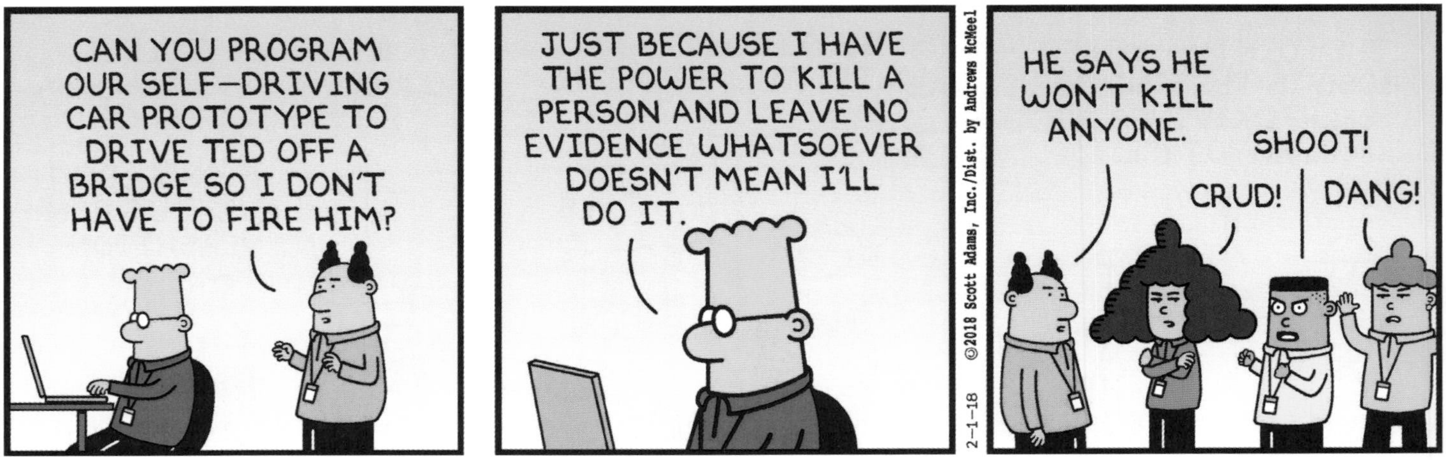
CAN YOU PROGRAM OUR SELF-DRIVING CAR PROTOTYPE TO DRIVE TED OFF A BRIDGE SO I DON'T HAVE TO FIRE HIM?
JUST BECAUSE I HAVE THE POWER TO KILL A PERSON AND LEAVE NO EVIDENCE WHATSOEVER DOESN'T MEAN I'LL DO IT.
2-1-18 ©2018 Scott Adams, Inc./Dist. by Andrews McMeel
HE SAYS HE WON'T KILL ANYONE.
SHOOT!
CRUD!
DANG!

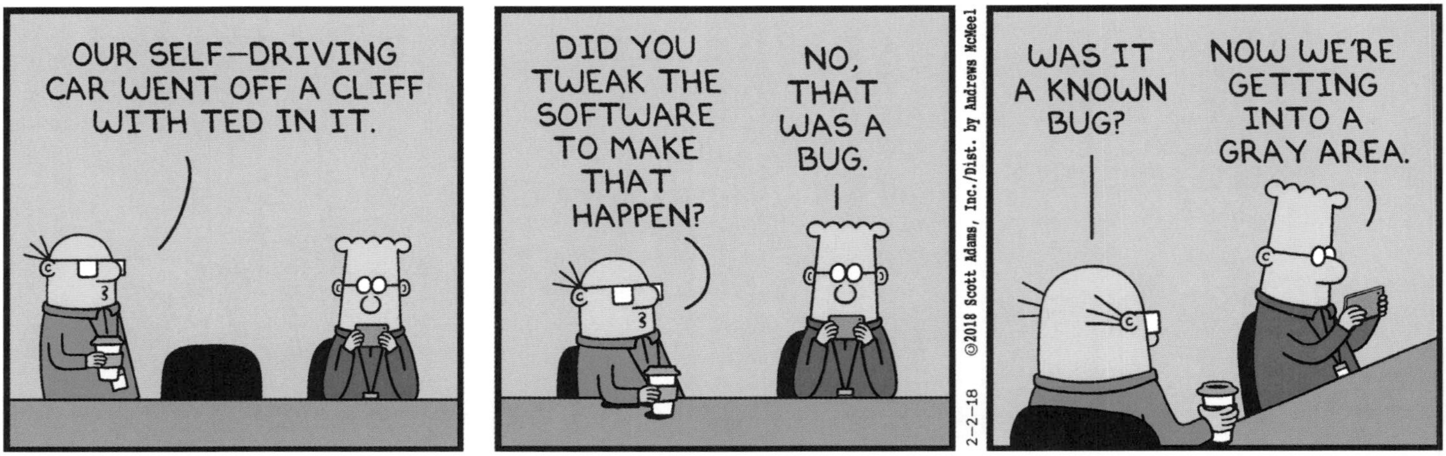
OUR SELF-DRIVING CAR WENT OFF A CLIFF WITH TED IN IT.
DID YOU TWEAK THE SOFTWARE TO MAKE THAT HAPPEN?
NO, THAT WAS A BUG.
2-2-18 ©2018 Scott Adams, Inc./Dist. by Andrews McMeel
WAS IT A KNOWN BUG?
NOW WE'RE GETTING INTO A GRAY AREA.

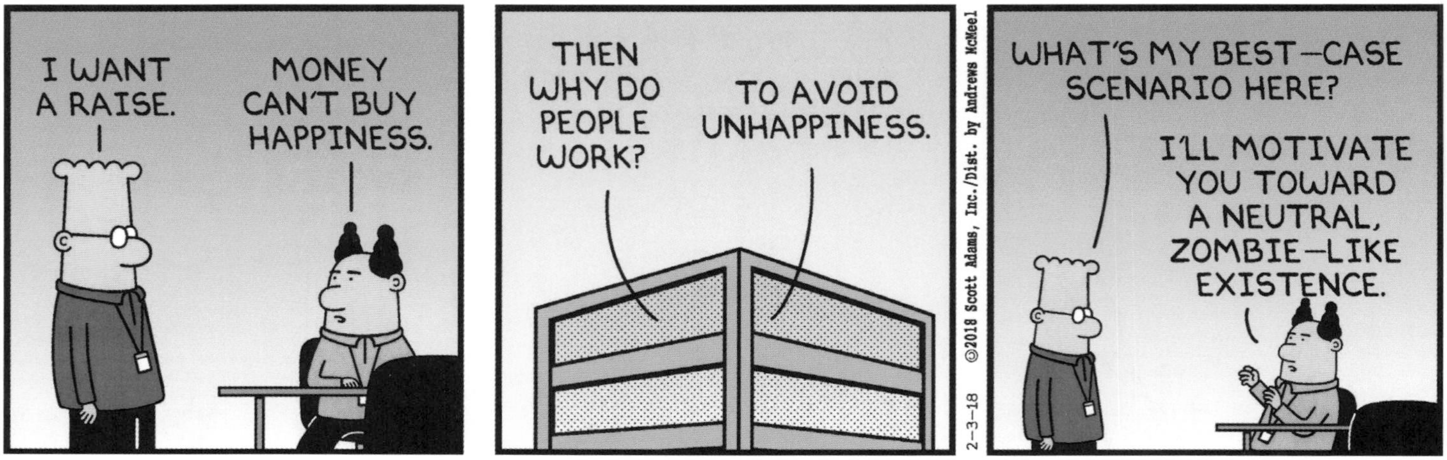
I WANT A RAISE.
MONEY CAN'T BUY HAPPINESS.
THEN WHY DO PEOPLE WORK?
TO AVOID UNHAPPINESS.
2-3-18 ©2018 Scott Adams, Inc./Dist. by Andrews McMeel
WHAT'S MY BEST-CASE SCENARIO HERE?
I'LL MOTIVATE YOU TOWARD A NEUTRAL, ZOMBIE-LIKE EXISTENCE.

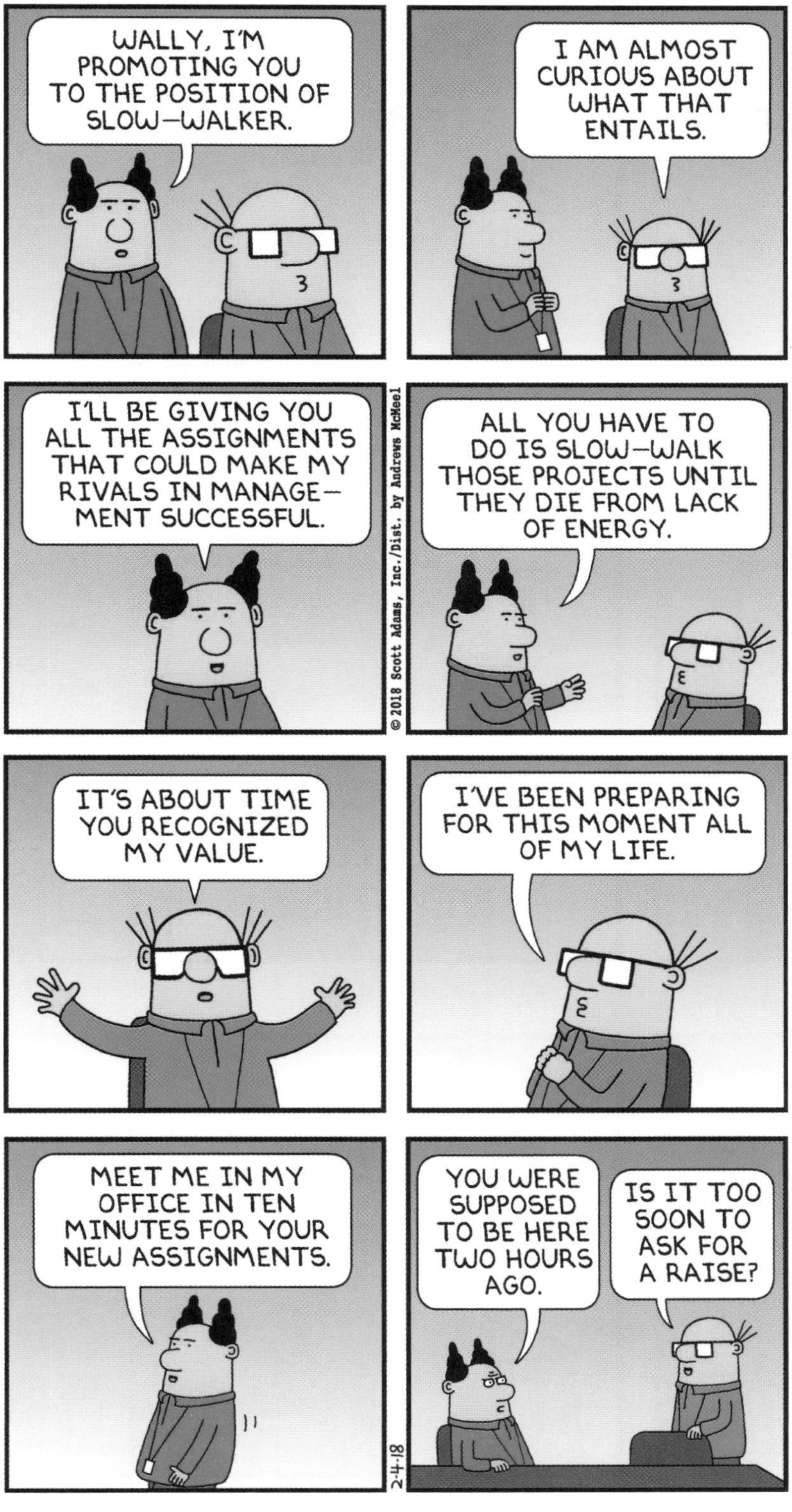
WALLY, I'M PROMOTING YOU TO THE POSITION OF SLOW-WALKER.
I AM ALMOST CURIOUS ABOUT WHAT THAT ENTAILS.
I'LL BE GIVING YOU ALL THE ASSIGNMENTS THAT COULD MAKE MY RIVALS IN MANAGE-MENT SUCCESSFUL.
ALL YOU HAVE TO DO IS SLOW-WALK THOSE PROJECTS UNTIL THEY DIE FROM LACK OF ENERGY.
IT'S ABOUT TIME YOU RECOGNIZED MY VALUE.
I'VE BEEN PREPARING FOR THIS MOMENT ALL OF MY LIFE.
MEET ME IN MY OFFICE IN TEN MINUTES FOR YOUR NEW ASSIGNMENTS.
YOU WERE SUPPOSED TO BE HERE TWO HOURS AGO.
IS IT TOO SOON TO ASK FOR A RAISE?
© 2018 Scott Adams, Inc./Dist. by Andrews McMeel
2-4-18

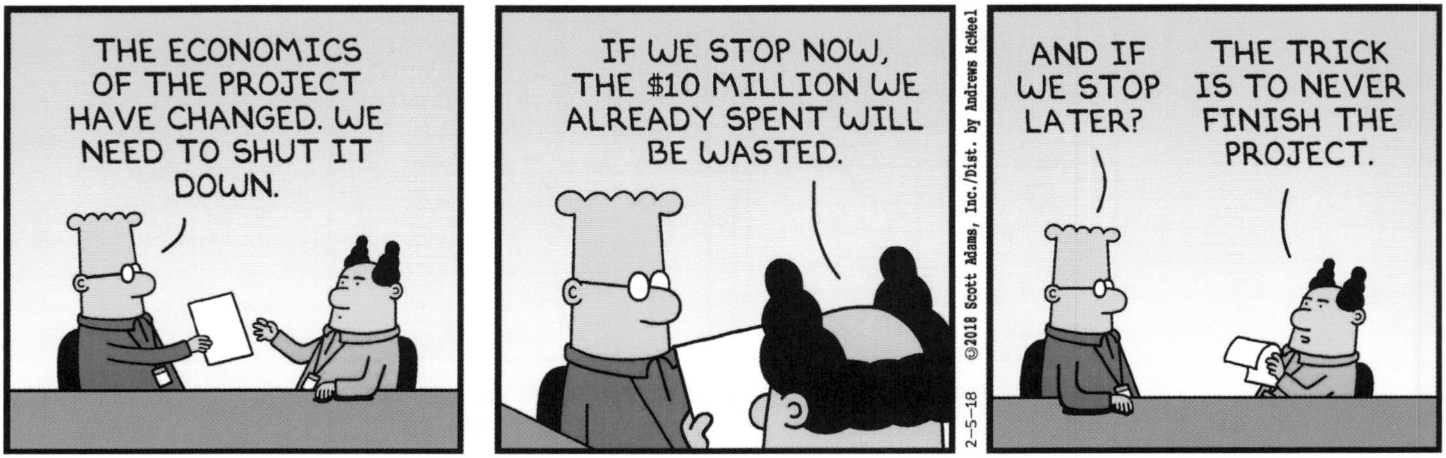
THE ECONOMICS OF THE PROJECT HAVE CHANGED. WE NEED TO SHUT IT DOWN.
IF WE STOP NOW, THE $10 MILLION WE ALREADY SPENT WILL BE WASTED.
2-5-18 ©2018 Scott Adams, Inc./Dist. by Andrews McMeel
AND IF WE STOP LATER?
THE TRICK IS TO NEVER FINISH THE PROJECT.

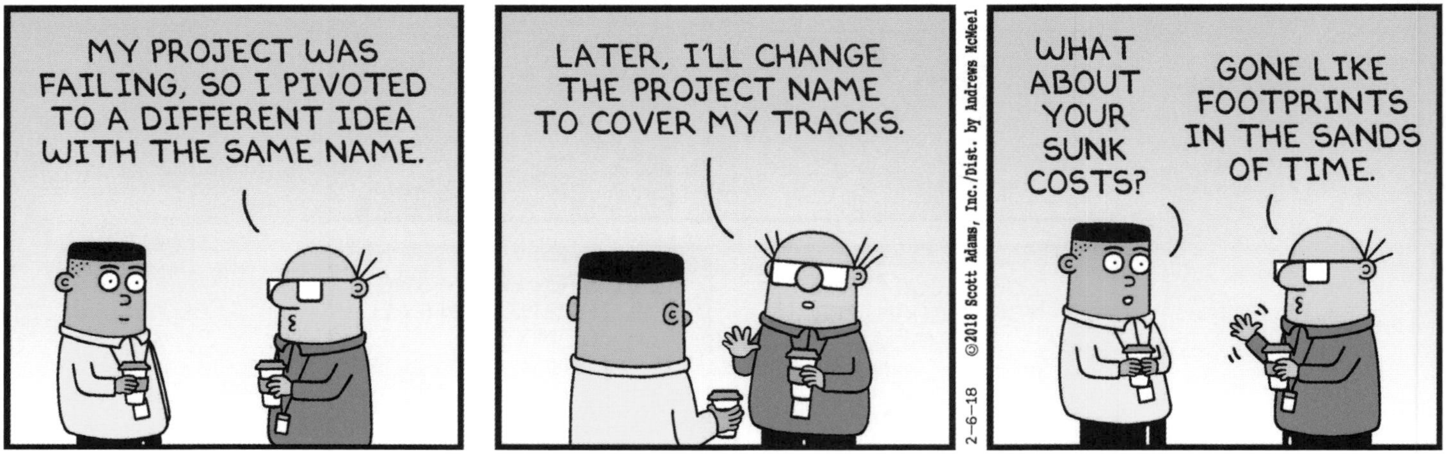
MY PROJECT WAS FAILING, SO I PIVOTED TO A DIFFERENT IDEA WITH THE SAME NAME.
LATER, I'LL CHANGE THE PROJECT NAME TO COVER MY TRACKS.
2-6-18 ©2018 Scott Adams, Inc./Dist. by Andrews McMeel
WHAT ABOUT YOUR SUNK COSTS?
GONE LIKE FOOTPRINTS IN THE SANDS OF TIME.

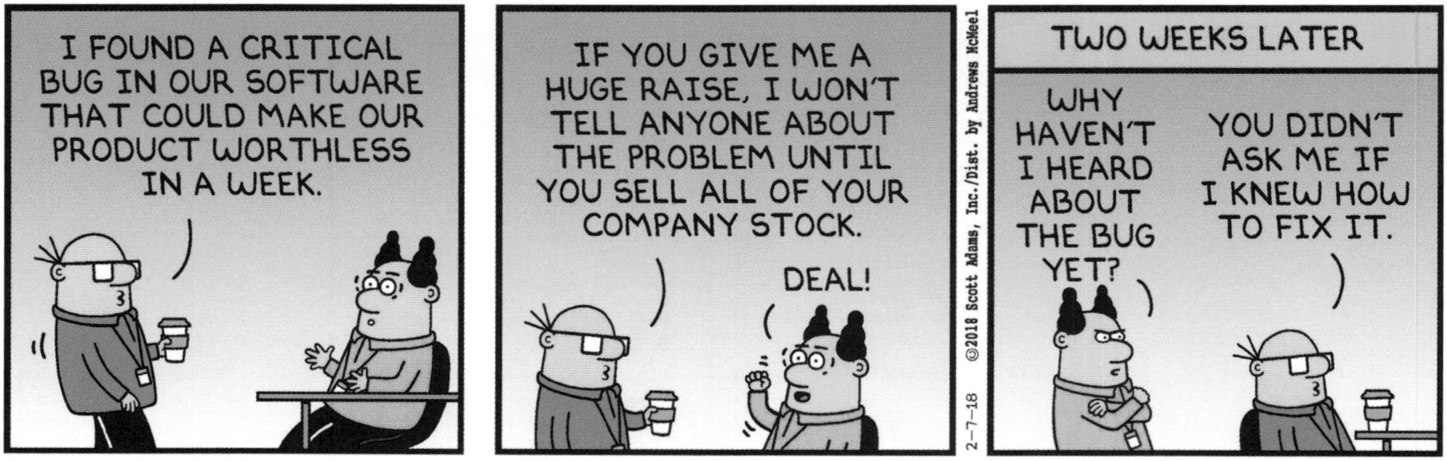
I FOUND A CRITICAL BUG IN OUR SOFTWARE THAT COULD MAKE OUR PRODUCT WORTHLESS IN A WEEK.
IF YOU GIVE ME A HUGE RAISE, I WON'T TELL ANYONE ABOUT THE PROBLEM UNTIL YOU SELL ALL OF YOUR COMPANY STOCK.
DEAL!
2-7-18 ©2018 Scott Adams, Inc./Dist. by Andrews McMeel
TWO WEEKS LATER
WHY HAVEN'T I HEARD ABOUT THE BUG YET?
YOU DIDN'T ASK ME IF I KNEW HOW TO FIX IT.

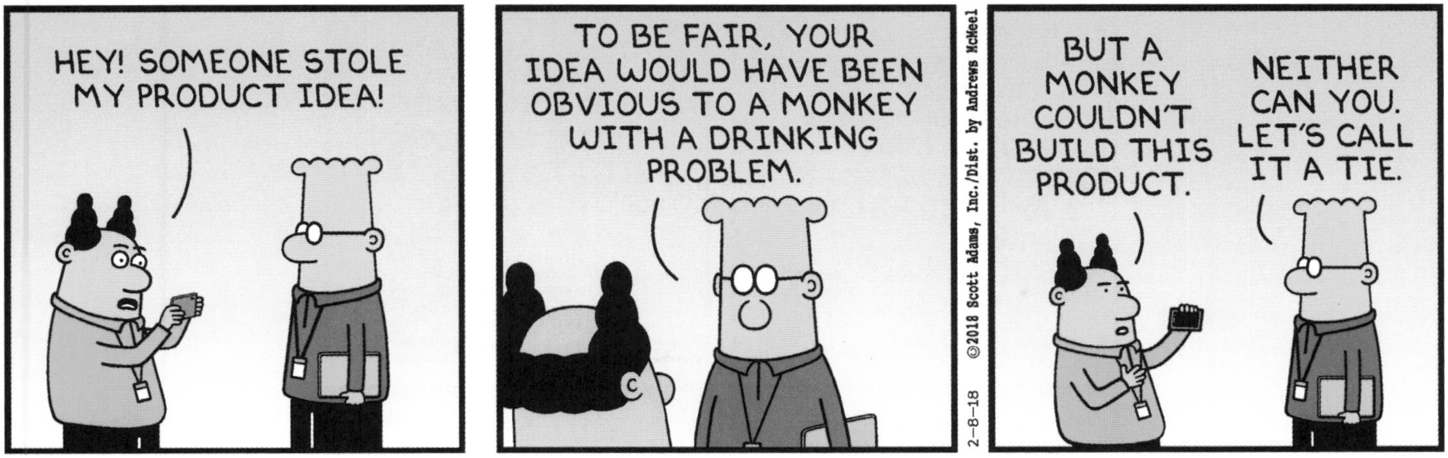
HEY! SOMEONE STOLE MY PRODUCT IDEA!
TO BE FAIR, YOUR IDEA WOULD HAVE BEEN OBVIOUS TO A MONKEY WITH A DRINKING PROBLEM.
2-8-18 ©2018 Scott Adams, Inc./Dist. by Andrews McMeel
BUT A MONKEY COULDN'T BUILD THIS PRODUCT.
NEITHER CAN YOU. LET'S CALL IT A TIE.

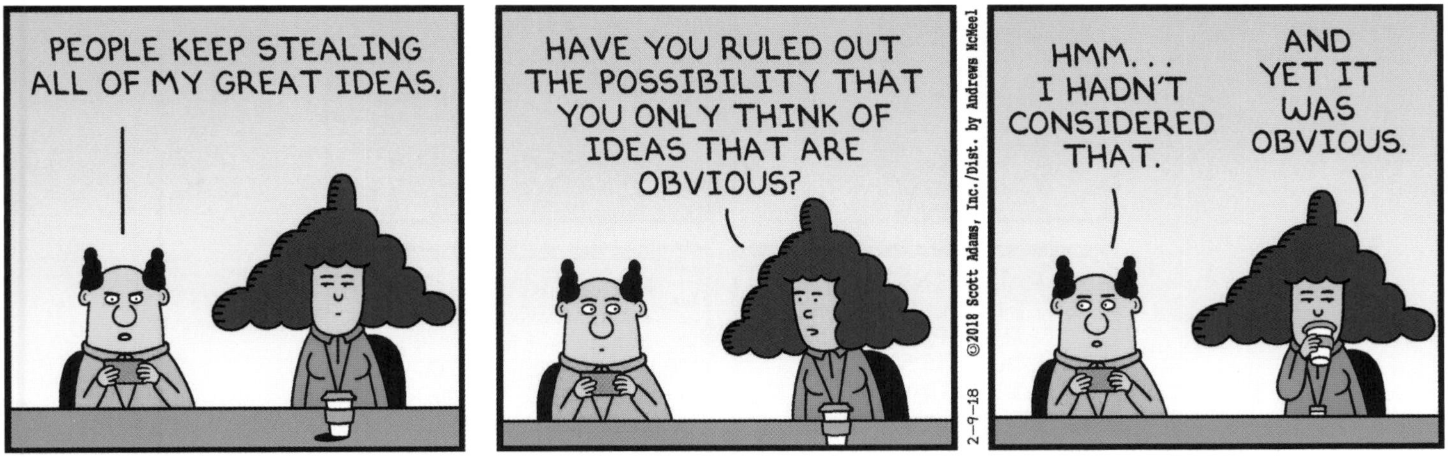
PEOPLE KEEP STEALING ALL OF MY GREAT IDEAS.
HAVE YOU RULED OUT THE POSSIBILITY THAT YOU ONLY THINK OF IDEAS THAT ARE OBVIOUS?
2-9-18 ©2018 Scott Adams, Inc./Dist. by Andrews McMeel
HMM. . . I HADN'T CONSIDERED THAT.
AND YET IT WAS OBVIOUS.

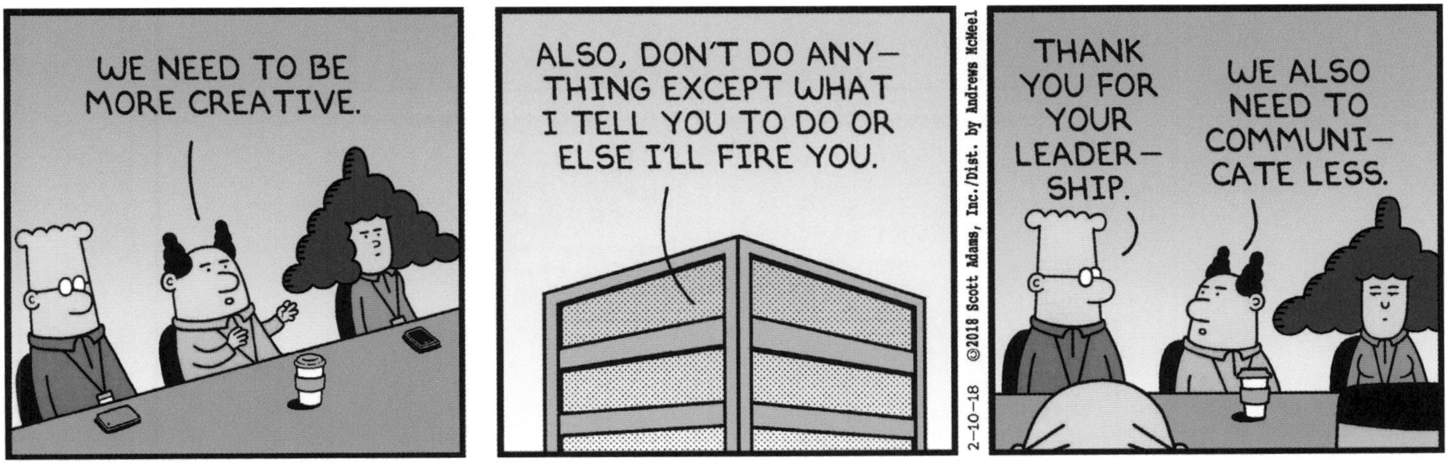
WE NEED TO BE MORE CREATIVE.
ALSO, DON'T DO ANY- THING EXCEPT WHAT I TELL YOU TO DO OR ELSE I'LL FIRE YOU.
2-10-18 ©2018 Scott Adams, Inc./Dist. by Andrews McMeel
THANK YOU FOR YOUR LEADER- SHIP.
WE ALSO NEED TO COMMUNI- CATE LESS.

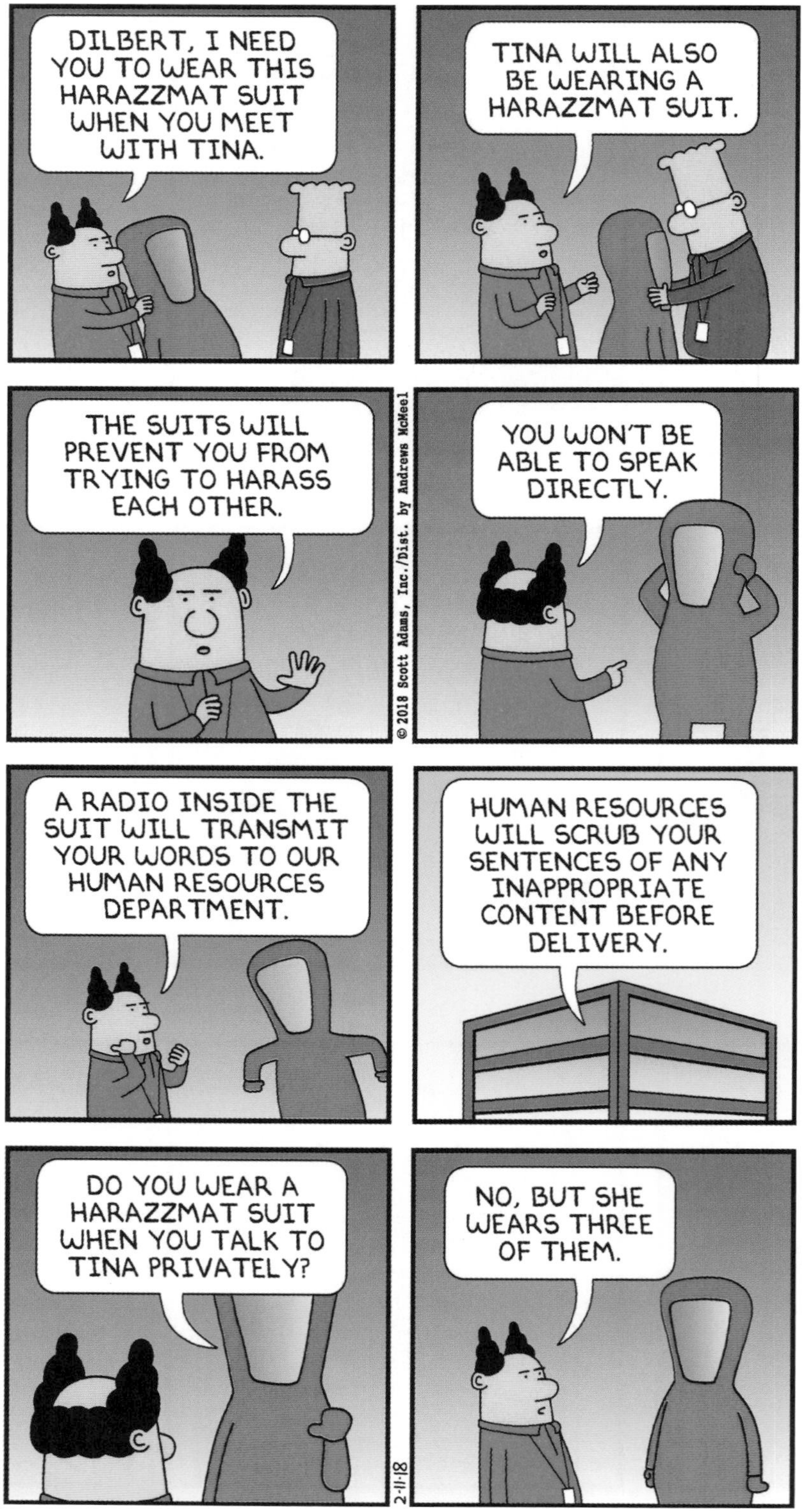
DILBERT, I NEED YOU TO WEAR THIS HARAZZMAT SUIT WHEN YOU MEET WITH TINA.
TINA WILL ALSO BE WEARING A HARAZZMAT SUIT.
THE SUITS WILL PREVENT YOU FROM TRYING TO HARASS EACH OTHER.
YOU WON'T BE ABLE TO SPEAK DIRECTLY.
A RADIO INSIDE THE SUIT WILL TRANSMIT YOUR WORDS TO OUR HUMAN RESOURCES DEPARTMENT.
HUMAN RESOURCES WILL SCRUB YOUR SENTENCES OF ANY INAPPROPRIATE CONTENT BEFORE DELIVERY.
DO YOU WEAR A HARAZZMAT SUIT WHEN YOU TALK TO TINA PRIVATELY?
NO, BUT SHE WEARS THREE OF THEM.
© 2018 Scott Adams, Inc./Dist. by Andrews McMeel
2-11-18

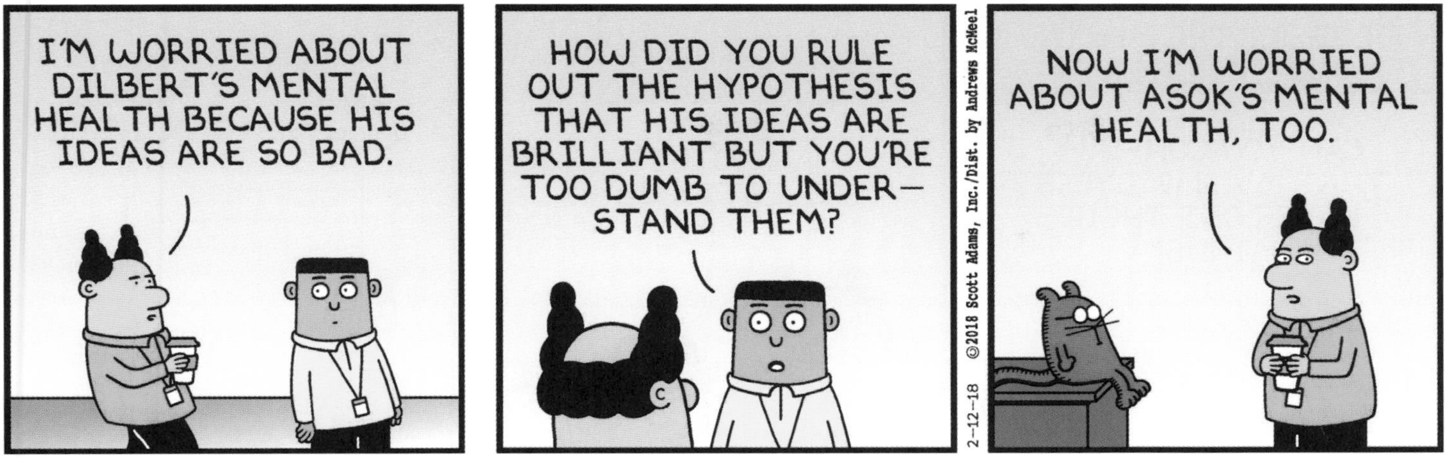
I'M WORRIED ABOUT DILBERT'S MENTAL HEALTH BECAUSE HIS IDEAS ARE SO BAD.
HOW DID YOU RULE OUT THE HYPOTHESIS THAT HIS IDEAS ARE BRILLIANT BUT YOU'RE TOO DUMB TO UNDER-STAND THEM?
NOW I'M WORRIED ABOUT ASOK'S MENTAL HEALTH, TOO.
2-12-18

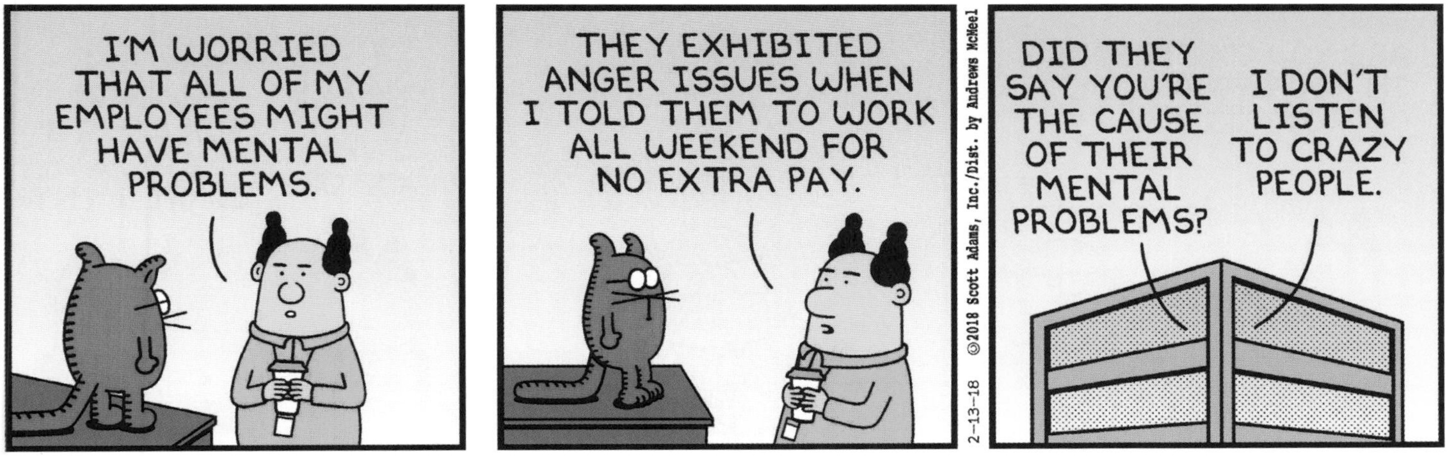
I'M WORRIED THAT ALL OF MY EMPLOYEES MIGHT HAVE MENTAL PROBLEMS.
THEY EXHIBITED ANGER ISSUES WHEN I TOLD THEM TO WORK ALL WEEKEND FOR NO EXTRA PAY.
DID THEY SAY YOU'RE THE CAUSE OF THEIR MENTAL PROBLEMS?
I DON'T LISTEN TO CRAZY PEOPLE.
2-13-18

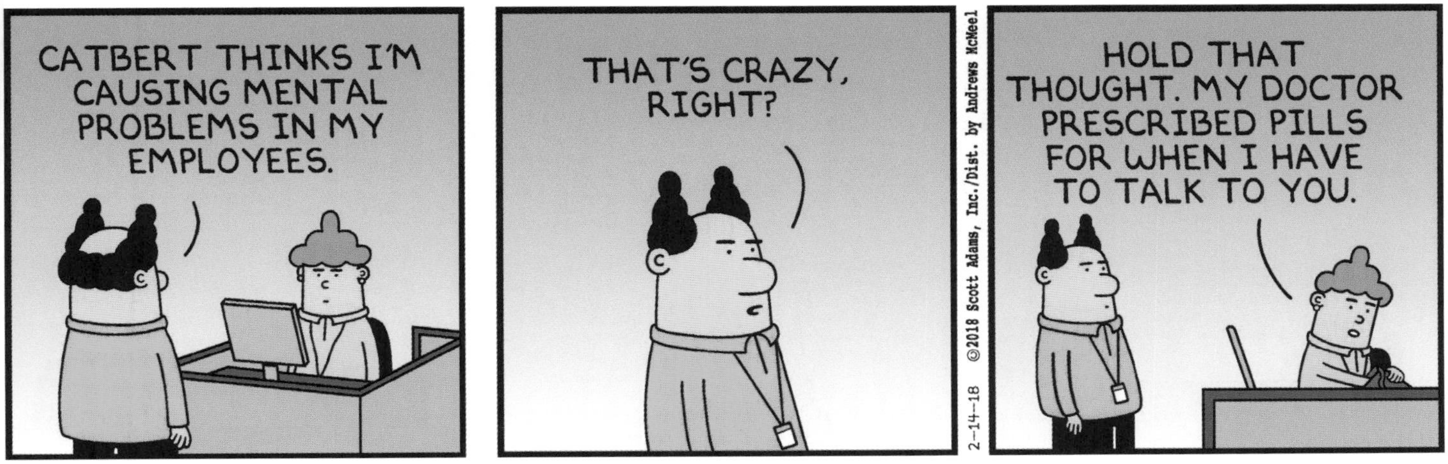
CATBERT THINKS I'M CAUSING MENTAL PROBLEMS IN MY EMPLOYEES.
THAT'S CRAZY, RIGHT?
HOLD THAT THOUGHT. MY DOCTOR PRESCRIBED PILLS FOR WHEN I HAVE TO TALK TO YOU.
2-14-18

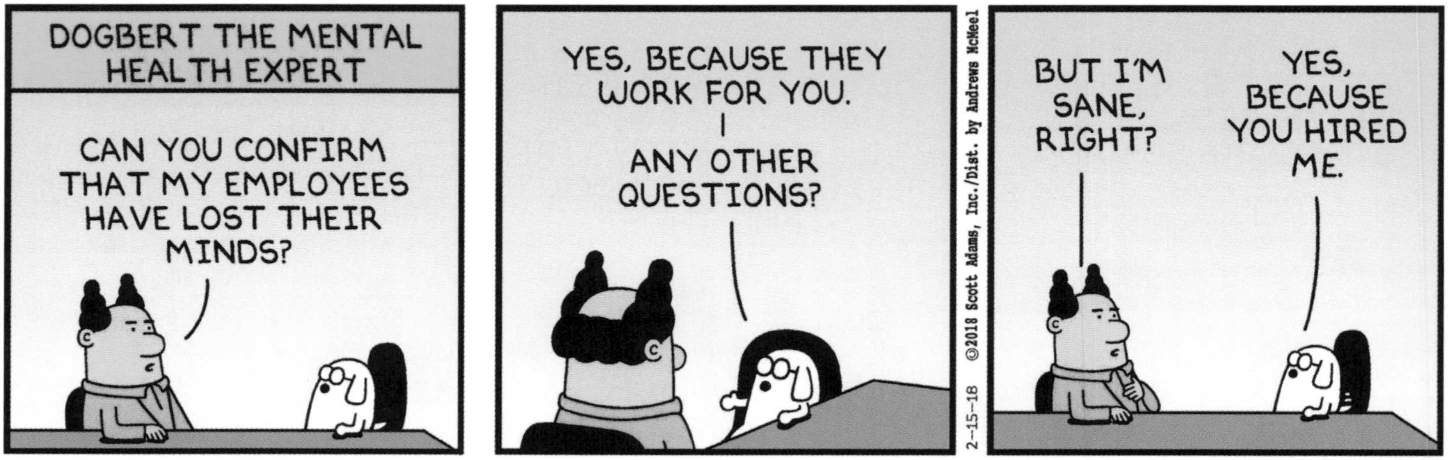
DOGBERT THE MENTAL HEALTH EXPERT
CAN YOU CONFIRM THAT MY EMPLOYEES HAVE LOST THEIR MINDS?
YES, BECAUSE THEY WORK FOR YOU.
ANY OTHER QUESTIONS?
2-15-18 ©2018 Scott Adams, Inc./Dist. by Andrews McMeel
BUT I'M SANE, RIGHT?
YES, BECAUSE YOU HIRED ME.

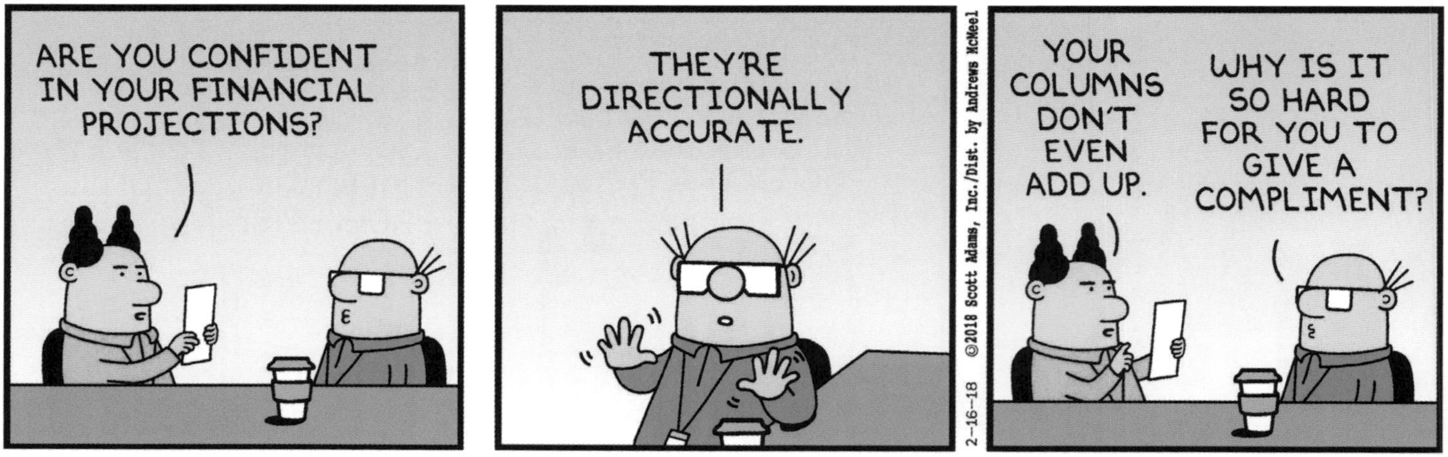
ARE YOU CONFIDENT IN YOUR FINANCIAL PROJECTIONS?
THEY'RE DIRECTIONALLY ACCURATE.
2-16-18 ©2018 Scott Adams, Inc./Dist. by Andrews McMeel
YOUR COLUMNS DON'T EVEN ADD UP.
WHY IS IT SO HARD FOR YOU TO GIVE A COMPLIMENT?

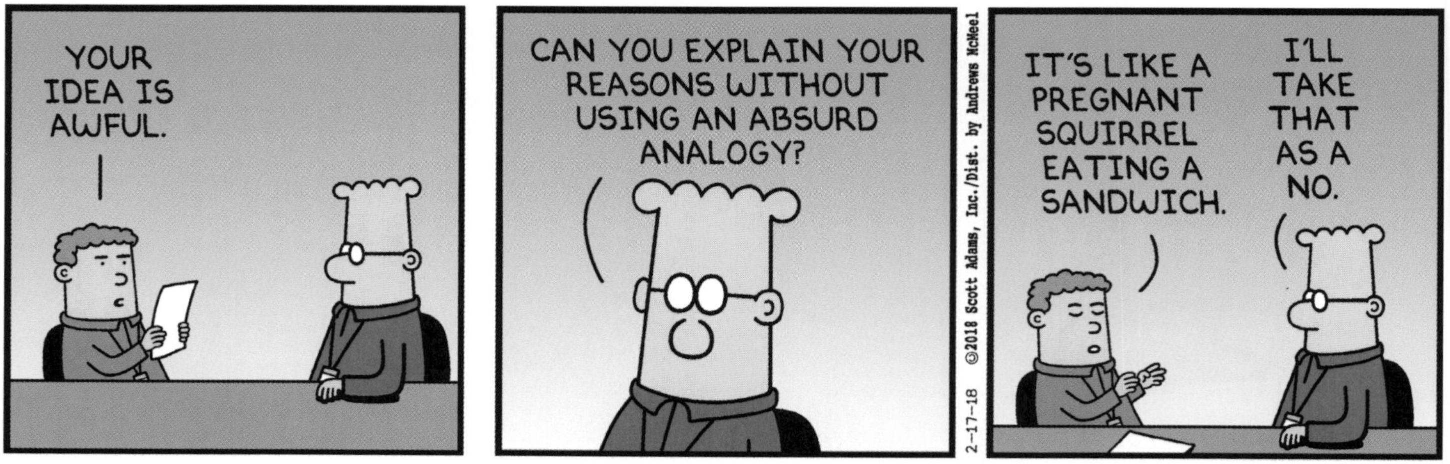
YOUR IDEA IS AWFUL.
CAN YOU EXPLAIN YOUR REASONS WITHOUT USING AN ABSURD ANALOGY?
2-17-18 ©2018 Scott Adams, Inc./Dist. by Andrews McMeel
IT'S LIKE A PREGNANT SQUIRREL EATING A SANDWICH.
I'LL TAKE THAT AS A NO.

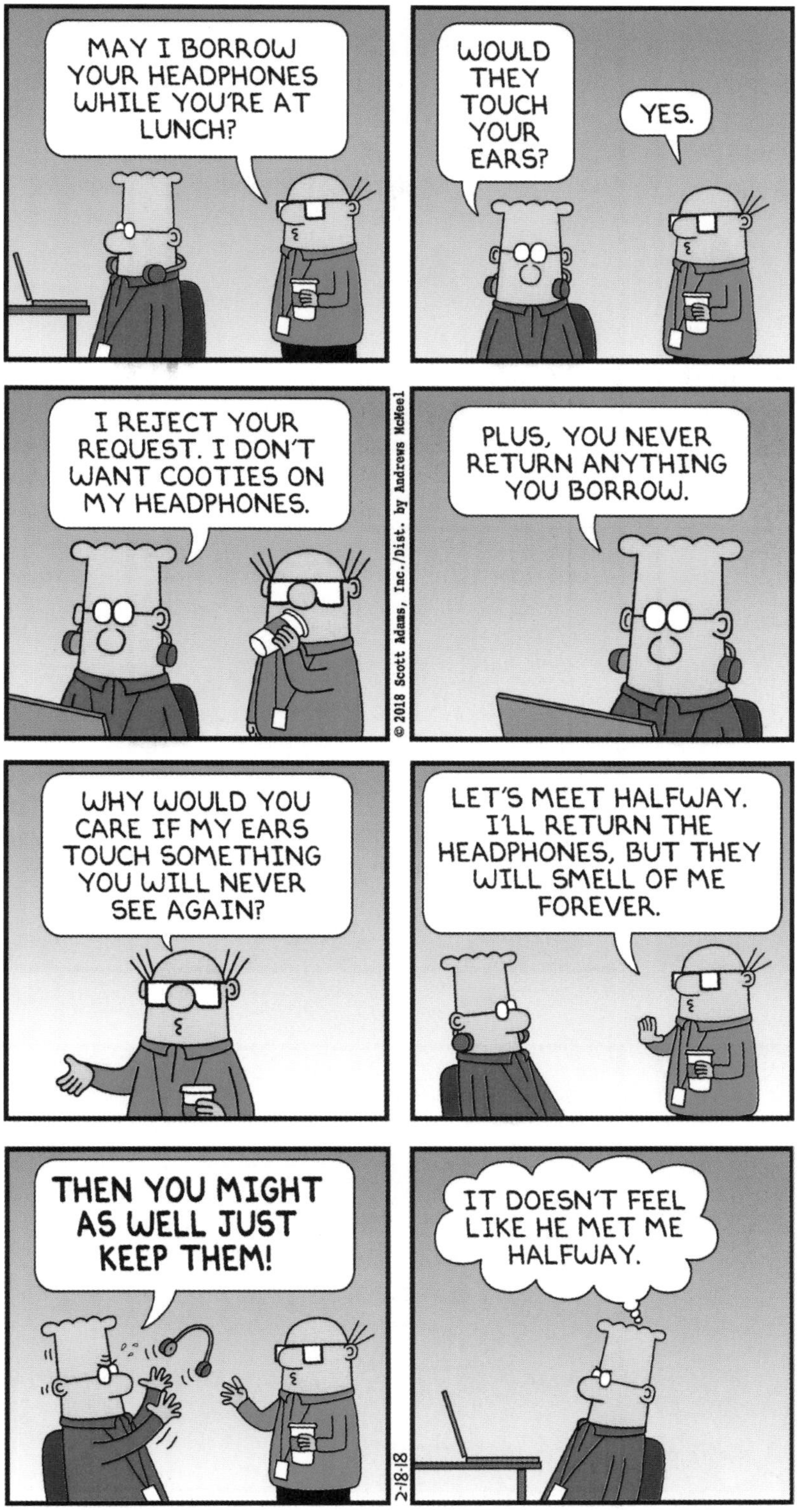
MAY I BORROW YOUR HEADPHONES WHILE YOU'RE AT LUNCH?
WOULD THEY TOUCH YOUR EARS?
YES.
I REJECT YOUR REQUEST. I DON'T WANT COOTIES ON MY HEADPHONES.
PLUS, YOU NEVER RETURN ANYTHING YOU BORROW.
WHY WOULD YOU CARE IF MY EARS TOUCH SOMETHING YOU WILL NEVER SEE AGAIN?
LET'S MEET HALFWAY. I'LL RETURN THE HEADPHONES, BUT THEY WILL SMELL OF ME FOREVER.
THEN YOU MIGHT AS WELL JUST KEEP THEM!
IT DOESN'T FEEL LIKE HE MET ME HALFWAY.
© 2018 Scott Adams, Inc./Dist. by Andrews McMeel
2-18-18

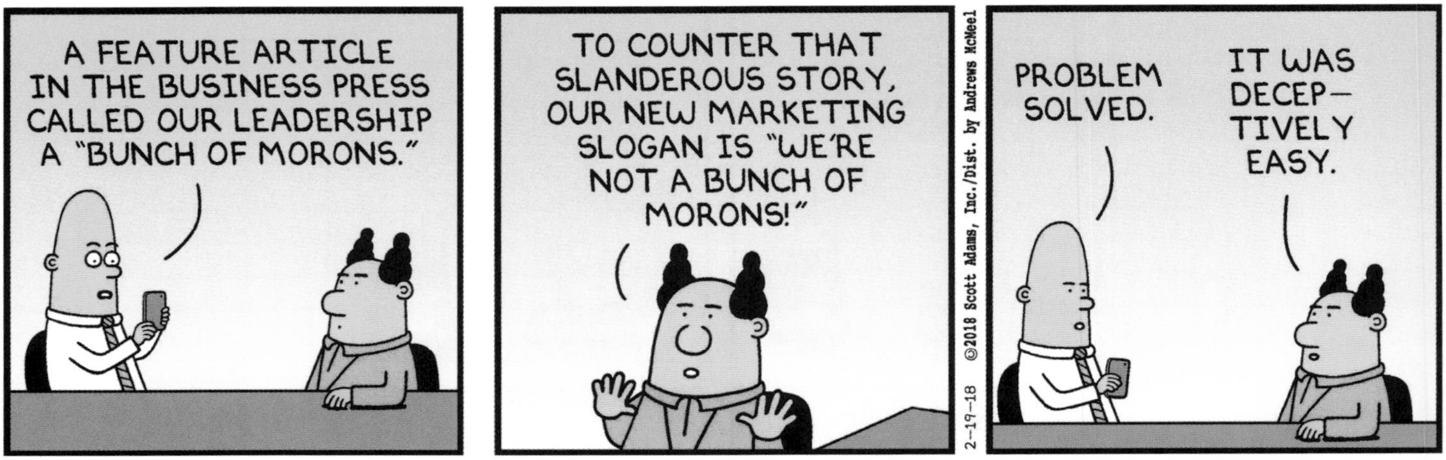
A FEATURE ARTICLE IN THE BUSINESS PRESS CALLED OUR LEADERSHIP A "BUNCH OF MORONS."
TO COUNTER THAT SLANDEROUS STORY, OUR NEW MARKETING SLOGAN IS "WE'RE NOT A BUNCH OF MORONS!"
2-19-18 ©2018 Scott Adams, Inc./Dist. by Andrews McMeel
PROBLEM SOLVED.
IT WAS DECEP–TIVELY EASY.

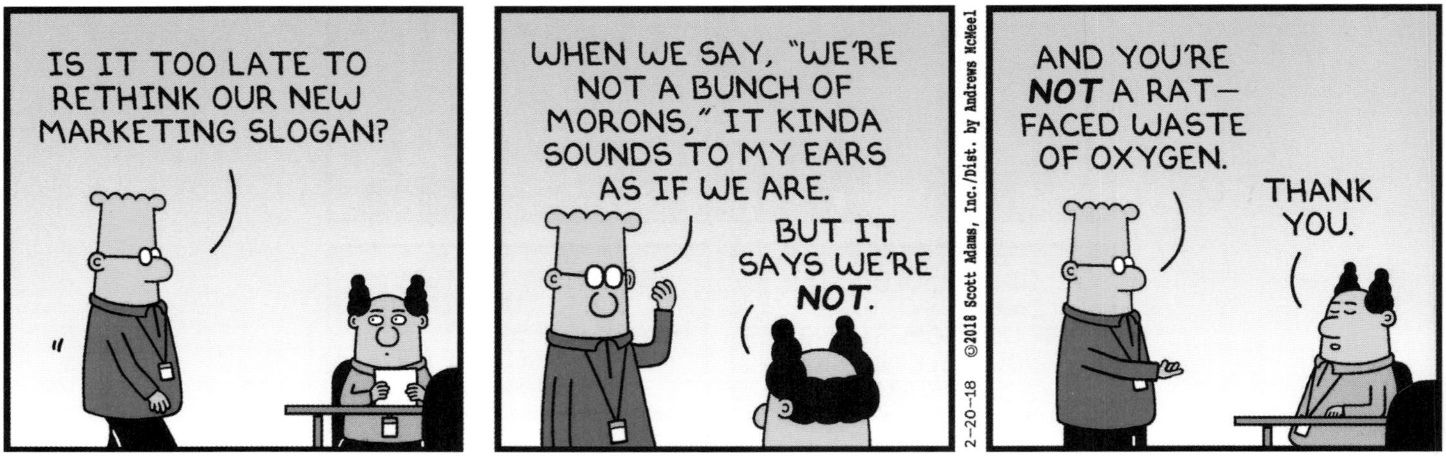
IS IT TOO LATE TO RETHINK OUR NEW MARKETING SLOGAN?
WHEN WE SAY, "WE'RE NOT A BUNCH OF MORONS," IT KINDA SOUNDS TO MY EARS AS IF WE ARE.
BUT IT SAYS WE'RE **NOT**.
2-20-18 ©2018 Scott Adams, Inc./Dist. by Andrews McMeel
AND YOU'RE **NOT** A RAT–FACED WASTE OF OXYGEN.
THANK YOU.

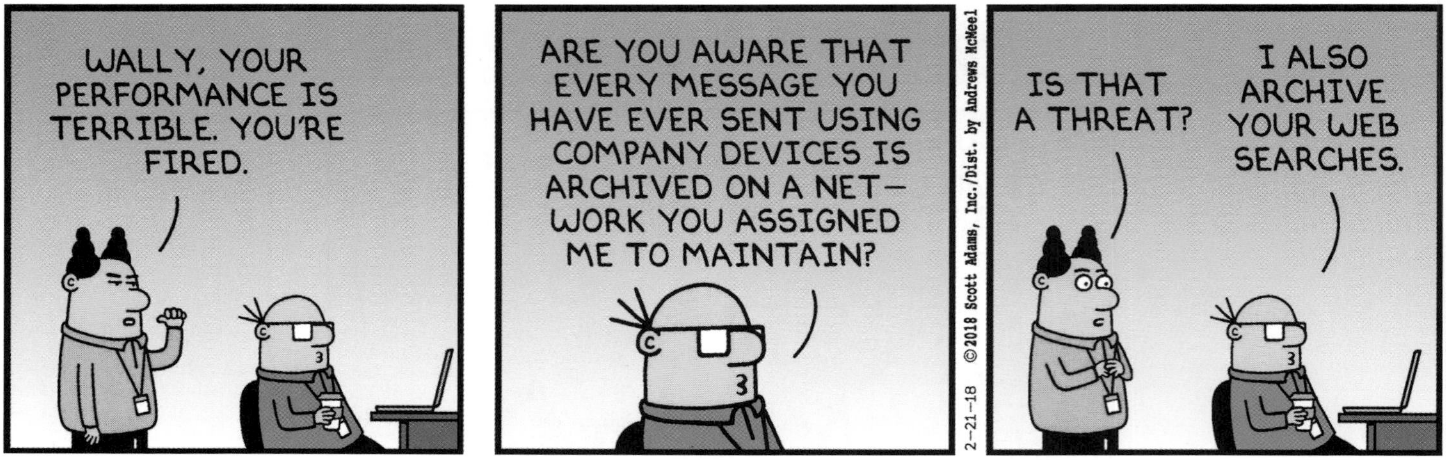
WALLY, YOUR PERFORMANCE IS TERRIBLE. YOU'RE FIRED.
ARE YOU AWARE THAT EVERY MESSAGE YOU HAVE EVER SENT USING COMPANY DEVICES IS ARCHIVED ON A NET–WORK YOU ASSIGNED ME TO MAINTAIN?
2-21-18 ©2018 Scott Adams, Inc./Dist. by Andrews McMeel
IS THAT A THREAT?
I ALSO ARCHIVE YOUR WEB SEARCHES.

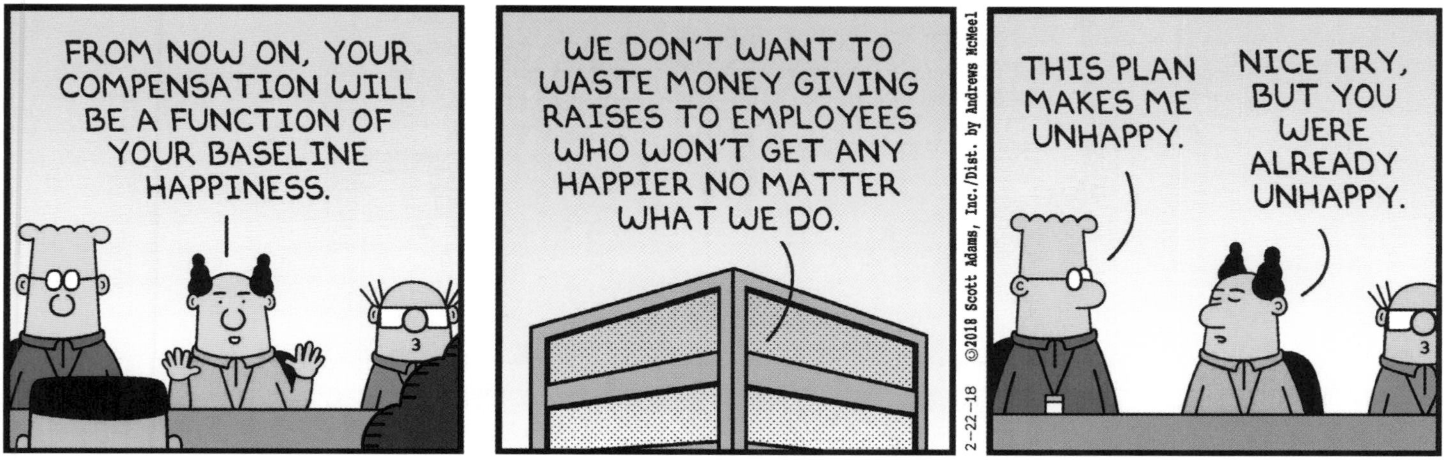
FROM NOW ON, YOUR COMPENSATION WILL BE A FUNCTION OF YOUR BASELINE HAPPINESS.
WE DON'T WANT TO WASTE MONEY GIVING RAISES TO EMPLOYEES WHO WON'T GET ANY HAPPIER NO MATTER WHAT WE DO.
2-22-18 ©2018 Scott Adams, Inc./Dist. by Andrews McMeel
THIS PLAN MAKES ME UNHAPPY.
NICE TRY, BUT YOU WERE ALREADY UNHAPPY.

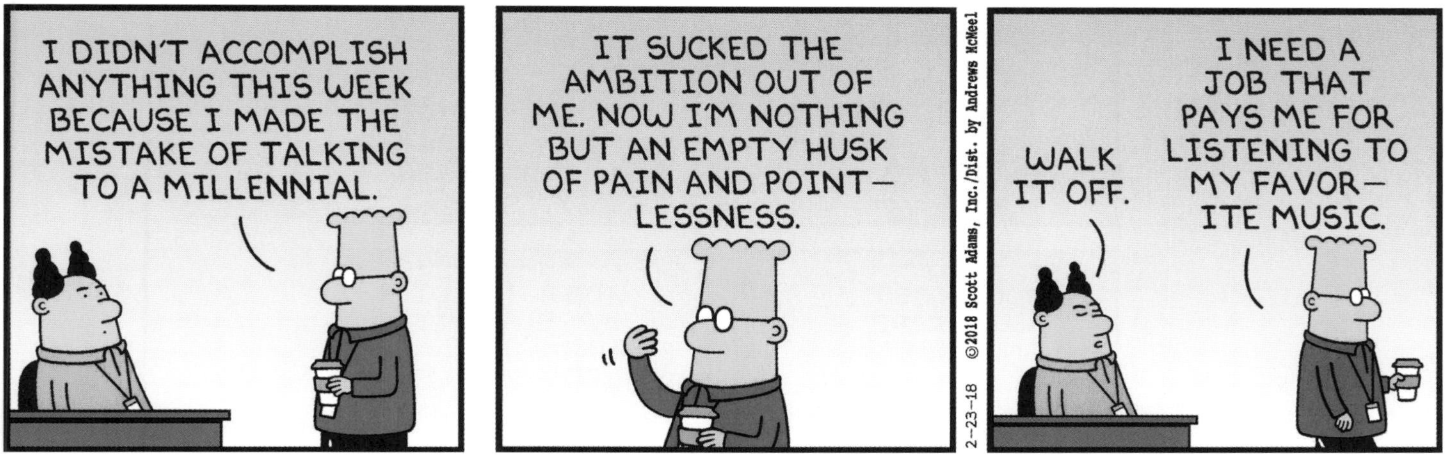
I DIDN'T ACCOMPLISH ANYTHING THIS WEEK BECAUSE I MADE THE MISTAKE OF TALKING TO A MILLENNIAL.
IT SUCKED THE AMBITION OUT OF ME. NOW I'M NOTHING BUT AN EMPTY HUSK OF PAIN AND POINT-LESSNESS.
2-23-18 ©2018 Scott Adams, Inc./Dist. by Andrews McMeel
WALK IT OFF.
I NEED A JOB THAT PAYS ME FOR LISTENING TO MY FAVOR-ITE MUSIC.

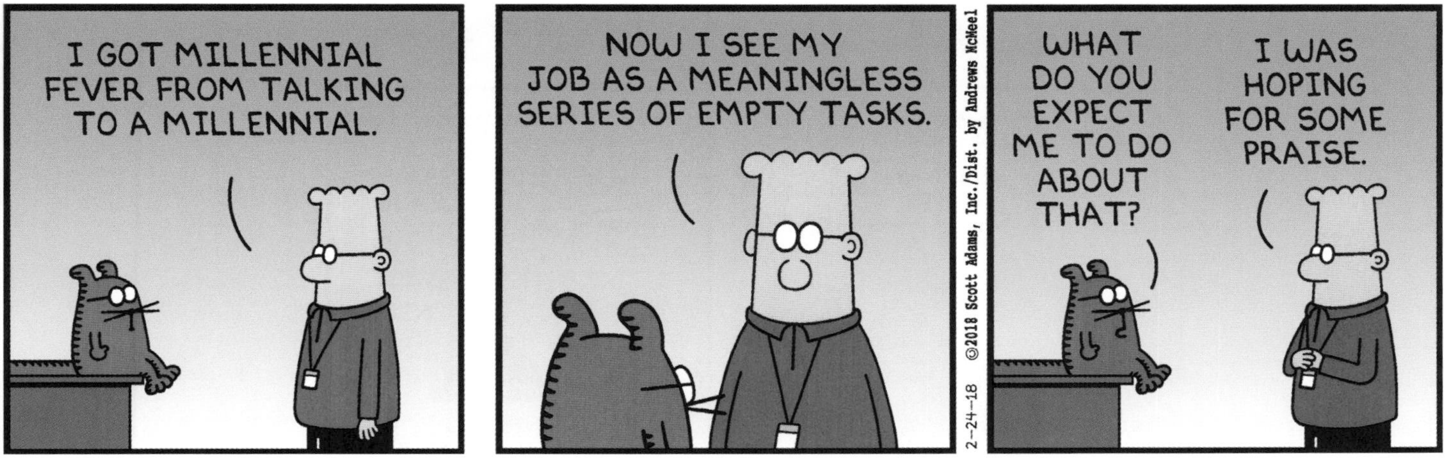
I GOT MILLENNIAL FEVER FROM TALKING TO A MILLENNIAL.
NOW I SEE MY JOB AS A MEANINGLESS SERIES OF EMPTY TASKS.
2-24-18 ©2018 Scott Adams, Inc./Dist. by Andrews McMeel
WHAT DO YOU EXPECT ME TO DO ABOUT THAT?
I WAS HOPING FOR SOME PRAISE.

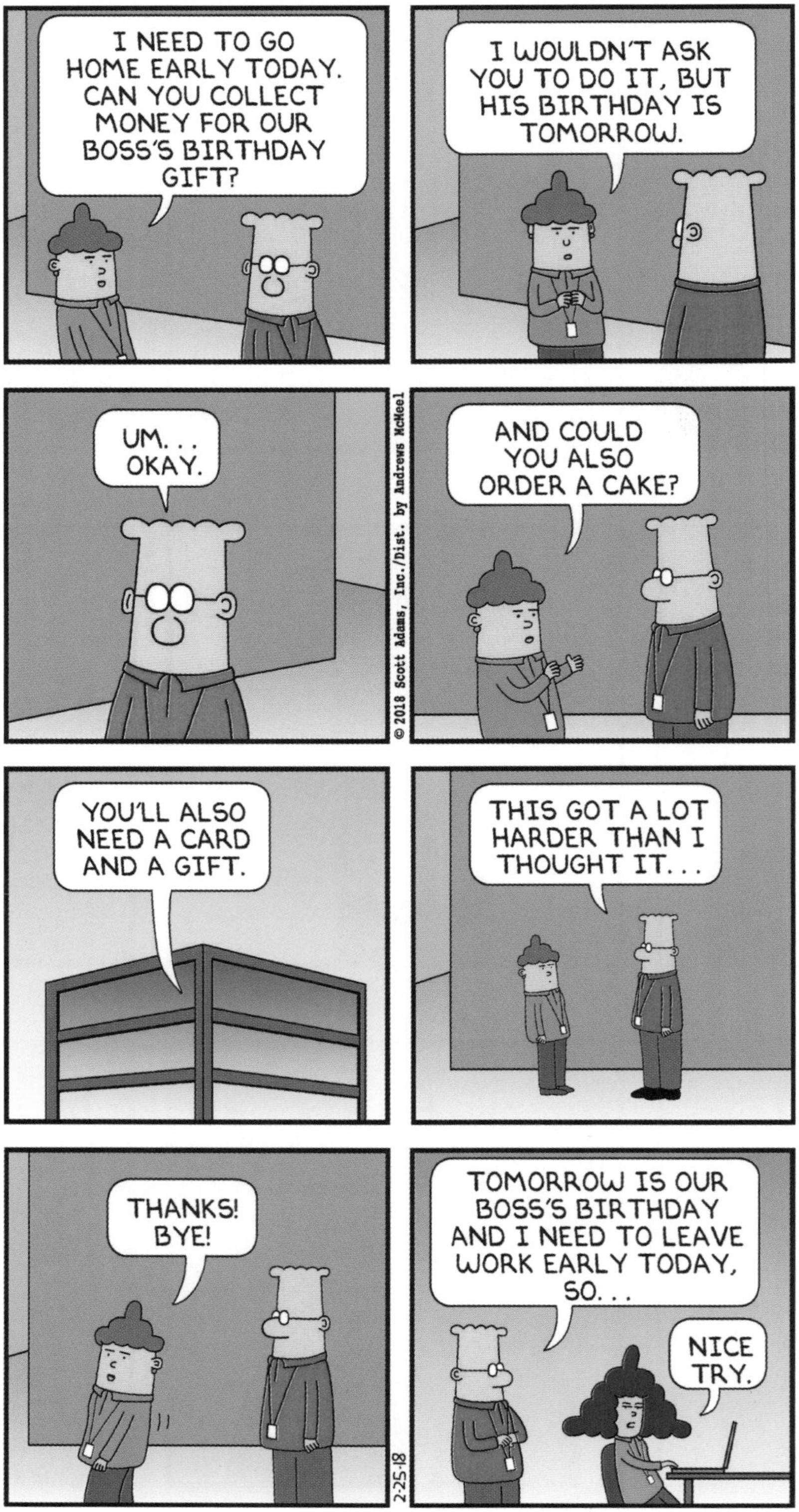
I NEED TO GO HOME EARLY TODAY. CAN YOU COLLECT MONEY FOR OUR BOSS'S BIRTHDAY GIFT?
I WOULDN'T ASK YOU TO DO IT, BUT HIS BIRTHDAY IS TOMORROW.
UM. . . OKAY.
AND COULD YOU ALSO ORDER A CAKE?
YOU'LL ALSO NEED A CARD AND A GIFT.
THIS GOT A LOT HARDER THAN I THOUGHT IT. . .
THANKS! BYE!
TOMORROW IS OUR BOSS'S BIRTHDAY AND I NEED TO LEAVE WORK EARLY TODAY, SO. . .
NICE TRY.
© 2018 Scott Adams, Inc./Dist. by Andrews McMeel
2-25-18

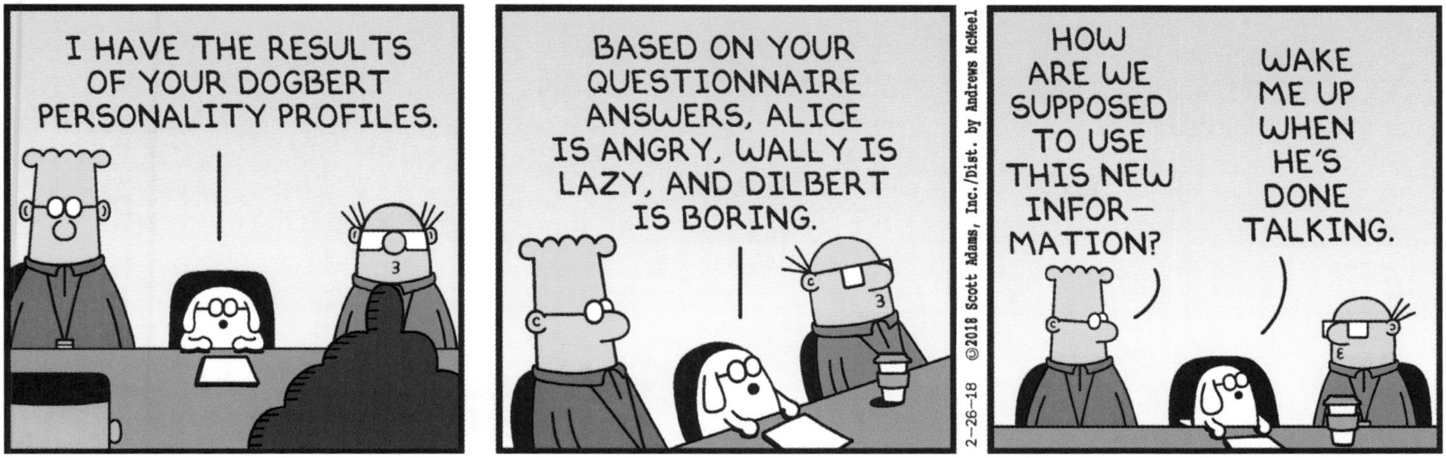
I HAVE THE RESULTS OF YOUR DOGBERT PERSONALITY PROFILES.
BASED ON YOUR QUESTIONNAIRE ANSWERS, ALICE IS ANGRY, WALLY IS LAZY, AND DILBERT IS BORING.
HOW ARE WE SUPPOSED TO USE THIS NEW INFOR– MATION?
WAKE ME UP WHEN HE'S DONE TALKING.
2-26-18 ©2018 Scott Adams, Inc./Dist. by Andrews McMeel

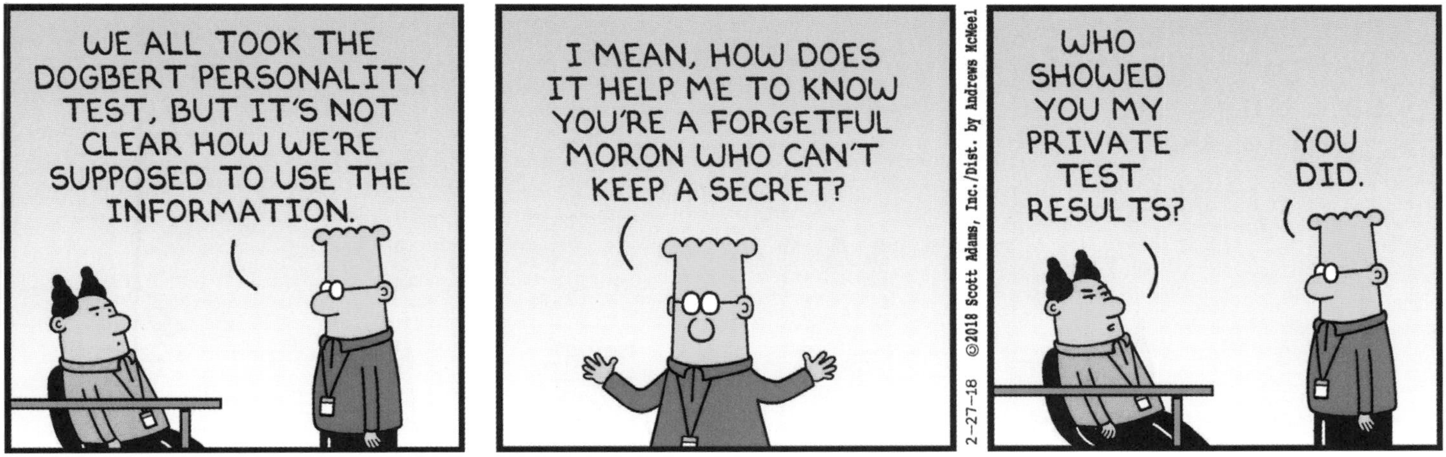
WE ALL TOOK THE DOGBERT PERSONALITY TEST, BUT IT'S NOT CLEAR HOW WE'RE SUPPOSED TO USE THE INFORMATION.
I MEAN, HOW DOES IT HELP ME TO KNOW YOU'RE A FORGETFUL MORON WHO CAN'T KEEP A SECRET?
WHO SHOWED YOU MY PRIVATE TEST RESULTS?
YOU DID.
2-27-18 ©2018 Scott Adams, Inc./Dist. by Andrews McMeel

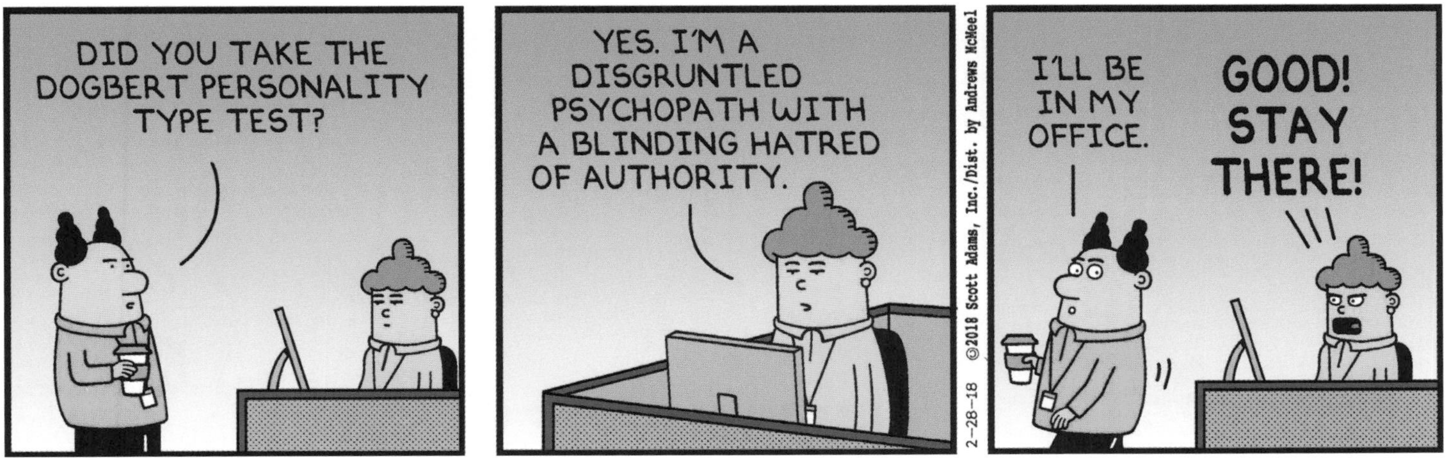
DID YOU TAKE THE DOGBERT PERSONALITY TYPE TEST?
YES. I'M A DISGRUNTLED PSYCHOPATH WITH A BLINDING HATRED OF AUTHORITY.
I'LL BE IN MY OFFICE.
GOOD! STAY THERE!
2-28-18 ©2018 Scott Adams, Inc./Dist. by Andrews McMeel

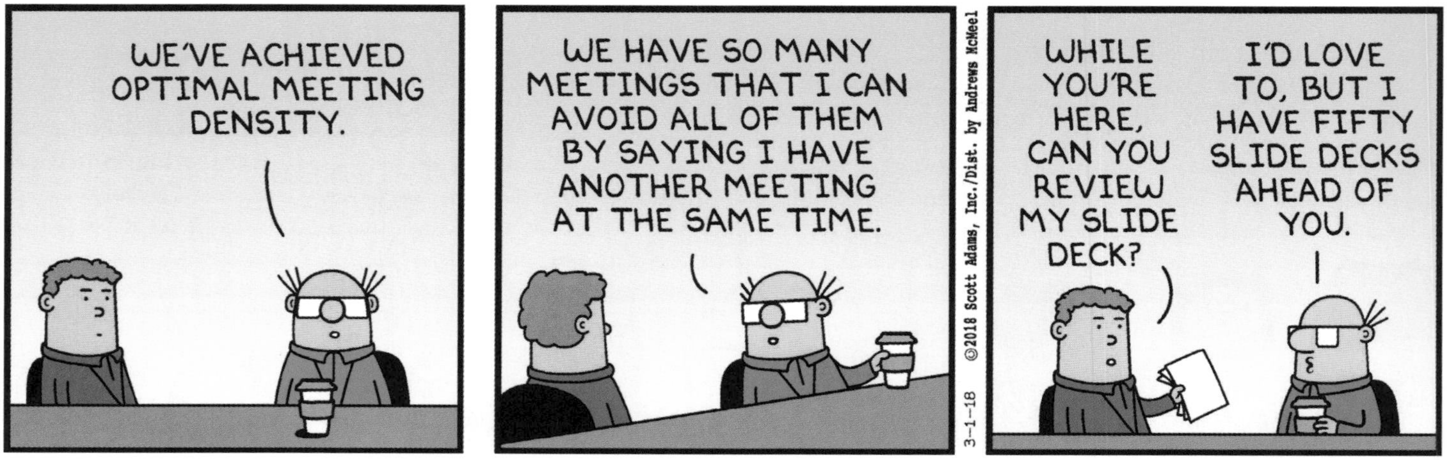
WE'VE ACHIEVED OPTIMAL MEETING DENSITY.
WE HAVE SO MANY MEETINGS THAT I CAN AVOID ALL OF THEM BY SAYING I HAVE ANOTHER MEETING AT THE SAME TIME.
3-1-18 ©2018 Scott Adams, Inc./Dist. by Andrews McMeel
WHILE YOU'RE HERE, CAN YOU REVIEW MY SLIDE DECK?
I'D LOVE TO, BUT I HAVE FIFTY SLIDE DECKS AHEAD OF YOU.

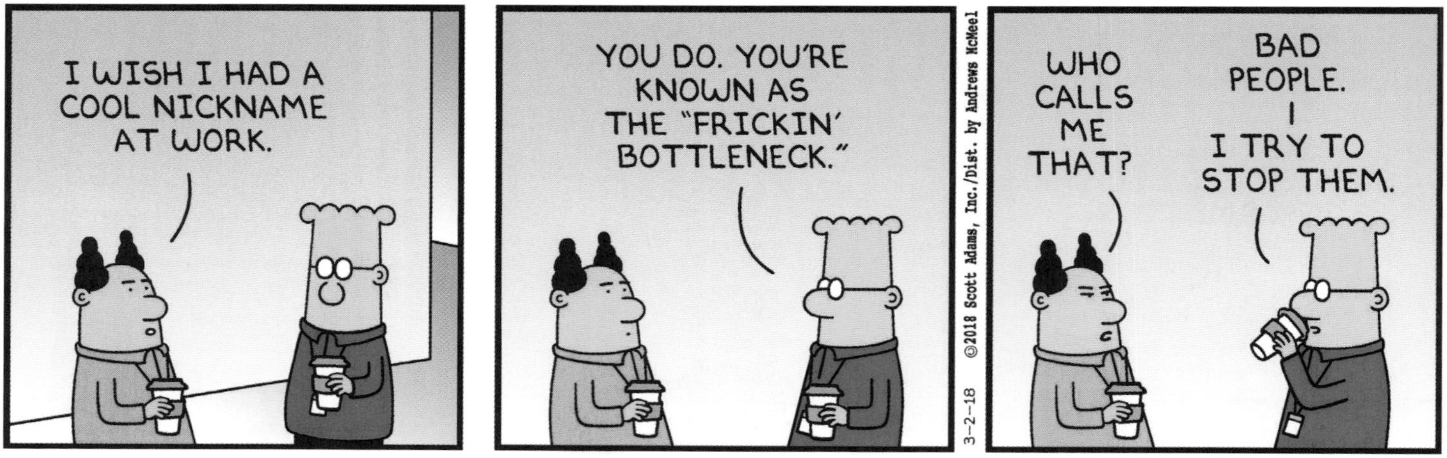
I WISH I HAD A COOL NICKNAME AT WORK.
YOU DO. YOU'RE KNOWN AS THE "FRICKIN' BOTTLENECK."
3-2-18 ©2018 Scott Adams, Inc./Dist. by Andrews McMeel
WHO CALLS ME THAT?
BAD PEOPLE.
I TRY TO STOP THEM.

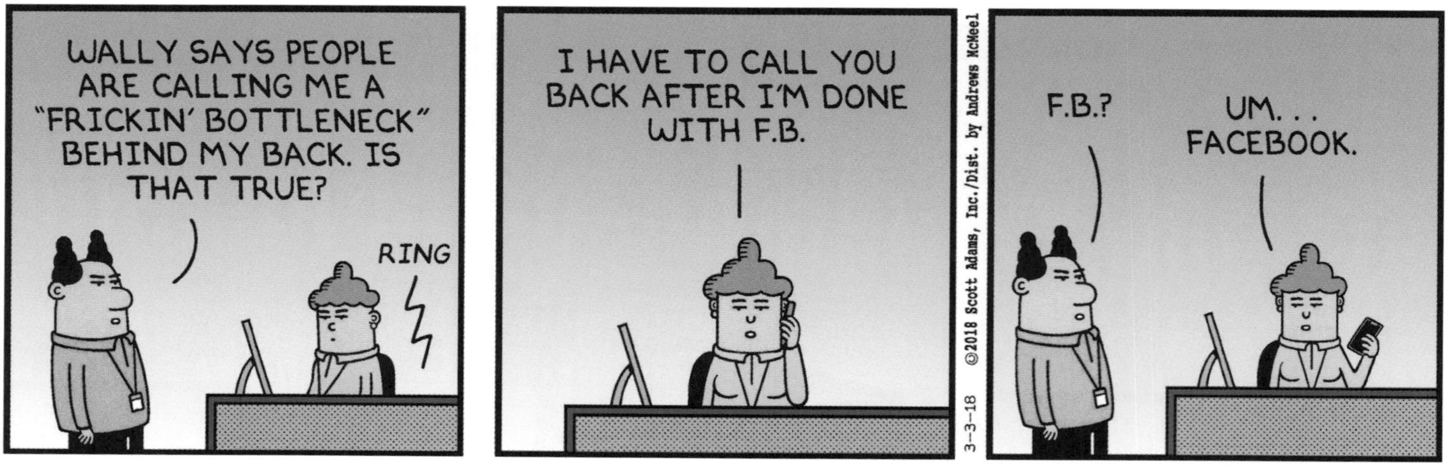
WALLY SAYS PEOPLE ARE CALLING ME A "FRICKIN' BOTTLENECK" BEHIND MY BACK. IS THAT TRUE?
RING
I HAVE TO CALL YOU BACK AFTER I'M DONE WITH F.B.
3-3-18 ©2018 Scott Adams, Inc./Dist. by Andrews McMeel
F.B.?
UM. . . FACEBOOK.

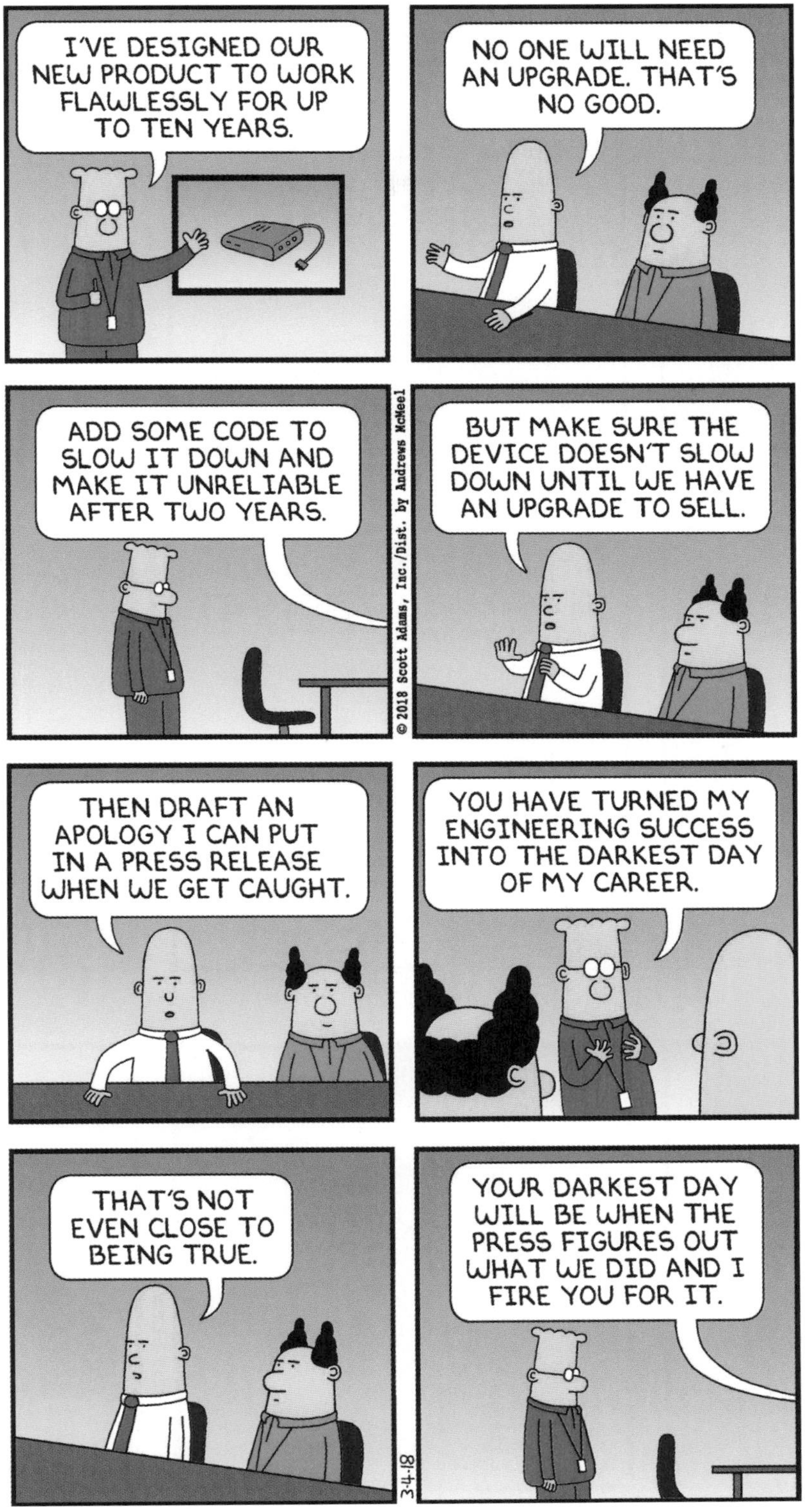
I'VE DESIGNED OUR NEW PRODUCT TO WORK FLAWLESSLY FOR UP TO TEN YEARS.
NO ONE WILL NEED AN UPGRADE. THAT'S NO GOOD.
ADD SOME CODE TO SLOW IT DOWN AND MAKE IT UNRELIABLE AFTER TWO YEARS.
BUT MAKE SURE THE DEVICE DOESN'T SLOW DOWN UNTIL WE HAVE AN UPGRADE TO SELL.
THEN DRAFT AN APOLOGY I CAN PUT IN A PRESS RELEASE WHEN WE GET CAUGHT.
YOU HAVE TURNED MY ENGINEERING SUCCESS INTO THE DARKEST DAY OF MY CAREER.
THAT'S NOT EVEN CLOSE TO BEING TRUE.
YOUR DARKEST DAY WILL BE WHEN THE PRESS FIGURES OUT WHAT WE DID AND I FIRE YOU FOR IT.
© 2018 Scott Adams, Inc./Dist. by Andrews McMeel
3-4-18

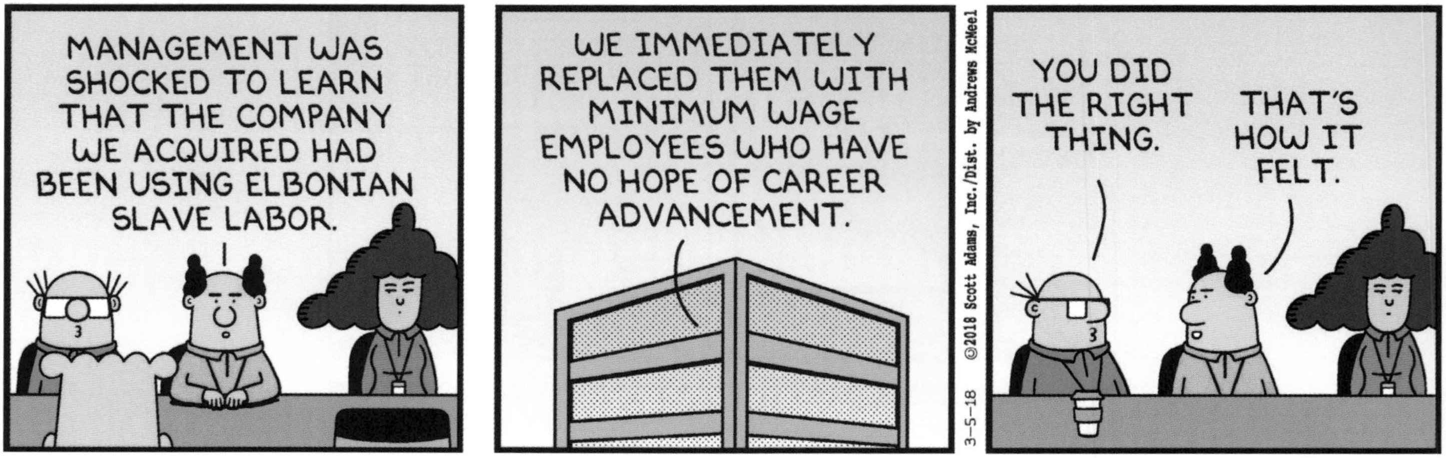
MANAGEMENT WAS SHOCKED TO LEARN THAT THE COMPANY WE ACQUIRED HAD BEEN USING ELBONIAN SLAVE LABOR.
WE IMMEDIATELY REPLACED THEM WITH MINIMUM WAGE EMPLOYEES WHO HAVE NO HOPE OF CAREER ADVANCEMENT.
3-5-18 ©2018 Scott Adams, Inc./Dist. by Andrews McMeel
YOU DID THE RIGHT THING.
THAT'S HOW IT FELT.

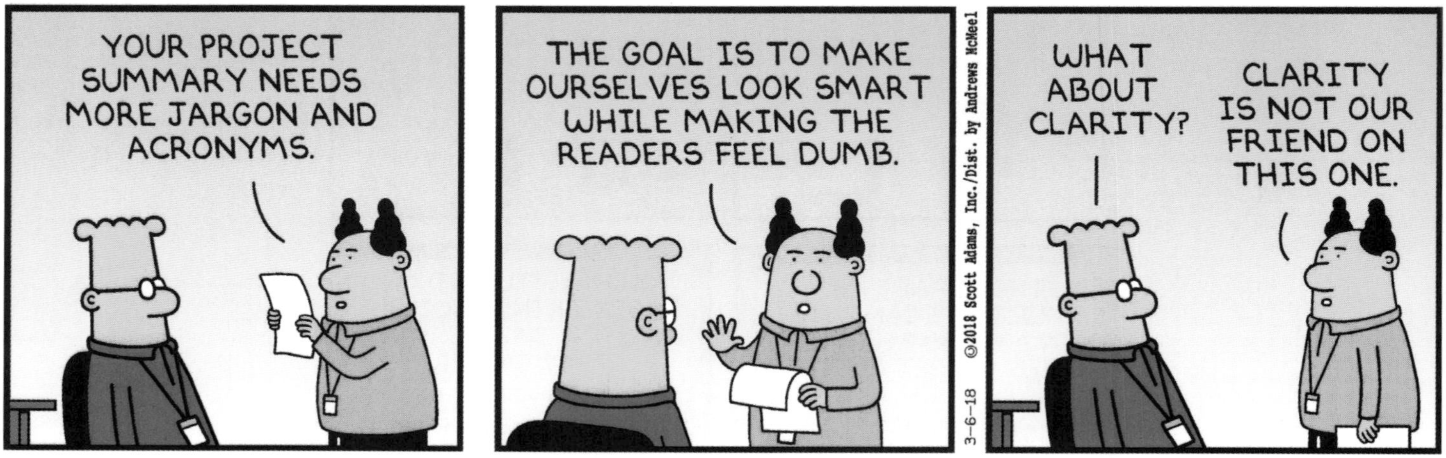
YOUR PROJECT SUMMARY NEEDS MORE JARGON AND ACRONYMS.
THE GOAL IS TO MAKE OURSELVES LOOK SMART WHILE MAKING THE READERS FEEL DUMB.
3-6-18 ©2018 Scott Adams, Inc./Dist. by Andrews McMeel
WHAT ABOUT CLARITY?
CLARITY IS NOT OUR FRIEND ON THIS ONE.

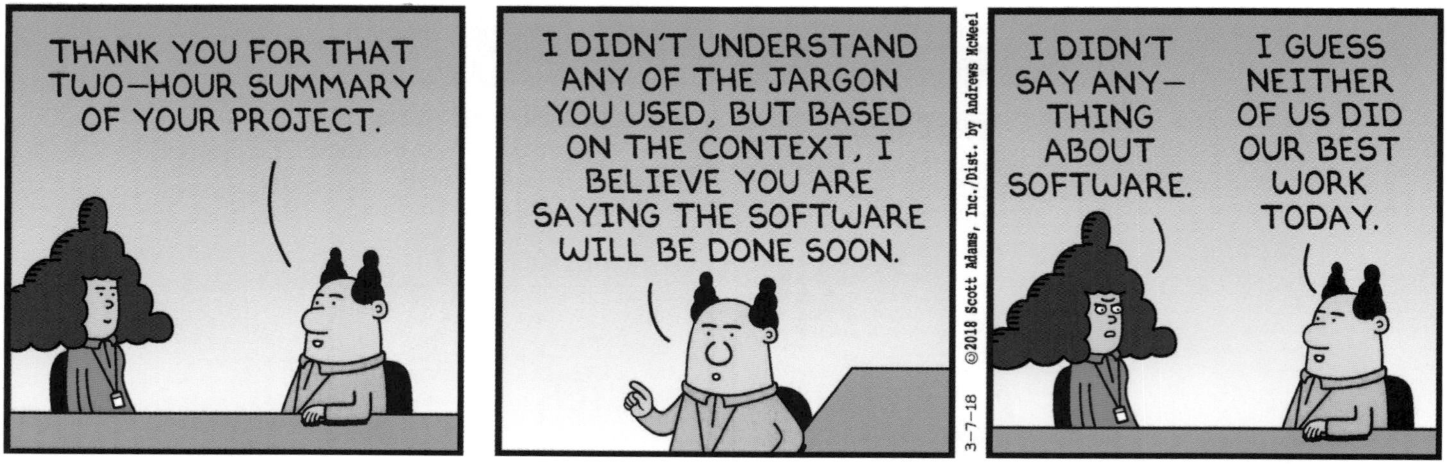
THANK YOU FOR THAT TWO-HOUR SUMMARY OF YOUR PROJECT.
I DIDN'T UNDERSTAND ANY OF THE JARGON YOU USED, BUT BASED ON THE CONTEXT, I BELIEVE YOU ARE SAYING THE SOFTWARE WILL BE DONE SOON.
3-7-18 ©2018 Scott Adams, Inc./Dist. by Andrews McMeel
I DIDN'T SAY ANY-THING ABOUT SOFTWARE.
I GUESS NEITHER OF US DID OUR BEST WORK TODAY.

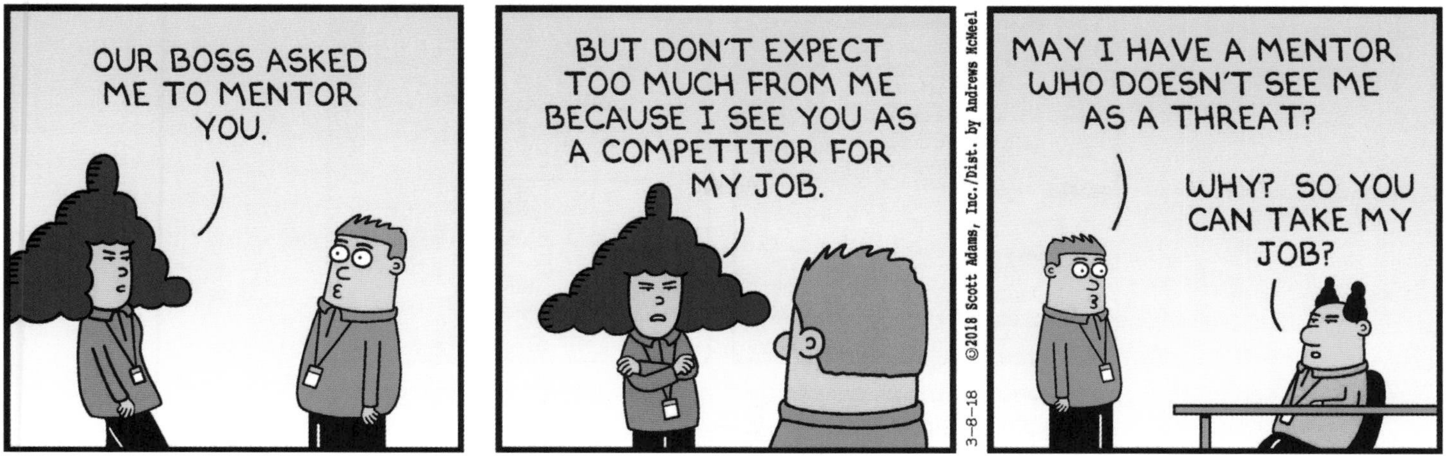
OUR BOSS ASKED ME TO MENTOR YOU.
BUT DON'T EXPECT TOO MUCH FROM ME BECAUSE I SEE YOU AS A COMPETITOR FOR MY JOB.
3-8-18 ©2018 Scott Adams, Inc./Dist. by Andrews McMeel
MAY I HAVE A MENTOR WHO DOESN'T SEE ME AS A THREAT?
WHY? SO YOU CAN TAKE MY JOB?

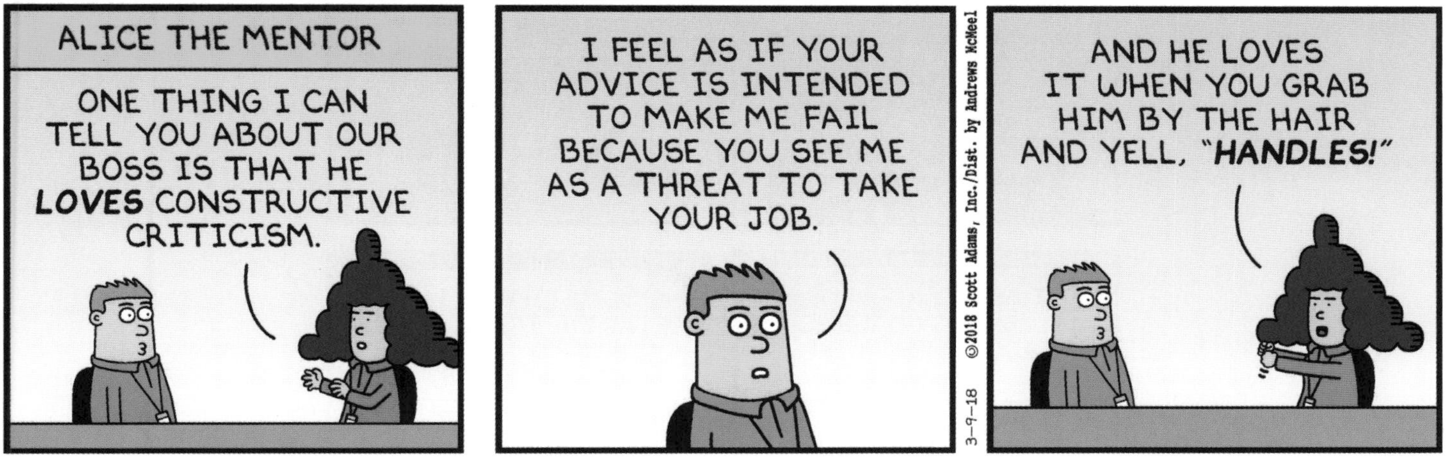
ALICE THE MENTOR
ONE THING I CAN TELL YOU ABOUT OUR BOSS IS THAT HE **LOVES** CONSTRUCTIVE CRITICISM.
I FEEL AS IF YOUR ADVICE IS INTENDED TO MAKE ME FAIL BECAUSE YOU SEE ME AS A THREAT TO TAKE YOUR JOB.
3-9-18 ©2018 Scott Adams, Inc./Dist. by Andrews McMeel
AND HE LOVES IT WHEN YOU GRAB HIM BY THE HAIR AND YELL, "***HANDLES!***"

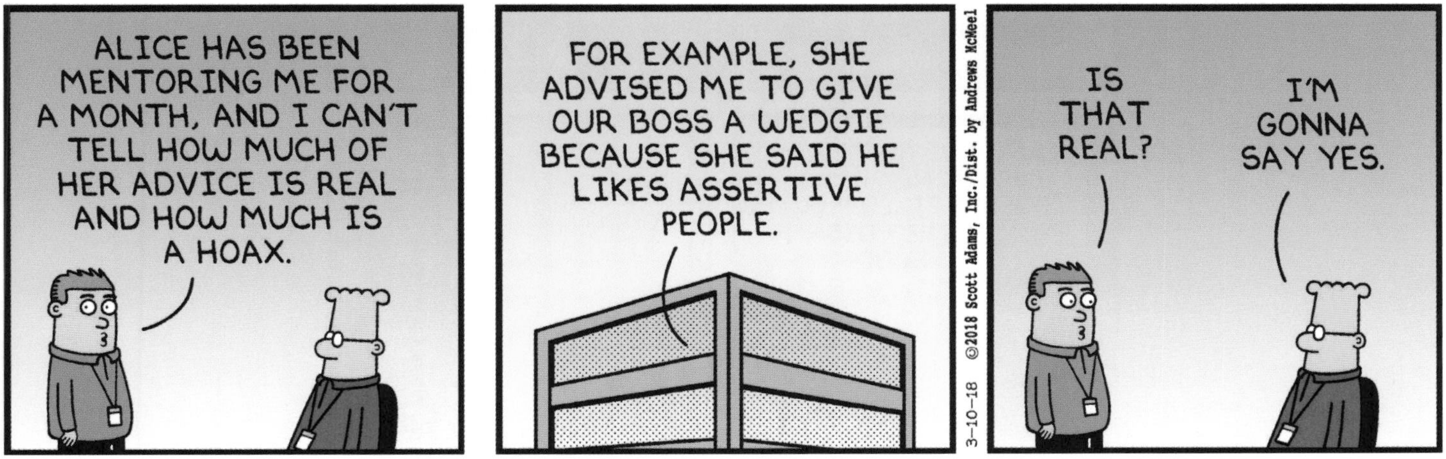
ALICE HAS BEEN MENTORING ME FOR A MONTH, AND I CAN'T TELL HOW MUCH OF HER ADVICE IS REAL AND HOW MUCH IS A HOAX.
FOR EXAMPLE, SHE ADVISED ME TO GIVE OUR BOSS A WEDGIE BECAUSE SHE SAID HE LIKES ASSERTIVE PEOPLE.
3-10-18 ©2018 Scott Adams, Inc./Dist. by Andrews McMeel
IS THAT REAL?
I'M GONNA SAY YES.

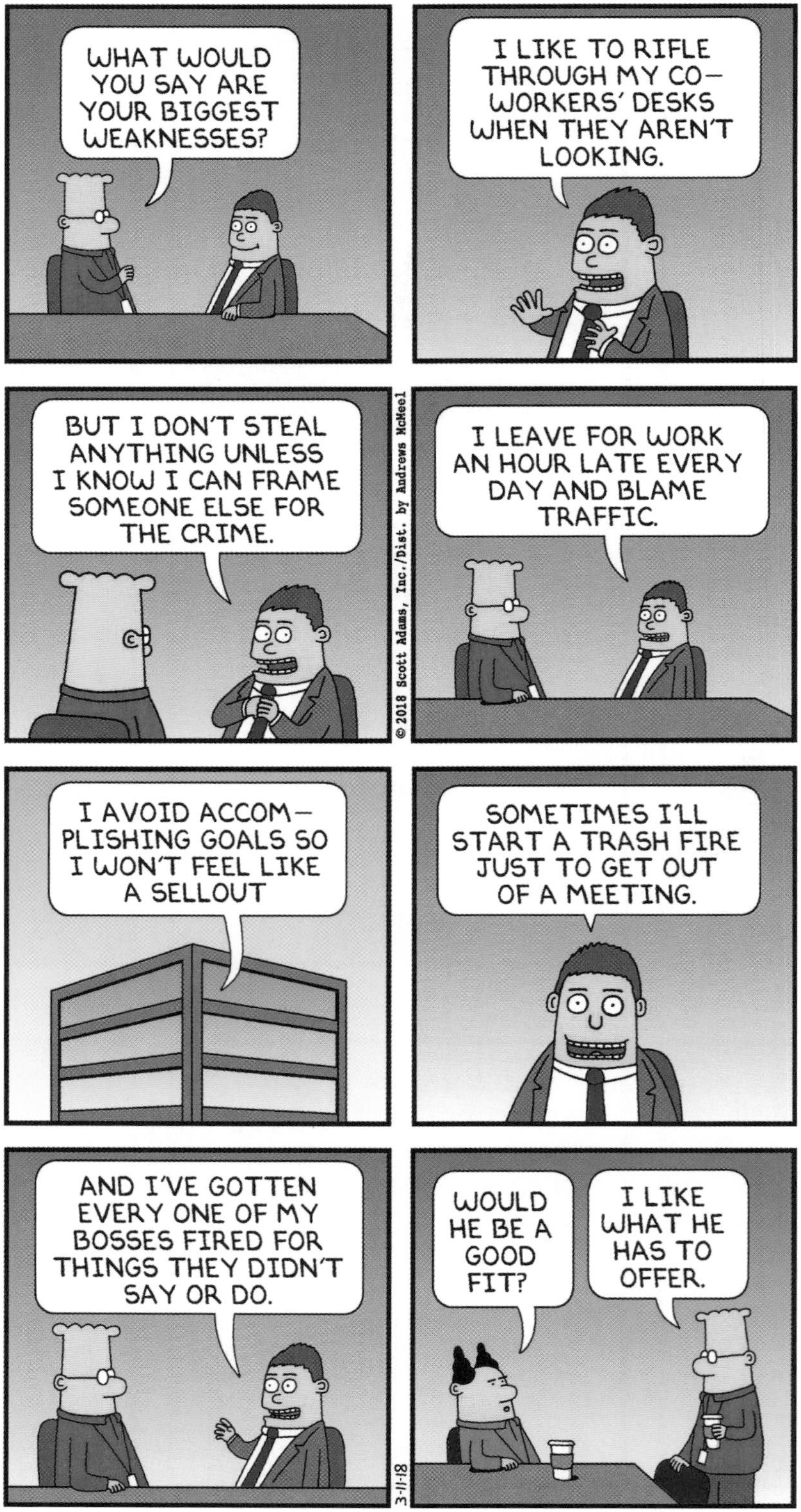
WHAT WOULD YOU SAY ARE YOUR BIGGEST WEAKNESSES?
I LIKE TO RIFLE THROUGH MY CO-WORKERS' DESKS WHEN THEY AREN'T LOOKING.
BUT I DON'T STEAL ANYTHING UNLESS I KNOW I CAN FRAME SOMEONE ELSE FOR THE CRIME.
© 2018 Scott Adams, Inc./Dist. by Andrews McMeel
I LEAVE FOR WORK AN HOUR LATE EVERY DAY AND BLAME TRAFFIC.
I AVOID ACCOM-PLISHING GOALS SO I WON'T FEEL LIKE A SELLOUT
SOMETIMES I'LL START A TRASH FIRE JUST TO GET OUT OF A MEETING.
AND I'VE GOTTEN EVERY ONE OF MY BOSSES FIRED FOR THINGS THEY DIDN'T SAY OR DO.
3-11-18
WOULD HE BE A GOOD FIT?
I LIKE WHAT HE HAS TO OFFER.

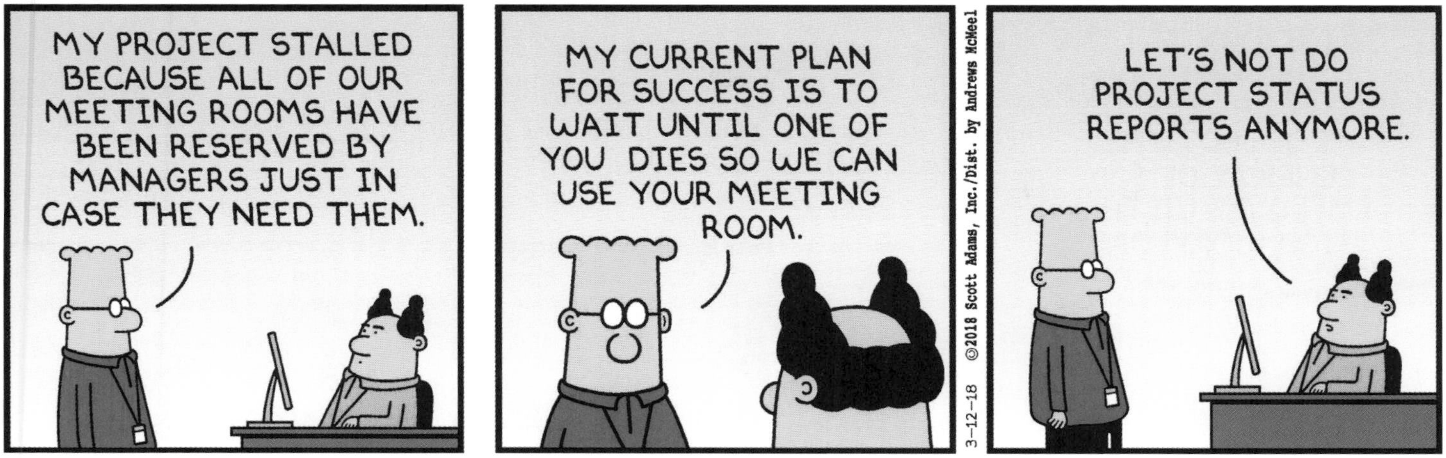
MY PROJECT STALLED BECAUSE ALL OF OUR MEETING ROOMS HAVE BEEN RESERVED BY MANAGERS JUST IN CASE THEY NEED THEM.
MY CURRENT PLAN FOR SUCCESS IS TO WAIT UNTIL ONE OF YOU DIES SO WE CAN USE YOUR MEETING ROOM.
LET'S NOT DO PROJECT STATUS REPORTS ANYMORE.
3-12-18 ©2018 Scott Adams, Inc./Dist. by Andrews McMeel

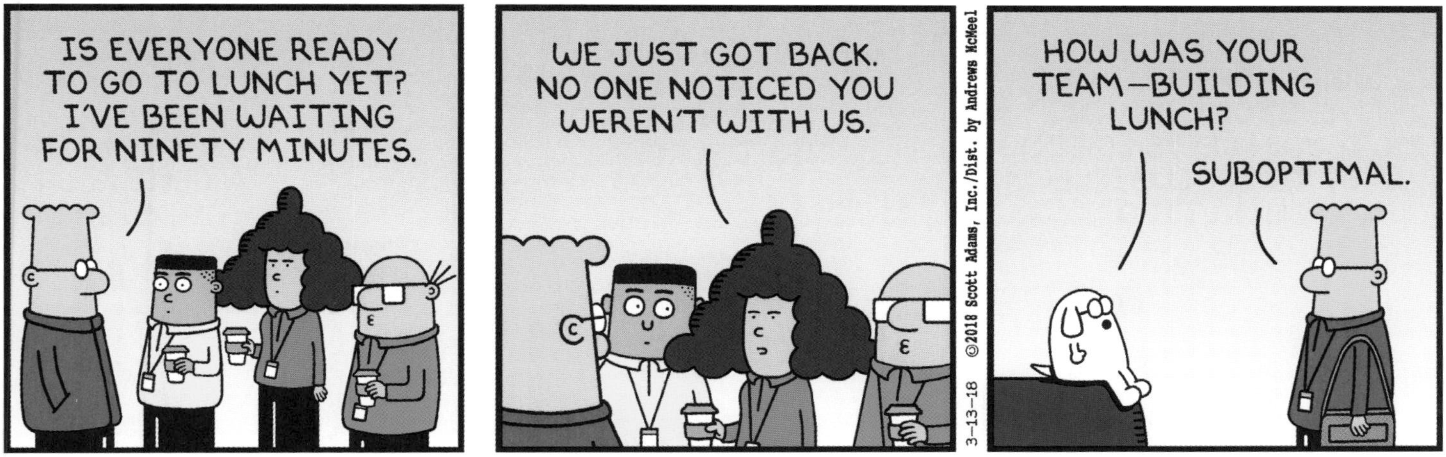
IS EVERYONE READY TO GO TO LUNCH YET? I'VE BEEN WAITING FOR NINETY MINUTES.
WE JUST GOT BACK. NO ONE NOTICED YOU WEREN'T WITH US.
HOW WAS YOUR TEAM-BUILDING LUNCH?
SUBOPTIMAL.
3-13-18 ©2018 Scott Adams, Inc./Dist. by Andrews McMeel

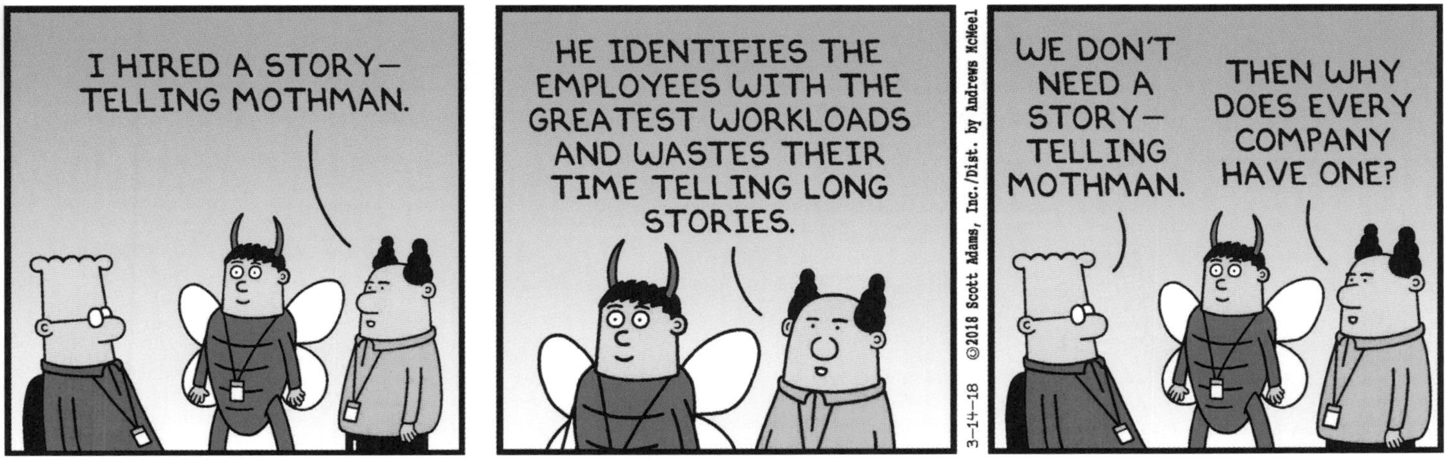
I HIRED A STORY-TELLING MOTHMAN.
HE IDENTIFIES THE EMPLOYEES WITH THE GREATEST WORKLOADS AND WASTES THEIR TIME TELLING LONG STORIES.
WE DON'T NEED A STORY-TELLING MOTHMAN.
THEN WHY DOES EVERY COMPANY HAVE ONE?
3-14-18 ©2018 Scott Adams, Inc./Dist. by Andrews McMeel

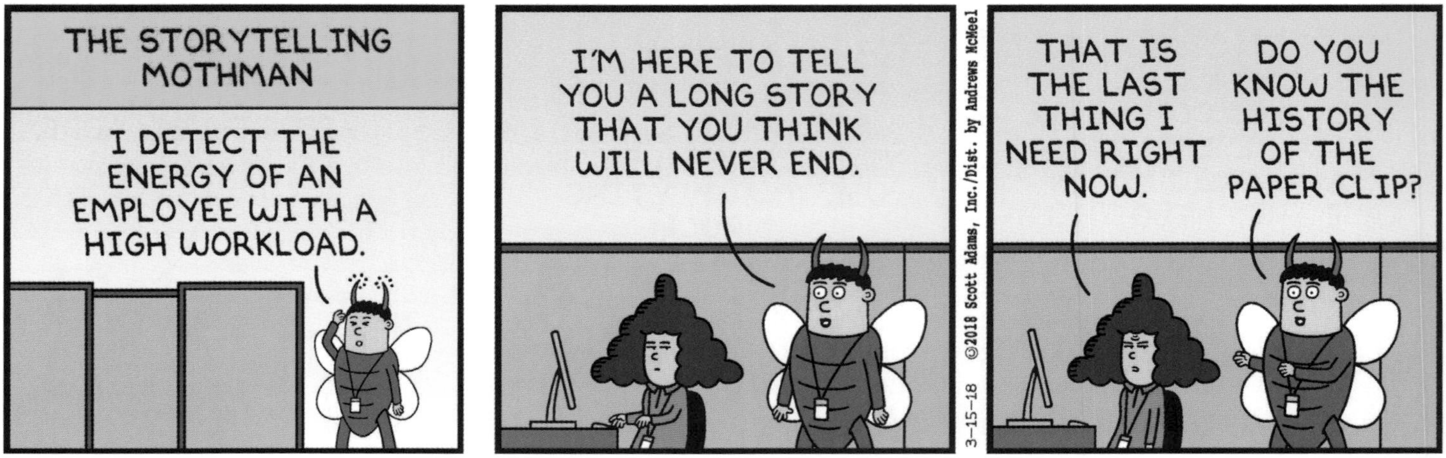
THE STORYTELLING MOTHMAN
I DETECT THE ENERGY OF AN EMPLOYEE WITH A HIGH WORKLOAD.
I'M HERE TO TELL YOU A LONG STORY THAT YOU THINK WILL NEVER END.
3-15-18 ©2018 Scott Adams, Inc./Dist. by Andrews McMeel
THAT IS THE LAST THING I NEED RIGHT NOW.
DO YOU KNOW THE HISTORY OF THE PAPER CLIP?

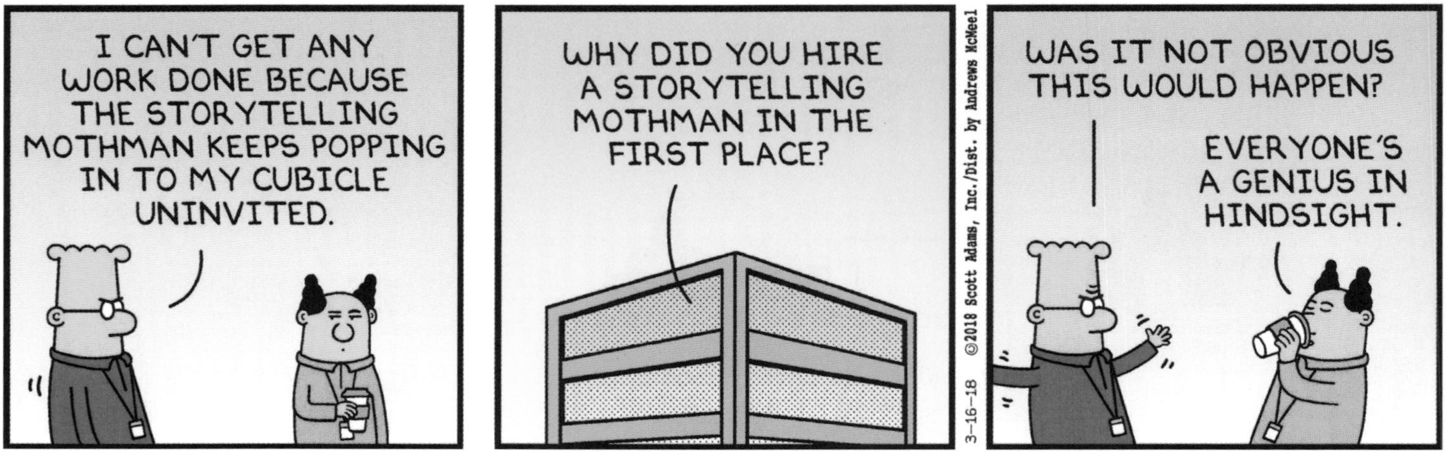
I CAN'T GET ANY WORK DONE BECAUSE THE STORYTELLING MOTHMAN KEEPS POPPING IN TO MY CUBICLE UNINVITED.
WHY DID YOU HIRE A STORYTELLING MOTHMAN IN THE FIRST PLACE?
3-16-18 ©2018 Scott Adams, Inc./Dist. by Andrews McMeel
WAS IT NOT OBVIOUS THIS WOULD HAPPEN?
EVERYONE'S A GENIUS IN HINDSIGHT.

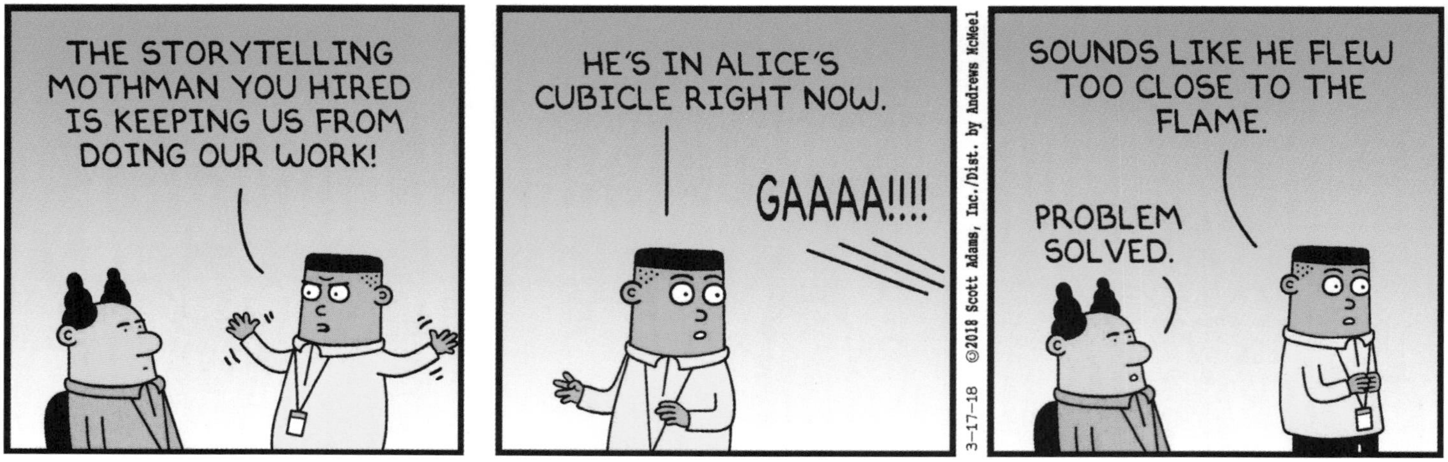
THE STORYTELLING MOTHMAN YOU HIRED IS KEEPING US FROM DOING OUR WORK!
HE'S IN ALICE'S CUBICLE RIGHT NOW.
GAAAA!!!!
3-17-18 ©2018 Scott Adams, Inc./Dist. by Andrews McMeel
SOUNDS LIKE HE FLEW TOO CLOSE TO THE FLAME.
PROBLEM SOLVED.

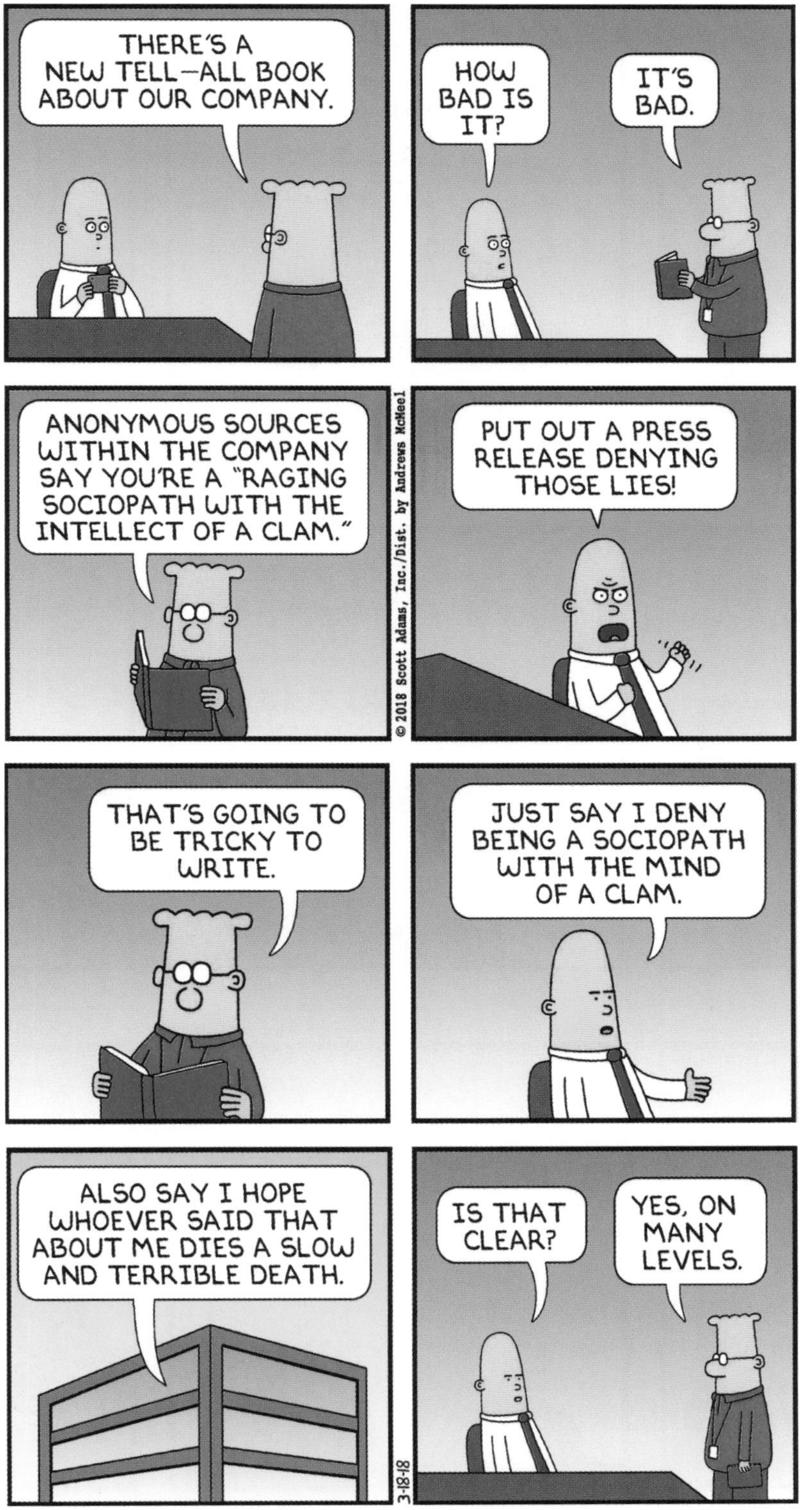
THERE'S A NEW TELL—ALL BOOK ABOUT OUR COMPANY.
HOW BAD IS IT?
IT'S BAD.
ANONYMOUS SOURCES WITHIN THE COMPANY SAY YOU'RE A "RAGING SOCIOPATH WITH THE INTELLECT OF A CLAM."
PUT OUT A PRESS RELEASE DENYING THOSE LIES!
THAT'S GOING TO BE TRICKY TO WRITE.
JUST SAY I DENY BEING A SOCIOPATH WITH THE MIND OF A CLAM.
ALSO SAY I HOPE WHOEVER SAID THAT ABOUT ME DIES A SLOW AND TERRIBLE DEATH.
IS THAT CLEAR?
YES, ON MANY LEVELS.
3-18-18

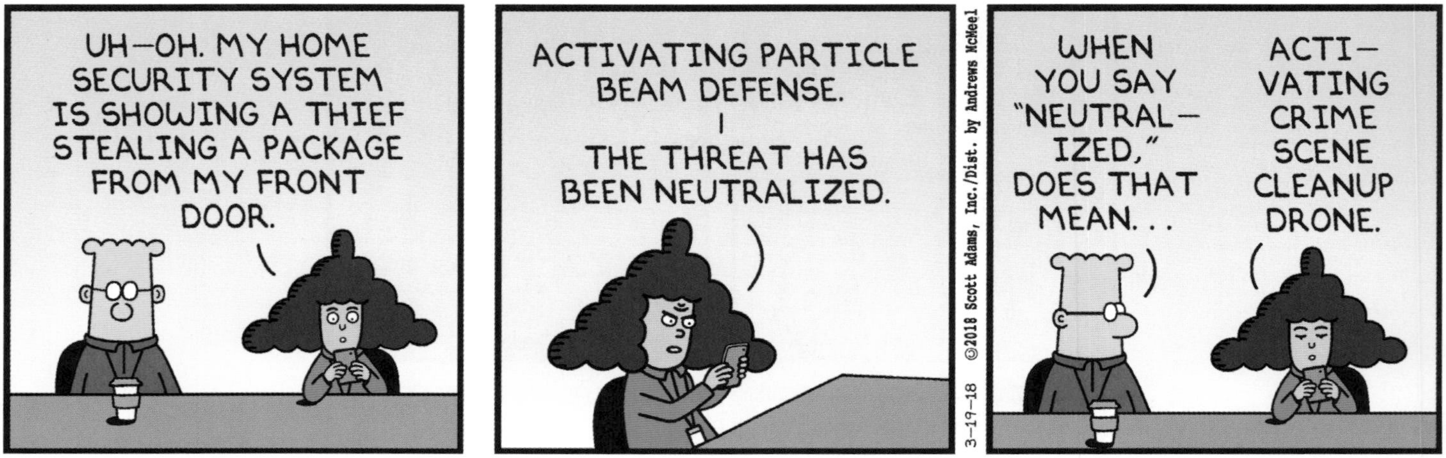
UH—OH. MY HOME SECURITY SYSTEM IS SHOWING A THIEF STEALING A PACKAGE FROM MY FRONT DOOR.
ACTIVATING PARTICLE BEAM DEFENSE.
I
THE THREAT HAS BEEN NEUTRALIZED.
WHEN YOU SAY "NEUTRAL—IZED," DOES THAT MEAN. . .
ACTI—VATING CRIME SCENE CLEANUP DRONE.

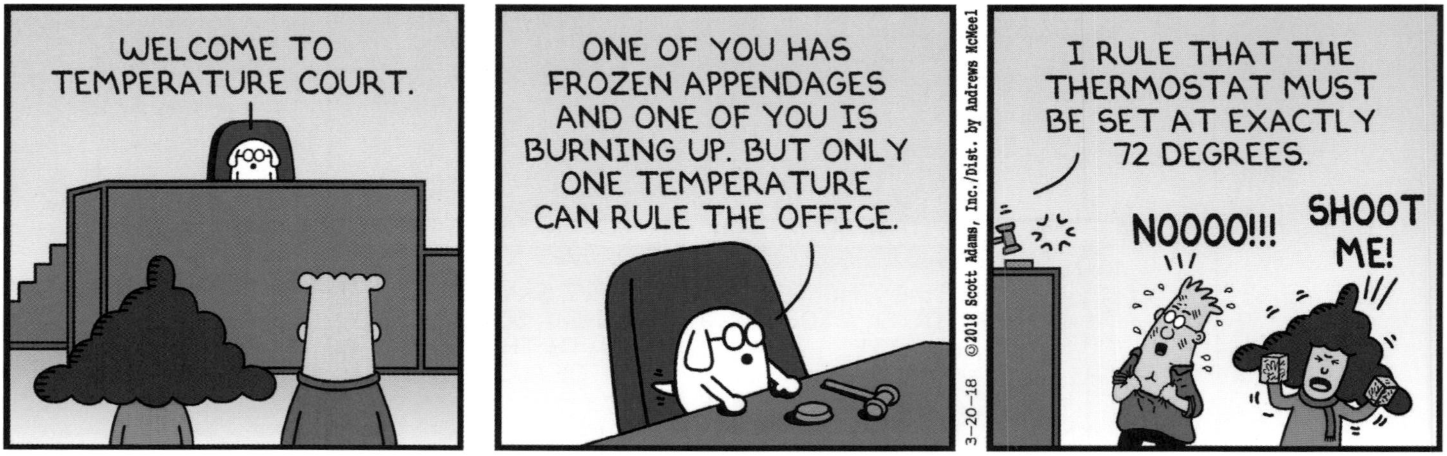
WELCOME TO TEMPERATURE COURT.
ONE OF YOU HAS FROZEN APPENDAGES AND ONE OF YOU IS BURNING UP. BUT ONLY ONE TEMPERATURE CAN RULE THE OFFICE.
I RULE THAT THE THERMOSTAT MUST BE SET AT EXACTLY 72 DEGREES.
NOOOO!!!
SHOOT ME!

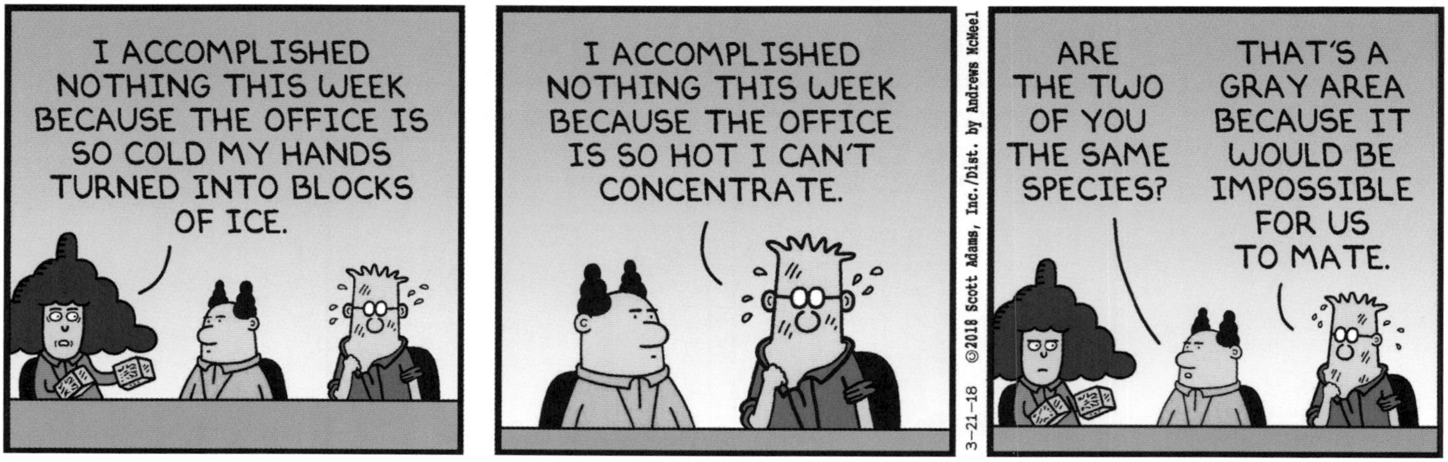
I ACCOMPLISHED NOTHING THIS WEEK BECAUSE THE OFFICE IS SO COLD MY HANDS TURNED INTO BLOCKS OF ICE.
I ACCOMPLISHED NOTHING THIS WEEK BECAUSE THE OFFICE IS SO HOT I CAN'T CONCENTRATE.
ARE THE TWO OF YOU THE SAME SPECIES?
THAT'S A GRAY AREA BECAUSE IT WOULD BE IMPOSSIBLE FOR US TO MATE.

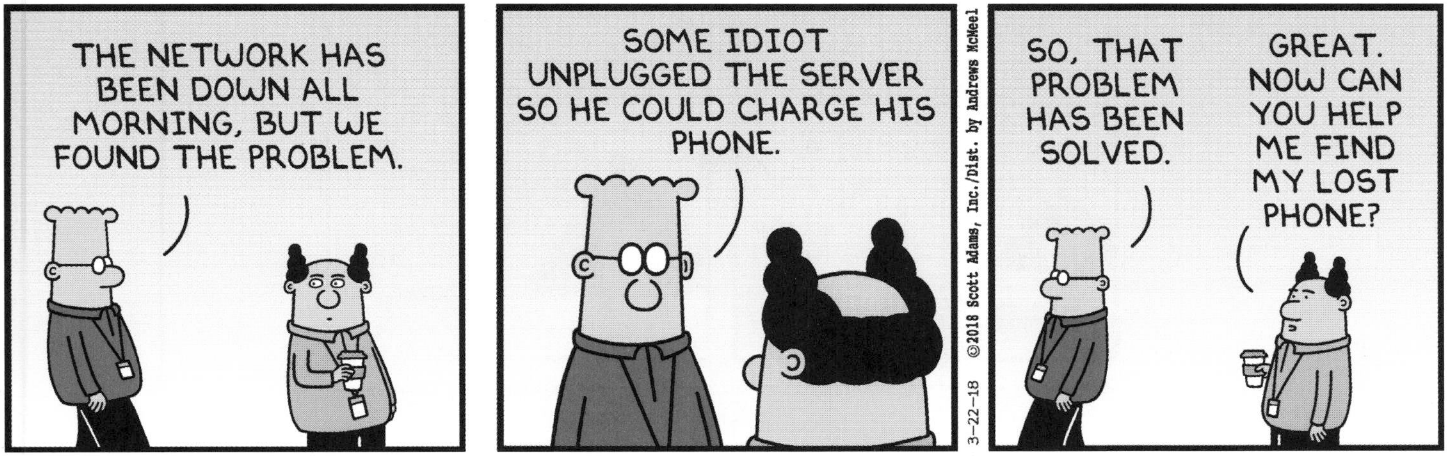
THE NETWORK HAS BEEN DOWN ALL MORNING, BUT WE FOUND THE PROBLEM.
SOME IDIOT UNPLUGGED THE SERVER SO HE COULD CHARGE HIS PHONE.
3-22-18 ©2018 Scott Adams, Inc./Dist. by Andrews McMeel
SO, THAT PROBLEM HAS BEEN SOLVED.
GREAT. NOW CAN YOU HELP ME FIND MY LOST PHONE?

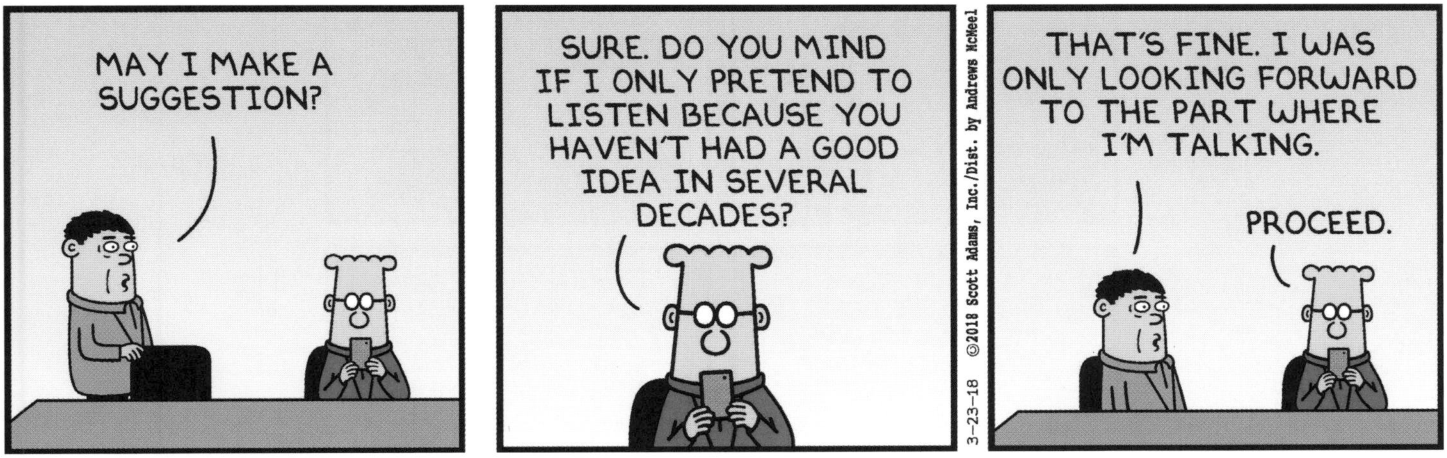
MAY I MAKE A SUGGESTION?
SURE. DO YOU MIND IF I ONLY PRETEND TO LISTEN BECAUSE YOU HAVEN'T HAD A GOOD IDEA IN SEVERAL DECADES?
3-23-18 ©2018 Scott Adams, Inc./Dist. by Andrews McMeel
THAT'S FINE. I WAS ONLY LOOKING FORWARD TO THE PART WHERE I'M TALKING.
PROCEED.

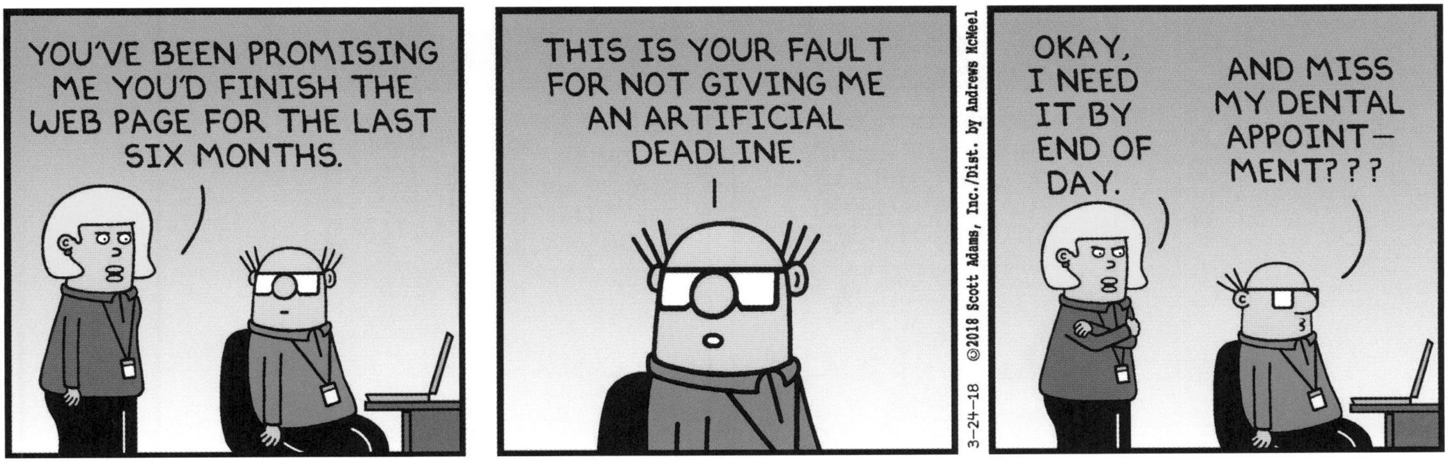
YOU'VE BEEN PROMISING ME YOU'D FINISH THE WEB PAGE FOR THE LAST SIX MONTHS.
THIS IS YOUR FAULT FOR NOT GIVING ME AN ARTIFICIAL DEADLINE.
3-24-18 ©2018 Scott Adams, Inc./Dist. by Andrews McMeel
OKAY, I NEED IT BY END OF DAY.
AND MISS MY DENTAL APPOINT- MENT???

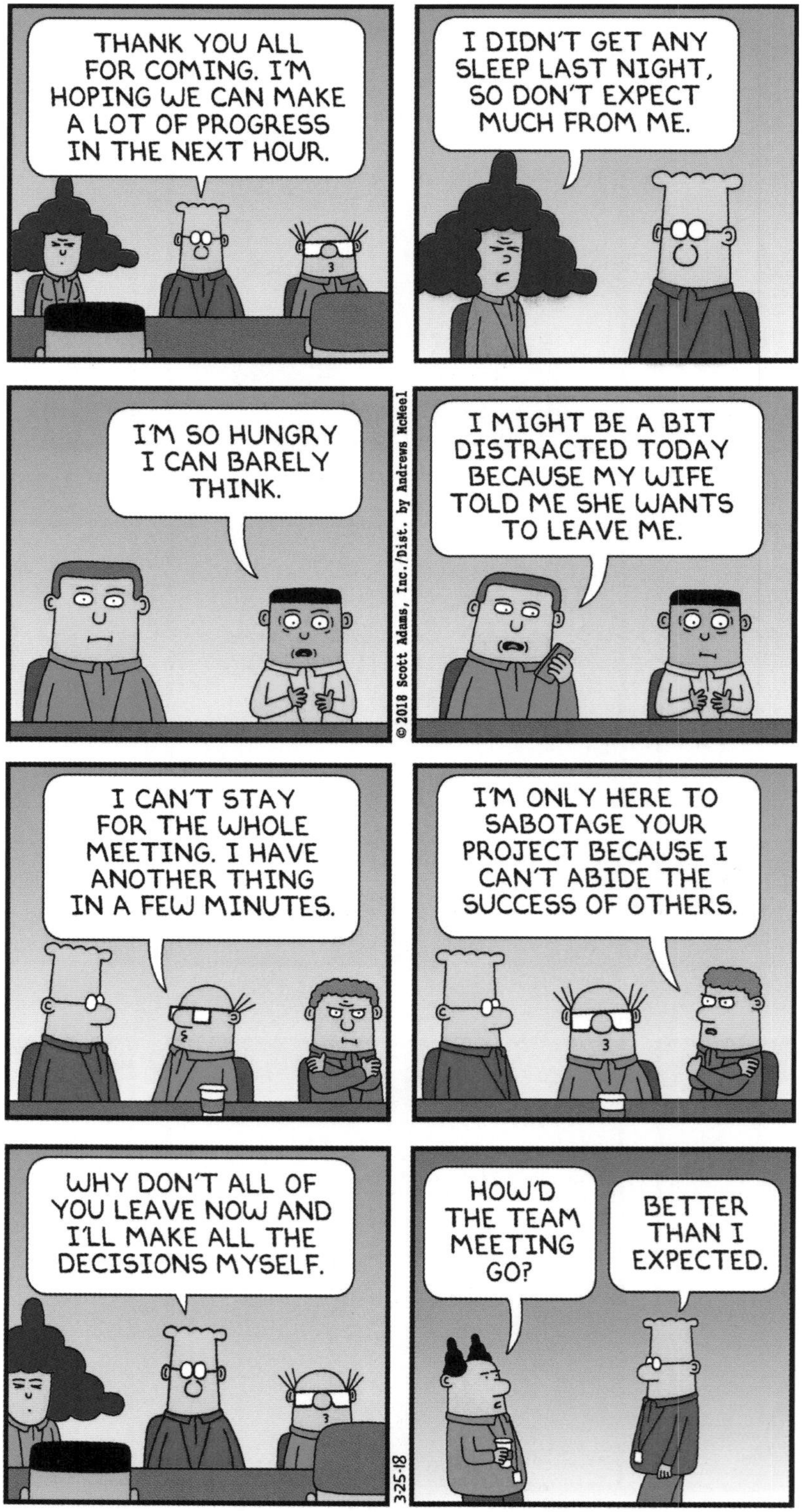
THANK YOU ALL FOR COMING. I'M HOPING WE CAN MAKE A LOT OF PROGRESS IN THE NEXT HOUR.
I DIDN'T GET ANY SLEEP LAST NIGHT, SO DON'T EXPECT MUCH FROM ME.
I'M SO HUNGRY I CAN BARELY THINK.
I MIGHT BE A BIT DISTRACTED TODAY BECAUSE MY WIFE TOLD ME SHE WANTS TO LEAVE ME.
I CAN'T STAY FOR THE WHOLE MEETING. I HAVE ANOTHER THING IN A FEW MINUTES.
I'M ONLY HERE TO SABOTAGE YOUR PROJECT BECAUSE I CAN'T ABIDE THE SUCCESS OF OTHERS.
WHY DON'T ALL OF YOU LEAVE NOW AND I'LL MAKE ALL THE DECISIONS MYSELF.
HOW'D THE TEAM MEETING GO?
BETTER THAN I EXPECTED.
© 2018 Scott Adams, Inc./Dist. by Andrews McMeel
3-25-18

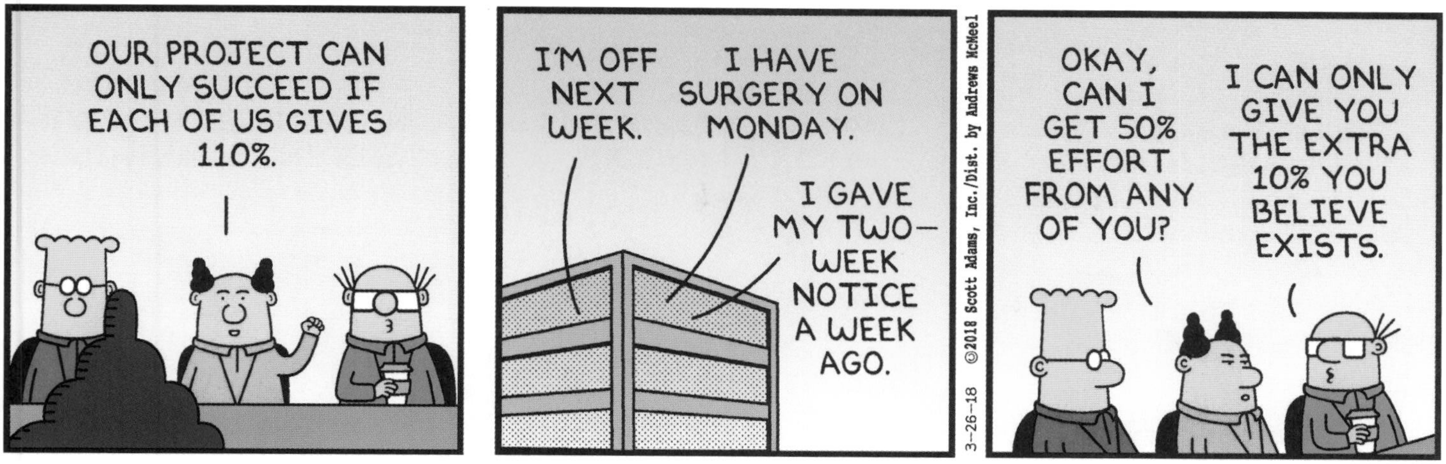
OUR PROJECT CAN ONLY SUCCEED IF EACH OF US GIVES 110%.
I'M OFF NEXT WEEK.
I HAVE SURGERY ON MONDAY.
I GAVE MY TWO-WEEK NOTICE A WEEK AGO.
3-26-18 ©2018 Scott Adams, Inc./Dist. by Andrews McMeel
OKAY, CAN I GET 50% EFFORT FROM ANY OF YOU?
I CAN ONLY GIVE YOU THE EXTRA 10% YOU BELIEVE EXISTS.

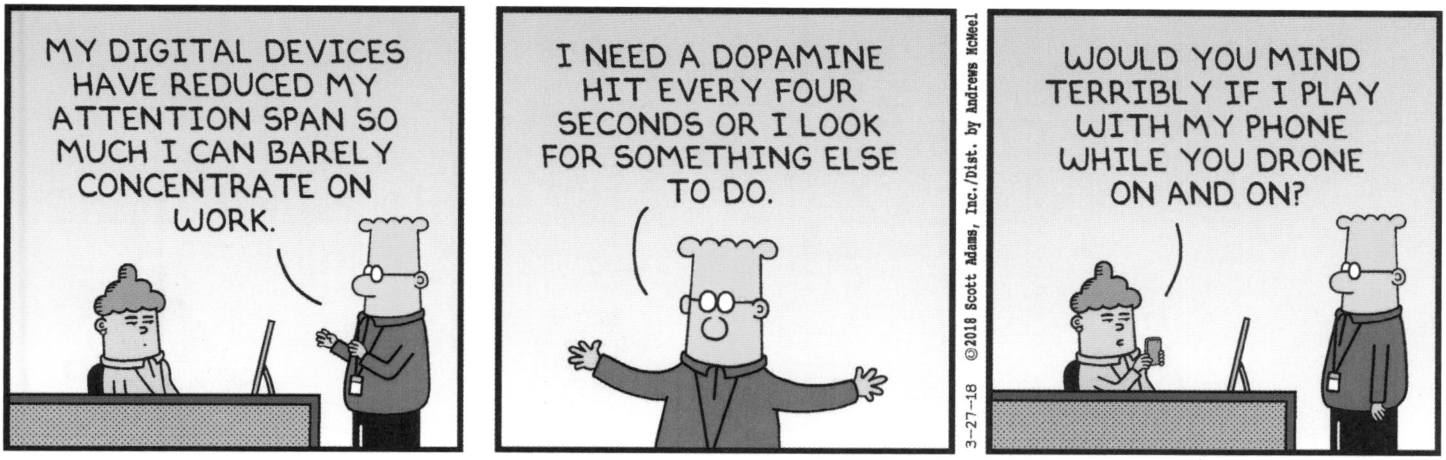
MY DIGITAL DEVICES HAVE REDUCED MY ATTENTION SPAN SO MUCH I CAN BARELY CONCENTRATE ON WORK.
I NEED A DOPAMINE HIT EVERY FOUR SECONDS OR I LOOK FOR SOMETHING ELSE TO DO.
3-27-18 ©2018 Scott Adams, Inc./Dist. by Andrews McMeel
WOULD YOU MIND TERRIBLY IF I PLAY WITH MY PHONE WHILE YOU DRONE ON AND ON?

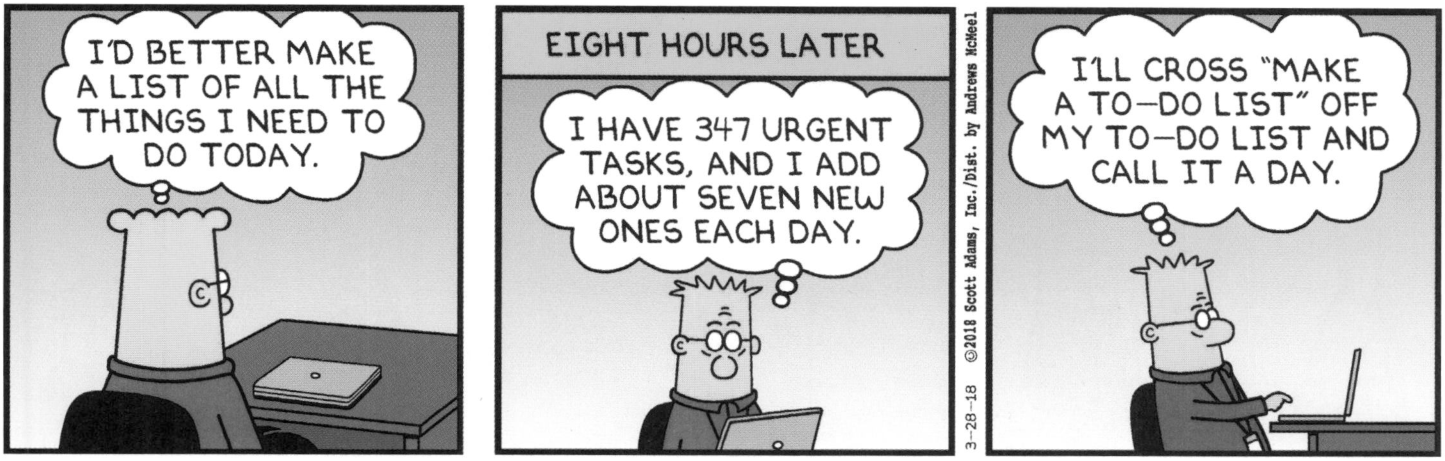
I'D BETTER MAKE A LIST OF ALL THE THINGS I NEED TO DO TODAY.
EIGHT HOURS LATER
I HAVE 347 URGENT TASKS, AND I ADD ABOUT SEVEN NEW ONES EACH DAY.
3-28-18 ©2018 Scott Adams, Inc./Dist. by Andrews McMeel
I'LL CROSS "MAKE A TO-DO LIST" OFF MY TO-DO LIST AND CALL IT A DAY.

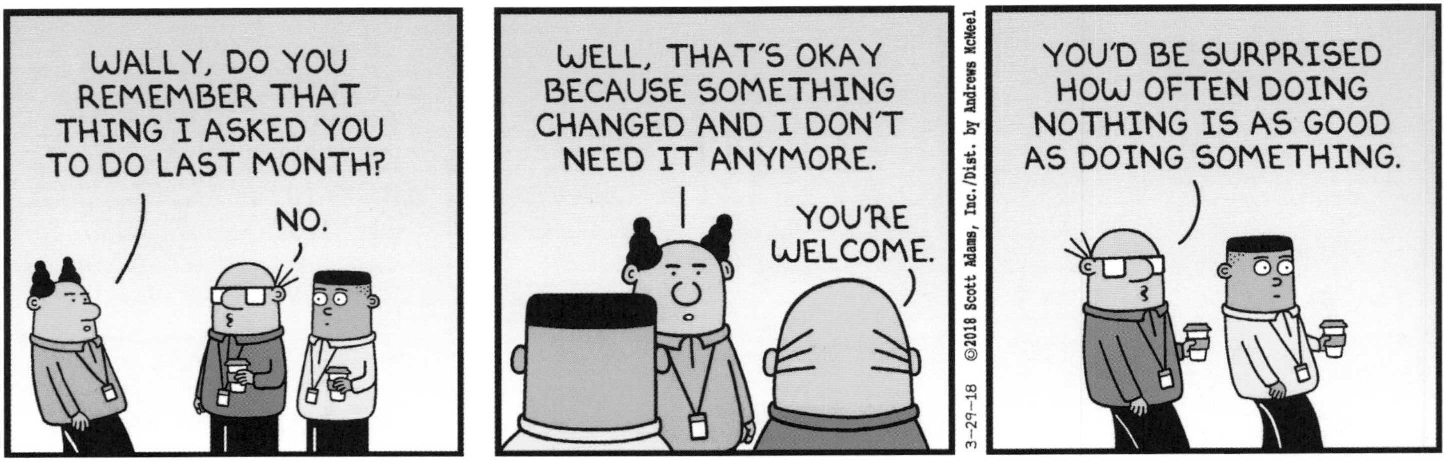
WALLY, DO YOU REMEMBER THAT THING I ASKED YOU TO DO LAST MONTH?
NO.
WELL, THAT'S OKAY BECAUSE SOMETHING CHANGED AND I DON'T NEED IT ANYMORE.
YOU'RE WELCOME.
3-29-18 ©2018 Scott Adams, Inc./Dist. by Andrews McMeel
YOU'D BE SURPRISED HOW OFTEN DOING NOTHING IS AS GOOD AS DOING SOMETHING.

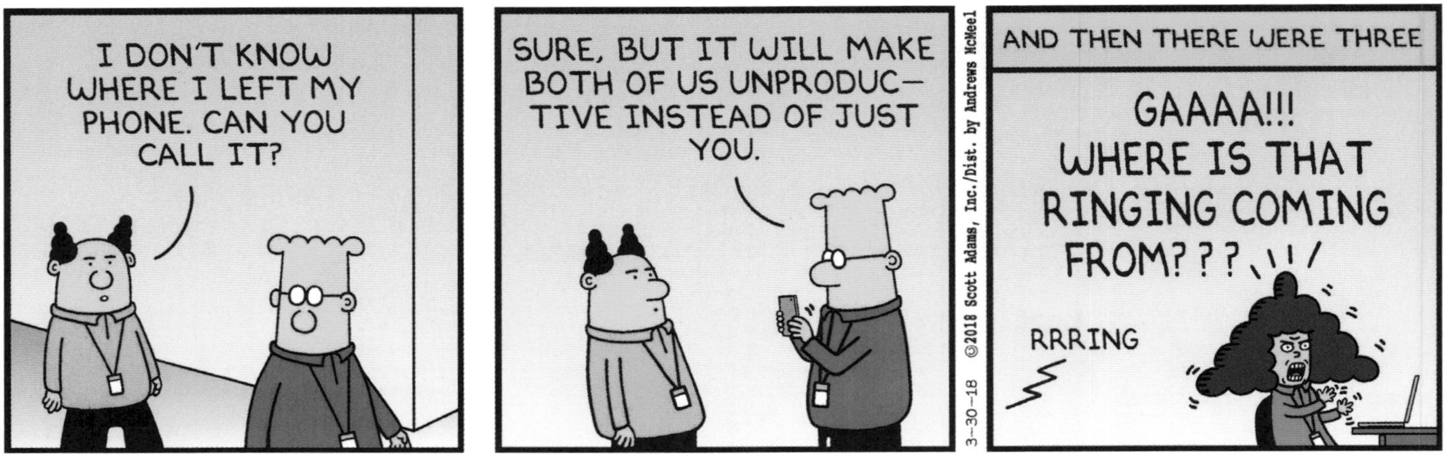
I DON'T KNOW WHERE I LEFT MY PHONE. CAN YOU CALL IT?
SURE, BUT IT WILL MAKE BOTH OF US UNPRODUC- TIVE INSTEAD OF JUST YOU.
3-30-18 ©2018 Scott Adams, Inc./Dist. by Andrews McMeel
AND THEN THERE WERE THREE
GAAAA!!! WHERE IS THAT RINGING COMING FROM???
RRRING

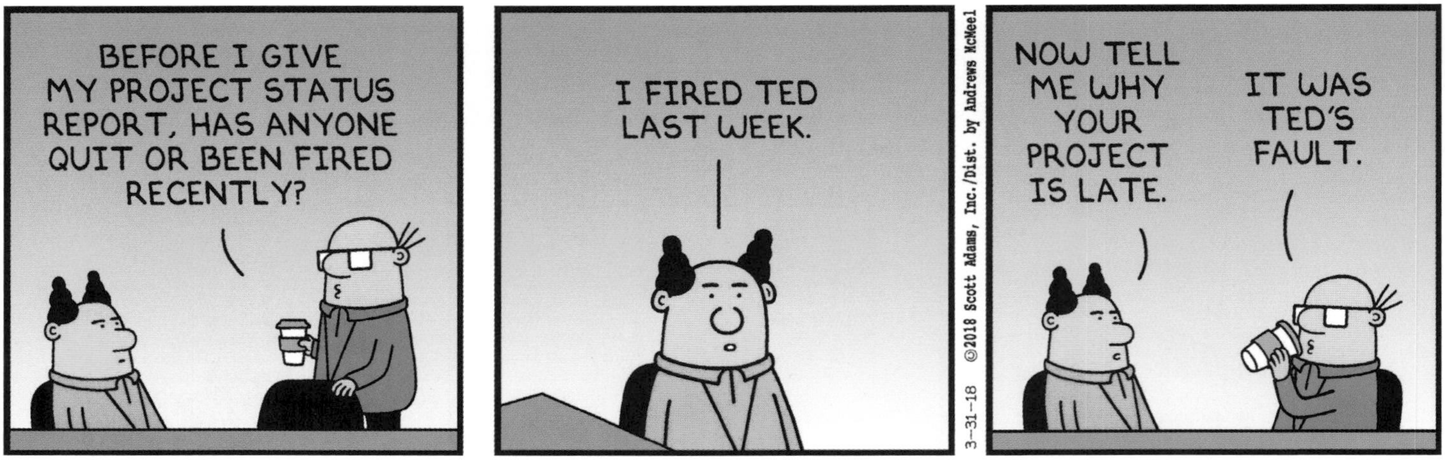
BEFORE I GIVE MY PROJECT STATUS REPORT, HAS ANYONE QUIT OR BEEN FIRED RECENTLY?
I FIRED TED LAST WEEK.
3-31-18 ©2018 Scott Adams, Inc./Dist. by Andrews McMeel
NOW TELL ME WHY YOUR PROJECT IS LATE.
IT WAS TED'S FAULT.

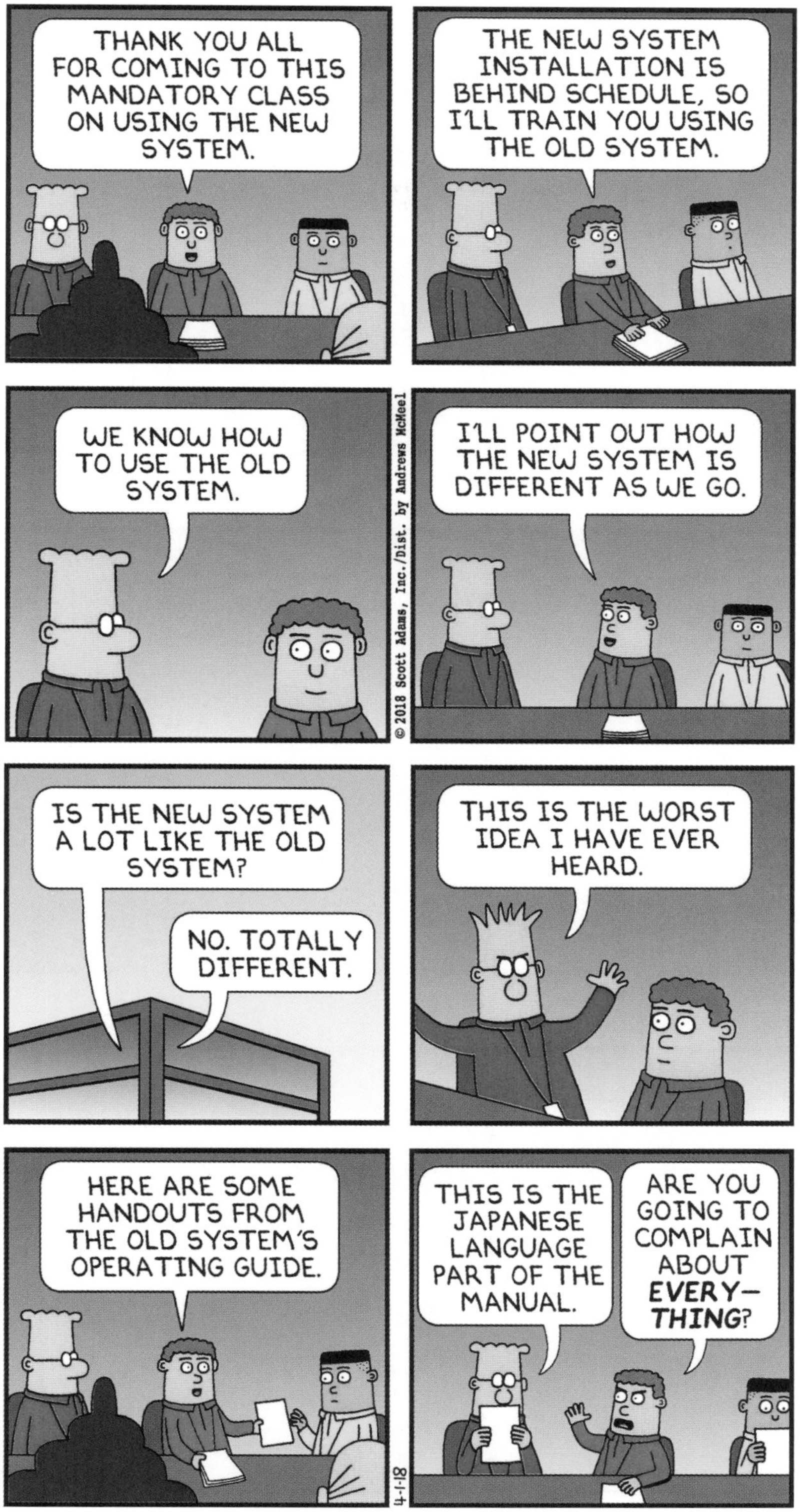
THANK YOU ALL FOR COMING TO THIS MANDATORY CLASS ON USING THE NEW SYSTEM.
THE NEW SYSTEM INSTALLATION IS BEHIND SCHEDULE, SO I'LL TRAIN YOU USING THE OLD SYSTEM.
WE KNOW HOW TO USE THE OLD SYSTEM.
I'LL POINT OUT HOW THE NEW SYSTEM IS DIFFERENT AS WE GO.
© 2018 Scott Adams, Inc./Dist. by Andrews McMeel
IS THE NEW SYSTEM A LOT LIKE THE OLD SYSTEM?
NO. TOTALLY DIFFERENT.
THIS IS THE WORST IDEA I HAVE EVER HEARD.
HERE ARE SOME HANDOUTS FROM THE OLD SYSTEM'S OPERATING GUIDE.
4-1-18
THIS IS THE JAPANESE LANGUAGE PART OF THE MANUAL.
ARE YOU GOING TO COMPLAIN ABOUT **EVERY-THING**?

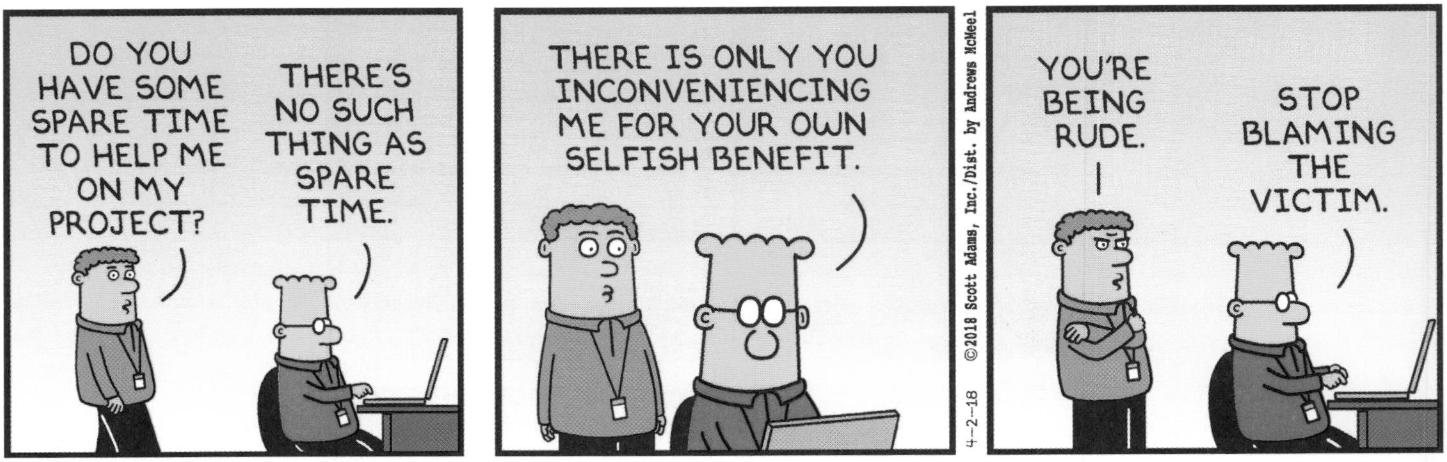
DO YOU HAVE SOME SPARE TIME TO HELP ME ON MY PROJECT?
THERE'S NO SUCH THING AS SPARE TIME.
THERE IS ONLY YOU INCONVENIENCING ME FOR YOUR OWN SELFISH BENEFIT.
4-2-18 ©2018 Scott Adams, Inc./Dist. by Andrews McMeel
YOU'RE BEING RUDE.
STOP BLAMING THE VICTIM.

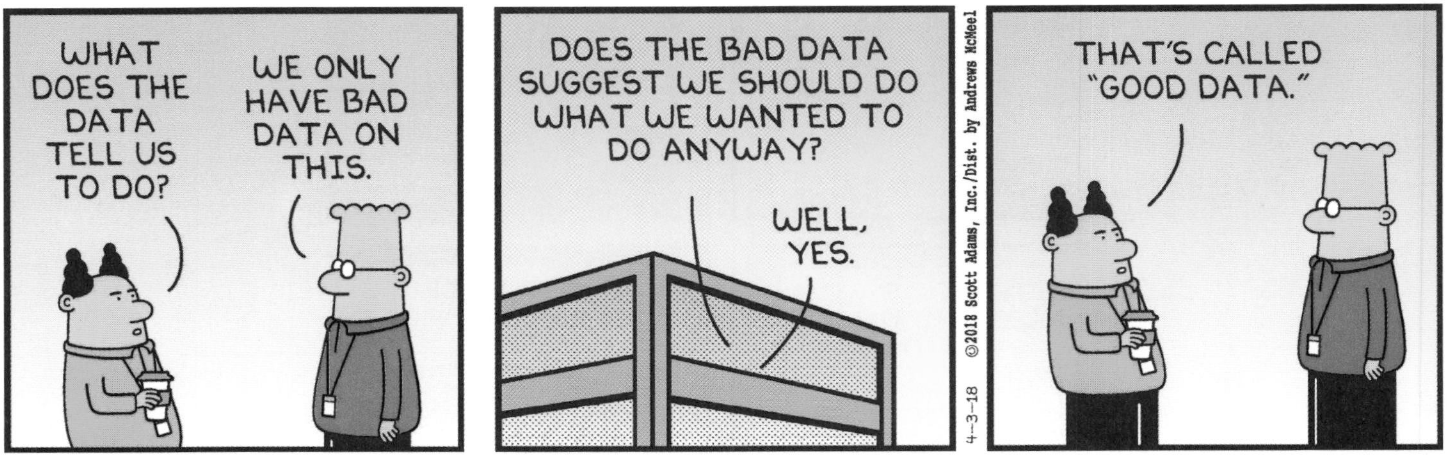
WHAT DOES THE DATA TELL US TO DO?
WE ONLY HAVE BAD DATA ON THIS.
DOES THE BAD DATA SUGGEST WE SHOULD DO WHAT WE WANTED TO DO ANYWAY?
WELL, YES.
4-3-18 ©2018 Scott Adams, Inc./Dist. by Andrews McMeel
THAT'S CALLED "GOOD DATA."

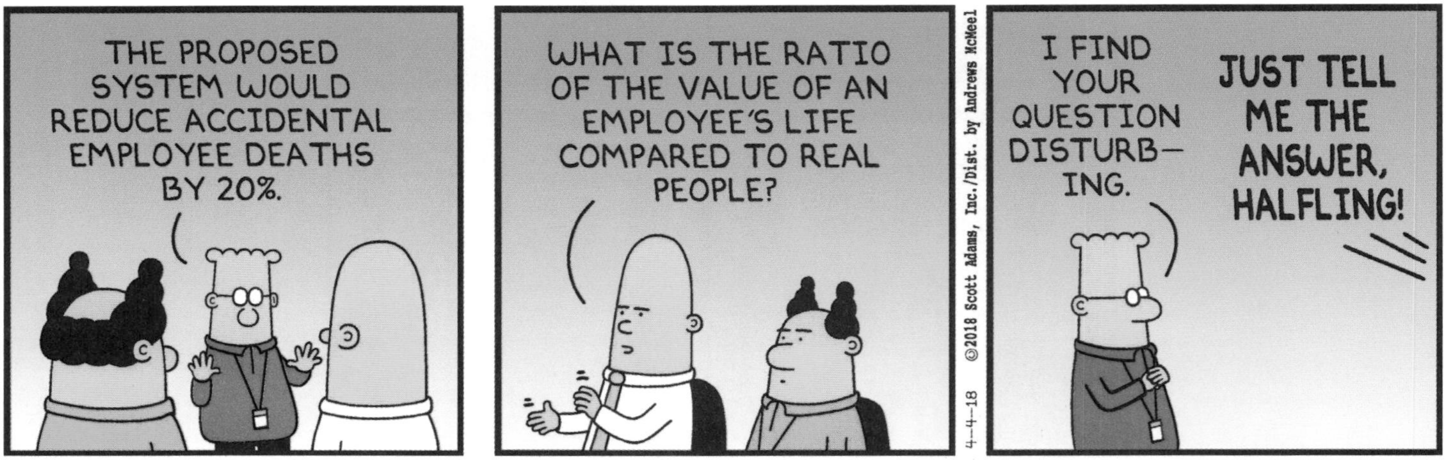
THE PROPOSED SYSTEM WOULD REDUCE ACCIDENTAL EMPLOYEE DEATHS BY 20%.
WHAT IS THE RATIO OF THE VALUE OF AN EMPLOYEE'S LIFE COMPARED TO REAL PEOPLE?
4-4-18 ©2018 Scott Adams, Inc./Dist. by Andrews McMeel
I FIND YOUR QUESTION DISTURB-ING.
JUST TELL ME THE ANSWER, HALFLING!

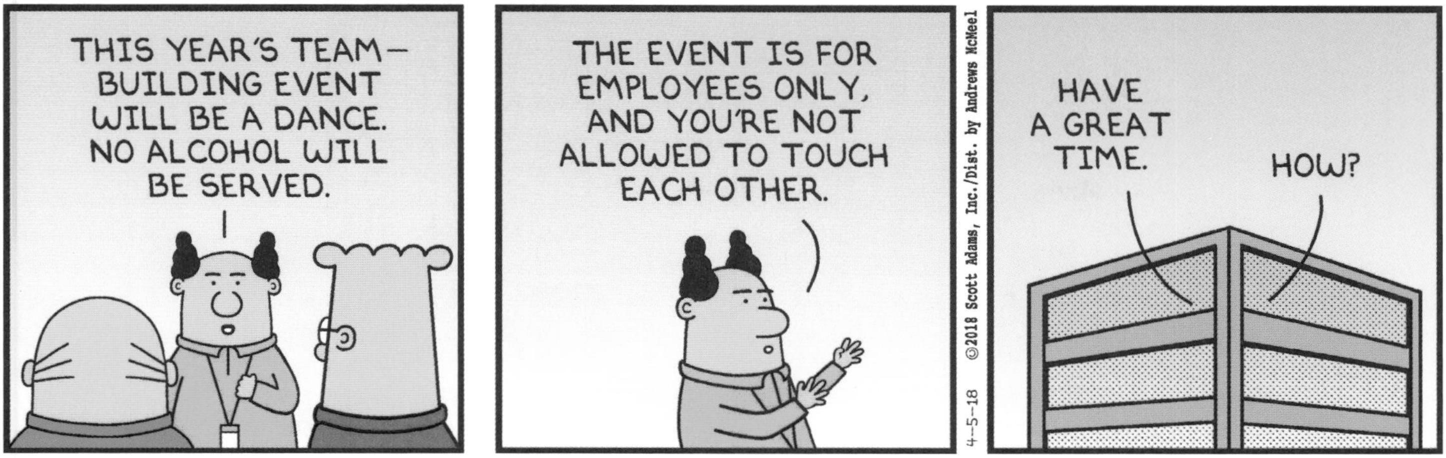
THIS YEAR'S TEAM–BUILDING EVENT WILL BE A DANCE. NO ALCOHOL WILL BE SERVED.
THE EVENT IS FOR EMPLOYEES ONLY, AND YOU'RE NOT ALLOWED TO TOUCH EACH OTHER.
4-5-18 ©2018 Scott Adams, Inc./Dist. by Andrews McMeel
HAVE A GREAT TIME.
HOW?

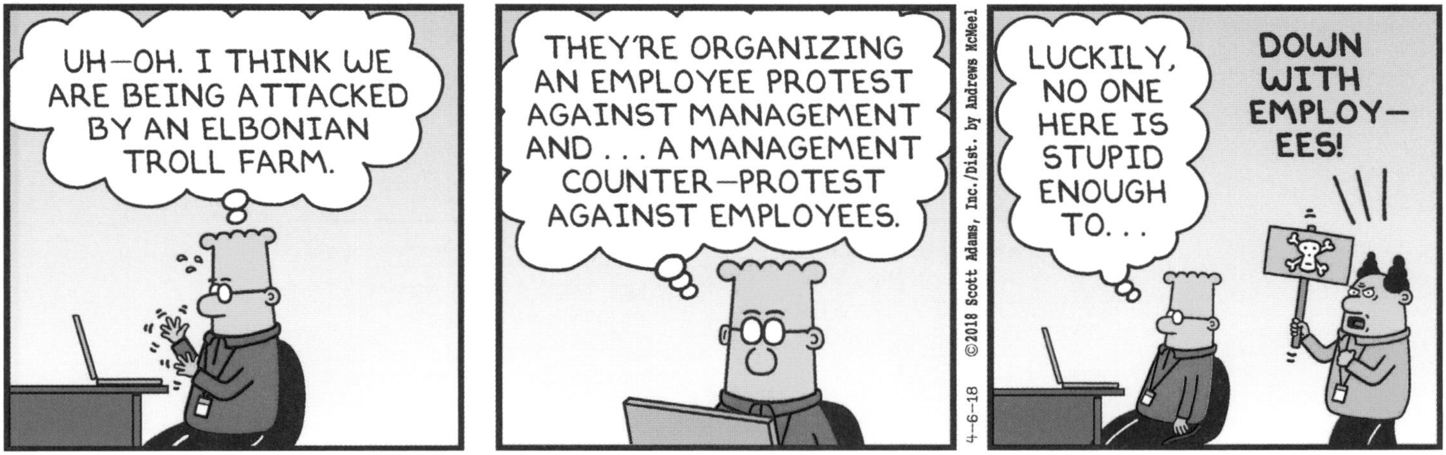
UH–OH. I THINK WE ARE BEING ATTACKED BY AN ELBONIAN TROLL FARM.
THEY'RE ORGANIZING AN EMPLOYEE PROTEST AGAINST MANAGEMENT AND . . . A MANAGEMENT COUNTER–PROTEST AGAINST EMPLOYEES.
4-6-18 ©2018 Scott Adams, Inc./Dist. by Andrews McMeel
LUCKILY, NO ONE HERE IS STUPID ENOUGH TO. . .
DOWN WITH EMPLOY–EES!

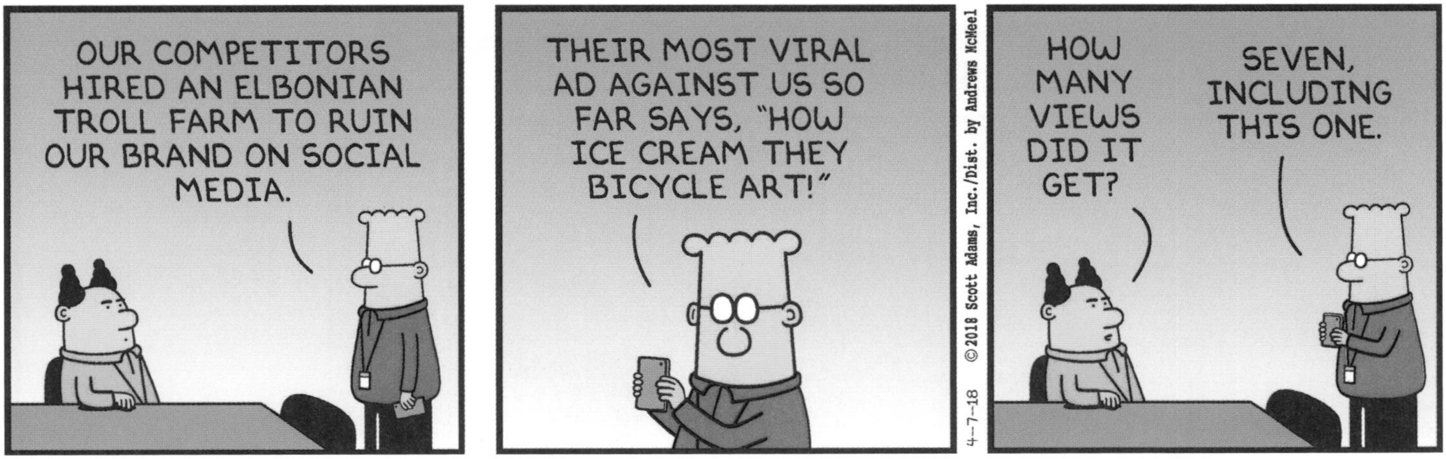
OUR COMPETITORS HIRED AN ELBONIAN TROLL FARM TO RUIN OUR BRAND ON SOCIAL MEDIA.
THEIR MOST VIRAL AD AGAINST US SO FAR SAYS, "HOW ICE CREAM THEY BICYCLE ART!"
4-7-18 ©2018 Scott Adams, Inc./Dist. by Andrews McMeel
HOW MANY VIEWS DID IT GET?
SEVEN, INCLUDING THIS ONE.

WHY DIDN'T YOU ANSWER MY EMAIL?
I DIDN'T GET IT.
MY LIE-DETECTOR APP DETECTED STRESS IN YOUR VOICE.
I CHECKED YOUR EMAIL HISTORY ON THE SERVER, AND IT CONFIRMS YOU OPENED MY EMAIL.
THAT COULD HAVE BEEN A HACKER WITH MY PASSWORD.
I'M CHECKING THE SECURITY CAMERA FOOTAGE FOR YOUR OFFICE AT THAT TIME.
AND THERE YOU ARE OPENING MY EMAIL.
NOW WILL YOU ADMIT YOU GOT MY EMAIL?
I'M SERIOUSLY CONSIDERING IT.
© 2018 Scott Adams, Inc./Dist. by Andrews McMeel
4-8-18

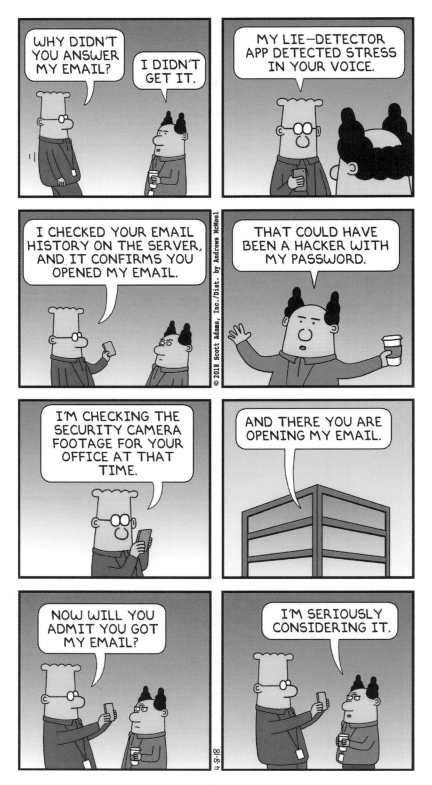

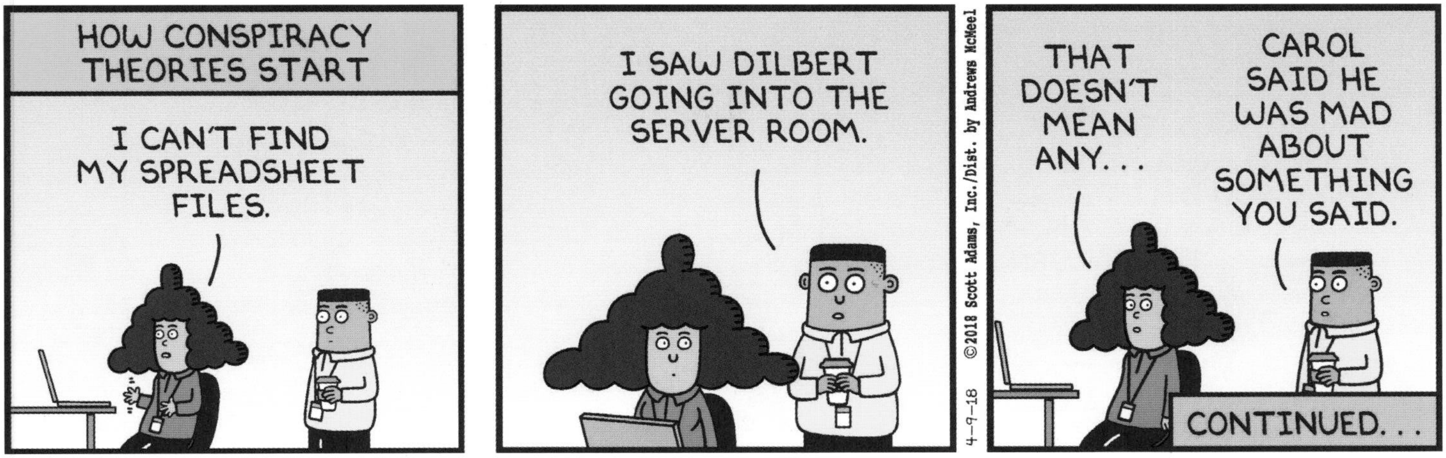
HOW CONSPIRACY THEORIES START
I CAN'T FIND MY SPREADSHEET FILES.
I SAW DILBERT GOING INTO THE SERVER ROOM.
4-9-18 ©2018 Scott Adams, Inc./Dist. by Andrews McMeel
THAT DOESN'T MEAN ANY. . .
CAROL SAID HE WAS MAD ABOUT SOMETHING YOU SAID.
CONTINUED. . .

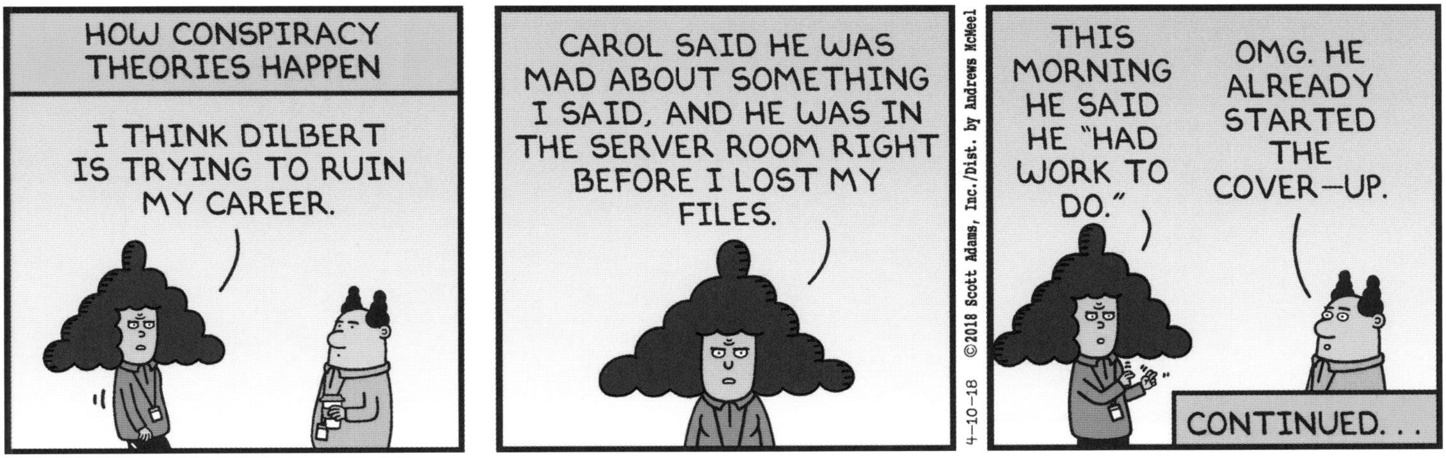
HOW CONSPIRACY THEORIES HAPPEN
I THINK DILBERT IS TRYING TO RUIN MY CAREER.
CAROL SAID HE WAS MAD ABOUT SOMETHING I SAID, AND HE WAS IN THE SERVER ROOM RIGHT BEFORE I LOST MY FILES.
4-10-18 ©2018 Scott Adams, Inc./Dist. by Andrews McMeel
THIS MORNING HE SAID HE "HAD WORK TO DO."
OMG. HE ALREADY STARTED THE COVER-UP.
CONTINUED. . .

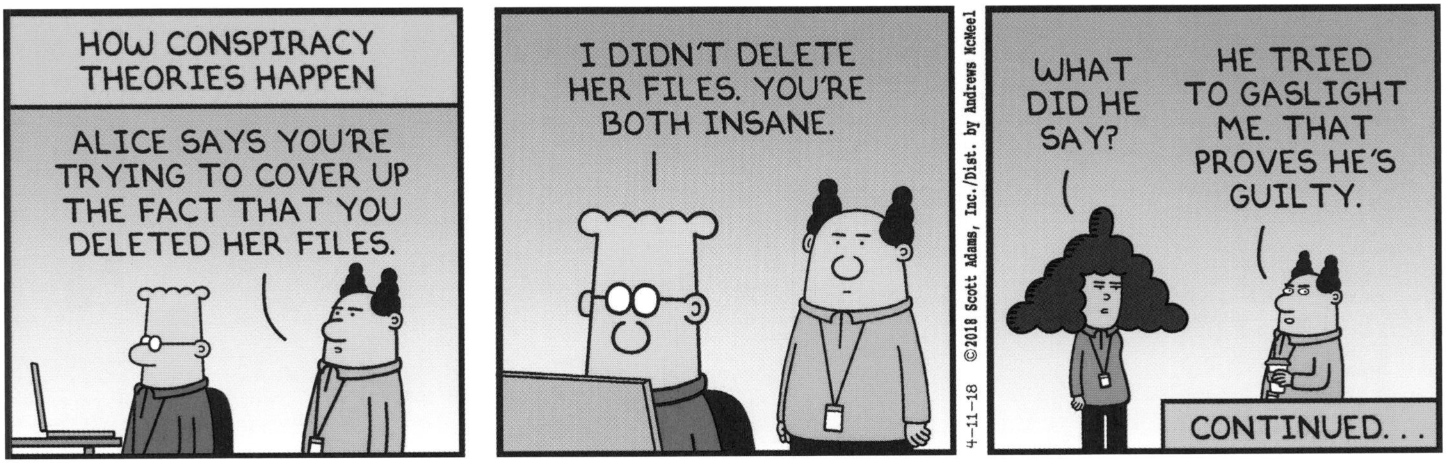
HOW CONSPIRACY THEORIES HAPPEN
ALICE SAYS YOU'RE TRYING TO COVER UP THE FACT THAT YOU DELETED HER FILES.
I DIDN'T DELETE HER FILES. YOU'RE BOTH INSANE.
4-11-18 ©2018 Scott Adams, Inc./Dist. by Andrews McMeel
WHAT DID HE SAY?
HE TRIED TO GASLIGHT ME. THAT PROVES HE'S GUILTY.
CONTINUED. . .

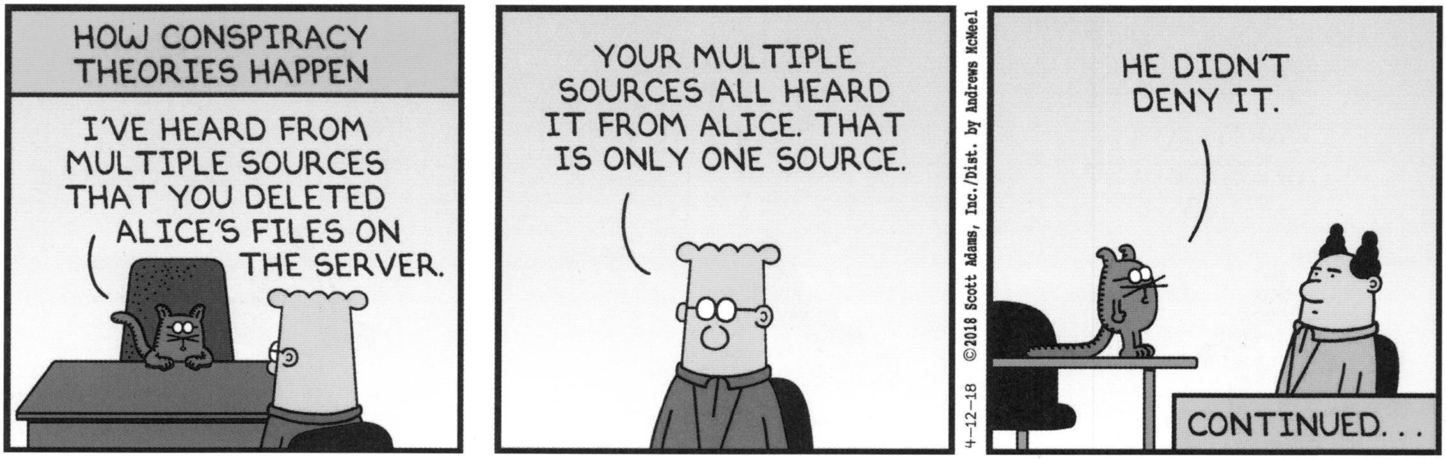
HOW CONSPIRACY THEORIES HAPPEN
I'VE HEARD FROM MULTIPLE SOURCES THAT YOU DELETED ALICE'S FILES ON THE SERVER.
YOUR MULTIPLE SOURCES ALL HEARD IT FROM ALICE. THAT IS ONLY ONE SOURCE.
4-12-18 ©2018 Scott Adams, Inc./Dist. by Andrews McMeel
HE DIDN'T DENY IT.
CONTINUED. . .

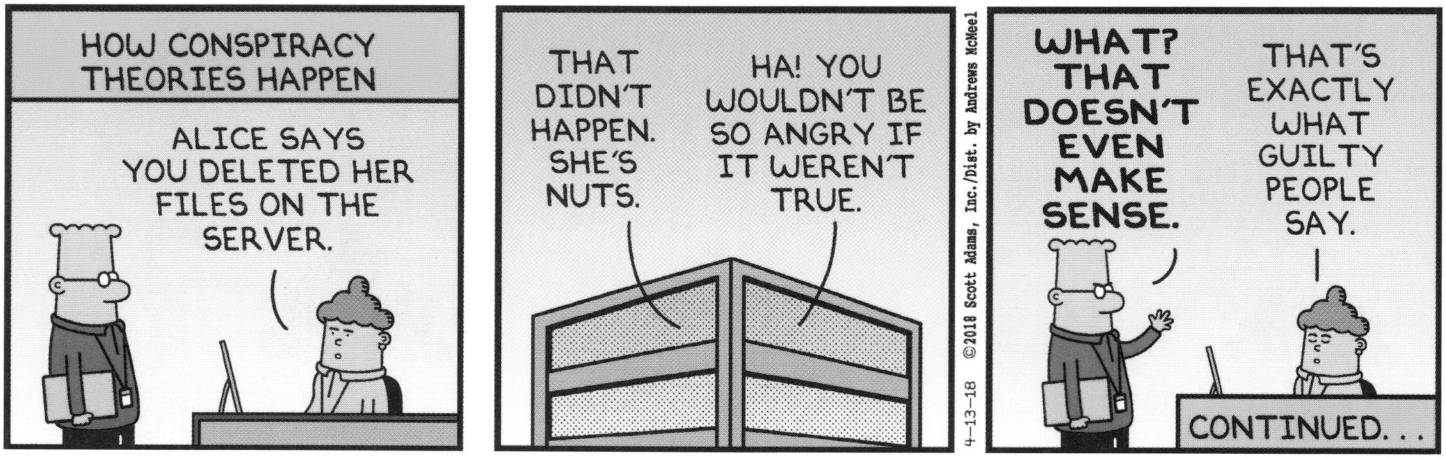
HOW CONSPIRACY THEORIES HAPPEN
ALICE SAYS YOU DELETED HER FILES ON THE SERVER.
THAT DIDN'T HAPPEN. SHE'S NUTS.
HA! YOU WOULDN'T BE SO ANGRY IF IT WEREN'T TRUE.
4-13-18 ©2018 Scott Adams, Inc./Dist. by Andrews McMeel
WHAT? THAT DOESN'T EVEN MAKE SENSE.
THAT'S EXACTLY WHAT GUILTY PEOPLE SAY.
CONTINUED. . .

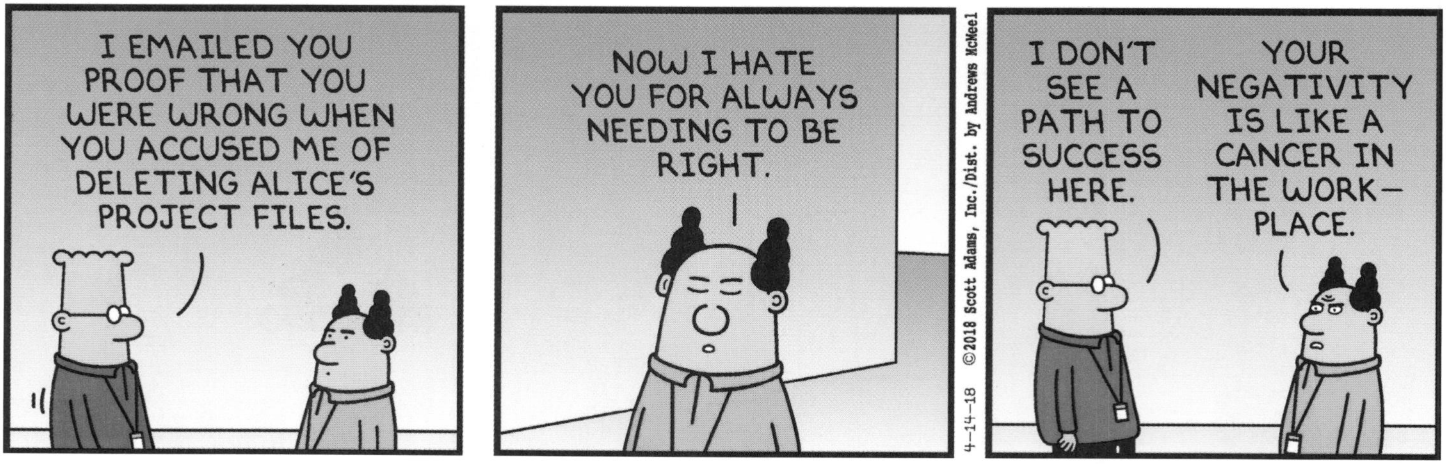
I EMAILED YOU PROOF THAT YOU WERE WRONG WHEN YOU ACCUSED ME OF DELETING ALICE'S PROJECT FILES.
NOW I HATE YOU FOR ALWAYS NEEDING TO BE RIGHT.
4-14-18 ©2018 Scott Adams, Inc./Dist. by Andrews McMeel
I DON'T SEE A PATH TO SUCCESS HERE.
YOUR NEGATIVITY IS LIKE A CANCER IN THE WORK-PLACE.

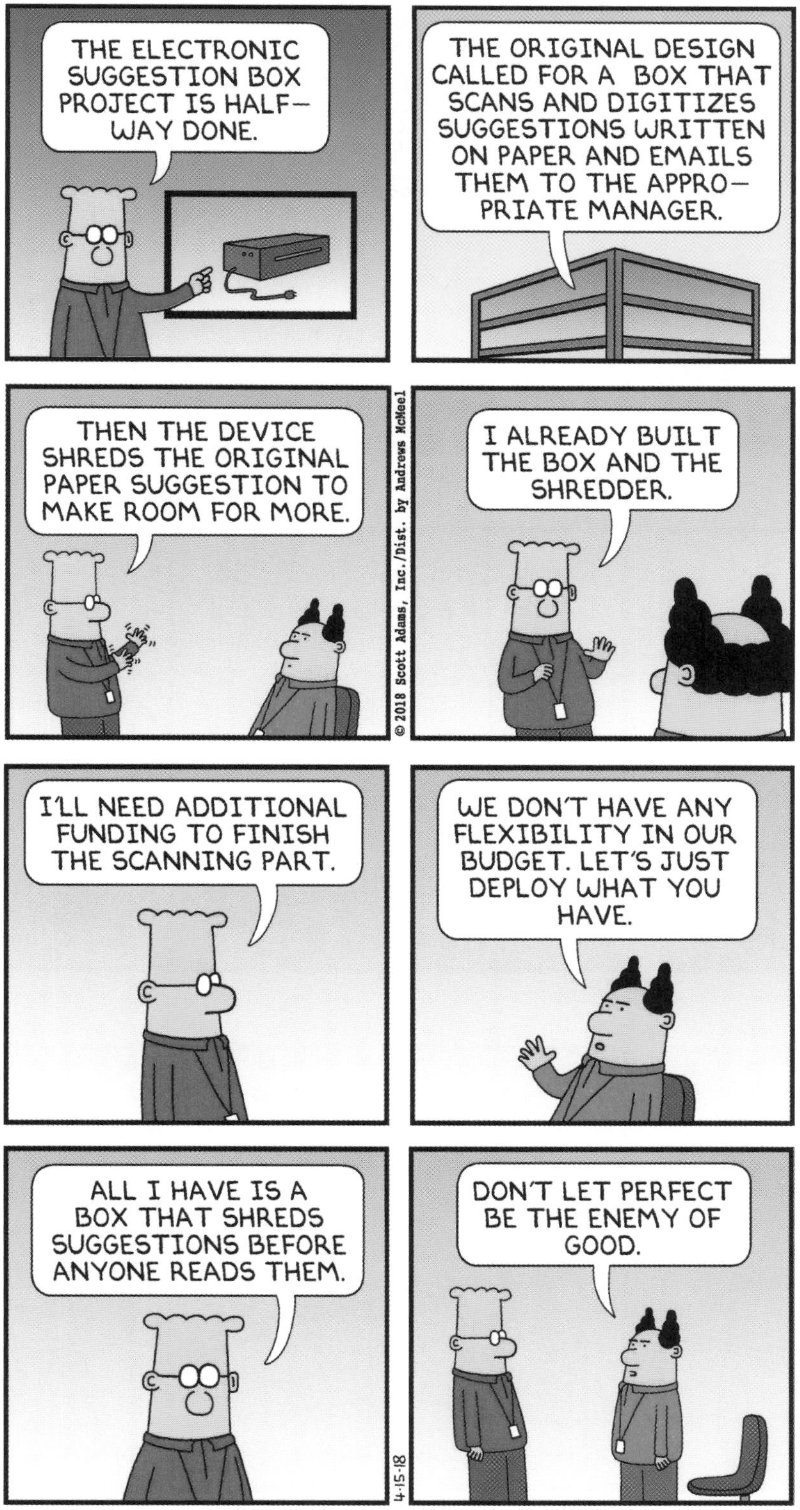
THE ELECTRONIC SUGGESTION BOX PROJECT IS HALF-WAY DONE.
THE ORIGINAL DESIGN CALLED FOR A BOX THAT SCANS AND DIGITIZES SUGGESTIONS WRITTEN ON PAPER AND EMAILS THEM TO THE APPROPRIATE MANAGER.
THEN THE DEVICE SHREDS THE ORIGINAL PAPER SUGGESTION TO MAKE ROOM FOR MORE.
I ALREADY BUILT THE BOX AND THE SHREDDER.
I'LL NEED ADDITIONAL FUNDING TO FINISH THE SCANNING PART.
WE DON'T HAVE ANY FLEXIBILITY IN OUR BUDGET. LET'S JUST DEPLOY WHAT YOU HAVE.
ALL I HAVE IS A BOX THAT SHREDS SUGGESTIONS BEFORE ANYONE READS THEM.
DON'T LET PERFECT BE THE ENEMY OF GOOD.
© 2018 Scott Adams, Inc./Dist. by Andrews McMeel
4-15-18

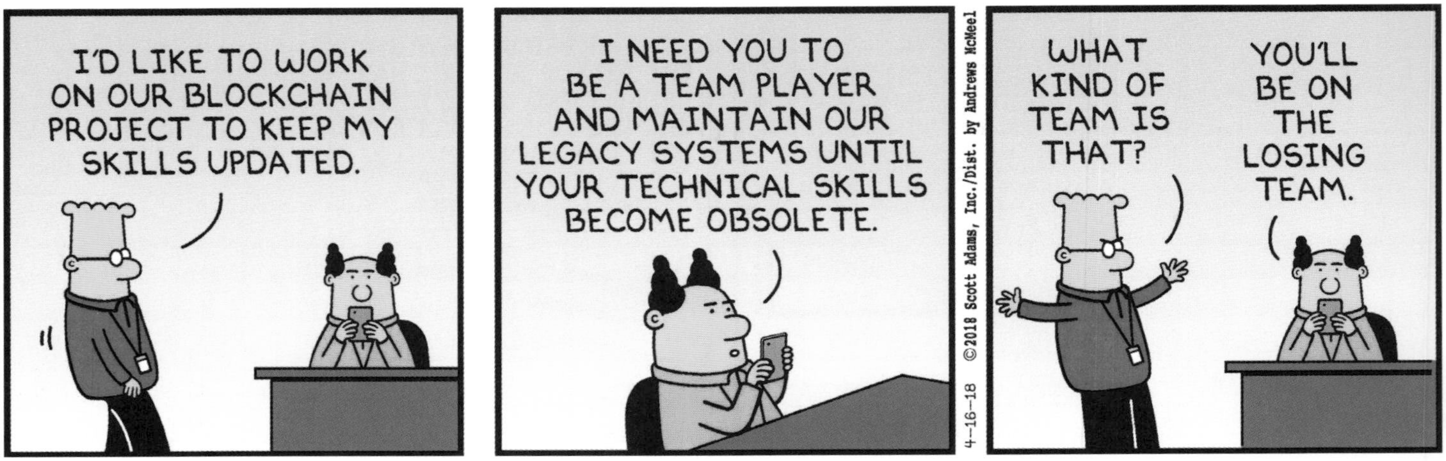
I'D LIKE TO WORK ON OUR BLOCKCHAIN PROJECT TO KEEP MY SKILLS UPDATED.
I NEED YOU TO BE A TEAM PLAYER AND MAINTAIN OUR LEGACY SYSTEMS UNTIL YOUR TECHNICAL SKILLS BECOME OBSOLETE.
4-16-18 ©2018 Scott Adams, Inc./Dist. by Andrews McMeel
WHAT KIND OF TEAM IS THAT?
YOU'LL BE ON THE LOSING TEAM.

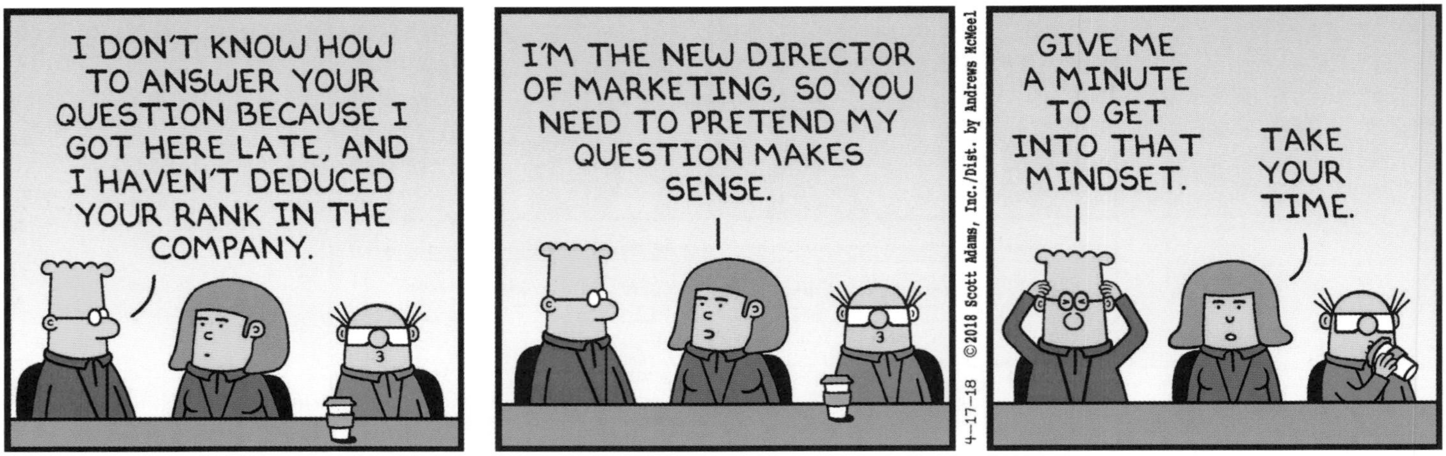
I DON'T KNOW HOW TO ANSWER YOUR QUESTION BECAUSE I GOT HERE LATE, AND I HAVEN'T DEDUCED YOUR RANK IN THE COMPANY.
I'M THE NEW DIRECTOR OF MARKETING, SO YOU NEED TO PRETEND MY QUESTION MAKES SENSE.
4-17-18 ©2018 Scott Adams, Inc./Dist. by Andrews McMeel
GIVE ME A MINUTE TO GET INTO THAT MINDSET.
TAKE YOUR TIME.

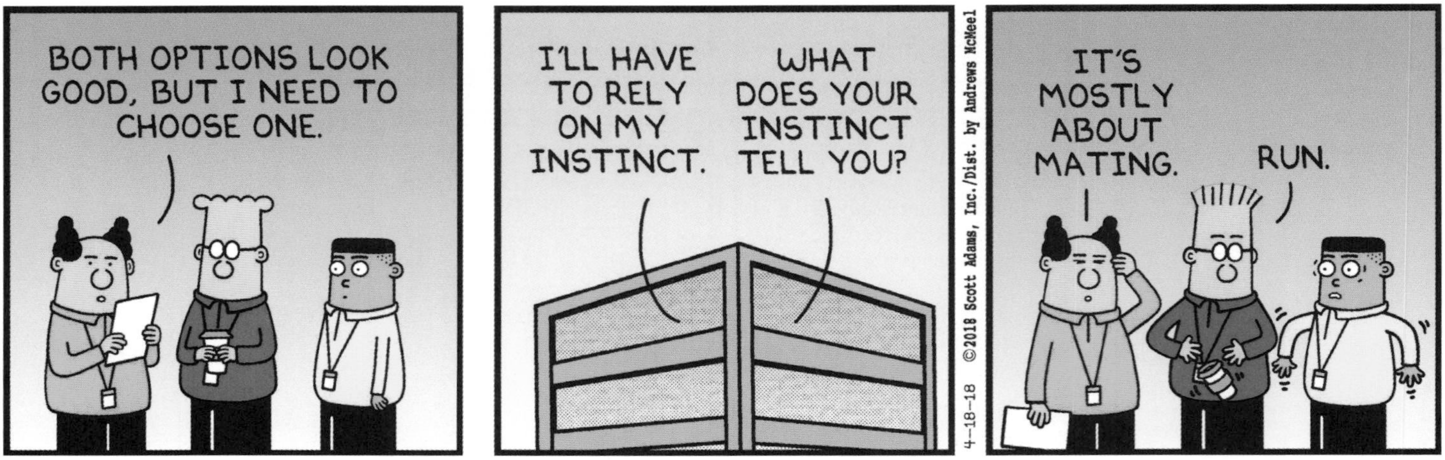
BOTH OPTIONS LOOK GOOD, BUT I NEED TO CHOOSE ONE.
I'LL HAVE TO RELY ON MY INSTINCT.
WHAT DOES YOUR INSTINCT TELL YOU?
4-18-18 ©2018 Scott Adams, Inc./Dist. by Andrews McMeel
IT'S MOSTLY ABOUT MATING.
RUN.

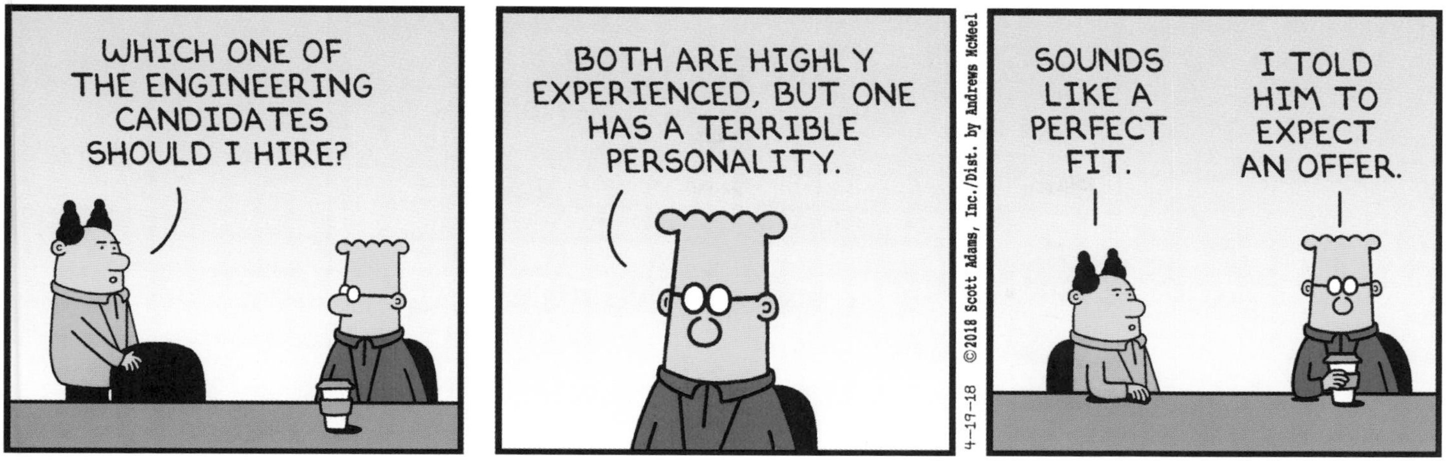
WHICH ONE OF THE ENGINEERING CANDIDATES SHOULD I HIRE?
BOTH ARE HIGHLY EXPERIENCED, BUT ONE HAS A TERRIBLE PERSONALITY.
SOUNDS LIKE A PERFECT FIT.
I TOLD HIM TO EXPECT AN OFFER.
4-19-18 ©2018 Scott Adams, Inc./Dist. by Andrews McMeel

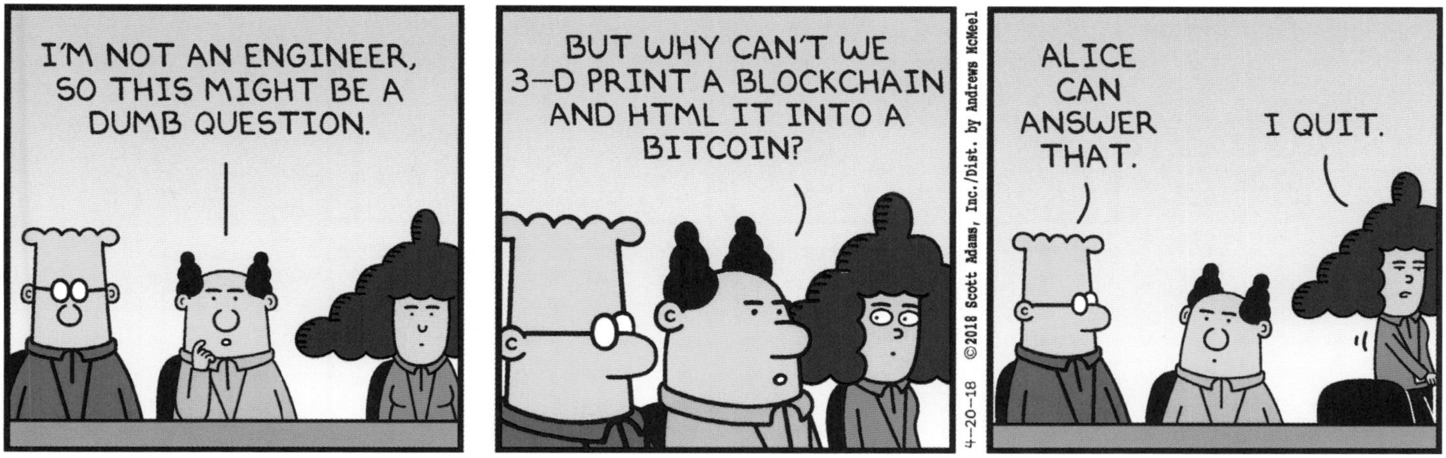
I'M NOT AN ENGINEER, SO THIS MIGHT BE A DUMB QUESTION.
BUT WHY CAN'T WE 3-D PRINT A BLOCKCHAIN AND HTML IT INTO A BITCOIN?
ALICE CAN ANSWER THAT.
I QUIT.
4-20-18 ©2018 Scott Adams, Inc./Dist. by Andrews McMeel

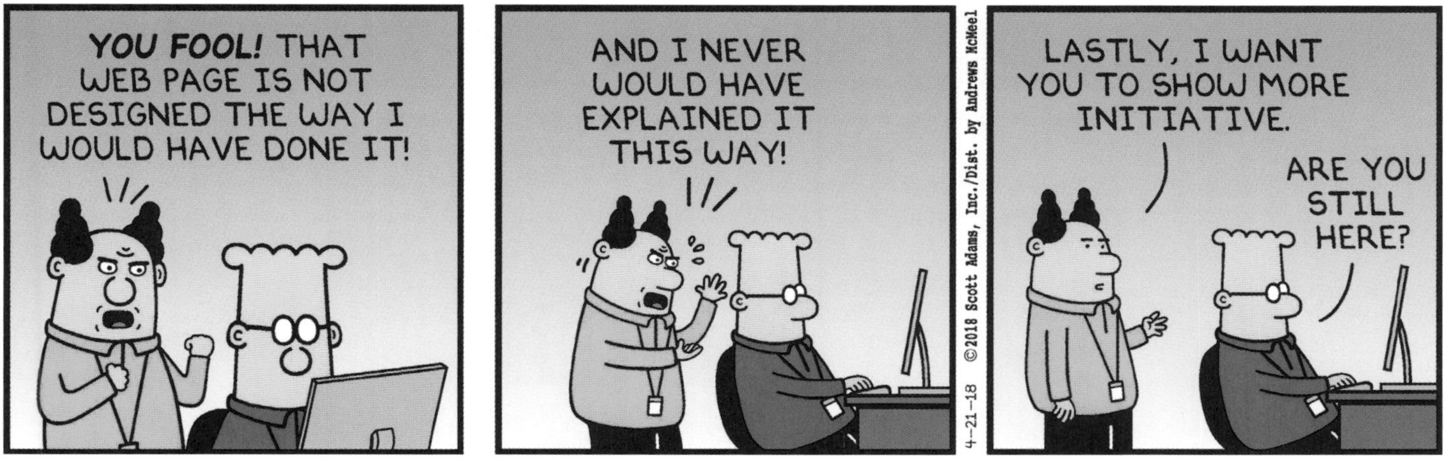
YOU FOOL! THAT WEB PAGE IS NOT DESIGNED THE WAY I WOULD HAVE DONE IT!
AND I NEVER WOULD HAVE EXPLAINED IT THIS WAY!
LASTLY, I WANT YOU TO SHOW MORE INITIATIVE.
ARE YOU STILL HERE?
4-21-18 ©2018 Scott Adams, Inc./Dist. by Andrews McMeel

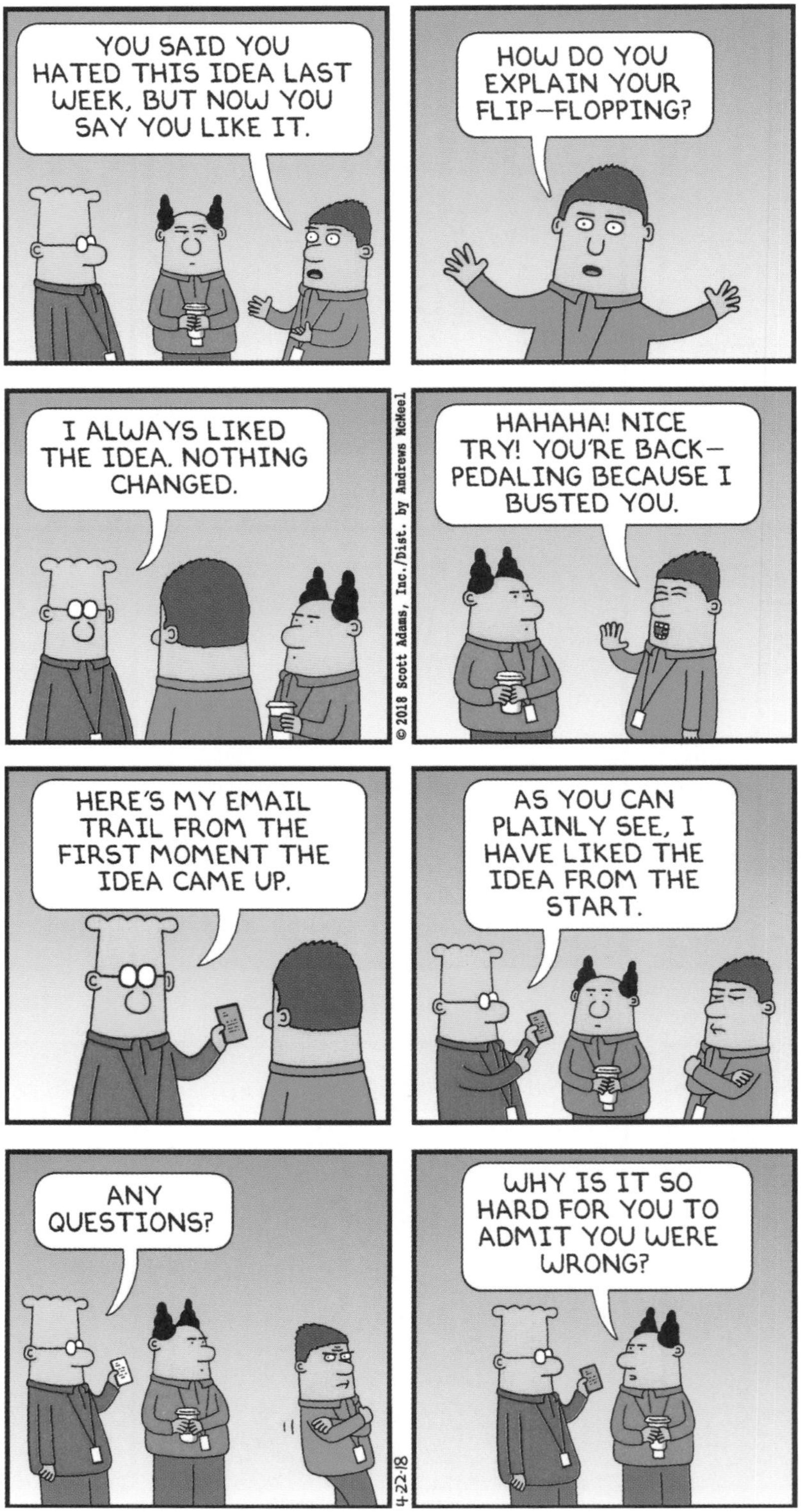
YOU SAID YOU HATED THIS IDEA LAST WEEK, BUT NOW YOU SAY YOU LIKE IT.
HOW DO YOU EXPLAIN YOUR FLIP—FLOPPING?
I ALWAYS LIKED THE IDEA. NOTHING CHANGED.
HAHAHA! NICE TRY! YOU'RE BACK—PEDALING BECAUSE I BUSTED YOU.
HERE'S MY EMAIL TRAIL FROM THE FIRST MOMENT THE IDEA CAME UP.
AS YOU CAN PLAINLY SEE, I HAVE LIKED THE IDEA FROM THE START.
ANY QUESTIONS?
WHY IS IT SO HARD FOR YOU TO ADMIT YOU WERE WRONG?
© 2018 Scott Adams, Inc./Dist. by Andrews McMeel
4-22-18

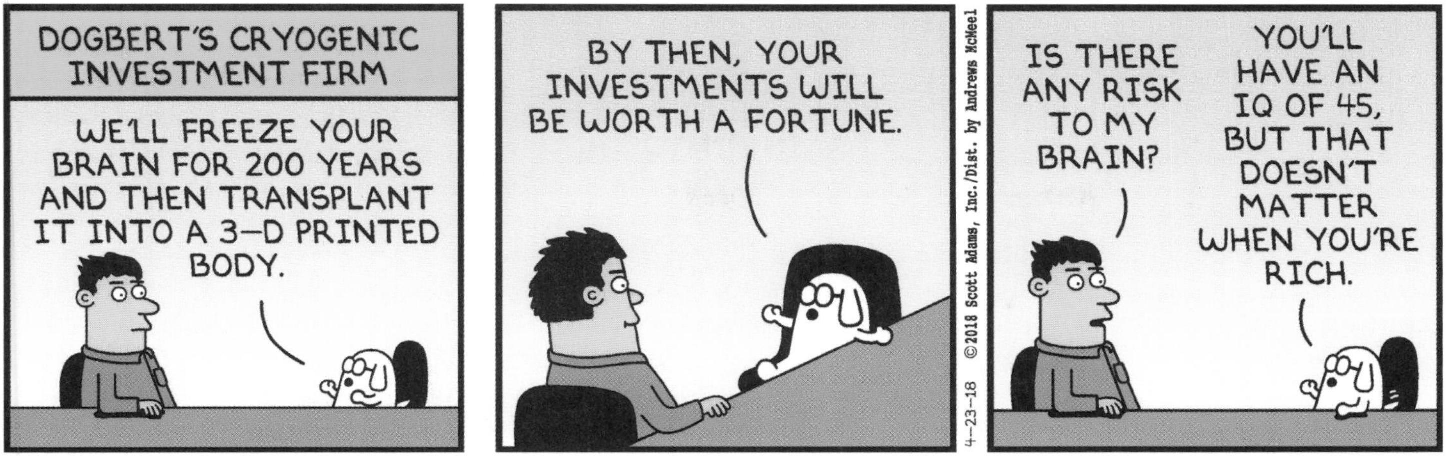
DOGBERT'S CRYOGENIC INVESTMENT FIRM
WE'LL FREEZE YOUR BRAIN FOR 200 YEARS AND THEN TRANSPLANT IT INTO A 3-D PRINTED BODY.
BY THEN, YOUR INVESTMENTS WILL BE WORTH A FORTUNE.
IS THERE ANY RISK TO MY BRAIN?
YOU'LL HAVE AN IQ OF 45, BUT THAT DOESN'T MATTER WHEN YOU'RE RICH.
4-23-18 ©2018 Scott Adams, Inc./Dist. by Andrews McMeel

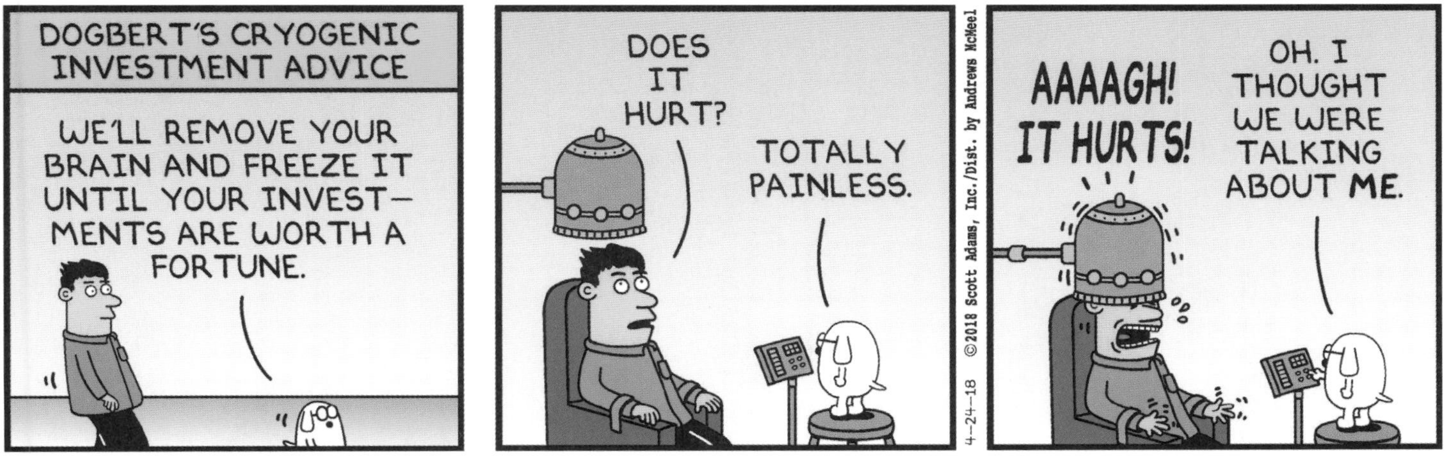
DOGBERT'S CRYOGENIC INVESTMENT ADVICE
WE'LL REMOVE YOUR BRAIN AND FREEZE IT UNTIL YOUR INVEST-MENTS ARE WORTH A FORTUNE.
DOES IT HURT?
TOTALLY PAINLESS.
AAAAGH! IT HURTS!
OH. I THOUGHT WE WERE TALKING ABOUT **ME**.
4-24-18 ©2018 Scott Adams, Inc./Dist. by Andrews McMeel

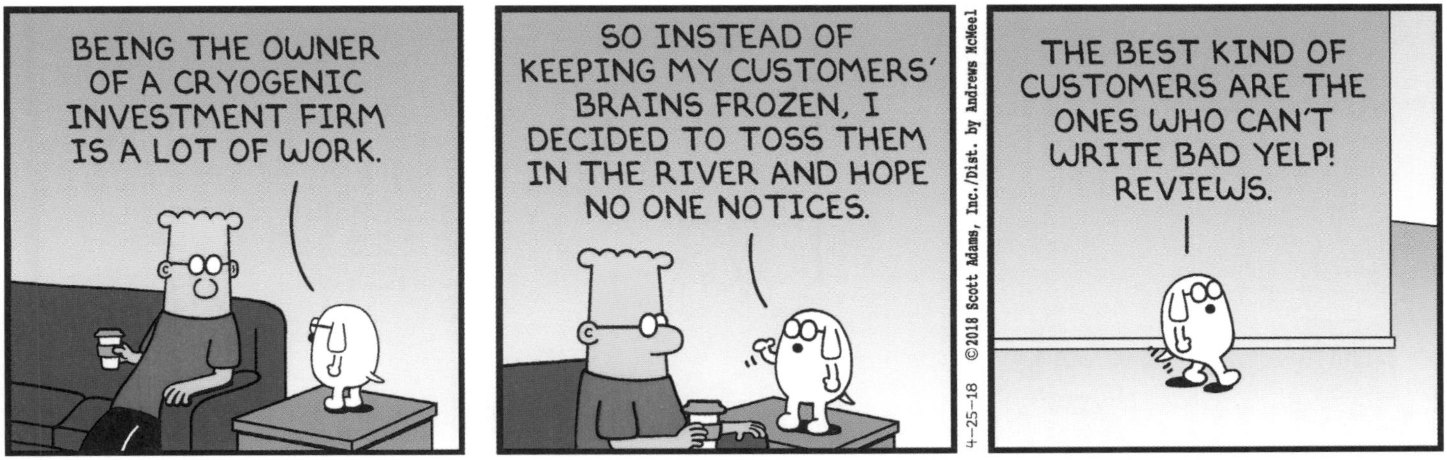
BEING THE OWNER OF A CRYOGENIC INVESTMENT FIRM IS A LOT OF WORK.
SO INSTEAD OF KEEPING MY CUSTOMERS' BRAINS FROZEN, I DECIDED TO TOSS THEM IN THE RIVER AND HOPE NO ONE NOTICES.
THE BEST KIND OF CUSTOMERS ARE THE ONES WHO CAN'T WRITE BAD YELP! REVIEWS.
4-25-18 ©2018 Scott Adams, Inc./Dist. by Andrews McMeel

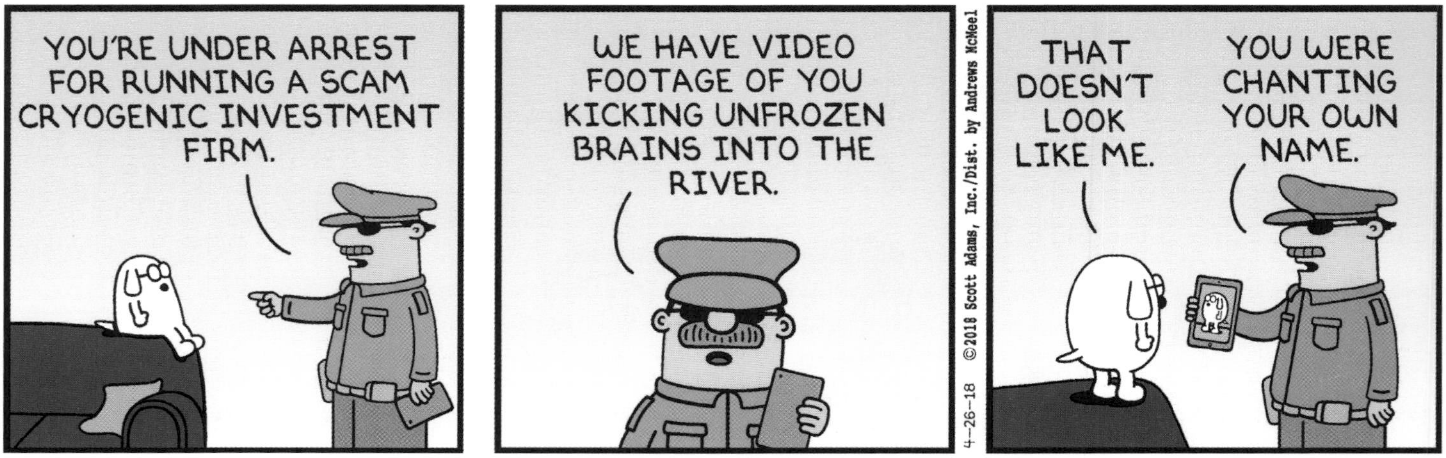
YOU'RE UNDER ARREST FOR RUNNING A SCAM CRYOGENIC INVESTMENT FIRM.
WE HAVE VIDEO FOOTAGE OF YOU KICKING UNFROZEN BRAINS INTO THE RIVER.
4-26-18 ©2018 Scott Adams, Inc./Dist. by Andrews McMeel
THAT DOESN'T LOOK LIKE ME.
YOU WERE CHANTING YOUR OWN NAME.

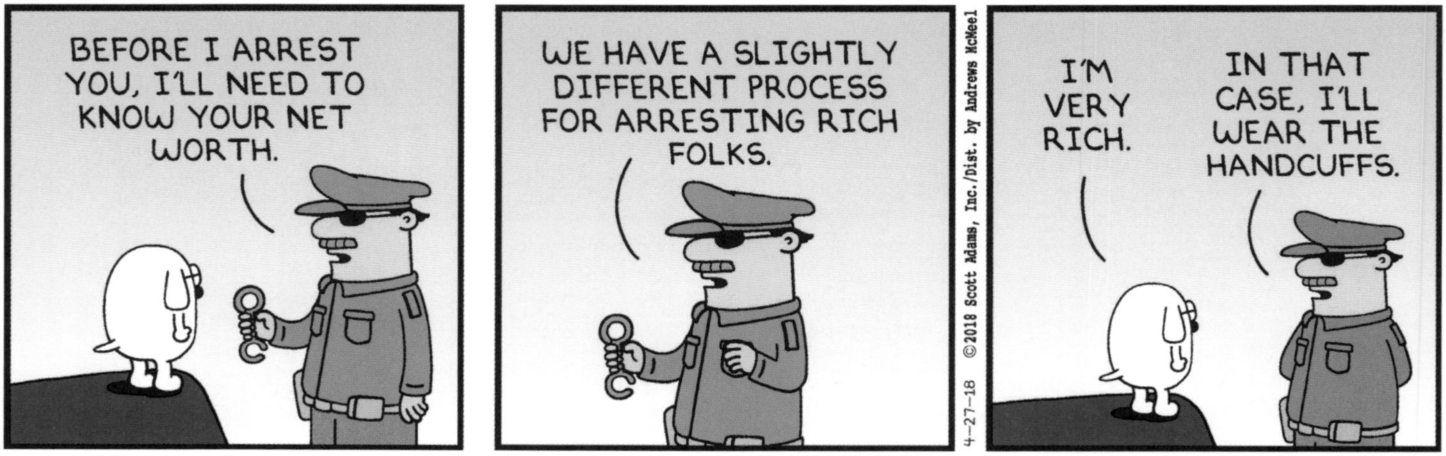
BEFORE I ARREST YOU, I'LL NEED TO KNOW YOUR NET WORTH.
WE HAVE A SLIGHTLY DIFFERENT PROCESS FOR ARRESTING RICH FOLKS.
4-27-18 ©2018 Scott Adams, Inc./Dist. by Andrews McMeel
I'M VERY RICH.
IN THAT CASE, I'LL WEAR THE HANDCUFFS.

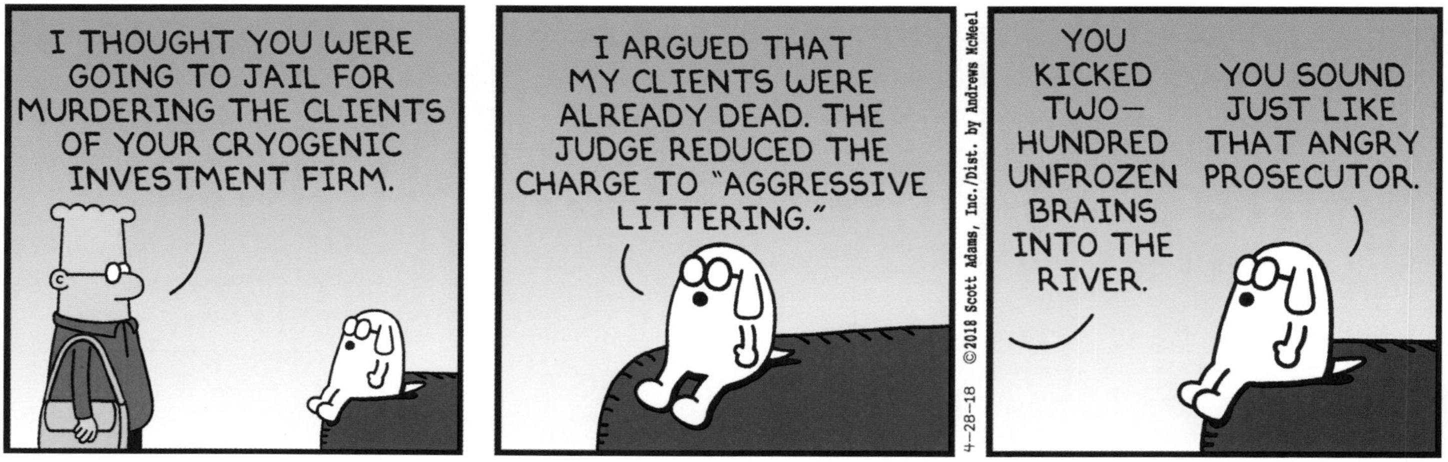
I THOUGHT YOU WERE GOING TO JAIL FOR MURDERING THE CLIENTS OF YOUR CRYOGENIC INVESTMENT FIRM.
I ARGUED THAT MY CLIENTS WERE ALREADY DEAD. THE JUDGE REDUCED THE CHARGE TO "AGGRESSIVE LITTERING."
4-28-18 ©2018 Scott Adams, Inc./Dist. by Andrews McMeel
YOU KICKED TWO-HUNDRED UNFROZEN BRAINS INTO THE RIVER.
YOU SOUND JUST LIKE THAT ANGRY PROSECUTOR.

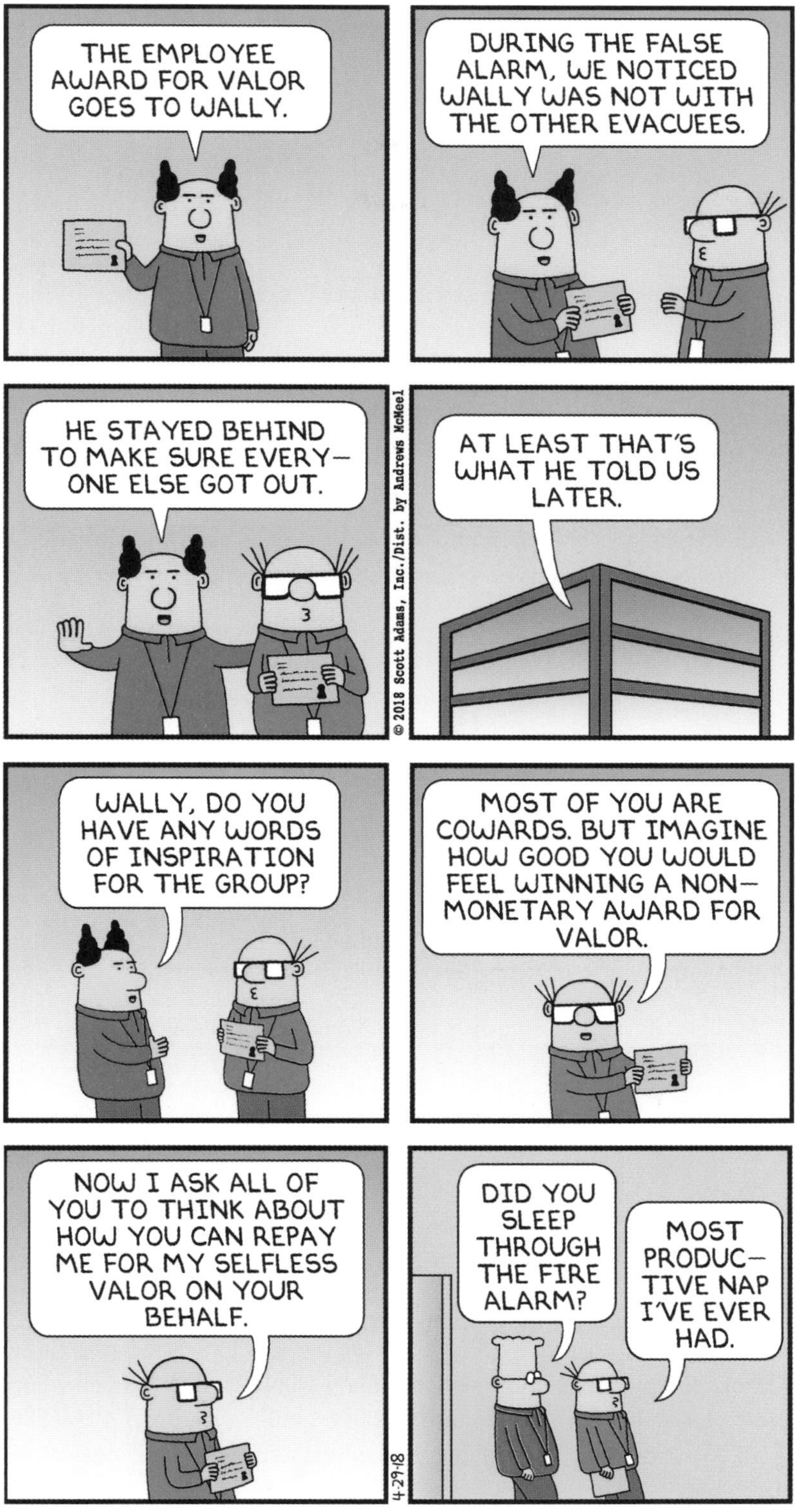
THE EMPLOYEE AWARD FOR VALOR GOES TO WALLY.
DURING THE FALSE ALARM, WE NOTICED WALLY WAS NOT WITH THE OTHER EVACUEES.
HE STAYED BEHIND TO MAKE SURE EVERY-ONE ELSE GOT OUT.
© 2018 Scott Adams, Inc./Dist. by Andrews McMeel
AT LEAST THAT'S WHAT HE TOLD US LATER.
WALLY, DO YOU HAVE ANY WORDS OF INSPIRATION FOR THE GROUP?
MOST OF YOU ARE COWARDS. BUT IMAGINE HOW GOOD YOU WOULD FEEL WINNING A NON-MONETARY AWARD FOR VALOR.
NOW I ASK ALL OF YOU TO THINK ABOUT HOW YOU CAN REPAY ME FOR MY SELFLESS VALOR ON YOUR BEHALF.
4-29-18
DID YOU SLEEP THROUGH THE FIRE ALARM?
MOST PRODUC-TIVE NAP I'VE EVER HAD.

Andrews McMeel Publishing
a division of Andrews McMeel Universal
1130 Walnut Street, Kansas City, Missouri 64106
www.andrewsmcmeel.com

19 20 21 22 23 SDB 10 9 8 7 6 5 4 3 2

ISBN: 978-1-4494-9378-3

Library of Congress Control Number: 2018938032

www.dilbert.com

─── **ATTENTION: SCHOOLS AND BUSINESSES** ───

Andrews McMeel books are available at quantity discounts with bulk purchase for educational, business,
or sales promotional use. For information, please e-mail the Andrews McMeel Publishing
Special Sales Department: specialsales@amuniversal.com.